TRANSFORMING THE HERMENEUTIC CONTEXT

SUNY series, Intersections:
Philosophy and Critical Theory

Rodolphe Gasché and Mark C. Taylor, Editors

Transforming the Hermeneutic Context

From Nietzsche to Nancy

Edited by

Gayle L. Ormiston and Alan D. Schrift

STATE UNIVERSITY OF NEW YORK PRESS

Published by
State University of New York Press, Albany

For information, address State University of New York
Press, State University Plaza, Albany, NY 12246

Library of Congress Cataloging-in-Publication Data

Transforming the hermeneutic context : from Nietzsche to Nancy /
  edited by Gayle L. Ormiston and Alan D. Schrift.
      p. cm.—(SUNY series, intersections. Philosophy and
  critical theory)
    Bibliography: p.
    Includes index.
    ISBN 0-7914-0134-0.—ISBN 0-7914-0135-9 (pbk.)
    1. Hermeneutics. I. Ormiston, Gayle L., 1951– . II. Schrift,
  Alan D., 1955– . III. Series: Intersections (Albany, N.Y.)
  BD241.T7   1990
  121'.68—dc19   89-4172
                                                         CIP

10 9 8 7 6 5 4 3 2

To Lynn and Rachel,

G. L. O.

To Jill,

A. D. S.

Contents

Preface

There are certain unavoidable risks incurred in any attempt to cata-
logue a tradition. When this project began, we hoped to present certain
canonical statements on hermeneutics from the nineteenth and twentieth
centuries with certain current perspectives on the "practices" of interpretation theory that stand both within and apart from what might be called
the "classical hermeneutical tradition." In the process of deciding which
representative texts to include, we realized that the breadth and depth of
such an endeavor made impractical the binding of these diverse interpretive
perspectives within one volume. Faced with eliminating or abridging certain selections, or dividing the project into two books that would reflect our
"original intention" to juxtapose both familiar and contemporary voices
within the tradition, the choice was clear. Because of our commitment to
presenting relatively complete expressions that display both recognized and
unexpected continuities, we divided the material in terms of the marked
differences between the authors' interpretations of interpretive practices.
We believe *Transforming the Hermeneutic Context: From Nietzsche to
Nancy* can stand alone. But we hope the connections with its companion,
The Hermeneutic Tradition: From Ast to Ricoeur, will be as apparent to the
reader as they have been to its editors throughout the life of the project.

There are many individuals and institutions without whose assistance
the completion of this project would not have been possible. For their en-
couragement and valuable support, we wish to thank our families, friends,
and colleagues. Special thanks are due to Eric Blondel, Fred Dallmayr, Rodolphe Gasché, David E. Linge, Jean-Luc Nancy, Richard Palmer, Paul
Ricoeur, John Sallis, and Calvin O. Schrag. For their time and expertise in
generously contributing their translations, we thank Timothy Bahti, Mary
Ann Caws, Peter Caws, and Robert Eben Sackett. Further, we would like to
acknowledge the financial, secretarial, and computer services support provided by the University of Colorado at Colorado Springs, Grinnell College,
Denison University, Purdue University, and the University of California at
Riverside. Additional major funding was supplied to Gayle L. Ormiston by
the University of Colorado's Committee on Research and Creative Works
and the President's Fund for the Humanities, and to Alan D. Schrift by the
American Council of Learned Societies Fellowship for Modern Society and

Values and the Grinnell College Grant Board. And for their valuable assistance during the preparation of the final manuscript, we thank Carola Sautter, Dana Foote, and Susan Zorn.

Finally, above all we would like to express our individual and joint appreciation and thanks to Lynn and Jill for their unwavering support during the several years it took to complete our work.

G. L. O. and A. D. S.

Acknowledgments

We gratefully acknowledge the kind permission of the following publishers, authors, and translators to reprint, and in some cases translate, the works included in this volume.

Random House, Inc., for kind permission to reprint excerpts from Friedrich Nietzsche, *Beyond Good and Evil,* translated by Walter Kaufmann, copyright © by Vintage Books/Random House, 1966; Friedrich Nietzsche, *On the Genealogy of Morals* and *Ecce Homo,* translated by Walter Kaufmann, copyright © by Vintage Books/Random House, 1969; Friedrich Nietzsche, *The Gay Science,* translated by Walter Kaufmann, copyright © by Vintage Books/Random House, 1974; and Friedrich Nietzsche, *The Will to Power,* edited by Walter Kaufmann, translated by R. J. Hollingdale and Walter Kaufmann, copyright © Vintage Books/Random House, 1968. Reprinted by Permission of Viking Penguin, Inc., from *The Portable Nietzsche,* edited and translated by Walter Kaufman, Friedrich Nietzsche, "On Truth and Lies in an Extra-Moral Sense" and *Twilight of The Idols,* copyright © 1954 The Viking Press, Inc., renewed © 1982 by Viking Penguin, Inc.

Anne Foucault, Denys Foucault, Francine Fruchaud, and Henri Fruchaud, for permission to translate and reprint Michel Foucault, "Nietzsche, Freud, Marx," originally published in *Nietzsche, Cahiers du Royaumont* (Paris: Les Éditions de Minuit, 1964), pages 183–200.

Eric Blondel, for permission to translate and publish "Interpreting Texts With and Without Nietzsche." Copyright © by Eric Blondel, 1986.

The University of Chicago Press and Julia Kristeva, for permission to reprint Julia Kristeva, "Psychoanalysis and the Polis," translated by Margaret Waller, *Critical Inquiry* 9 (1982): 77–92. Copyright © by the University of Chicago Press, 1982.

Arien Mack, Editor, *Social Research,* and Jacques Derrida, for permission to reprint Jacques Derrida, "Sending: On Representation," translated by Mary Ann Caws and Peter Caws, *Social Research* 49, no. 2 (1982): 294–326. Copyright © by Jacques Derrida, 1982.

J. B. Metzlersche Verlagsbuchhandlung, for permission to translate and reprint Manfred Frank, "The Interpretation of a Text," originally published in *Erkenntnis und Literatur,* edited by D. Harth and P. Gebhardt as

"Textauslegung," pages 123–60. Copyright © by J. B. Metzlersche Verlagsbuchhandlung, 1982.

Verlag Ferdinand Schöningh KG, for permission to translate and reprint Werner Hamacher, "Hermeneutic Ellipses: Writing the Hermeneutical Circle in Schleiermacher," originally published in *Texthermeneutik*, edited by Ulrich Nassen, as "Hermeneutischen Ellipsen: Schrift und Zirkel bei Schleiermacher," pages 113–48. Copyright © by Verlag Ferdinand Schöningh KG.

Éditions Galilée and Jean-Luc Nancy, for permission to translate and reprint "Sharing Voices," originally published as *Le partage des voix* (Paris: Éditions Galilée, 1982). Copyright © by Éditions Galilée, 1982.

Editors' Introduction

Gayle L. Ormiston and Alan D. Schrift

I know not what to say to it; but experience makes it manifest, that so many interpretations dissipate the truth, and break it . . . Who will not say that glosses augment doubts and ignorance, since there is no book to be found, either human or divine, which the world busies itself about, whereof the difficulties are cleared by interpretation. The hundredth commentator passes it on to the next, still more knotty and perplexed than he found it. When were we ever agreed among ourselves: "this book has enough; there is now no more to be said about it?" . . . do we find any end to the need of interpreting? is there, for all that, any progress or advancement toward peace, or do we stand in need of any fewer advocates and judges? . . . There is more ado to interpret interpretations than to interpret things; and more books upon books than upon any other subject; we do nothing but comment upon one another. Every place swarms with commentaries . . . Is it not the common and final end of all studies? Our opinions are grafted upon one another; the first serves as a stock to the second, the second to the third, and so forth . . .

—Michel de Montaigne, *Essays*[1]

The "Experience" of Interpretation: "there are only interpretations . . ."

Montaigne's comments on interpretation, cited here, appear in an essay entitled "Of Experience." In this essay, Montaigne begins with an allusion to Aristotle's famous dictum: "All men by nature desire to know."[2] Montaigne writes: "There is no desire more natural than that of knowledge. We try all ways that can lead us to it; where reason is wanting, we therein employ experience."[3] What follows this paraphrase is a *gloss;* it is an interpretation of the thought that opens Aristotle's *Metaphysics,* introducing the single, very complex theme which, momentarily, orders Montaigne's musings. In short, the gloss "interprets" Aristotle while it simultaneously

1

"interprets" *itself,* inserting itself into the Aristotelian text and tradition. Beyond offering an exegesis of the thought that organizes Montaigne's commentary, in a provisional fashion, there is a rewriting, indeed a reformulation, of a thought which eclipses the epistemological and metaphysical tradition that binds Montaigne.

By way of a *commentary* that turns away from itself, toward a different text, *and* that turns in on itself, Montaigne articulates a line of inquiry inextricably inscribed in a certain epistemological and metaphysical tradition of Western thought. Montaigne's text, then, announces a sentiment that has come to regulate and provide a refuge for a particular current in contemporary philosophical analysis: "there are only interpretations of interpretations." The name given to this inquiry, and the line(s) of thought it has produced, is *"hermeneutics."* It is the purpose of the selections collected in this volume, under the title *Transforming the Hermeneutic Context: From Nietzsche to Nancy,* to trace certain *paths* traversed within selected discourse(s) and tradition(s) of hermeneutics in the nineteenth and twentieth centuries. To be sure, like Montaigne's *Essays,* each of the selections presented in this volume can be seen as an interpretation of interpretations, announcing once again—rethinking and rewriting—hermeneutics and its fundamental motifs.

It must be noted explicitly, then, that the selections included here do not emerge outside the context of the hermeneutic tradition; they are grafted to that tradition; they presuppose that tradition. In fact, the issues and themes presented in this text, and incorporated in *The Hermeneutic Tradition: From Ast to Ricoeur,*[4] and the debates and polemics that mark the tradition(s) of hermeneutics account for the production of a very intricate history or series of graftings. To trace the paths traversed and ordered within selected discourses of the hermeneutic tradition is to give an account of the continuities that bind apparently incommensurable interpretations of the hermeneutic tradition itself. Moreover, it is to give an account of the differences generated in any attempt to rupture with that tradition and the simultaneous transformation (dissemination) of the tradition. With both *The Hermeneutic Tradition* and *Transforming the Hermeneutic Context,* then, we hope to present certain thematic linkages between the so-called "tradition" of hermeneutics, as represented in *The Hermeneutic Tradition,* and the alleged nontraditional practices of interpretation reflected in this volume. Toward this end, it seems fitting at this juncture to provide a sketch of *The Hermeneutic Tradition.*

Divided into two parts—"The Hermeneutic Legend" (part I) and "Hermeneutics and Critical Theory: Dialogues on Methodology" (part II)—, *The Hermeneutic Tradition* presents readings representative of what is referred to as "traditional" hermeneutic theory and "post-Heideggerian" hermeneutics. In effect, the selections from Friedrich Ast, Friedrich Schleiermacher, Wilhelm Dilthey, and Martin Heidegger help to identify the tradition of hermeneutics according to certain lines of thought and styles of discourse and, as such, create the "historical" background against which the issues and themes pursued in this text will be configured.

In terms of certain post-Heideggerian lines of debate—the polemics inaugurated in Hans-Georg Gadamer's *Truth and Method*—that surround the hermeneutic project, the selections by Gadamer, Emilio Betti, Jürgen Habermas, and Paul Ricoeur address two intertwining points of contention: (1) the "universality" and methodology of the hermeneutic project, as it is stated in Gadamer's philosophical hermeneutics, and the "objective status" of interpretation argued for by Betti, as it pertains to the Diltheyan notion of *Geisteswissenschaften;* and (2) how the hermeneutic claim of "universality" contends with or accommodates the critique of ideology, as articulated by Habermas. With respect to their historical and philosophical import, the debates presented in this context are germinal. They incorporate and cast anew certain fundamental concerns expressed in the writings of Ast, Schleiermacher, Dilthey, and Heidegger. The textual exchanges between Gadamer and Betti, Gadamer and Habermas, and Ricoeur and Gadamer and Habermas can be cast not only against the historical context of the other selections that appear in *The Hermeneutic Tradition*. These texts demonstrate once more, in a different context, and in their respective ways, the force of Montaigne's remark regarding the experience of interpretation: "[W]e do nothing but comment upon one another." "Our opinions are grafted upon one another; the first serves as a stock to the second, the second to the third, and so forth . . . " Interpretations—interpretations of interpretations—can do no more nor less than "dissipate the truth [the tradition], and break it . . . "[5] while at the same time refer to it as a complete, fixed, and organized whole.

*
* *

Where reason, in its different forms and capacities, takes into account the resemblance and similitude among ideas and objects, Montaigne claims that the conclusions which can be drawn from these comparisons are always "unsure" and incomplete. "There is no quality so universal in this image of things, as diversity and variety."[6] Resemblance and similitude simultaneously betray and employ difference(s). As such, dissimilitude, difference, and dissimulation intrude upon all of our works, judgments, and pronouncements. "Resemblance does not so much make one, as difference makes another. Nature has obliged herself to make nothing other, that was not unlike."[7]

What promise does this condition hold for those analyses interested in explicating the "nature" of knowledge? If knowledge claims are "grounded" in the otherness of that point where resemblance and difference converge, the "nature" of knowledge can be neither certain nor uncertain. As a consequence, the authority as well as the legitimacy of epistemological claims, and those metaphysical and ontological claims made regarding the "nature" of understanding, and our understanding of nature, must be suspended. The only recourse we have, the only "law" to which we can turn to adjudicate the differences and legitimate our assertions, is *interpretation*—to comment upon, to analyze the announcements, the discourses, the texts offered in behalf and in support of various theoretical and practical positions.

Resemblance, difference, and similitude converge in acts of interpretation; through individual *acts* of interpreting, our sensibilities are challenged, our expectations are confirmed or subverted. Thus, whatever claims to truth are advanced, even about the concept "truth" itself, the authority and the significance—the "truth"—of these claims is dispersed, placed in circulation through a proliferation of interpretations. "We exchange one word for another, and often for one less understood."[8] And so, Montaigne asks, is this not our common experience, in the end, in all fields of study?

In the idiom of contemporary, Western philosophical discourse, the exchange of "one word for another" is an analogue for the substitution of one interpretation for another. To invoke two technical terms taken from the grammatology of Jacques Derrida, we might say it is the "supplementation" or "reinscription" of interpretation by interpretation:[9] that is to say, it is the grafting of one text to others, the "sharing" or "multiplication" of voices in dialogue, as identified by Jean-Luc Nancy.[10] In fact, Montaigne's gloss offers an apt description of the context in which, and the conditions out of which, today, one encounters the question of interpretation in philosophy, literary criticism, film studies, art criticism, the theories of "natural" and "social" science, jurisprudence, psychoanalysis, feminist theory, theology, and other fields. If "there are only interpretations . . . of interpretations," then the systematic pursuit of "truth"—"truth" as the *object* of inquiry—or the search for axiological, epistemological, and metaphysical foundations, will never be brought to completion. Is this not a central consequence of the hermeneutical circle, or, at the very least, of the chain of discourses and interpretations which identify and determine the "hermeneutical circle"?[11] The search after truth, as it were, is deferred, diverted, caught in a network of contextually bound and generated commentaries. Here we begin to see how the proposition that "there are only interpretations of interpretations" is intertwined with and conditioned by certain classical problems. In particular, one may consider the question of reference, especially as it emanates from what Hegel calls "the desire for *absolute knowledge.*"

The problem of reference arises in this context for the following reasons. The desire for/of absolute knowledge is the desire to make present the fundamental unity or ground of knowledge and understanding through the unveiling of *self-evident* first principles and truths. But there is a more significant presumption which involves reference and signification. The ideal object of this desire—"truth," metaphysical "first principles" of "self" and "God," the Kantian "thing in-itself," or Husserlian transcendental conditions—is presumed to stand outside or independent of the linguistic framework, the interpretive context in which it is *"re-presented."* Here interpretation—hermeneutics, more appropriately—intervenes; it must come to terms with certain questions regarding the status of its *object,* the representation of that object, and the relation(s) between our commentaries, "interpretations," and the object *itself.*

Does interpretation lead or extend beyond itself? Does it refer to an "external" world, a specific field of objects that stands outside the linkage of interpretations? Is there a necessary connection assumed between interpretation and its object, a "text" or *the* ("intended") meaning of a text? Does interpretation exhaust itself in its attempt to reveal *its* object? Does it exhaust its object in this attempt? In the language of semiology, we might ask, analogously, if there is a necessary connection assumed between signifier and signified.[12] If interpretation *is* connected to the world in varying ways, what conditions make this connection possible? Is language not the medium for making such links and references? If so, is language anything other than a system of signs, coherent and systematic marks for representation and communication? What would allow for any kind of reference outside the system? Or is language to be understood as an open-ended system of signs and traces that refer only to other signs and traces ad infinitum? Does not the determination of referential conditions and possibilities itself introduce the question of interpretation? Is this determination not an interpretive intervention?

As these questions indicate, interpretation, hermeneutics, and the attendant claim that "there are only interpretations . . ." are not merely conditioned by the desire for absolute knowledge and the problem of reference. The act of interpreting—always and already bound to a chain of interpretations, which is not to say a predetermined meaning or set of possible meanings—stands in complicity with the desire for absolute knowledge: interpretation works on behalf of absolute knowledge *and* it struggles to free itself from the all-encompassing framework of the desire for absolute knowledge. Interpretation, or what Montaigne calls "the need to interpret,'' mediates, and, in effect, is mediated by this desire. As a consequence of this complicity, the act of interpreting, especially if comprehended as an act of *creating connections*, reintroduces the question of unity and harmony, that is to say, *totality*. Creating connections could be understood in accordance to Wilhelm Dilthey's notion of *Zusammenhang*,[13] as well as Julia Kristeva's reformulation of the (Aristotelian and) Stoic conception of interpretation, where ''to interpret'' means ''to make a connection'' (p. 90). It reformulates, it translates, if you will, the question of the unity of knowledge and understanding into questions concerning the unity of sign and signified, of word and object, the harmony of language and reality, of thought and reality, of thought and action. Given this set of conditions, we might answer Montaigne's question ''Do we find any end to the need of interpreting?'' by asking ''How could we find an end to this need when interpretation disguises itself in so many ways, when interpretation masks itself and its desire for absolute knowledge in the drive toward satiety?'' How could we find an end to this need to interpret when, apparently, by its very production and introduction, interpretation defers and transforms its object, and the path it follows (or blazes) in its desire to reveal its object? Is this not a condition which perpetuates the need to interpret?

   ''Like everything metaphysical,'' writes Ludwig Wittgenstein in *Zettel*, ''the harmony between thought and reality is to be found in the grammar of the language.''[14] Like Montaigne's gloss on the Aristotelian metaphysical text and tradition, Wittgenstein's remark points directly to a general issue emanating from the question of interpretation: the congruence and compatibility of discourse (language, interpretation) and the ''meaning'' of human-being, thereby raising the question of understanding the discourse of others. If, in general, the condition of discourse is one where we are unable to thwart the need to interpret, then it should come as no surprise that finally, today, ''after two thousand years'' of submission to the axiom ''the Word became flesh'' (Kristeva, p. 99), we are coming to recognize the far-reaching implications of having ''achieved a discourse on discourse, an interpretation of interpretation'' (*ibid.*). And yet, to recognize this achievement is to acknowledge our quandary: the word, propositions, words on words, interpretations mediate and betray our understanding, our acts, the experience of interpretation.[15]

   With the recognition of this condition, what fascinates the imagination, and what provokes the critical skills and sensibilities of our discourse today, is the *difference* of interpretation, that is to say, the conflict(s) that arise(s) in and through the attempts to offer a commentary on another text, discourse, or analysis. However, one might ask: ''What hangs on this difference—the difference of interpretation?'' Here the difference, the conflict, and the incommensurability of interpretation(s) (or Wittgensteinian "language-games") demonstrates, ironically, how the proposition "there are only interpretations . . ." cannot be granted the status of law, cannot be taken as a first principle nor as the last word. Stated otherwise: interpretation cannot be taken for granted; meaning is not a given with interpretation; its path(s) must be determined.[16] The proposition is, itself, an announcement of the conditions which make interpretation possible as the interpretation of interpretation. It subverts its own claim to "truth." But this is only one concern among many, and the fascination with interpretation theory or hermeneutics does not end here, nor is it to be limited to the issues addressed in this discussion.

Today, one can imagine a contemporary Montaigne asking whether there is a book, any text, that presents *the* word, *another* gospel, a "new" testament regarding a particular subject matter or thematic complex. Is there a text, today, that espouses a certain critical perspective or theory, about which one could say it has offered the last word, about which one could assert that a consensus has been reached? At the very least, can one agree with its proclamation about how to reach consensus in order to re-solve certain philosophical and political dilemmas? Is there a philosophical or political position, for example, taken toward specific questions which would bring one to the point of claiming that "there is now no more to be said about it"? By advancing any one of these claims, would we not do so both in opposition to the desire for absolute knowledge *and* in its name, both against the desire of *philo-sophia and* in its name as well?

The themes and questions identified in this all-too-provisional-and-all-too-brief exegesis of Montaigne's text are announced, suspended from a specific historical epoch and cultural and intellectual context. The issues and questions posed in Montaigne's essay, as they relate to the question of interpretation, have been translated into a foreign context and idiom, and displaced and rewritten for a purpose completely different from what may have given rise to their expression in Montaigne's *Essays.* In this regard, the displacement and translation of "Montaigne"—the proper name, the text, the questions, the interpretations, and so forth—illustrate some of the *consequences* engendered by the proposition that "there are only interpretations . . . of interpretations." "We come to what is tangible and conceivably practical," writes Charles Sanders Peirce, as the "ground" for the determination of meaning(s). Is this not what hangs on the difference of interpretation, or the *differance* of interpretation, to reiterate Derrida's neologism? Groundings? Foundations? Privileged sources? The practice of interpretation, or "active interpretation," is this ground. It provides its *own* condition of possibility, but one which always shifts under one's feet, and one which is fissured and fails to secure certainty. "[T]here is no distinction of meaning so fine as to consist in anything but a possible difference of practice."[17]

Like Montaigne's gloss of Aristotle, the reading of Montaigne's text is a reading between the lines, the insertion of disparate, different assumptions and interests between the lines of another text. If "there are only interpretations . . . ," then each gloss, each reading, becomes a textual intervention and provocation. Such a reading withdraws the "unity" of a text—here the totality of Montaigne's "thought"; it is always and already working toward other purposes, already attempting to achieve other ends. Like Montaigne's gloss, the reading of Montaigne's text, as it relates to the conditions surrounding the question of interpretation in a particular tradition of contemporary Western thought, is always selective, fragmentary, and incomplete, while remaining constitutive of its object and itself. As Michel Foucault remarks, an interpretation "always has to interpret itself . . . [it] cannot fail to return to itself" (p. 66). This is the "experience" of interpretation to which Montaigne refers: interpretation finds itself always positioned, as it comments on other "texts," to comment on itself endlessly, "always correcting itself" (ibid.). This is the "life of interpretation" (ibid.), and this "experience," this practice, this "life," constituting the complex domain of hermeneutics, is the subject for the essays included in this volume.

To advance the proposition that "there are only interpretations of interpretations," or to focus, however provisionally, on the "life of interpretation," then, is to survey one site, among many, in the field of hermeneutics whereby the question of interpretation (both as a problematic and as the subject of an interrogation) can be isolated. It is not an attempt to reduce the question of interpretation or hermeneutics to any one specific theme or set of issues. It is, however, to take account of the heterogeneity of the so-called "hermeneutic tradition."

Moreover, to advance this proposition, to provide this focus, is not an attempt to perpetuate or to give primacy of place to an aloof or disengaged academic debate (though one cannot prohibit this as a possible consequence). At the most rudimentary level of comprehension, interpretation—the exchange of words for words, what others might call "dialogue"—is concerned with the "world," "reality," the historical, cultural, political, economic, technological context or setting into which it is inserted, and against which it is asserted. Interpretation does not release or disengage us from the world. To the contrary, it is through interpretation that we engage the world, our surroundings; through the act of interpretation the world becomes what it is, a "text."[18] Interpretation sets the stage for engagement: we draw the world closer to us through words and language. As with any text, we represent its heterogeneity to ourselves and others; we demonstrate our comprehension of this world through words and language; we articulate our needs and desires, our joys and disappointments, our questions and insights, on the basis of interpretation(s).[19] On the basis of this kind of engagement, these interpretive interventions, we seek and determine, again provisionally, the rules which regulate our actions. But, if our interpretive interventions and provocations lead in these directions, do they not already engage certain assumptions regarding basic categories of thought, and their attendant dichotomies—categories that regulate our efforts to comprehend action and discourse? Is the determination of these presumed categories not itself an *issue* of interpretation?

Furthermore, to advance the proposition that "there are only interpretations . . . ," to insist upon the "experience" of interpretation as a transitory point of focus, is one way to bring into relief a complex set of issues which traverses the history of hermeneutics. The concern with interpreting the words or speech of an other, for example, in light of the duplicitous character of language, is given one of its earliest treatments by Plato's Socrates in the *Cratylus*. Hermes, as his *name* indicates (herald and messenger of other gods, the god of science and cunning, the protector of boundaries, or so the story goes), is an interpreter, "or messenger, or thief, or liar, or bargainer; all that sort of thing has a great deal to do with language." (408a–b).[20] Hermes is represented as a "contriver of tales or speeches." That "speech signifies all things, and is always turning them round and round" (408c), as Socrates announces somewhat ironically, has little to do with Hermes himself. What is important, in this context, is not that Hermes is responsible for the duplicitous character of language and interpretation, except that he "invented language and speech." It is more to the point to note that if Hermes is responsible, it is because he "invents" through the *use* of language. Throughout the dialogues of Plato, as Jean-Luc Nancy points out through his reading of *Ion* (p. 237), it is "the word" which mediates the experience of "all things." *Use* creates, ordering the linguistic field which it engages and the interpretive boundaries of that field. Thus, it is the self-production, the self-effacement of language, in this case the dialogue, which twists and turns words through their use, that determines (1) *how* one understands the ideas and objects one encounters, (2) *what* one understands *about* these ideas and objects, and (3) *that* understanding is possible. Linguistic meaning is determined in and through the dialogue, itself the scene or stage on which the experience of interpretation is played out.[21]

The experience of interpretation, as Montaigne's text insinuates, founds itself on the recognition that language, in a general and systematic fashion, and individual acts of interpretation, in particular, generate the conditions and limits of and for the possibility of understanding. As already noted, Plato's dialogues—specifically, the *Cratylus* and *Ion*—take into account this feature of interpretation and understanding. In a concomitant fashion, Aristotle's *Peri hermēneias* (*De Interpretatione, On Interpretation*), a text which by *name* alone, if not by content, has become the ostensible source for many of the themes and questions addressed in the discourse of hermeneutics, argues for the "linguistic" determination of meaning.[22]

On Interpretation is one of six treatises included in Aristotle's *Organon*. The *Organon*, in general, deals with issues of logic: the principles of argumentation and the techniques of proof or demonstration. Within this domain, *On Interpretation* holds an *intermediary* position among the first three of the six treatises; its subject—*hermēneia*, interpretation—mediates the concerns of *Categories*, which precedes it in the *Organon*, and the *Prior Analytics*, which follows it. Where the *Categories* articulates the classical notion of Substance (chapter 5), the differentiation of substance according to the categories of objects of thought (chapter 4), and uncombined simple terms (chapter 2), the subject of *On Interpretation* is the combination of terms in propositions, the relation of terms, and how any understanding of propositions includes the expression of "truth" or "falsity" (4 17a 1–8). The *Prior Analytics*, then, is concerned with the derivation of inference based upon a set or combination of propositions that, in the end, is expressive of the relation between thought and what it predicates (1 24b 15–20).

The subject of *On Interpretation* is decidedly linguistic, even though at the outset its problematic overlaps with that of *De Anima* (*On the Soul*) (1 16a 7–8). But for Aristotle's purposes, *hermēneia* is to be separated from rhetoric and poetry. *On Interpretation* analyzes the character of propositions: a proposition is a sentence that expresses something true or false about the world. According to Aristotle, "propositions correspond with facts" (9 19a 33–34). Other kinds of sentences or statements, such as a prayer (4 17a 4), poetry, and a question and an answer (*Poetics* 19 1456b 8–10), are subsumed by the study of rhetoric or poetics.

All propositions, according to Aristotle, simple or complex, indicate a fact or facts, by way of universal and particular affirmation or negation. Propositions are significant because they are presentations of either "mental experience" or "spoken words," depending on whether they are expressed as spoken words or written words. "Spoken words are the symbols [representations] of mental experience and written words are the symbols [representations] of spoken words" (*On Interpretation* 1 16a 3–4). Thus, every proposition has meaning because it is the function of the *combination* and *disjunction* of symbols. As Socrates' depiction of Hermes' "invention"

of language points out, meaning is created by use, by "the limitation of convention" (2 16a 19–29). A noun or a name, a sentence or a proposition, has meaning, or is part of meaningful discourse, because it *represents, expresses* something about some-thing. The connections, the relations that exist between the symbol and that which it represents, between spoken words and mental experience, between written words and spoken words, are not natural, but the products of "convention."[23]

In the idiom of Montaigne's discourse on interpretation, we can see how Aristotle's concern with understanding propositions, which are themselves "symbols," "representations," "interpretations" of facts, and as such "correspond" with facts, can be comprehended according to another proposition, "there are only interpretations . . . " The proposition makes an announcement; it announces the experience, the life of interpretation, through the interpretation of the other.

*

* *

The point here is not to gloss over the differences that distinguish the ancient texts of Plato and Aristotle from each other and the texts of Montaigne, or for that matter any of the texts selected for this volume. Indeed, if there is one moment in the experience or life of interpretation which we would hope to celebrate and to embrace, it is the *difference/différance* of interpretation (reading, writing, understanding) that makes possible the continued reiteration of terms, ideas, and concepts from one philosophical epoch to another. We are situated within certain historically and linguistically different contexts, and the repetition of terms, ideas, and concepts entails the transformation of their force and significance. To reiterate: as the epigraph from Montaigne notes, "Our opinions [interpretations] are grafted upon one another; the first serves as a stock to the second, the second to the third, and so forth." When we reinscribe these hermeneutic motifs, when we trace the paths blazed in their formulation, we interpret, we translate, these motifs according to a different set of desires and interests. And yet, "whatever and however we may try to think, we think within the sphere of tradition."[24] This interpretive transformation involves the displacement of old concepts; it involves leaping, as Wittgenstein says, "from one level of thought to another."[25] The task, then, is to record the difference(s)/*différance* of interpretation, the experience of interpretation, not by blurring the conflicts and confrontations but by affirming the differences and points of divergence and appropriation as making possible a preliminary articulation of the proposition "there are only interpretations . . . of interpretations."

Interpretation and Transformation of the Hermeneutic Context:
The Postmodernity of Interpretation

The selections and essays comprising this book provide readings which not only reinscribe certain basic hermeneutic themes, but as such effect a dissemination, a scattering, of themes across a field of diverse perspectives and orientations. In spite of the eclectic character of the assays brought together here, in their respective ways, the writers presented in this collection share certain concerns—concerns that traverse the history of hermeneutics—with the writers brought together in *The Hermeneutic Tradition:* questions surrounding the character and goals of interpretation; the effects of interpretative intervention; the representation, multiplication, and articulation of alternate voices in philosophical, political, and poetic exchange; and the desire to expose and, perhaps, to work up against the "limits" of language imposed by traditional conceptions of interpretation and understanding, all the while remaining painfully aware that limits are established through use.

To borrow an image which plays a central role in Jean-Luc Nancy's "Sharing Voices," it seems appropriate to say that the "authors" represented here are analogues, though no more nor less so than the "authors" included in *The Hermeneutic Tradition* in this regard, of the Greek rhapsodes described in Plato's *Ion.* Just as the rhapsode is an interpreter of a poet, who is an interpreter—*creator,* "inventor"—of the myths regarding the gods, the authors represented in this section are interpreters of the words, the declarations, the writings, which constitute the "hermeneutic tradition." Each provides a theatrical interpretation of some question or theme already articulated or inscribed within the tradition. Each offers an "inspired" performance, an announcement of some theme or question issued by the hermeneutic tradition—if not the "thought" and words of a "poet." In this regard, these authors—indeed, all of us—are tethered to the tradition, as the iron rings in *Ion* are linked to one another by a magnetic force. The force of magnetism "passes through the rings, which are able to act (*poiein*) in their turn like the magnet, and attract other rings" p. 234). And yet, as Nancy notes, even though this constitutes " 'a very long series of rings suspended from one another' " (*Ion* 533 c), the rings, the voices, the interpretations of interpretation, are not "chained" to one another. They are "suspended from one another." In this way, they remain "*unchained* (in every manner one can imagine it), and they hold together" (Nancy, p. 234).

The *suspension* of hermeneutic themes, then, is also a fragmentation of the hermeneutic legend. It entails the displacement of those themes, those points of connection, and the transformation of what, in effect, can be called the "hermeneutic context"—the conditions and settings of and for the life of interpretation. Further, suspension of the hermeneutic question in the writings of Nietzsche, Foucault, Blondel, Kristeva, Derrida, Frank, Hamacher, and Nancy sets the stage for exploring what we call the "postmodernity" of interpretation.

We do not intend for the selections contained in this text to be associated or identified with the contemporary movement known as "postmodernism." Nor do we intend to offer these selections as representative of so-called "postmodern theories of interpretation" and, in doing so, oppose them to the selections constituting *The Hermeneutic Tradition.* There is an overwhelming number of art forms (architecture, film, dance, painting), theories of literary criticism, historiography, and psychoanalysis, as well as of philosophical perspectives, which fall under the rubric of "postmodernism." By drawing attention to the "postmodernity" of interpretation, we wish only to erect markers which indicate what others have called a "condition,"[26] an "occasion,"[27] an "awareness,"[28] or even a "turn" or "sensibility."[29] Referring to "postmodernity," we wish to mark out what seems to be the nascent condition of interpretation, whether one is concerned with issues of method, objectivity, ideology-critique, or the dissemination of interpretation through interpretation. To refer to the "postmodernity of interpretation" is to refer to the possibilities of hermeneutics, the possibilities of histories and traditions, the possibilities of interpretation. As such, this possibility, this condition, is "always already there"— that is to say, it is always and already a *current issue,* never limited in its effects to a specific historical moment. Passing from hand to hand, as it were, the word, "interpretation" always circulates—suspending, fragmenting, decentering, but always transforming its object and subject in the experience of interpretation. The postmodernity of interpretation indicates the ever-present possibilities of otherness, the difference(s) of sign and its object, of interpretation and the text that mark(s) the life of interpretation.

With the fragments and essays presented in this context, the themes of (textual) universality and legitimacy are suspended. The universality of the "ontology of prior understanding" and the legitimacy of ideology-critique, for example, assumes particular goals, ends which are informed by privileged categories and rules. The selections contained in this text, in general, emphasize *the act* of interpretation, *the performative* character of interpretation, where the performance is not governed or regulated by a set of preestablished, prosaic principles or categories. Instead, the questions of communication, understanding, interpretation, and representation are used, radicalized in an elliptical fashion, as Hamacher suggests in his reading of Schleiermacher (p. 200), to show how the principles or categories thought to regulate "interpretation" are put forward, sent forth in the act(s) of communication (dialogue), the *event(s)* of interpretation, the production of representation. Unity, universality, and legitimation are fictive consequences of interpretation, set forth in the multiplication of interpretive strategies and devices. In this way, the hermeneutic legend is transfigured, the hermeneutical context transformed. Displacement and fragmentation, rather than the unity and harmony of either a generalized or regionalized "hermeneutics," prefigure the discourse on interpretation.

Under the domains of "traditional" and "post-Heideggerian" hermeneutics, the task is to articulate universal principles and conditions of understanding and, thus, to overcome those obstacles that hinder and prohibit understanding a "text." In short, understanding and meaningful discourse unfold concomitantly. On the one hand, with Ast certain principles are required to achieve an understanding of the "one idea" that guides a text as a whole.[30] Schleiermacher's general hermeneutics is designed to uncover the interpretive techniques which function universally within understanding. The task of interpretation, then, according to Schleiermacher, is "to understand the discourse just as well as and even better than its creator."[31] On the other hand, this theme is expressed, in a similar manner, in *Truth and Method*. According to Gadamer, the "assimilation of what is said" in the tradition, "to the point that it becomes one's own," is the goal of understanding.[32] In fact, the appropriation of the foreign, "that something *distant* has to be brought close, a certain strangeness overcome, a bridge built between the once and the now,"[33] is the "hermeneutical problem" broadly construed.

This desire for and of understanding, the need to know which interpretation is supposed to satisfy, is exactly what is suspended in the readings of the hermeneutic tradition presented here. It is with Friedrich Nietzsche that the challenge to the tradition of Ast, Schleiermacher, Dilthey, Heidegger, Gadamer, Betti, Habermas, and Ricoeur receives its initial proclamation. If we apply Nietzsche's comments regarding *"the origin of our concept of knowledge,"* found in *The Gay Science*, the "hermeneutical problem" can be understood as the desire *to reduce* the strange to the familiar. But, for Nietzsche's purposes, what is more significant is that the desire to know is easily satisfied once it becomes a *rule*. He writes: "What is familiar means what we are used to so that we no longer marvel at it, our everyday, some *rule* in which we are stuck, anything at all in which we feel at home. Look, isn't our need for knowledge precisely this need for the familiar, the will to uncover under everything strange, unusual, and questionable something that no longer disturbs us?" (p. 48) Beginning with Nietzsche, disquietude, fragmentation, and the heterogeneity of interpretation are embraced and celebrated, not so much as an end which interpretation is to realize but as a *function* of interpretive intervention, as a predicate of the life of interpretation.

There is one thread which joins Nietzsche with and yet suspends his texts from the tradition of hermeneutics: " 'to understand' means merely: to be able to express something new in the language of something old and familiar" (p. 53). To the extent that the words "understand" and "knowledge" have any meaning, according to the rule of common usage, "the world" is comprehensible, "knowable" (*ibid*). But, Nietzsche continues, "it is *interpretable* otherwise, it has no meanings behind it, but countless meanings.—'Perspectivism' " (*ibid.*). According to Nietzsche, we cannot extricate ourselves from the play of perspectives and interpretations. The classical notions of "a timeless knowing subject," "pure reason," "absolute spirituality," and "knowledge in itself" are pure fictions on which rests the security of understanding. There is *"only* a perspective seeing, *only* a perspective 'knowing' " (p. 47), but if the "world" can be interpreted in other ways, if it has "become 'infinite' for us all over again," then "we cannot reject the possibility that it *may include infinite interpretations*" (p. 49).

Furthermore, if there are no limits "to the ways in which the world can be interpreted," as Nietzsche asserts in the fragments of *The Will to Power* (section 600, p. 56 below), and if there are only interpretations produced from definite perspectives, the world ("being" or "life," as Blondel argues for Nietzsche) is always and only an "apparent" world, "not a fact but a fable and approximation" based on "a meager sum of observations"(p. 57). The "truth" of the world, then, is in a constant "state of becoming, as a falsehood changing but never getting near the: truth for—there is no 'truth' " (*ibid.*). The "truth" of the world, of life of being, the truth of our knowledge *about* the world, the truth of our understanding *of* the world, is cast as a fiction, but one which has been interpreted as something else. "Truths are illusions," writes Nietzsche in an often cited early essay, "about which one has forgotten that this is what they are" (p. 43).

For Nietzsche, to embrace the lack of certainty engendered by the possibility of infinite interpretations is not to embrace nihilism. On the contrary, it is only through interpretation that "meaning," in any sense of the word, can be introduced into the world. Meaning or truth are not *already there;* they are produced, interpreted according to a particular scheme which cannot be discarded (p. 54), a scheme which is itself the product of interpretive interventions in the world. Thus, interpretation is, according to Nietzsche, "a *process in infinitum,*" an active determination and affirmation of life itself; a *sign* or symptom of "growth or decline" (p. 56).

The relationship between semiology (semeiotic) and the perspectival and interpretive character of life in Nietzsche's writings is another theme to be explored in an attempt to comprehend the life of interpretation. As a sign or symptom of a particular perspective, interpretation always and already signifies other interpretations: interpretations which, as in the case of "truth," have been forgotten, buried in the attempts to overcome other, perhaps narrower, interpretations. It is this connection between semiology and interpretation (or hermeneutics in general) which acts as a point of reference in the selections by Foucault, Blondel, and Kristeva.

In "Nietzsche, Freud, Marx," Michel Foucault addresses what he calls "some themes concerning *the techniques of interpretation.*" Foucault's concern with "techniques of interpretation" is, in effect, an interest in analyzing "two kinds of suspicions" encountered in the discourse on language. Foucault first addresses the suspicion that "language does not say exactly what it means. The meaning that one grasps, and that is immediately manifest, is perhaps in reality only a lesser meaning that shields, restrains, and despite everything transmits another meaning, the meaning 'underneath it' " (p. 59). The use of language engenders a second suspicion in that "in some way [language] overflows its properly verbal form, and there are many other things in the world that speak, and that are not language" (*ibid.*).

The identification of these two suspicions is, ostensibly, the deployment of Foucault's own interpretive technique. By associating the first suspicion with the concepts of '*allegoria*' and '*hyponïa,*' and the second suspicion with the concept of '*semaïnon*' [*semêion*], Foucault juxtaposes the fundamental concepts that found "anew the possibility of a hermeneutic" in the sixteenth and seventeenth centuries and then, again, in the nineteenth century with Nietzsche, Freud, and Marx. But these founding concepts and suspicions provide more than a way to comprehend the ground on which a hermeneutic is possible. They identify two contrasting tendencies in interpretive techniques which can be traced in texts like the first book of *Capital, The Birth of Tragedy, On The Genealogy of Morals,* and *The Interpretation of Dreams.* According to Foucault, these texts, and the interpretive techniques used in them, are significant because "we interpret ourselves according to these techniques" and today we read Nietzsche, Freud, and Marx in accordance with them. The consequence is that we are always thrown into and return in "a perpetual play of mirrors," that is to say, interpretive representations in which we see ourselves according to an assemblage of classical conceptions of *resemblance* (p. 60).

Tracing the differences and resemblances of two specific themes in the texts of Nietzsche, Freud, and Marx, that is, the transformation of the "space in which signs can be signs" and, in particular, the "incompleteness of interpretation," Foucault identifies what he calls the "postulates of modern hermeneutics": "If interpretation can never be brought to an end, it is simply because there is nothing to interpret. There is nothing absolutely primary to interpret, because at bottom everything is already interpretation. Each sign is in itself not the thing that presents itself to interpretation, but the interpretation of other signs" (p. 64). Interpretation can only seize another interpretation which is buried within the system of discourse.

In this regard, Marx does not interpret history as such, or the "history of relations of production." Instead Marx interprets a "relation that . . . is already giving itself as an interpretation." It is an interpretation of relations which represents the material conditions of production as "nature." Freud does not interpret signs or symptoms of diseases; he does not discover any-*thing*—"traumatism"—beneath these symptoms. Rather, he interprets interpretations; each sign, each symptom, refers to a fantasy— itself an interpretation—to be interpreted. And, finally, in Nietzsche's texts, interpretations are already interpretations "which have already seized one another." As already indicated in the discussion of Nietzsche, there is no "truth," there is no "transcendental signified," in Nietzsche's eyes. "Words themselves are nothing other than interpretations; throughout their history, they interpret before being signs, and in the long run they signify only because they are only essential interpretations" (p. 65): that is to say, as Nietzsche notes in the first essay of *On the Genealogy of Morals,* words impose interpretations on the world.

Foucault's concern with "techniques of interpretation," then, pertains not only to how the relationship between semiology and hermeneutics is conceived; it pertains, as well, to the question of how this relationship is put into practice. On the one hand, if one believes that "there are signs, signs that exist primarily, originally, actually, like coherent, pertinent, and systematic marks," in other words, signs which refer to an arcane object, a *signified,* then one practices a hermeneutic that marks the "death of interpretation." It would be a hermeneutic that "gives up the violence, the incompleteness, the infinity of interpretations, so as to create a reign of terror where the mark rules" (p. 67). On the other hand, a hermeneutic that affirms the "life of interpretation," that is the belief that "there is nothing but interpretations," affirms the violence of life, as Nietzsche would say, the incompleteness and fragmentation of interpretation. This would be a hermeneutic that "envelopes around itself the intermediate region of madness and pure language," where interpretation never stops implicating itself.

The difference between the two suspicions is a difference discerned only in practice, a difference in technique. But this difference presupposes another difference, another interpretation: it is a question of whether signs designate *objects* which stand outside the system of signs, or whether signs designate as their objects other interpretations, suspended within a chain of interpretations. It is this difference which leads Foucault to claim that *"hermeneutics and semiology are two ferocious enemies."*

For Eric Blondel, in "Interpreting Texts With and Without Nietzsche," and Julia Kristeva, in "Psychoanalysis and the Polis," interpretation (the possibility of hermeneutics) and semiology are decidedly interrelated. The contentious quality of their intersection, found in Foucault's discussion, is missing in the texts of Blondel and Kristeva. Interpretation and signs are never placed in isolation from one another; the possibility of the one always carries with it the possibility of the *other*.

"Interpreting Texts With and Without Nietzsche" presents an account of the relation between interpretation and sign that demands interpretation on the basis of the very ambiguity, ambivalence, uncertainty, and multiplicity of the subject which it addresses—interpretation. In order to articulate the ambiguity and multiplicity of perspectives announced at the outset, Blondel presents three "portraits," three texts, three parables, which introduce the "theoretical problem of interpretation" but which also, in the end, evoke Nietzsche's conception of interpretation. Blondel claims that he will focus on two portraits, one presented in a text of Balzac's and one from a text of Proust's. But, as one will see, Blondel presents a portrait of Nietzsche, as well, in his analysis of Nietzsche's conception of interpretation.

The three portraits depict how the texts of Balzac, Proust, and Nietzsche present themselves as "interpreting texts." Here "interpreting texts" signifies both "the interpretation of texts," that is to say, a commentary on a text, and "texts which interpret," that is, a text that practices interpretation by assuming its own object to be interpretive. Blondel uses Balzac as a parable of "interpretation *on*" a text, and he uses Proust as a parable of "interpretation *in*" a text (p. 69). Nietzsche is placed in reserve, suspended for the moment as the frame through which the texts and Balzac and Proust can be read. And yet, Nietzsche is inserted always into the readings of Balzac and Proust. According to Blondel's portrait, Nietzsche's texts practice and maintain the play of both styles of interpretation.

All three portraits are "strictly *interpretive*" enterprises, simultaneously descriptive and intuitive. First Blondel focuses on an excerpt from Balzac's *Father Goriot* in which the character Vautrin is introduced. According to Blondel, Balzac attempts to provide a portrait which describes Vautrin's character, nature, and personality. It is a portrait that "wishes to reach the truth," desires to reveal the truth of (a) being by outlining "the concept of human being." In order to achieve this end, Balzac's attempt can only proceed on the basis of signs. The truth of Vautrin's character, his being, is revealed in the interpretation of signs. As such, the portrait is forever incomplete and wanting, always ambiguous. As it attempts to decode signs, the portrait "obscures" its subject or object, all the while appearing to be certain of its task. Blondel claims that Balzac's portrait of Vautrin is "a non-portrait," "an anti-portrait," a "non-descriptive portrait." It is a "mask." Despite what appears to be the well-defined character of Vautrin, the portrait "reveals and insists upon its conjectural and interpretive character." Desiring to present Vautrin, the portrait "dismantles its own interpretive apparatus." We learn from Balzac, according to Blondel, that "we cannot trust any appearances, any signs, in truth not even *this* discourse which wishes to be truthful" (p. 72).

Next, Blondel offers a reading of Proust's description of Madame Swann taken from *Remembrance of Things Past*. Whereas Balzac, according to Blondel, leaves the ambiguity and interpretive character of a portrait to be surmised or understood, though never explicitly stated, Proust thematizes these characteristics. For Proust, the portrait involves both the "practice" of interpretation as well as the "placement in the abyss of this practice." Conscious of itself, "interpretation . . . takes for its object interpreting itself" (*ibid.*).In this portrait of Madame Swann, Proust presents a set of observations which focus upon "(a) simple and brute reality . . . ; (b) the interpretation of exterior signs . . . ; and (c) factual reality. . . ." This account brings to light (1) reality's ambiguity, (2) how interpretation is always precarious, illusory, and subject to error, and (3) how reality must be "committed" to interpretation because of its inherently "enigmatic character" (p. 74). According to Blondel, Proust's text, his portrait of Madame Swann, is a reflection on the concept of the sign. Reality, then, is an "ensemble of signs," and our knowledge of this reality is radically contingent and can only be interpretive knowledge, never explicative or objective knowledge.

In the portraits offered by Balzac and Proust, Blondel emphasizes the ambiguity of signs and the context in which they are inscribed. Both characters are masks of themselves: Vautrin is also known as Jacques Collin, a convict, and Madame Swann is known otherwise, in another set of circumstances that intrude upon her life as Swann's wife, as Odette de Crécy, the prostitute. In Balzac's text, the portrait unravels a riddle created by interpretation, whereas in the Proust text, interpretation is explicitly thematized. In each case, the "object" of the portrait is ambiguous by nature and status. It can only "give/conceal" itself, writes Blondel, and always at the "risk of an interpretation." "The risk of interpretation, then, creates the relations with the riddle, the mystery, soothsaying" (p. 75).

To say that reality, or being, is an "ensemble of signs" and must be interpreted as such is to invoke a fundamental theme in Nietzsche's conception of interpretation: "interpretation is simultaneously other than and the same as the text." Blondel's portrait of Nietzsche's texts, as texts which comment on *and* interpret in a text, emphasizes this theme. The object of interpretation is being; thus, being *is as* it is interpreted. In the Nietzschean text, according to Blondel, being remains enigmatic and unthinkable, unfathomable, except by the interpretation of signs. In that case, "Being *is* not; it designates, it signifies" some-*thing* other than what it is (p. 80). Moreover, interpretation must be understood as a philological metaphor of *ontological* significance, according to which "the world is a text" and "being is deciphered." Interpretation, for Nietzsche, is being, and "being is interpretation." In these terms, Blondel notes exactly how interpretation makes "being *be* . . . " through "a movement of metaphoric displacement" in which *it*—interpretation *and* being—is always caught by and slips away from apprehension.

Focusing on the "political" dimension of interpretation, Julia Kristeva maintains that in comparison to "Marxism in the United States" and "post-Heideggerian 'deconstructivism'," it is psychoanalysis, à la Freud, which offers the only "theoretical breakthrough" capable of mobilizing radical thought. The "decentering" of the "speaking-subject" by psychoanalysis leads to "the very foundations of language" (p. 89)—that is to say, it leads directly to the birth of interpretation in the sign-signified relation. How psychoanalysis, or what Kristeva terms "analytic interpretation," moves in this direction is the organizing motif of "Psychoanalysis and the Polis."

Presented initially at a conference on the "Politics of Interpretation," Kristeva's text accepts the premise that "there are political implications inherent in the act of interpretation itself, whatever meaning that interpretation bestows" (p. 90). Like Nietzsche, like Foucault, and like Blondel (among others), Kristeva argues that every act of interpretation introduces, assumes, a certain perspective or position from which meaning is conferred upon an object which is always an enigma. But it is *how* the object is identified, according to which specific conception of interpretation the object is determined, that interests Kristeva.

Every act of interpretation arises out of the "desire to give meaning" to the world. According to Kristeva, the *desire* to give meaning—always an indication of a lack—receives its most acute expression with the interpretive act which desires to give "political meaning" to something. According to Kristeva, the desire to give meaning is not an innocent desire or attitude. It is given through the need of the speaking-subject "to reassure himself of his image and his identity faced with an object," to position him- or herself in relation to the *other*. Without this confrontation between "subject" and "object," the speaking-subject lacks identity and placement in the world.

Such is the decentered condition of the speaking-subject. "Political interpretation is thus the apogee of the obsessive quest for A Meaning" (*ibid.*).
Psychoanalysis radicalizes interpretation; it "cuts through political illusions, fantasies, and beliefs to the extent that they consist in providing
only one meaning, an uncriticizable ultimate Meaning, to human behavior."
In this manner, the intervention of analytic interpretation thwarts the desire—the desire to provide an answer, to interpret—to render any discourse,
political or other, as a new "religion," "the final explanation" (*ibid.*).
Psychoanalytic interpretation understands that the delusions of the patients
are the "equivalents of the [interpretive] constructions" built up in the
"course of an analytic treatment—attempts at explanation and cure."[34]
Psychoanalysis can provide only "a discourse on a discourse, an interpretation of interpretation," where the object of analytic discourse is a patient's delusions.

In order to substantiate her claims regarding the revolutionary character, and potential, of analytic interpretation, Kristeva returns to the Stoic
conception of interpretation rather than, and juxtaposed to, a Platonic conception. According to Kristeva's account, the Stoic conception envisions
interpretation as an "epistemological and ethical attitude." It is not to be
confused with or reduced to the Platonic notion of *theory,* because this "assumes a prior knowledge of the ideal Forms to which all action and creation is subordinate." In effect, the Platonic conception of interpretation as
theory searches for an end to its activity, an object that is to be revealed; it
seeks an "ultimate Meaning." On the other hand, the Stoic conception envisions interpretation as not only an act whereby one "'interprets'" or "'attempts to understand'" the words of God but also as an act whereby one
makes "connections" between the words and works of God and subsequent
action (*ibid.*). "To make connections" implies, in this context, going beyond the sign-signified relation. It indicates that more than one connection
is possible, more than one interpretation is possible; it indicates that the
possibility of interpretation itself is given in the sign-signified relation, a
relation bound by the desire to give meaning.

Kristeva admits that an analysis of this relationship must acknowledge
an inherent circularity. On the one hand, grounded in the sign-signified relation, hermeneutics produces its own "'preselected'" object, "'enclosing the
enigmatic (interpretable) object within the interpretive theory's preexistent
system." The "logic" of hermeneutics requires, according to the model of
the hermeneutical circle, that interpretation (as theory) project an "object
onto a theoretical place at a distance, outside its grasp, thereby eliciting the
very possibility of interrogation (Heidegger's *Sachverhalt*)" (p. 91). In
Kristeva's eyes, on the other hand, it seems that given this "hermeneutic
tautology," interpretation of this particular kind "harbors its object."

Kristeva does not pursue the question of "whether interpretation is a circle or a spiral." It is too much a Platonic issue which does not take into account the innovation of the Stoic conception. Whereas the Platonic-Heideggerian conception of interpretation generates and maintains *distance* between interpretation and object, between theory and practice, the Stoic-Kristevian model attempts to eliminate this gap, this classic binary polarization. What makes this elimination possible is "the field of subjectivity": when one interprets, makes connections, one *creates* the interpretable object; one encounters an object not preselected to fit within an already enclosed system. Such a possibility is the possibility of "posthermeneutic and perhaps even postinterpretive" interpretation (p. 92), where the object is unnameable, positioned beyond the logic of hermeneutics.

The difference in the confrontation of subject and object, or what in other terms would be described as the realization of the desire for meaning, is a difference in forms of interpretive intervention. If one accepts the Platonic-Heideggerian conception of interpretation *as theory,* then "the object may succumb to the interpretive interventions of the interpreter," which leads to various forms of domination. However, if one accepts the conception of interpretation, informed by the Stoics, Marx, Freud, by which interpretation is seen "as transformation and as cure," then "the object could reveal to the interpreter the unknown of his theory and permit the constitution of a new theory" (*ibid.*). In this case, discourse is renewed, its desire to give meaning is transmuted, it becomes a desire to create an-other discourse, an-other object, an-other interpretation. Here the interpreter is no longer satisfied with the presentation of an *object* within the interpretive space of hermeneutics. Rather the interpreter, Kristeva's "speaking-subject," "renounces the game of *indebtedness, proximity,* and *presence* hidden within the connotations of the concept of interpretation." (*ibid.*). "Breaking out of the enclosure of the presentness of meaning, the *new* 'interpreter' no longer interprets: he speaks, he 'associates,' because there is no longer an object of interpretation; there is, instead, the setting off of semantic, logical, phantasmatic, and indeterminable sequences" (*ibid.*). As a result, the "metalinguistic" status of interpretation is canceled. If there is to be an "ob-ject" of interpretation, it will be the dissemination of interpretation which seeks to rupture the closure of the hermeneutic logic.

Within Jacques Derrida's texts, the question of interpretation is polymorphic. The form in which the question of interpretation, and hermeneutics in general, appears depends on the context and organizing theme of his speculations. Interpretation is inserted always into a chain of metaphysical terms, that is, a series of equally overdetermined terms taken from the

history of philosophy, psychoanalysis, and literature. These terms are reinscribed, diverted from their "original" context and path, and are given different uses throughout his texts. Interpretation is thus determined by the
other terms in this chain, or other "interpretations" or "representations"
of this chain, but only to the extent that it comes to replace or to place
"under erasure" those terms, subvert their significant unity through its use,
through its having been inserted into the series. Within this chain one can
locate terms (concepts) such as *arché-writing, sign, trace, supplement, différance, gram, grafting, writing, metaphor, spacings, translation, envoi(s),
representation,* and so forth.[35]

Derrida's relation to the hermeneutic tradition of Western thought is
best understood in terms of the "undecidability" of interpretive interventions. As opposed to what he calls "the hermeneutic project,"[36] Derrida
positions "the transformative activity of interpretation."[37] According to
this juxtaposition, hermeneutics "postulates a true sense of the text,"[38] a
true meaning hidden in the text, but a meaning which is, as yet, inarticu-
lable except by the intervention of a specific interpretive strategy. The "active transformation of interpretation," then, is not bound by a desire for an
ultimate meaning, nor is it grounded in the desire to pursue the truth (or
essence) of being—as if one could announce the *presence* of this truth or
represent its essence in interpretation. But this is not to establish a hierarchy of interpretive strategies or to assign entitlements among a closed set of
possible performative interventions. Interpretation—the life or "play" of
interpretation—enjoins the necessity of choice, suspends the prescription
that one mode of interpretive intervention is to be preferred and, as such,
pursued because of its promise to produce the truth, being, the truth of
being. According to Derrida,

> there are thus two interpretations of interpretation, of structure, of
> sign, of play. The one seeks to decipher, dreams of deciphering a
> truth or an origin which escapes play and the order of the sign, and
> which lives the necessity of interpretation as an exile. The other,
> which is no longer turned toward the origin, affirms play and tries to
> pass beyond man and humanism, the name of man being the name of
> that being who, throughout the history of metaphysics or of ontothe-
> ology—in other words, throughout his entire history—has dreamed
> of full presence, the reassuring foundation, the origin and end of
> play.[39]

There can be no choice between these two interpretations. Their irreducible differences are the differences which make possible interpretation:
the contextual transformation of interpretation. "Interpretation will be nei-

ther hermeneutical nor exegetical readings but performative interventions in the political rewriting of the text and of its destination."[40]

Derrida's announcements regarding the differences of interpretation simultaneously reveal his relation to the hermeneutic tradition. Even though interpretation entails the "systematic" rewriting of "the text and its destination," a disruption of the hermeneutic program, this does not entail an escape from or rupture of the closure of metaphysics, in this case, the hermeneutical circle. Rather it indicates that the hermeneutical circle is one among many "performative [interpretive] interventions" to be redirected, diverted, reinscribed, to be sent elsewhere. This repetition is bequeathed by the legacy—the "life"—of interpretation.[41] All breaks with or ruptures in the tradition, then, are "always, and fatally, reinscribed in an old cloth that must be continually, interminably undone."[42] But, for Derrida, one can produce and affirm rupture only by "repeating what is implicit in the founding concepts and the original problematic, by using against the edifice the instruments or stones available in the house."[43]

That *everything*—interpretation, translation, writing, reading, representation—"begins by referring back [*par le renvoi*], that is to say, does not begin" is a theme Derrida pursues in "Sending: On Representation" (p. 136). In its own fashion and according to its own protocols, "Sending: On Representation" represents one of many contexts in which Derrida engages the hermeneutic question, particularly as an issue both suspended from and suspended in Heidegger's texts.[44] Tracing the philological development of *representation, repraesentatio, Vorstellung,* and *Darstellung,* in conjunction with the renderings received in Heidegger's meditations on Being as *Anwesenheit,* Derrida uses the concept of "representation," in its various lexical, semantic, and historical determinations, to challenge two conditions which are assumed for the purpose of "fixing the meaning of a word or overcoming the polysemy of a name": "the existence of an invariant under the diversity of semantic transformations on the one hand, the possibility of determining a context which would saturate the meaning on the other hand" (pp. 110–11). In effect, Derrida is engaged in an intervention that traverses the scope and breadth of his texts: the subversion and redirection of the search for essences, foundations, origins.

The belief in these two conditions regarding the possible fixation of a word's meaning is one of the "bad effects of philosophy." It arises from a practice, and a theoretical base, that attempts "to think what a concept means in itself, to think what representation is, the essence of representation in general" (p. 111). Of course, Derrida's comments regarding representation apply, in general, to interpretation. Where he claims that representation "is the interpretation of the essence of what is as an object of representation," one could substitute "interpretation" for "representation.'' According to the hermeneutic project, a project which Derrida identifies with the *Geschick des Seins* of which Heidegger speaks, interpretation seeks to comprehend and to articulate the essence of its object. *"Representation"* has become "the most general category to determine the apprehension of whatever it is that is of concern or interest in any relation at all" p. 118). As such, for Derrida representation is already *pre*-sent as interpretation.

To think of interpretation or representation in terms other than those of hermeneutical or exegetical readings—that is, presentations of a sustained meaning or sense—is to think of interpretation according to its sending (*envoi*), not as a sending of itself but as the dissemination "of the other, of others" (p. 132). According to Derrida's own *envois,*[45] there can be no representation of representation, if one means by this the *re*-presentation of the essence of representation. Representation is not representable. It does not enclose itself. In a similar fashion, there can be no representation of interpretation, no "interpretation of interpretation" if one means by this phrase the representation or interpretation of the essence of "interpretation." Like *Anwesenheit* (according to Derrida's reading of Heidegger's text), neither representation nor interpretation presents a simple unity, nor can either be comprehended as one. Representation—interpretation—"is already divided and differentiated, it marks the place of a cut, of a division, of a dissension [*Zwiespalt*]" (p. 124). The representation of interpretation, the interpretation of interpretation "issues forth only on the basis of the other, the other in itself without itself" (p. 136), where *the other* signifies difference. For Derrida, every representation *is* already an interpretive intervention that *is* already the *sending* of another sort(ie). Just as every sending, every *envoi,* is a retracing, a *renvoi* which returns to no simple origin but to "a multiplicity of *renvois,* so many different traces referring back to other traces and to traces of others" (*ibid.*), so too is every interpretation a sending, what Montaigne calls a "grafting" of one interpretation to another where "the first serves as a stock to the second, the second to the third, and so forth."

The final three selections, by Manfred Frank, Werner Hamacher, and Jean-Luc Nancy, explore in different ways the Derridean theme that "everything begins by referring back . . . to other traces and to traces of others." Frank and Hamacher refer back to Schleiermacher; Nancy retraces Heidegger by way of Plato. The grafting of one thought to another does not permit the presentation of an author's thought *as such,* as a whole or a unity, complete unto itself. And Frank, Hamacher, and Nancy do not attempt such a unifying presentation. Instead, they engage certain lines of thought, motifs, and questions which have been repeated so often within the hermeneutic tradition that they have come to be recognized in a standard form as the tradition. The differences which once constituted their announcements have been obliterated. As a consequence, certain themes and texts are forgotten, certain questions are presented as if they are already resolved, eclipsed by the identification of categories and postulates which have come to organize hermeneutics. By referring back to certain fundamental axioms of the hermeneutic tradition, Frank, Hamacher, and Nancy thus are able to recall and reinsert other themes suspended and marginalized by the life of interpretation itself.

In "The Interpretation of a Text," Manfred Frank sends the hermeneutic tradition back to the texts of Friedrich Schleiermacher in order to insert Jean-Paul Sartre into the hermeneutic tradition. In this context, Sartre's "hermeneutic method" of "regressive analysis" and "progressive synthesis" is contrasted with the structural analysis of codes offered by Roland Barthes, the poststructuralist reading of Saussurean semiological *difference*, as it is articulated and rewritten in Derrida's texts, and the "pragmatic" speech-act theories of J. L. Austin and John Searle. According to Frank, Sartre's work in *Search for a Method* and *The Family Idiot* understands the force and significance of Schleiermacher's claim that "interpretation [*Auslegung*] is art" (p. 159, cf. Hamacher, p. 196).[46] Tracing a theme he attributes to Schleiermacher, Frank writes that "the unity of the text . . . is not a function of its grammar but of the intellectual mobility of its reader whose . . . creative power, through interpretation, makes up for the absence of a textual unity."[47]

The point at which Schleiermacher's texts and Sartre's texts converge is where both claim that "every interpretation remains *in the final analysis* hypothetical" (p. 161). As Frank notes, Sartre discusses understanding (*Verstehen*) as a "hypothesis."[48] By necessity one can only present a hypothesis in order to comprehend "that which is not disclosed through the convention of discourse and of words, that which is radically 'new' in an expression" (*ibid.*). It is this hypothetical, conjectural character of understanding which differentiates "textual interpretation" from the codified, canonic procedures of science and hermeneutics as theory.

In order "to understand the text at first as well as and then even better than its author," Schleiermacher claims that one must comprehend its "style." Style is the *individual use* of discourse that allows the text to express something new and different. According to Frank, for Schleiermacher the "main-ideas" of a text are not "the products of an extratextual intervention of the interpreting subject" (p. 150). The "main-ideas" are already woven into the fabric of signs and grammar; thus, the text for Schleiermacher is a "work" fabricated, a "deed-thing" (*Tat-sache*), a "meaningful thing that owes its existence to the *deed* of an individual who creates meaning" (p. 147). Deciphering or decoding a particular text is possible only when any text is composed of signs that "give each expression a lasting and quite particular interpretation." But interpretation does not limit itself to a decoding of expressions in which a meaning is hidden. Instead, according to Schleiermacher, and it is the assertion of this point which leads Frank to Sartre, "the allocations of significance to particular expressions (can) slip away from obligatory rules in the course of the story (of the text-reader communication) and consequently appeal to the reader's collaboration in the creation of meaning." At this point, according to Schleiermacher (and Frank), " 'the hermeneutic operation extends to the psychological side' " (p. 158).

Rather than remaining at a level of understanding where a text is grasped as a "form without a world, abstracted from situations, and without an author," Schleiermacher stresses the importance of extending the scope of interpretation to the "other side" of textual analysis, where interpretation is technical interpretation: "*the complete understanding of style*" (p. 159). It is at this juncture that Frank inserts Sartre. Sartre's hermeneutic method of regressive analysis and progressive synthesis applies simultaneously to an individual and to a work.

Outside of his autobiography, *The Words*, and *The Critique of Dialectical Reason*, Sartre's work on Gustav Flaubert in *The Family Idiot* stands as his masterwork in the application of this method. As the subject of regressive analysis, Flaubert—individual and "text"—is "imaginary," a work of art. "With him," Sartre writes, "I am at the border, the barrier of dreams."[49] Here Sartre crosses over to Schleiermacher's "other side," "where one no longer analyzes but interprets the text," where "textual analysis," for Schleiermacher, "becomes textual hermeneutics" (*ibid.*). As the subject of progressive synthesis, then, Flaubert can only be an "imaginary person." Sartre once claimed that what he describes as Flaubert is "throughout the book, Flaubert the way I imagined him to have been, but since I used what I think were rigorous methods, this should also be Flaubert as he really is, as he really was."[50]

As Frank shows, Schleiermacher's appeal to the "other side" or the "psychological" side of interpretation is an appeal to the productivity of the subject, ambiguously identified in terms of the style of both individual (discourse) and work. In Schleiermacher's terms, as Frank notes, this is "the objective-subjective, historical *and* divining method of interpretation" (p. 167). Here "divination" means the attempt at guessing by which "original act . . . the author discovered meaning." Frank asserts that this is the positive formulation of Schleiermacher's hermeneutics. "No one guarantees the interpreter that he actually has touched the author's individual style (or, put more cautiously, the textual subject's), or even that he has spanned the distance of time separating his world from the world of his text" (p. 168).

Rather, at best textual interpretation remains conjectural; comprehension remains imprecise in its "word-for-word reconstitution" of an exchange. As Sartre writes regarding his task in dealing with Flaubert in *The Family Idiot*,

> comprehension is a personal act. If the listener repeats what he has heard, he is merely lending his voice to a transcendent object that is realized through his voice and then flies off toward new tongues. If he *comprehends*, he reshapes the well-worn path *for himself*. In the end, the act is completely his own. . . And in the spiral garland must be seen, too, *myself in the Other;* language expresses human relationship, but it is the relationship of those who seek out words—to support them, to censure them, to reject them—in each individual. The Other in me makes my language, which is my way of being in the Other.[51]

Werner Hamacher also sends the general discussion of interpretation back to the texts of Schleiermacher. In "Hermeneutic Ellipses: Writing the Hermeneutical Circle in Schleiermacher," Hamacher argues that Schleiermacher's formulation of the question of style and the method of divinatory interpretation systematically calls into question the conditions of understanding. However, in his criticisms of (1) theories which limit hermeneutics to regional fields of study, such as sacred biblical texts or the writings of classical authors, and (2) Ast's claim that "hermeneutics is the art of discovering, with necessary insight, the thoughts of the writer from out of his own discourse," Schleiermacher's own position retains elements of these classical theories. According to Hamacher, this is so because Schleiermacher deployed an arsenal of arguments borrowed from those whom he attacked. By focusing on these residual elements, Hamacher claims that the radical character of Schleiermacher's hermeneutic project can be grasped apart from the standard appropriation and use made of it in the history of hermeneutics.

In Hamacher's account, Schleiermacher is dispatched to assist in the elaboration of a "literary hermeneutics." Although judged by traditional standards too "regional" or specialized, a "literary hermeneutics" may claim "universality" on the grounds that its "object" holds "within the sphere of both a general as well as fundamental hermeneutics" (p. 194). When a literary hermeneutics is grounded in the fundamental motifs of Schleiermacher's hermeneutics, Hamacher claims that its possibility must be comprehended in terms of its oscillation between a regional hermeneutics and a metahermeneutics: "Oscillating between both, it uncovers as the latter the general conditions of understanding, as the former the particular, material and historical modifications which traverse every pretension toward universal validity'' (*ibid.*).

There is an unavoidable irony involved in Hamacher's attempt which he readily acknowledges. If a literary hermeneutics mediates itself as a regional hermeneutics *and* as a metahermeneutics, if it accents the interpretive breach between the particular and the general (where a "hinged articulation" becomes the basic structure of the hermeneutic circle), then hermeneutics, as theory and as practice, carries out its own "permanent dismantling of the hermeneutic paradigm of (self-)presentation and of living speech, without being able to replace it by another" paradigm (*ibid.*).[52] Hamacher cites the following reason in support of this claim: the medium conditioning the possibility of a literary hermeneutics of this kind also conditions its impossibility. That medium is, as Hamacher says, "graphic"— writing (p. 193).

The "schema of oscillation" is not one that can be characterized as "a movement between" polar opposites. Instead, Hamacher argues, the movement between general and particular, transcendental and empirical, is a function of the oscillation: the oscillation is the condition of the possibility and impossibility of mediation, of understanding the part in the whole and the whole in the part; the placement in-between is the condition of interpretation. As such, the hermeneutical circle is, already, rhetorically, metaphorically, elliptically displaced.

The attempt "to discover the thoughts of an author" through mimetic representation will never grasp "the stylistic peculiarity of the text" nor the "living expression" bursting through at a particular moment (p. 183). "The web of the communicative net tied by language and history, and reconstructed by the linguistic and historical *Wissenschaften,* is never so tight that the individuality of an author couldn't succeed in slipping through it" (p. 179). To achieve an understanding of the author and text, as noted by Manfred Frank, requires a "divinatory procedure." The domain of hermeneutics encompasses all modes of individual expression or "living discourse" (*lebendige Rede*), and it cannot be bound by the strictures of "necessary insight." Rather, the hermeneutic field, for Schleiermacher and Hamacher, is one of possibility, "the realization of possibilities, none of which can make a claim for the sufficient representation of the truth" (p. 180).

In his desire to overcome the theological and rationalistic presumptions of Astian hermeneutics, Schleiermacher gives primacy of place to speech over writing. But, as Hamacher is ready to point out, though an ostensibly traditional move on Schleiermacher's part, this does not tell the whole story. Schleiermacher's definition of the relation between speech and writing sets him apart from the Platonic-Aristotelian tradition. Writing is a special mode of speech, albeit "arrested," "fixed," and "held." As a result, the hermeneutic principles which have been developed for the divinatory understanding of "a moment of life bursting forth" in living expression can be applied legitimately to the interpretation of writing.

Writing preserves "living speech," but it is a virulent condition; it simultaneously promotes possible loss of life. As fixed speech, writing presents the danger of destroying the entire hermeneutic project, as Schleiermacher construes it, by petrifying the means by which meaning is produced. To avoid this situation, Schleiermacher claims that it is by memory that both forms of articulation are joined "into an impermeable amalgam." Hamacher explains that for Schleiermacher, "memory, like writing, is given the task of 'fixing' the particular, so that one might be able to return to it from out of the series of all the other particulars of a given whole that are grasped in the course of understanding" (p. 184). In an analogous fashion, divinatory understanding or psychological interpretation is defined as the comprehension of particulars from "out of the whole," in "living expression." Thus, one might say that memory breathes life into arrested speech. But this resuscitation does not allow for a full recovery or recuperation; there is no return to an "original" condition. Memory and writing recreate the whole out of its parts, and the parts in conjunction with the whole. Speech is necessarily recast in a different light. According to Hamacher, then, "writing is . . . at once the condition of possibility and the ground of impossibility" for understanding (p. 185). As such, writing is also the condition for a "literary hermeneutics."

To understand writing as a mode of speech, one must understand it as supplementing speech. Fixing the object of hermeneutics, writing elevates it to an objective status. Moreover, writing creates the conditions of oscillation: it makes possible the move from the general to the particular, from the whole to the part, from the transcendental to the empirical. Meaning, then, is never present; it is always deferred. Totality, wholeness, is always elliptical. So, Hamacher claims, if writing constitutes "the problematic instituting and necessary condition of every sign-system," as Schleiermacher's texts suggest, "then a hermeneutics which directs itself toward the literal constitution of texts, and whose themes are the specific forms of fictionality of verbal constructs, can raise the ironic claim of staking out the foundation of every fundamental hermeneutics and, as a regional one, the field of every general hermeneutics" (p. 194). In Hamacher's terms, such a literary hermeneutics would be in the position "to indicate scripturality [Schriftlichkeit] as the perpetually self-decentering structure of every thinkable form of articulation and experience" (ibid.).

Given this set of conditions, the move from whole to part, from transcendental to empirical and back again, the divinatory desire to interpret the living moment necessarily generates gaps and differences. The production of totalities is fragmentary, a function of the hermeneutical circle's fracture. When discussing the effect writing has on the hermeneutical circle, Hamacher writes:

The part is never demonstrably part of *its* whole, the whole never the whole of *its* parts. The hermeneutical circle opens itself, and makes every closure into a heuristic hermeneutic fiction—admittedly employable, economizing the deficit of understanding, and yet one that can neither accommodate itself to the ideal of perfect understanding, nor eliminate the loss, constitutive of language and understanding, which ellipses bring with them. Understanding cannot remain within the limits of the economy of the circle, within the limits of the whole, for this whole is itself the result of rhetorical-grammatical tropes and as such the subcode of a language game that for its part is not codifiable (pp. 201–02).

All interpretive acts perpetuate this condition for Hamacher and Schleiermacher. Divination necessarily fails in its "appropriation" of the other's thought; there can be no return to an origin, to the "author" as source. So it must supplement this lack by going beyond what is given, announcing what is not given. Interpretation must "give back" what has been lost in the pursuit of meaning by going to "the other side," by becoming its other(s).[53] Such a giving back will be analogous to the "sending back" (*renvois*) about which Derrida speaks, an elliptical move that suspends and opens up, as well as being suspended from and opened by, the circulation of the hermeneutical circle.

The last selection is Jean-Luc Nancy's "Sharing Voices." Nancy's text explores what he calls "the modern misinterpretation of interpretation," the "misinterpretation of the risk of interpretation—or of *hermēneia*."[54] For Nancy the question of interpretation is, of course, not *one* question; it is already divided, as its *history* indicates.[55] It is a complex of questions that deals with hermeneutics as a problematic determined through the history of philosophy; with the concept of "interpretation" and what delimits that concept; with the concepts of *technē, mimēsis,* and *logos;* and with interpretation as an "entire thematic" that has become "the modern substitute for 'truth'." Today, in spite of—and perhaps because of—the fundamental role assigned to the motif of interpretation, every issue submitted to this motif "remains caught in an interpretation of what 'interpretation' itself gives to thought" (p. 211). According to Nancy, then, the overwhelming acceptance of interpretation as the means by which an arcane truth or primoridal meaning can be recovered marks the "misinterpretation of interpretation."

Nancy retraces Heidegger's appeal to the authority of the hermeneutic motif in *Being and Time* and the alleged abandonment of the term "hermeneutics" by Heidegger following *Being and Time*. According to Nancy's reading of Heidegger's texts, the abandonment of the term "hermeneutics" should not be confused with or taken as an abandonment of the hermeneutic thematic. On the contrary, Heidegger affirms once again the significance of the hermeneutic motif to his thought in a twofold manner. First, he makes an oblique reference to hermeneutics, specifically the "hermeneutic relation," that is, the hermeneutic circle, in a post–*Being and Time* text titled "Dialogue on Language." And, second, this reference appears in the context of a "conversation" on the nature and essence of language and speech which not only refers explicitly to Plato's *Ion*, and the treatment of *hermēneuein* presented in that dialogue, but which enacts the very structure of that dialogue, "the most ancient philosophical document concerning *hermēneia*."

Heidegger's dialogue, like Plato's *Ion*, does not issue an analytic of "hermeneutics," language, or speech. The dialogue—Heidegger's or Plato's or "dialogue" in general—presents *itself*, presents *the dialogue* as the "announcement" of the dialogue's meaning, of the hermeneutic relation, of the hermeneutic circle. Like Plato's dialogue, the exchange must proceed or unfold "not from the men who speak it, but from an address, from a challenge to men by *Sprache* [language] itself" (p. 226). This will be the case, according to Nancy, if one is talking about Homer's interpretation of the gods or Ion's interpretation of Homer or Plato's interpretation of Ion on Homer or Heidegger's interpretation of the hermeneutic circle in Plato, and so on. The "hermeneutic relation" can only be *announced;* it does not allow itself to be revealed or exposed as such. It is, though quite differently in each instance, a question of "divination."

Thus, whereas Ion's performance of Homeric poetry announces the meaning of Homer's poems by "*making him speak his own words,*" Heidegger's dialogue on language and speech is understood according to what would be its "primordial," preinterpretive signification. It is a sending, a dispatch "carrying the announcement and communicating knowledge." The "art of understanding the other," which could be recast in contemporary (Gadamerian) hermeneutic terms of "understanding that which is foreign," is "carried out," "performed," "represented and presented in the work of art which is the 'Dialogue'." The "meaning" of the poem, the "dialogue," or the contemporary philosophic "text" is delivered "in delivering" the poem, the dialogue, and the history of philosophy.

Nancy's reading of Heidegger and, by extension, Plato turns on the articulation of the hermeneutic circle, as it is announced in the history of philosophy (and hermeneutics) from Schleiermacher to Heidegger, through

Heidegger to Bultmann's and Gadamer's interpretation of Heidegger, and beyond to Ricoeur, Frank, and Hamacher.[56] Furthermore, Nancy shows *how*, in Heidegger's texts, hermeneutics is interlaced with the concept of "preunderstanding" and the translation of *hermēneuein* as *Auslegung*.

Nancy claims there is good reason to doubt the "hermeneutic" interpretations of Heidegger's text provided by Gadamer and Bultmann. In particular, he questions Gadamer's interpretation of the relation established by Heidegger between the hermeneutic circle and preunderstanding (or prejudices) (p. 216). But his claim is not made in an attempt to restore or to recover, to set in place as it were, the "proper" meaning of Heidegger's text. It is an attempt to show, in Heidegger's own words, that even if Heidegger's text is engaged in the pursuit of the "primordial meaning" of hermeneutics, that is to say, as a way to present the meaning of the question of being, it is a delivery that is always diverted and led elsewhere by its relation to the hermeneutic circle.

> The circle as such flies into pieces; it contracts at a certain point, or else it disconnects [*affole*] its circularity to the point of rendering impossible the coincidence of a beginning and a result. It will not be a question, in the investigation, of leading to the meaning of a being . . . as origin of being-there . . . It will be a question of letting— the "question"—display itself *insofar as it is* the "meaning" of being which is "pre-supposed" in the being of the questioning-being (p. 218).

"Primordial meaning," so-called, is achieved through *Auslegung, hermēneuein,* "which *announces* to the comprehension of Being, included in being-there, the authentic meaning of Being in general and the fundamental structures of its own being."[57] Joined with Heidegger's treatment of *logos* as "*letting-something-be-seen,*" "interpretation" or *hermēneuein* is neither a method for interpretation nor an operation of interpretive construction: it is quite simply an announcement of that which has been constituted already; it is a bringing into speech of "the meaning of being" (p. 220). The hermeneutic circle provides a temporarily privileged and necessarily fictional access to the circle itself. *Auslegung,* interpretation as announcement of meaning, anticipates itself. Thus, "understanding," in Heidegger's text, according to Nancy, "is possible only by the anticipation of meaning which creates meaning itself."

Dialogue provides the medium for "living expression," or what Schleiermacher, Frank, and Hamacher call "a moment of life bursting forth" in the presentation or announcement of the other. Dialogue is constituted, arises from and against, the background of differences. As Nancy announces it through others, dialogue is the medium and condition for the sharing of "an originary difference" between interpretive voices—*logos*. In effect, the announcement of differences, of hermeneutic difference as the condition of interpretation and the effect of interpretation, is shared in and through dialogue. Given this set of conditions, to fix "interpretation," to fix the task of interpretation as the final disclosure of hidden meanings and truths, would entail the forfeiture of exchange. Interpretation as *hermēneia*, the declarative, imitative act which passes on and reabsorbs the "*alterity*"of meaning in the exchange of dialogue, provides the meaning to interpretation. There is no object of interpretation; interpretation entails more than providing a comment on another text. It is the announcement of the other in the presentation of the self as other.

The sharing of the dialogue is a sharing of *hermēneia*, "the *voice* of the divine" (p. 236). "And this voice is first of all," Nancy asserts, "shared voices, the differentiation between singular voices. In other words, there is no *one* divine voice, nor perhaps a divine voice in general"; there is only the "divine" participation in the voice of the other—the *difference* of "being-outside-of-oneself," of "the sharing of voices" (p. 237), such as would be the "delirium" of interpretation about which Kristeva writes.

To speak, then, of sharing, dialogue, and the hermeneutic circle is to speak according to another set of determinations about the *life* of interpretation, "the interpretation of interpretations." If " 'hermeneutics' is then the *meaning* of the circle," and "the 'circle' is nothing other than the relation of interpretation which circulates in the circle as the inaccurate expression" of meaning, then interpretation is and will be, always and already, the maintenance of life itself, where the "meaning" of this "life" and the rules that are to govern it remain in the foreground, yet to be determined. These are the stakes of interpretation, the risks of dialogue from which there is no escape.

Notes

1. Michel de Montaigne, *Essays*, translated by Charles Cotton and edited by W. Carew Hazlitt (New York: A. L. Burt, Publisher, 1892). Book II, chapter XLIV, pp. 563–64, 565–66.

2. Aristotle, *Metaphysics*, 980a, *The Basic Works of Aristotle*, edited by Richard McKeon (New York: Random House, 1941). For the sake of comparison, Montaigne's text should be juxtaposed to Aristotle's. The complete first paragraph of the *Metaphysics* reads as follows: "All men by nature desire to know. An indication of this is the delight we take in our senses; for even apart from their usefulness they are loved for themselves; and above all others the sense of sight. For not only with

a view to action, but even when we are not going to do anything, we prefer seeing (one might say) to everything else. The reason is that this, most of all the senses, makes us know and brings to light many differences between things."

3. Montaigne, *Essays*, II, XLIV, p. 561.

4. Gayle L. Ormiston and Alan D. Schrift, editors, *The Hermeneutic Tradition: From Ast to Ricoeur* (Albany: State University of New York Press, 1990). Subsequent reference to the selections included in *The Hermeneutic Tradition* will be cited by the abbreviation HT with page numbers.

5. Montaigne, *Essays*, II, XLIV, p. 566.

6. *Ibid.*

7. *Ibid.*

8. *Ibid.*

9. Jacques Derrida, *Of Grammatology,* translated by Gayatri Chakravorty Spivak (Baltimore, Md.: Johns Hopkins University Press, 1974). See especially part II, chapter 4: "From/Of the Supplement to the Source: The Theory of Writing," especially pp. 275–95 and pp. 303–4.

10. Jean-Luc Nancy, "Sharing Voices," pp. 211–59 below. The French title of Nancy's text is *Le partage des voix* (Paris: Éditions Galilée, 1982). The ambiguity of *partage* should not be overlooked: its field of designation covers sharing, multiplying, distributing, and differentiating, as well as fate, destiny, and determination. Moreover, *voix* is simultaneously the singular "voice" and the plural "voices." As Montaigne's comments indicate, interpretation is the interpretation(s) of interpretation(s): in this regard, as Nancy notes, politically and poetically we each share and multiply our voice(s) with the voice(s) of others—we each have a stake in determining the path(s) of our dialogues. Subsequent references to the selections included in this volume will appear parenthetically in the text.

11. To be sure, the "hermeneutical circle" has been the locus of hermeneutical discourse, but this does not signify consensus regarding the character and function of the "circle." The differences in "interpreting" the hermeneutical circle are clearly indicated in general by each of the selections contained in HT. More recent discussions, valuations, and revaluations of this primary hermeneutical theme will be found in the selections by Blondel, Kristeva, Frank, Hamacher, and Nancy below.

12. Although not an issue foreign to the developments of either field, the relational mapping that can be drawn between the discourse of semiology (and Peircean semeiotic) and hermeneutics remains uncharted for the most part. However, this is not to say that this problem has not been discussed. Ricoeur has addressed the intersection of semiology and hermeneutics in many of his texts; see, for example, *The Conflict of Interpretations,* edited by Don Ihde (Evanston, Ill.: North-

western University Press, 1974) and *The Rule of Metaphor: Multi-Disciplinary Studies of the Creation of Meaning in Language,* translated by Robert Czerny et al. (Toronto: University of Toronto Press, 1977). In *Truth and Method,* Gadamer is critical of what he calls the "instrumental theory of signs"; *Truth and Method,* translated by Garrett Barden and John Cumming (New York: Seabury Press, 1977); see pp. 87, 134, and 377ff.

The problem receives direct comment and analysis from Nietzsche, Foucault, Blondel, and Kristeva. The lines of contention are distinct in each case. As an example, on the one hand, Michel Foucault claims that *"hermeneutics and semiology are two ferocious enemies"* and that their differences must always be recalled (p. 67 below). On the other hand, Julia Kristeva writes that "the birth of interpretation [and hermeneutics] is considered the birth of semiology, since the semiological sciences relate a sign (an event-sign) to a signified in order to *act* accordingly," that is, "to interpret" or "to make connections," "consistently, consequently" (p. 90 below).

13. See Wilhelm Dilthey, *Plan der Fortsetzung zum Aufbau der geschichtlichen Welt in den Geisteswissenschaften* and *Ideen über eine beschreibende und zergliedernde Psychologie, Gesammelte Schriften,* volumes 7 and 5 (Stuttgart: B. G. Teubner, 1958). *Zusammenhang* has a variety of meanings, given the context of Dilthey's text. In some instances it covers "connection," "interrelation," "internal structure," "coherence," "system." He writes in the *Plan der Fortsetzung:* "We understand *Zusammenhang. Zusammenhang* and understanding correspond to each other" (p. 257). And in the *Ideen* we find the following statement: "Life exists everywhere only as *Zusammenhang"* (p. 144). Cf. the English translation by Richard M. Zaner and Kenneth L. Heiges, Wilhelm Dilthey, *Descriptive Psychology and Historical Understanding* (The Hague: Nijhoff, 1977), p. 28.

14. Ludwig Wittgenstein, *Zettel,* translated by G. E. M. Anscombe (Berkeley: University of California Press, 1967), section 55.

15. See, for example, Martin Heidegger's formulation of this problem as it is articulated in *On the Way to Language,* translated by Peter Hertz and Joan Stambaugh (New York: Harper and Row, 1971) and *Identity and Difference,* translated by Joan Stambaugh (New York: Harper and Row, 1969). In a very simple, direct, and historically (metaphysically) bound manner, Heidegger identifies the difficulty which faces "interpretation," especially in *Identity and Difference.* First, he asserts that the withdrawal, the "step back," from metaphysics would remain "unaccomplished, and the path which it opens and points out would remain untrod." Why? Because the challenge to thought in this regard, the challenge of withdrawing from metaphysics, "lies in language." He continues:

> Our Western languages are languages of metaphysical thinking, each in its own way. It must remain an open question whether the nature of Western languages is in itself marked with the exclusive brand of metaphysics, and thus marked permanently by onto-theo-logic, or whether these languages offer other possibilities of utterance . . . The little word "is," which speaks every-

where in our language, and tells of Being even where It does not appear expressly, contains the whole destiny of Being [*das ganze Geschick des Seins*] (p.73).

There is an interesting point of comparison to be found in Aristotle's *Peri hermēneias*. In a section which deals explicitly with the "little word 'is'," (3 16b 19–25), Aristotle claims that even though verbs are "substantial and have significance" they do so because the one who expresses them "fixes" the attention of the hearer. But verbs do not bear any "existential import" in and of themselves—and, for Aristotle, this is especially true for the verb "*to be.*" Something must be added—a subject and a predicate. "To be," "being," and "is" indicate nothing by themselves, but *can only imply copulation, a possible or potential connection with the world.* Moreover, in Aristotle's eyes, to form a conception of the "copula" apart from the terms coupled or conjoined is impossible. (In anticipation, cf., Manfred Frank, "The Interpretation of a Text," pp. 145–76 below, and Werner Hamacher, "Hermeneutic Ellipses: Writing the Hermeneutical Circle in Schleiermacher," pp. 178–210 below.

The point here is this: if "is" carries and contains the "*whole* destiny of Being," if "is" refers to "Being" even where "It does not appear expressly," and if "our Western languages" or "language" in general carries the mark of metaphysics, it is not because language, in and of itself, whatever "It" may be, has an inherent metaphysical or onto-theo-logical orientation. It is because language *is used* toward the realization of certain metaphysical and onto-theo-logical ends. So, for Heidegger to claim that "is" contains "the whole destiny of Being," he must note that it is the *use* of the copula, as Aristotle indicates, what can be termed its "iterative structure," which allows it to refer to "Being" in any capacity whatsoever.

In "Sending: On Representation," Jacques Derrida examines the "possibility" of a "step back" from metaphysics (pp. 107–18 below). In order to "step back" from metaphysics and onto-theo-logy, there must be a different use of language, one which accepts and affirms the "iterative structure" of language as its condition for *use* and *articulation.* To "step back," as Derrida points out, one would have to withdraw from the "metaphysical/onto-theo-logical" representational use of language. In "Sending: On Representation," Derrida concerns himself with just that possibility.

16. Cf. Ludwig Wittgenstein, *Philosophical Grammar,* edited by Rush Rhees and translated by Anthony Kenny (Berkeley: University of California Press, 1974). According to Wittgenstein's notes which constitute this text, nothing has, already, a specific interpretation. In other words, there are no predetermined interpretations of images, pictures, signs, and so on. Rather, Wittgenstein claims that "what gives an image an interpretation is the *path* on which it lies" (section 99).

17. Charles Sanders Peirce, *Collected Papers,* edited by Charles Hartshorne and Paul Weiss (Cambridge, Mass.: Harvard University Press, 1931–35), 5.400.

18. For Eric Blondel, the interplay between semiology and interpretation, that is, *metaphor,* as articulated in Nietzsche's texts, indicates anew in what ways

"being" is, "life" is, "existence" is what it is. Language is not only the means of expressing our understanding, but through this articulation the world is allowed "to be." Cf. Eric Blondel, "Nietzsche's Style of Affirmation: The Metaphors of Genealogy," in *Nietzsche as Affirmative Thinker*, edited by Yirmiyahu Yovel (Dordrecht: Nijhoff, 1986), pp. 132–46; "Nietzsche: Life as Metaphor," in *The New Nietzsche: Contemporary Styles of Interpretation*, edited by David B. Allison (Cambridge, Mass.: MIT Press, 1987), pp. 150–75; and "Interpreting Texts With and Without Nietzsche," pp. 69–88 below.

19. E. D. Hirsch, well known for his defense of a hermeneutic approach that privileges the author's intention in the determination of the meaning of a text, strikes an interesting note in this regard in his most recent text, *Cultural Literacy: What Every American Needs to Know*, (Boston: Houghton Mifflin Company, 1987), p. 48: "All continuing experience is partial and fragmented . . . Our cognitive life takes place through a small window of attention that is framed by short-term memory. We use past knowledge to interpret this window of experience, to place momentary fragments within larger wholes that give them a function and a place. . . In our minds these transitory fragments can acquire meaning only by being placed within larger, not presently visible wholes that are based on past knowledge." One should not be misled here. Beyond its present context and use, Hirsch's remark must be examined in terms of the purposes for which he makes this claim, that is, the realignment of "national" educational goals with the realization of a "cultural" *telos*.

20. David Hoy begins his discussion in *The Critical Circle* by citing the same passage from the *Cratylus*. "Words . . . have the power to reveal, but they also conceal, speech can signify all things, but it also turns things this way and that." On the basis of this acknowledgment, and with the recognition that today Hermes is absent, Hoy claims that "the modern age needs hermeneutics"; it needs an understanding of "the methodology of interpretation of texts." See *The Critical Circle: Literature, History, and Philosophical Hermeneutics* (Berkeley: University of California Press, 1978), p. 1.

21. Cf. Martin Heidegger, "A Dialogue on Language between a Japanese and an Inquirer," in *On the Way to Language*; Gadamer, *Truth and Method*, especially part III, pp. 364ff. and 404–6; and Nancy, "Sharing Voices," pp. 230–48 below.

22. Aristotle, *On Interpretation*, translated by E. M. Edghill, in *The Basic Works of Aristotle*, edited by Richard McKeon. Aristotle's text is taken as a symbol for the historical importance of hermeneutics. Today, very little use is made of this short text. To paraphrase Aristotle, one might say that *On Interpretation* is a significant text in the history of hermeneutics by its *name* alone because it has become a symbol for the questions and concerns which dominate current discourse in this field. In other words, for a name to have meaning it must become a symbol, and a symbol has meaning only because it is bound to the "conventions" of a linguistic system. Today, hermeneutics provides the necessary system of conventions.

23. Cf. Ricoeur, *The Conflict of Interpretations*, p. 4.

24. Heidegger, *Identity and Difference*, p. 41.

25. Wittgenstein, *Philosophical Grammar*, section 99.

26. Cf. Jean-François Lyotard, *The Postmodern Condition: A Report on Knowledge*, translated by Geoff Bennington and Brian Massumi (Minneapolis: University of Minnesota Press, 1984), pp. 79–81. Consider Lyotard's "working" definition of the "postmodern": "A work can become modern only if it is first postmodern. Postmodernism thus understood is not modernism at its end but in the nascent state, and this state is constant." And again: "The postmodern would be that which, *in the modern*, puts forward the unpresentable in presentation itself; that which denies itself the solace of good forms, the consensus of a taste which would make it possible to share collectively the nostalgia for the unattainable."

27. Cf. William V. Spanos, *Repetitions: The Postmodern Occasion in Literature and Culture* (Baton Rouge and London: Louisiana State University Press, 1987); see chapter 5, "Postmodern Literature and Its Occasion: Retrieving the Preterite Middle," pp. 189–276. Regarding the occasion of postmodernism, Spanos writes: "The measure of postmodern occasion form is, in other words, the differential measure of diaspora: not the inseminating Patriarchal Word that establishes a dynastic relationship between the temporal words, but of the disseminating words of contemporary man's [*sic*] orphanage, not of the One but of the many, not of Unity but of dispersal, not of Identity but of ontological difference" (p. 234).

28. Cf. Mark Taylor, editor, *Deconstruction in Context* (Chicago: University of Chicago Press, 1986), p. 34. "Postmodern awareness is born of the recognition that the past that was never present eternally returns as the future that never arrives to displace all contemporaneity and defer forever the presence of the modern."

29. Cf. Ihab Hassan, *The Postmodern Turn: Essays in Postmodern Theory and Culture* (Columbus: Ohio State University Press, 1987). It is interesting that in his review of specific themes found in Nietzsche's texts which can be associated with a "postmodern sensibility," Hassan lists "hermeneutics" along with the following: "the decenterment of man," "the vitality of the new," "the demystification of reason," "the refusal of unity," "the empty subject," "the liminality of language," "thinking in fictions," "the denial of origins," "the energetics of value," "ludic arts, the metaphysics of play," and "the collapse of being and becoming, a new ontology"; see pp. 46–51.

30. Ast, "Hermeneutics," sections 80–81, HT, pp. 46–47.

31. Schleiermacher, "*The Hermeneutics:* Outline of the 1819 Lectures," HT, p. 93.

32. Gadamer, *Truth and Method*, p. 360.

33. Hans-Georg Gadamer, "On the Scope and Function of Hermeneutics," in *Philosophical Hermeneutics*, edited and translated by David E. Linge (Berkeley: University of California Press, 1976), p. 22.

34. These phrases are taken from the epigraph to Kristeva's paper. She cites a passage from Freud's "Constructions in Analysis."

35. Indeed, Derrida's texts are replete with encounters with the hermeneutic tradition. The most recent "encounter," so-called, has been recorded in *Dialogue and Deconstruction: The Gadamer-Derrida Encounter,* edited by Richard Palmer and Diane Michelfelder (Albany: State University of New York Press, 1989). Other texts in which more nuanced and protracted engagements can be located are "Structure, Sign, and Play in the Discourse of the Human Sciences," in *Writing and Difference,* translated by Alan Bass (Chicago: University of Chicago Press, 1978), pp. 278–93; *Of Grammatology; Glas,* translated by John P. Leavey, Jr. (Lincoln: University of Nebraska Press, 1987); *Dissemination,* translated by Barbara Johnson (Chicago: University of Chicago Press, 1981); *Margins of Philosophy,* translated by Barbara Johnson (Chicago: University of Chicago Press, 1981); "Limited Inc., a b c . . . ," translated by Samuel Weber, *Glyph* 2 (1978): 162–54; *Spurs: Nietzsche's Styles/Éperons: Les styles de Nietzsche,* translated by Barbara Harlow (Chicago: University of Chicago Press, 1979); and *The Ear of the Other: Otobiography, Transference, Translation,* translated by Avital Ronell and Peggy Kamuf (New York: Schocken, 1985).

36. Derrida, *Spurs,* p. 107.

37. See Jacques Derrida, "La Question du Style," in *Nietzsche aujourd'hui, 10/18* (Paris: Union Générale d'Éditions, 1973), p. 291. Alex Argyros also notes the importance of Derrida's juxtaposition in his "The Warp of the World: Deconstruction and Hermeneutics," *Diacritics* 16, no. 3 (Fall 1986): 46–55.

38. Derrida, *Spurs,* p. 107.

39. Derrida, "Structure, Sign, and Play in the Discourse of the Human Sciences, in *Writing and Difference,* p. 292.

40. Derrida, *The Ear of the Other,* p. 32. The translation has been altered in this case [G.L.O.]. See *Otobiographies: L'enseignement de Nietzsche et la politique du nom propre* (Paris: Éditions Galilée, 1984), pp. 101–2.

41. Derrida, *The Post Card: From Socrates to Freud and Beyond,* translated by Alan Bass (Chicago: University of Chicago Press, 1987), p. 336.

42. Jacques Derrida, *Positions,* translated by Alan Bass (Chicago: University of Chicago Press, 1981), p. 24.

43. Derrida, "The Ends of Man," in *Margins of Philosophy,* p. 135.

44. It should be noted that, following *Being and Time,* Heidegger suspended use of the term "hermeneutic" to describe his attempt to think the *Geschick* of being. One moment where Heidegger returns—*renvoir* in Derrida's idiom—to the issue of *hermēneuein* is in "A Dialogue On Language between a Japanese and an Inquirer," in *On the Way to Language.* However, during the exchange on the term

"*hermēneuein,*" when asked to define the term, Heidegger has the inquirer decline by saying "I would like to leave the question open." Cf. Nancy's discussion of this statement in "Sharing Voices," pp. 226ff. below.

45. See the translators' note to Derrida's paper regarding the connotations associated with the use of *envoi* and *envois*. Moreover, in his postscript, Peter Caws speculates further about Derrida's relation to the tradition of philosophy known as the philosophy of language on the basis of Derrida's *envoi(s)*. See pp. 139–44 below.

46. Cf. Schleiermacher, "*The Hermeneutics:* Outline of the 1819 Lectures," HT, p. 87.

47. This line is taken from a portion of Frank's essay not translated in the present selection. See Manfred Frank, "Textauslegung," in *Erkenntnis und Literatur*, edited by D. Harth and P. Gebhardt (Stuttgart: J. B. Metzlersche Verlagsbuchhandlung, 1982), p. 139.

48. See Jean-Paul Sartre, *Search For a Method*, translated by Hazel Barnes (New York: Vintage Books, 1968), p. 153. One might imagine whether Sartre has Schleiermacher in mind when he asserts that in order to grasp "the meaning of human conduct, it is necessary to have at our disposal what German psychiatrists and historians called 'comprehension' [*Verstehen*]."

49. Jean-Paul Sartre, "The Itinerary of a Thought," in *Between Existentialism and Marxism,* translated by John Mathews (New York: William Morrow and Company, 1974), p. 44.

50. Jean-Paul Sartre, "On *The Idiot of the Family,*" in *Life/Situations: Essays Written and Spoken,* translated by Paul Aster and Lydia Davis (New York: Pantheon Books, 1977), p. 112.

51. Jean-Paul Sartre, *The Family Idiot*, volume I, translated by Carol Cosman (Chicago: University of Chicago Press, 1981), p. 12. Cf. "The Interpretation of a Text," p. 160 below, where Frank writes, recalling the contribution of August Boeckh to hermeneutics: "To record an individual expression and re-produce it in the act of reading (in other words, re-create it) does not then signify (and this is decisive) *articulating the same linguistic sequence again and indeed with like meaning,* but rather *undertaking another articulation of the same linguistic sequence.* For, says August Boeckh . . . , 'one can never produce the same thing again'."

52. Hamacher's presentation of this irony, this paradox, aligns itself, more or less, with Derrida's discussion of "the hinge" in *Of Grammatology,* pp. 65–73.

53. Cf. Aristotle, *On Interpretation,* 3 16b 19–25.

54. Nancy, *Le partage des voix,* p. 8. The "misinterpretation of the *risks* of interpretation—or of *hermēneia*" is a phrase which appears in Nancy's prefatory remarks to "Sharing Voices," which have not been included in this volume at Nancy's request.

55. The ambiguity attached to the use of "history" in this context cannot be resolved. Like so many other of the contributions included in this text and HT, Nancy's text insists upon the rendering of "history" according to its chronological connotation *and* the sense assigned to it as "destiny," "fate," the *Geschick* of which Heidegger's texts speaks, and the *envois* of Derrida's text.

56. Nancy notes that it is necessary to presuppose Hamacher's analysis of Schleiermacher. See note 10 to Nancy's text, p. 251 below.

57. Martin Heidegger, *Being and Time*, translated by John Macquarrie and Edward Robinson (New York: Harper and Row, 1962), section 7, C.

1

Interpretation

Friedrich Nietzsche

[. . .] What, then, is truth? A mobile army of metaphors, metonyms, and anthropomorphisms—in short, a sum of human relations, which have been enhanced, transposed, and embellished poetically and rhetorically, and which after long use seem firm, canonical, and obligatory to a people: truths are illusions about which one has forgotten that this is what they are; metaphors which are worn out and without sensuous power; coins which have lost their pictures and now matter only as metal, no longer as coins [. . .]

—"On Truth and Lies in an Extra-Moral Sense"

Supposing truth is a woman—what then? Are there not grounds for the suspicion that all philosophers, insofar as they were dogmatists, have been very inexpert about women? That the gruesome seriousness, the clumsy obtrusiveness with which they have usually approached truth so far have been awkward and very improper methods for winning a woman's heart? What is certain is that she has not allowed herself to be won—and today every kind of dogmatism is left standing dispirited and discouraged. *If* it is left standing at all! For there are scoffers who claim that it has fallen, that all dogmatism lies on the ground—even more, that all dogmatism is dying.

Speaking seriously, there are good reasons why all philosophical dogmatizing, however solemn and definitive its airs used to be, may nevertheless have been no more than a noble childishness and tyronism. And perhaps the time is at hand when it will be comprehended again and again *how little* used to be sufficient to furnish the cornerstone for such sublime and unconditional philosophers' edifices as the dogmatists have built so far: any old popular superstition from time immemorial (like the soul superstition which, in the form of the subject and ego superstition, has not even yet

ceased to do mischief); some play on words perhaps, a seduction by grammar, or an audacious generalization of very narrow, very personal, very
human, all too human facts . . .

Let us not be ungrateful to it, although it must certainly be conceded
that the worst, most durable, and most dangerous of all errors so far was a
dogmatists's error—namely, Plato's invention of the pure spirit and the
good as such. But now that it is overcome, now that Europe is breathing
freely again after this nightmare and at least can enjoy a healthier—sleep,
we, whose task is wakefulness itself, are the heirs of all that strength which
has been fostered by the fight against this error. To be sure, it meant standing truth on her head and denying *perspective,* the basic condition of all
life, when one spoke of spirit and the good as Plato did. Indeed, as a physician one might ask: "How could the most beautiful growth of antiquity,
Plato, contract such a disease? Did the wicked Socrates corrupt him after
all? Could Socrates have been the corrupter of youth after all? And did he
deserve his hemlock?" [. . .]

—Beyond Good and Evil, Preface

The falseness of a judgment is for us not necessarily an objection to a
judgment; in this respect our new language may sound strangest. The question is to what extent it is life-promoting, life-preserving, species-
preserving, perhaps even species-cultivating. And we are fundamentally
inclined to claim that the falsest judgments (which include the synthetic
judgments *a priori*) are the most indispensable for us; that without accept-
ing the fictions of logic, without measuring reality against the purely invented world of the unconditional and self-identical, without a constant
falsification of the world by means of numbers, man could not live—that
renouncing false judgments would mean renouncing life and a denial of life.
To recognize untruth as a condition of life—that certainly means resisting
accustomed value feelings in a dangerous way; and a philosophy that risks
this would by that token alone place itself beyond good and evil.

—Beyond Good and Evil, Section 4

Forgive me as an old philologist who cannot desist from the malice of
putting his finger on bad modes of interpretation: but "nature's conformity
to law," of which you physicists talk so proudly, as though—why, it exists
only owing to your interpretation and bad "philology." It is no matter of
fact, no "text," but rather only a naively humanitarian emendation and per-
version of meaning, with which you make abundant concessions to the dem-

ocratic instincts of the modern soul! "Everywhere equality before the law; nature is no different in that respect, no better off than we are"—a fine instance of ulterior motivation, in which the plebeian antagonism to everything privileged and autocratic as well as a second and more refined atheism are disguised once more. "*Ni Dieu, ni maitre*"—that is what you, too, want; and therefore "cheers for the law of nature!"—is it not so? But as said above, that is interpretation, not text; and somebody might come along who, with opposite intentions and modes of interpretation, could read out of the same "nature," and with regard to the same phenomena, rather the tyrannically inconsiderate and relentless enforcement of claims of power— an interpreter who would picture the unexceptional and unconditional aspects of all "will to power" so vividly that almost every word, even the word "tyranny" itself, would eventually seem unsuitable, or a weakening and attenuating metaphor—being too human—but he might, nevertheless, end by asserting the same about this world as you do, namely, that it has a "necessary" and "calculable" source, *not* because laws obtain in it, but because they are absolutely *lacking*, and every power draws its ultimate consequences at every moment. Supposing that this also is only interpretation—and you will be eager enough to make this objection?—well, so much the better.

—*Beyond Good and Evil*, Section 22

[. . .] Forgive me the joke of this gloomy grimace and trope; for I myself have learned long ago to think differently, to estimate differently with regard to deceiving and being deceived, and I keep in reserve at least a couple of jostles for the blind rage with which the philosophers resist being deceived. Why *not*? It is no more than a moral prejudice that truth is worth more than mere appearance; it is even the worst proved assumption there is in the world. Let at least this much be admitted: there would be no life at all if not on the basis of perspective estimates and appearances; and if, with the virtuous enthusiasm and clumsiness of some philosophers, one wanted to abolish the "apparent world" altogether—well, supposing *you* could do that, at least nothing would be left of your "truth" either. Indeed, what forces us at all to suppose that there is an essential opposition of "true" and "false"? Is it not sufficient to assume degrees of apparentness and, as it were, lighter and darker shadows and shades of appearance— different "values," to use the language of painters? Why couldn't the world *that concerns us*—be a fiction? And if somebody asked, "but to a fiction there surely belongs an author?"—couldn't one answer simply: *why*? Doesn't this "belongs" perhaps belong to the fiction, too? Is it not permitted to be a bit ironical about the subject no less than the predicate and object? Shouldn't philosophers be permitted to rise above faith in grammar? All due respect for governesses—but hasn't the time come for philosophy to renounce the faith of governesses?

—Beyond Good and Evil, Section 34

If this book is incomprehensible to anyone and jars on his ears, the fault, it seems to me, is not necessarily mine. It is clear enough, assuming, as I do assume, that one has first read my earlier writings and has not spared some trouble in doing so: for they are, indeed, not easy to penetrate. Regarding my *Zarathustra,* for example, I do not allow that anyone knows that book who has not at some time been profoundly wounded and at some time profoundly delighted by every word in it; for only then may he enjoy the privilege of reverentially sharing in the halcyon element out of which that book was born and in its sunlight clarity, remoteness, breadth, and certainty. In other cases, people find difficulty with the aphoristic form: this arises from the fact that today this form is *not taken seriously enough.* An aphorism, properly stamped and molded, has not been "deciphered" when it has simply been read; rather, one has then to begin its *exegesis,* for which is required an art of exegesis. I have offered in the third essay of the present book an example of what I regard as "exegesis" in such a case— an aphorism is prefixed to this essay, the essay itself is a commentary on it. To be sure, one thing is necessary above all if one is to practice reading as an *art* in this way, something that has been unlearned most thoroughly nowadays—and therefore it will be some time before my writings are "readable"—something for which one has almost to be a cow and in any case *not* a "modern man": *rumination.*

—On the Genealogy of Morals, Preface, Section 8

Suppose such an incarnate will to contradiction and antinaturalness is induced to *philosophize:* upon what will it vent its innermost contrariness? Upon what is felt, most certainly to be real and actual: it will look for error precisely where the instinct of life most unconditionally posits truth. It will, for example, like the ascetics of the Vedanta philosophy, downgrade physicality to an illusion; likewise pain, multiplicity, the entire conceptual antithesis "subject" and "object"—errors, nothing but errors! To renounce belief in one's ego, to deny one's own "reality"—what a triumph! not merely over the senses, over appearance, but a much higher kind of triumph, a violation and cruelty against *reason*—a voluptuous pleasure that reaches its height when the ascetic self-contempt and self-mockery of reason declares: *"there is* a realm of truth and being, but reason is *excluded* from it!"*

(Incidentally, even in the Kantian concept of the "intelligible character of things" something remains of this lascivious ascetic discord that loves to turn reason against reason: for "intelligible character" signifies in Kant that things are so constituted that the intellect comprehends just enough of them to know that for the intellect they are—*utterly incomprehensible.*)

But precisely because we seek knowledge, let us not be ungrateful to such resolute reversals of accustomed perspectives and valuations with which the spirit has, with apparent mischievousness and futility, raged against itself for so long: to see differently in this way for once, to *want* to see differently, is no small discipline and preparation of the intellect for its future "objectivity"—the latter understood not as "contemplation without interest" (which is a nonsensical absurdity), but as the ability *to control* one's Pro and Con and to dispose of them, so that one knows how to employ a *variety* of perspectives and affective interpretations in the service of knowledge.

Henceforth, my dear philosophers, let us be on guard against the dangerous old conceptual fiction that posited a "pure, will-less, painless, timeless knowing subject"; let us guard against the snares of such contradictory concepts as "pure reason," "absolute spirituality," "knowledge in itself": these always demand that we should think of an eye that is completely unthinkable, an eye turned in no particular direction, in which the active and interpreting forces, through which alone seeing becomes seeing *something,* are supposed to be lacking; these always demand of the eye an absurdity and a nonsense. There is *only* a perspective seeing, *only* a perspective "knowing"; and the *more* affects we allow to speak about one thing, the *more* eyes, different eyes, we can use to observe one thing, the more complete will our "concept" of this thing, our "objectivity," be. But to eliminate the will altogether, to suspend each and every affect, supposing we were capable of this—what would that mean but to *castrate* the intellect?—

—*On the Genealogy of Morals,* Third Essay, Section 12

The origin of our concept of "knowledge" ["*Erkenntnis*"]. —I take this explanation from the street. I heard one of the common people say, "he knew me right away" ["*er hat much erkannt*"]. Then I asked myself: What is it that the common people take for knowledge? What do they want when they want "knowledge"? Nothing more than this: Something strange is to be reduced to something *familiar* [*etwas Bekanntes*]. And we philosophers—have we really meant *more* than this when we have spoken of knowledge? What is familiar means what we are used to so that we no longer marvel at it, our everyday, some rule in which we are stuck, anything at all in which we feel at home. Look, isn't our need for knowledge precisely this need for the familiar, the will to uncover under everything strange, unusual, and questionable something that no longer disturbs us? Is it not the *instinct of fear that bids us to know?* And is the jubilation of those who attain knowledge not the jubilation over the restoration of a sense of security?

Here is a philosopher who fancied that the world was "known" when he had reduced it to the "idea." Was it not because the "idea" was so familiar to him and he was so well used to it—because he hardly was afraid of the "idea" any more?

How easily these men of knowledge are satisfied! Just have a look at their principles and their solutions of the world riddle with this in mind! When they find something in things—under them, or behind them—that is unfortunately quite familiar to us, such as our multiplication tables or our logic, or our willing and desiring—how happy they are right away! For "what is familiar is known" ["*was bekannt ist, ist erkannt*"]. On this they are agreed. Even the most cautious among them suppose that what is familiar is at least *more easily knowable* than what is strange, and that, for example, sound method demands that we start from the "inner world," from the "facts of consciousness," because this world is *more familiar* to us; and what we are used to is most difficult to "know"—that is, to see as a problem, that is, to see as strange, as distant, as "outside us."

The great certainty of the natural sciences in comparison with psychology and the critique of the elements of consciousness—one might almost say, with the *unnatural* sciences—is due precisely to the fact that they choose for their object what is *strange*, while it is almost contradictory and absurd to even *try* to choose for an object what is not strange.

—*The Gay Science*, Section 355

Our new "infinite."— How far the perspective character of existence extends or indeed whether existence has any other character than this; whether existence without interpretation, without "sense," does not become "nonsense"; whether, on the other hand, all existence is not essentially actively engaged in *interpretation* [*ob . . . nicht alles Dasein essentiell ein auslegendes Dasein ist.*] —that cannot be decided even by the most industrious and most scrupulously conscientious analysis and self-examination of the intellect; for in the course of this analysis the human intellect cannot avoid seeing itself in its own perspectives, and *only* in these. We cannot look around our own corner: it is a hopeless curiosity that wants to know what other kinds of intellects and perspectives there *might* be; for example, whether some beings might be able to experience time backward, or alternately forward and backward (which would involve another direction of life and another concept of cause and effect). But I should think that today we are at least far from the ridiculous immodesty that would be involved in decreeing from our corner that perspectives are permitted only from this corner. Rather has the world become "infinite" for us all over again, inasmuch as we cannot reject the possibility that *it may include infinite interpretations.* Once more we are seized by a great shudder; but who would feel inclined immediately to deify again after the old manner this monster of an unknown world? And to worship the unknown henceforth as "the Unknown One"? Alas, too many *ungodly* possibilities of interpretation are included in the unknown, too much devilry, stupidity, and foolishness of interpretation—even our own human, all too human folly, which we know.

—*The Gay Science,* Section 374

My demand upon the philosopher is known, that he take his stand *beyond* good and evil and leave the illusion of moral judgment *beneath* himself. This demand follows from an insight which I was the first to formulate: that *there are altogether no moral facts.* Moral judgments agree with religious ones in believing in realities which are no realities. Morality is merely an interpretation of certain phenomena—more precisely, a misinterpretation. Moral judgments, like religious ones, belong to a stage of ignorance at which the very concept of the real and the distinction between what is real and imaginary, are still lacking; thus "truth," at this stage, designates all sorts of things which we today call "imaginings." Moral judgments are therefore never to be taken literally: so understood, they always contain mere absurdity. Semeiotically, however, they remain invaluable; they reveal, at least for those who know, the most valuable realities of cultures and inwardnesses which did not know enough to "understand" themselves. Morality is mere sign language, mere symptomatology: one must know what it is all about to be able to profit from it.

—*Twilight of the Idols,* "The 'Improvers' of Mankind," Section 1

Learning to *think*: in our schools one no longer has any idea of this. Even in the universities, even among the real scholars of philosophy, logic as a theory, as a practice, as a *craft*, is beginning to die out. One need only read German books: there is no longer the remotest recollection that thinking requires a technique, a teaching curriculum, a will to mastery—that thinking wants to be learned like dancing *as* a kind of dancing. Who among Germans still knows from experience the delicate shudder which light feet in spiritual matters send into every muscle? The stiff clumsiness of the spiritual gesture, the bungling hand at grasping—that is German to such a degree that abroad one mistakes it for the German characteras such. The German has no fingers for nuances.

That the Germans have been able to stand their philosophers at all, especially that most deformed concept-cripple of all time, the *great* Kant, provides not a bad notion of German grace. For one cannot subtract dancing in every form from a noble education—to be able to dance with one's feet, with concepts, with words: need I still add that one must be able to do it with the pen too—that one must learn to *write*? But at this point I should become completely enigmatic for German readers.

—*Twilight of the Idols,* "What the Germans Lack," Section 7

What is a *belief*? How does it originate? Every belief is a considering-something-true.

The most extreme form of nihilism would be the view that *every* belief, every considering-something-true, is necessarily false because there simply is no *true world*. Thus: a *perspectival appearance* whose origin lies in us (in so far as we continually *need* a narrower, abbreviated, simplified world).

—That is the measure of strength to what extent we can admit to ourselves, without perishing, the merely *apparent* character, the necessity of lies.

To this extent, nihilism, as the denial of a truthful world, of being, might be *a divine way of thinking*.

—*The Will to Power,* Section 15

My attempt to understand moral judgments as symptoms and sign languages which betray the processes of physiological prosperity or failure, likewise the consciousness of the conditions for preservation and growth—a mode of interpretations of the same worth as astrology, prejudices prompted by the instincts (of races, communities, of the various stages of life, as youth or decay, etc.).

Applied to the specific Christian-European morality: Our moral judgments are signs of decline, of disbelief in life, a preparation for pessimism.

My chief proposition: there are no moral phenomena, there is only a moral interpretation of these phenomena. This interpretation itself is of extra-moral origin.

What does it mean that our interpretation has projected a *contradiction* into existence?—Of decisive importance: behind all other evaluations these moral evaluations stand in command. Supposing they were abolished, according to what would we measure then? And then of what value would be knowledge, etc., etc.? ? ?

—*The Will to Power,* Section 258

Insight: all evaluation is made from a definite perspective: that of the preservation of the individual, a community, a race, a state, a church, a faith, a culture.—Because we forget that valuation is always from a perspective, a single individual contains within him a vast confusion of contradictory valuations and consequently of contradictory drives. This is the expression of the diseased condition in man, in contrast to the animals in which all existing instincts answer to quite definite tasks.

This contradictory creature has in his nature, however, a great method of acquiring knowledge: he feels many pros and cons, he raises himself to justice—to comprehension beyond esteeming things good and evil.

The wisest man would be the one richest in contradictions, who has, as it were, antennae for all types of men—as well as his great moments of grand harmony—a rare accident even in us! A sort of planetary motion—

—*The Will to Power,* Section 259

Profound aversion to reposing once and for all in any one total view of the world. Fascination of the opposing point of view: refusal to be deprived of the stimulus of the enigmatic.

—*The Will to Power,* Section 470

I maintain the phenomenality of the inner world, too: everything of which we become conscious is arranged, simplified, schematized, interpreted through and through—the actual process of inner "perception," the causal connection between thoughts, feelings, desires, between subject and object, are absolutely hidden from us—and are perhaps purely imaginary. The "apparent *inner* world" is governed by just the same forms and procedures as the "outer" world. We never encounter "facts": pleasure and displeasure are subsequent and derivative intellectual phenomena—

"Causality" eludes us; to suppose a direct causal link between thoughts, as logic does—that is the consequence of the crudest and clumsiest observation. Between two thoughts all kinds of affects play their game: but their motions are too fast, therefore we fail to recognize them, we deny them—

"Thinking," as epistemologists conceive it, simply does not occur: it is a quite arbitrary fiction, arrived at by selecting one element from the process and eliminating all the rest, an artificial arrangement for the purpose of intelligibility—

The "spirit," something that thinks: where possible even "absolute, pure spirit"—this conception is a second derivative of that false introspection which believes in "thinking": first an act is imagined which simply does not occur, "thinking," and secondly a subject-substratum in which every act of thinking, and nothing else, has its origin: that is to say, both the deed and the doer are fictions.

—*The Will to Power,* Section 477

The phenomenalism of the "inner world." Chronological inversion, so that the cause enters consciousness later than the effect.—We have learned that pain is projected to a part of the body without being situated there—we have learned that sense impressions naively supposed to be conditioned by the outer world are, on the contrary, conditioned by the inner world; that we are always unconscious of the real activity of the outer world—The fragment of outer world of which we are conscious is born after an effect from outside has impressed itself upon us, and is subsequently projected as its "cause"—

In the phenomenalism of the "inner world" we invert the chronological order of cause and effect. The fundamental fact of "inner experience" is that the cause is imagined after the effect has taken place—The same applies to the succession of thoughts:—we seek the reason for a thought before we are conscious of it; and the reason enters consciousness first, and then its consequence—Our entire dream life is the interpretation of complex feelings with a view to possible causes—and in such a way that we are conscious of a condition only when the supposed causal chain associated with it has entered consciousness.

The whole of "inner experience" rests upon the fact that a cause for an excitement of the nerve centers is sought and imagined—and that only a cause thus discovered enters consciousness: this cause in no way corresponds to the real cause—it is a groping on the basis of previous "inner experiences," i.e., of memory. But memory also maintains the habit of the old interpretations, i.e., of erroneous causality—so that the "inner experience" has to contain within it the consequences of all previous false causal fictions. Our "outer world" as we project it every moment is indissolubly tied to the old error of the ground: we interpret it by means of the schematism of "things," etc.

"Inner experience" enters our consciousness only after it has found a language the individual understands—i.e., a translation of a condition into conditions familiar to him—; "to understand" means merely: to be able to express something new in the language of something old and familiar. E.g., "I feel unwell"—such a judgment presupposes a great and late neutrality of the observer—; the simple man always says: this or that makes me feel unwell—he makes up his mind about his feeling unwell only when he has seen a reason for feeling unwell.—I call that a *lack of philology;* to be able to read off a text as a text without interposing an interpretation is the last-developed form of "inner experience"—perhaps one that is hardly possible—

—*The Will to Power,* Section 479

Against positivism, which halts at phenomena—"There are only *facts*"—I would say: No, facts is precisely what there is not, only interpretations. We cannot establish any fact "in itself": perhaps it is folly to want to do such a thing.

"Everything is subjective," you say; but even this is interpretation. The "subject" is not something given, it is something added and invented and projected behind what there is.—Finally, is it necessary to posit an interpreter behind the interpretation? Even this is invention, hypothesis.

In so far as the word "knowledge" has any meaning, the world is knowable; but it is *interpretable* otherwise, it has no meaning behind it, but countless meanings.—"Perspectivism."

It is our needs that interpret the world; our drives and their For and Against. Every drive is a kind of lust to rule; each one has its perspective that it would like to compel all the other drives to accept as a norm.

—*The Will to Power,* Section 481

We set up a word at the point at which our ignorance begins, at which we can see no further, e.g., the word "I," the word "do," the word "suffer":—these are perhaps the horizon of our knowledge, but not "truths."

—*The Will to Power,* Section 482

Truth is the kind of error without which a certain species of life could not live. The value for *life* is ultimately decisive.

—*The Will to Power,* Section 493

Ultimate solution.— We believe in reason; this, however, is the philosophy of gray *concepts.* Language depends on the most naive prejudices.

Now we read disharmonies and problems into things because we think *only* in the form of language—and thus believe in the "eternal truth" of "reason" (e.g., subject, attribute, etc.).

We cease to think when we refuse to do so under the constraint of language; we barely reach the doubt that sees this limitation as a limitation.

Rational thought is interpretation according to a scheme that we cannot throw off.

—*The Will to Power,* Section 522

There are many kinds of eyes. Even the sphinx has eyes—and consequently there are many kinds of "truths," and consequently there is no truth.

—*The Will to Power,* Section 540

[. . .] Will to truth is a making firm, a making true and durable, an abolition of the false character of things, a reinterpretation of it into beings. "Truth" is therefore not something there, that might be found or discovered—but something that must be created and that gives a name to a process, or rather to a will to overcome that has in itself no end—introducing truth, as a *process in infinitum,* an active determining—not a becoming-conscious of something that is in itself firm and determined. It is a word for the "will to power." [. . .]

—*The Will to Power,* Section 552

A "thing-in-itself" just as perverse as a "sense-in-itself," a "meaning-in-itself." There are no "facts-in-themselves," for a sense must always be projected into them before there can be "facts."

The question "what is that?" is an imposition of meaning from some other viewpoint. "Essence," the "essential nature," is something perspective and already presupposes a multiplicity. At the bottom of it there always lies "what is that for *me*?" (for us, for all that lives, etc.)

A thing would be defined once all creatures had asked "what is that?" and had answered their question. Supposing one single creature, with its own relationships and perspectives for all things, were missing, then the thing would not yet be "defined."

In short: the essence of a thing is only an *opinion* about the "thing." Or rather: "it is considered" is the real "it is," the sole "this is."

One may not ask: "who then interprets?" for the interpretation itself is a form of the will to power, exists (but not as a "being" but as a process, a becoming) as an affect.

The origin of "things" is wholly the work of that which imagines, thinks, wills, feels. The concept "thing" itself just as much as all its qualities.—Even "the subject" is such a created entity, a "thing" like all others: a simplification with the object of defining the force which posits, invents, thinks, as distinct from all individual positing, inventing, thinking as such. Thus a capacity as distinct from all that is individual—fundamentally, action collectively considered with respect to all anticipated actions (action and the probability of similar actions).

—*The Will to Power,* Section 556

That things possess a constitution in themselves quite apart from interpretation and subjectivity, is a quite idle hypothesis: it presupposes that interpretation and subjectivity are not essential, that a thing freed from all relationships would still be a thing.

Conversely, the apparent *objective* character of things: could it not be merely a difference of degree within the subjective?—that perhaps that which changes slowly presents itself to us as "objectively" enduring, being, "in-itself"—that the objective is only a false concept of a genus and an antithesis *within* the subjective?

—*The Will to Power,* Section 560

[. . .] The belief that the world as it ought to be *is,* really exists, is a belief of the unproductive who do *not desire to create a world* as it ought to be. They posit it as already available, they seek ways and means of reaching it. "Will to truth"—*as the impotence of the will to create.* [. . .] *The fiction of a world* that corresponds to our desires: psychological trick and interpretation with the aim of associating everything we honor and find pleasant with this true world.

"Will to truth" at this stage is essentially an art of interpretation: which at least requires the power to interpret. [. . .]

Whoever is incapable of laying his will into things, lacking will and strength, at least lays some *meaning* into them, i.e., the faith that there is a will in them already.

It is a measure of the degree of strength of will to what extent one can do without meaning in things, to what extent one can endure to live in a meaningless world *because one organizes a small portion of it oneself.* [. . .]

—*The Will to Power,* Section 585A

Our values are interpreted *into* things.
Is there then any *meaning* in the in-itself?!
Is meaning not necessarily relative meaning and perspective?
All meaning is will to power (all relative meaning resolves itself into it).

—*The Will to Power,* Section 590

No limit to the ways in which the world can be interpreted; every interpretation a symptom of growth or of decline.

Inertia needs unity (monism); plurality of interpretations a sign of strength. Not to desire to deprive the world of its disturbing and enigmatic character!

—*The Will to Power,* Section 600

"Interpretation," the introduction of meaning—not "explanation" (in most cases a new interpretation over an old interpretation that has become incomprehensible, that is now itself only a sign). There are no facts, everything is in flux, incomprehensible, elusive; what is relatively most enduring is—our opinions.

—*The Will to Power,* Section 604

The ascertaining of "truth" and "untruth," the ascertaining of facts in general, is fundamentally different from creative positing, from forming, shaping, overcoming, willing, such as is of the essence of philosophy. To introduce a meaning—this task still remains to be done, assuming there is no meaning yet. Thus it is with sounds, but also with the fate of peoples: they are capable of the most different interpretations and direction toward different goals.

On a yet higher level is to *posit a goal* and mold facts according to it; that is, active interpretation and not merely conceptual translation.

—*The Will to Power,* Section 605

Ultimately, man finds in things nothing but what he himself has imported into them: the finding is called science, the importing—art, religion, love, pride. Even if this should be a piece of childishness, one should carry on with both and be well disposed toward both—some should find; others—*we* others!—should import!

—*The Will to Power,* Section 606

That the value of the world lies in our interpretation (—that other interpretations than merely human ones are perhaps somewhere possible—); that previous interpretations have been perspective valuations by virtue of which we can survive in life, i.e., in the will to power, for the growth of power; that every elevation of man brings with it the overcoming of narrower interpretations; that every strengthening and increase of power opens up new perspectives and means believing in new horizons—this idea permeates my writings. The world with which we are concerned is false, i.e., is not a fact but a fable and approximation on the basis of a meager sum of observations; it is "in flux," as something in a state of becoming, as a falsehood always changing but never getting near the truth: for—there is no "truth."

—*The Will to Power,* Section 616

Translated by Walter Kaufman and R. J. Hollingdale

2

Nietzsche, Freud, Marx*

Michel Foucault

This plan for a "round table,"[1] when it was proposed to me, appeared very interesting, but clearly quite puzzling. I suggest a subterfuge: some themes concerning *the techniques of interpretation* in Marx, Nietzsche, and Freud.

In reality, behind these themes there is a dream that one day it will be possible to make a kind of general corpus, an encyclopedia of all the techniques of interpretation that we can know from the Greek grammarians to our time. I think that few of the chapters of this great corpus of all the techniques of interpretation have thus far been drawn up. It seems to me that one could say, as a general introduction to this idea of a history of techniques of interpretation, that language, at least language in Indo-European cultures, has always given rise to two kinds of suspicions.

—First of all, the suspicion that language does not say exactly what it means [*le langage ne dit pas exactement ce qu'il dit*]. The meaning [*sens*] that one grasps, and that is immediately manifest, is perhaps in reality only a lesser meaning [*moindre sens*] that shields, restrains, and despite everything transmits another meaning, the meaning "underneath it" ["*d'en dessous*"]. This is what the Greeks called *allegoria* and *hyponoïa*.

—On the other hand, language gives rise to another suspicion: that in some way it overflows its properly verbal form, and that there are many other things in the world that speak, and that are not language. After all, it might be that nature, the sea, rustling trees, animals, faces, masks, crossed swords all speak. Perhaps there is some language articulating itself in a way that would not be verbal. This would be, if you wish, very crudely, the *semaïnon* of the Greeks.

These two suspicions, which we see appearing already in Greek texts, have not disappeared. They are still our contemporaries, as once again we have come to believe, precisely since the nineteenth century, that mute gestures, illnesses, all the confusion around us can speak as well. More than ever we are at the listening post of all this possible language, trying to overhear, beneath the words, a discourse that would be more essential.

I think that each culture, I mean each cultural form in Western civilization, has had its system of interpretation, its techniques, its methods, its way of suspecting that language means something other than what it says, and of suspecting that there is language elsewhere than in language. It seems in fact that there was an attempt to establish the system or the table, as they used to say in the seventeenth century, of all these systems of interpretation.

To understand what sort of system of interpretation the nineteenth century founded and, as a result, to what sort of system of interpretation we others, even now, belong, it seems to me that it would be necessary to take a distant reference, a type of technique as may have existed, for example, in the sixteenth century. At that time, resemblance was what gave *rise* to interpretation, at one and the same time its general site and the minimal unity that interpretation had to treat. There, where things were like each other, there, where *interpretation* would resemble itself, something wanted to be said and could be deciphered. The important role played by resemblance and all the notions that revolved like satellites around it in the cosmology, the botany, the zoology, and the philosophy of the sixteenth century are well known. To tell the truth, to our eyes as people of the twentieth century, this whole network of similitudes is fairly confused and entangled. In fact, this corpus of resemblance in the sixteenth century was perfectly organized. There were at least five exactly defined notions:

—The notion of convenience [*convenance,* propriety, expediency, fitness], *convenentia,* which is agreement (for example, of the soul to the body, or the animal series to the vegetable series).

—The notion of *sympatheïa,* sympathy, which is the identity of accidents in distinct substances.

—The notion of *emulatio,* which is the very curious parallelism of attributes in substances or in distinct beings, such that the attributes of one being are like the reflection of the other's attributes. (Thus Porta explains that the human face, with the seven parts that distinguish it, is the emulation of the sky with its seven planets.)

—The notion of *signatura,* the signature, which is the image of an invisible and hidden property among the visible properties of an individual.

—And then, of course, the notion of *analogie,* which is the identity of the relations between two or more distinct substances.

At that time, the theory of the sign and the techniques of interpretation rested in fact on a perfectly clear definition of all the possible types of resemblance, and they had established two types of completely distinct knowledge: *cognitio,* which was the passage, in some way lateral, from one resemblance to another; and *divinatio,* which was the deep knowledge [*connaissance en profondeur*], going from a superficial resemblance to a more profound resemblance. All these resemblances manifest the *consensus* of the world that lays their foundation; they resist the *simulacrum,* the false resemblance which rests on the discord between God and the Devil.

If these techniques of interpretation of the sixteenth century were left suspended by the evolution of Western thought in the seventeenth and eighteenth centuries, if the Baconian and Cartesian critique of resemblance certainly played a large part in their being put in parentheses, the nineteenth century, and quite singularly Marx, Nietzsche, and Freud, placed us once again in the presence of a new possibility of interpretation. They founded anew the possibility of a hermeneutic.

The first book of *Capital* and texts like *The Birth of Tragedy, On the Genealogy of Morals,* and the *Interpretation of Dreams* place us in the presence of these interpretive techniques. And the shock effect, the type of wound provoked in Western thought by these works, comes probably from something they reconstituted before our eyes that Marx, himself, moreover, called "hieroglyphs." This has put us in an uncomfortable situation, since these techniques of interpretation concern ourselves: since we interpret, we interpret ourselves according to these techniques. It is with these techniques of interpretation, in return, that we must question these interpreters who were Freud, Nietzsche, and Marx, so that we are always returned in a perpetual play of mirrors.

Freud says somewhere that there are three great narcissistic wounds in Western culture: the wound imposed by Copernicus; that made by Darwin, when he discovered that man was descended from the ape; and the wound made by Freud himself when he, in his turn, discovered that consciousness was based on the unconscious. I wonder whether we could not say that by involving us in an interpretive task that always reflects upon itself, Freud, Nietzsche, and Marx did not constitute around us, and for us, those mirrors which reflect to us the images whose inexhaustible wounds form our contemporary narcissism. In any case, and it is to this proposal that I would like to make some suggestions, it seems to me that Marx, Nietzsche, and Freud have not somehow multiplied the signs in the Western world. They have not given a new meaning to things which did not have any meaning. In reality they have changed the nature of the sign, and modified the way in which the sign in general could be interpreted.

The first question that I want to pose is this: have not Marx, Freud, and Nietzsche profoundly modified the distributive space [*répartition,* assessment] in which signs can be signs? At the time that I have taken for a point of reference, the sixteenth century, signs were disposed of in a homogeneous way in a space that was itself in all directions homogeneous. Signs of the earth turned back to the sky, but they turned back as well to the underground world; they turned back reciprocally, from man to animal, from animal to plant. From the nineteenth century on, that is, from Freud, Marx, and Nietzsche, signs are themselves stages in a much more differentiated space, according to a dimension that we could call depth, on the condition that one understand by that not interiority but, on the contrary, exteriority.

I am thinking in particular of the long debate with depth that Nietzsche never stopped maintaining. There is in the works of Nietzsche a critique of ideal depth, the depth of consciousness that he denounces as an invention of the philosophers. This depth would be a pure, interior search for truth. Nietzsche shows how depth implies resignation, hypocrisy, the mask, so that the interpreter, when he surveys signs in order to denounce them, must descend the length of the vertical line and show that this depth of interiority is in reality something other than what appears. It is necessary, therefore, that the interpreter descend, that he be, as he says, "the good excavator of the underworld."[2]

But when one interprets, one can in reality traverse this descending line only to restore the sparkling exteriority that has been covered up and buried. The fact is that whereas the interpreter must go himself to the bottom of things like an excavator, the movement of interpretation is, on the contrary, one that projects out over the depth, raised more and more above the depth, always leaving the depth below, exposed to ever greater visibility. The depth is now restored as an absolutely superficial secret, in such a way that the eagle's taking flight, the ascent of the mountain, all the verticality so important in Zarathustra, is, in the strict sense, the reversal of depth, the discovery that depth was only a game, and a crease [pli] in the surface. As the world becomes more profound under our gaze, one notices that everything that exercised the profundity of man was only child's play.

I wonder whether this spatiality, Nietzsche's play with profundity, could be compared to the apparently different game that Marx conducted with platitude. The concept of "platitude" is very important in the works of Marx. At the beginning of Capital,[3] he explains how, contrary to Perseus, he should bury himself in the uncertainty to show in fact that there are neither monsters nor profound enigmas. Instead one finds that all there is of profundity in the conception that the bourgeoisie have of money, of capital, of value, and so forth is in reality only platitude.

And, of course, it would be necessary to recall the interpretive space that Freud constituted, not only in the celebrated topology of Consciousness and the Unconscious, but equally in the rules that he formulated for psychoanalytic attention, and the deciphering by the analyst of what is said all along the spoken "chain." One should recall the spatiality, after all quite material, to which Freud attached so much importance, and which exposes the patient under the watchful gaze of the psychoanalyst.

The second theme I would like to propose to you, which is moreover somewhat tied to the former, would be to indicate that, beginning with these three men who now speak to us, interpretation at last became an endless task. To tell the truth, it was already that in the sixteenth century, but the signs were exchanged back and forth, quite simply because resemblance could only be limited. From the nineteenth century on, signs were linked in an inexhaustible as well as infinite network, not because they rested on a resemblance without border, but because there are irreducible gaps and openings.

The incompleteness of interpretation, the fact that it is always fragmented and initially remains suspended on itself, is met with again, I believe, in a sufficiently similar way in the works of Marx, Nietzsche, and Freud in the form of the denial of origination [*commencement*]: the denial of the "Robinsonade," said Marx; the distinction, so important in the works of Nietzsche, between the beginning and the origin; and the always incomplete character of the regressive and analytic practice in the works of Freud. It is above all in the works of Nietzsche and Freud, and to a lesser degree in those of Marx, that we see delineated this experience, which I believe to be so important for modern hermeneutics, that the further one goes in interpretation, the closer one approaches at the same time an absolutely dangerous region where interpretation is not only going to find its points of no return but where it is going to disappear itself as interpretation, bringing perhaps the disappearance of the interpreter himself. The existence that always approached some absolute point of interpretation would be at the same time that of a breaking point [*point de rupture*].

In the works of Freud, it is well known how progressively the discovery of this structurally open character of interpretation is forced structurally wide open. It was done first in a very allusive way, quite hidden by itself in the *Interpretation of Dreams*, when Freud analyzed his own dreams, and he invoked reasons of modesty or nondivulgence of a personal secret in order to interrupt himself. In the analysis of Dora, one sees appear this idea that interpretation must stop itself, unable to go to its conclusion in consideration of something that some years later will be called *transference*. And then, the inexhaustibility of analysis affirms itself across the entire study of transference in the infinite and infinitely problematic character of the relationship of the analyzed and the analyst, a relationship which is clearly constituent for psychoanalysis—one that opens the space in which it never stops deploying itself without ever being able to be finished.

In the works of Nietzsche also, it is clear that interpretation is always unfinished. What is philosophy for him if not a sort of philology always suspended, a philology without end, always further unfolded, a philology which would never be absolutely fixed? Why? It is, as he said in *Beyond Good and Evil*, because "to perish from absolute knowledge might be a basic characteristic of existence."[4] And yet he showed in *Ecce Homo* how he was near this absolute knowledge which makes up a part of the foundation of Being [*fondement de l'Etre*]—likewise, during Autumn, 1888 in Turin.

If one deciphers in the correspondence of Freud his constant anxiety from the moment when he discovered psychoanalysis, we can wonder whether the experience of Freud is not, at bottom, quite similar to that of Nietzsche. What is in question at the breaking point of interpretation, in this convergence of interpretation toward a point that renders it impossible, could well be something like the experience of madness—experience against which Nietzsche struggled and by which he was fascinated, experience against which Freud himself, all his life, had wrestled, not without anguish. This experience of madness would be the penalty for a movement of interpretation which approached the infinity of its center, and which collapsed, calcinated.

I believe that this essential incompleteness of interpretation is linked to two other equally fundamental principles, and with the two former ones that I have just mentioned, would constitute the postulates of modern hermeneutics. This one first: if interpretation can never be brought to an end, it is simply because there is nothing to interpret. There is nothing absolutely primary to interpret, because at bottom everything is already interpretation [*tout est déjà interprétation*]. Each sign is in itself not the thing that presents itself to interpretation, but the interpretation of other signs.

There is never, if you will, an *interpretandum* which is not already an *interpretans*, so that there is established in interpretation a relation of violence as much as of elucidation. In fact, interpretation does not illuminate an interpretive topic that would offer itself passively to it; it can only violently seize an interpretation already there, which it must reverse, return, shatter with blows of a hammer. This is seen already in the works of Marx, which do not interpret the history of relations of production, but which interpret a relation that, inasmuch as it presents itself as nature, is already giving itself as an interpretation. Likewise, Freud does not interpret signs, but interpretations. Indeed, what does Freud discover under symptoms? He does not discover, as one says, "traumatisms"—he brings to light *fantasies*, with their burden of anguish, that is to say, a nucleus which is already itself, in its own being, an interpretation. Anorexia, for example, is not sent back [*renvoie*] to weaning, as the signifier would refer [*renverrait*] to the signified; but anorexia as sign, as symptom to interpret, refers to the fantasies of the false maternal breast, which is itself an interpretation, which is already in itself a speaking body. That is why Freud did not have to interpret what his patients offered to him as symptoms in language other than that of his patients; his interpretation is the interpretation of an interpretation, in the terms in which that interpretation is given. It is well known that Freud invented the "superego" ["*surmoi*"] the day when a patient said to him: "I sense a dog over me" ["*je sens un chien sur moi*"].

In the same way, Nietzsche makes himself master of interpretations which have already seized one another. There is no original signified for Nietzsche. Words themselves are nothing other than interpretations; throughout their history, they interpret before being signs, and in the long run they signify only because they are only essential interpretations. Look at the famous etymology of *agathos*.[5] This is also what Nietzsche says when he says that words have always been invented by the upper classes: they do not indicate a signified; they impose an interpretation. Therefore it is not because there are primary and enigmatic signs that we are now dedicated [*voués*] to the task of interpretation, but because there are interpretations, because beneath everything they never stop being that which expresses the great texture of violent interpretations. This is the reason that there are signs, signs which prescribe to us the interpretation of their interpretation, which prescribe to us their reversal as signs. In this sense, it can be said that *Allegoria, Hyponoïa,* are *at the foundation of language and before it,* not what are slid under the words afterwards [*non pas ce qui s'est glissé après coup sous les mots*] in order to displace them and make them vibrate, but what give birth to words, what cause them to shine with a brilliance that is never fixed. This is also why, in the works of Nietzsche, the interpreter is the "truthful one ["*véridique*"]; he is the "genuine one" ["*véritable*"], not because he makes himself master of a sleeping truth in order to utter it, but because he declares the interpretation that all truth has the function of concealing. Perhaps this preeminence of interpretation in relation to signs is what is most decisive in modern hermeneutics.

The idea that interpretation precedes the sign implies that the sign may not be simple and benevolent being, as was still the case in the sixteenth century, when the plethora of signs—the fact that things were alike—simply proved the benevolence of God, and only a transparent veil separated the sign from the signified. On the other hand, from the nineteenth century on, beginning with Freud, Marx, and Nietzsche, it seems to me that the sign is going to become malevolent. I mean that there is in the sign an ambiguous quality and a slight suspicion of ill will and "malice." Moreover, insofar as the sign is already an interpretation which is not given as such, signs are interpretations which try to justify themselves, and not the reverse.

Thus functions money as one sees it defined in the *Critique of Political Economy,* and above all in the first book of *Capital.* Symptoms also function in the same way in the works of Freud. And in the works of Nietzsche, words, justice, the binary classification of Good and Evil, that is to say, signs, are masks. By acquiring this new function of covering up [*recouvrement,* recovery] the interpretation, the sign loses its simple being as signifier that it still possessed at the time of the Renaissance. Its own thickness comes almost to open itself, and all the negative concepts which had until then remained foreign to the theory of the sign can rush into the opening. This theory had known only the transparent moment and the negative penalty [*peine*] of the veil. Now the whole play of negative concepts, contradictions, oppositions, in short, the ensemble of that play of reactive forces that Deleuze has analyzed so well in his book on Nietzsche[6] has the power to organize itself in the interior of the sign.

"To put the dialectic back on its feet": if this expression must have a meaning, is it not to have justly replaced in the thickness of the sign, in that open, gaping space without end, in that space without real content or reconciliation, all this play of negativity that the dialectic finally uncapped in giving to it a positive sense?

Finally, the last characteristic of hermeneutics: interpretation finds itself before the obligation of interpreting itself endlessly, of always correcting itself. From here, two important consequences follow. The first is that interpretation will be henceforth always interpretation by the "who?": one does not interpret what there is in the signified, but one interprets, fundamentally, *who* has posed the interpretation. The origin [*principe*] of interpretation is nothing other than the interpreter, and this is perhaps the sense that Nietzsche gave to the word "*psychology.*"[7] The second consequence is that interpretation always has to interpret itself, and it cannot fail to return to itself. In opposition to the age of signs, which is a time when payments fall due, and in opposition to the age of the dialectic, which despite everything is linear, one has an age of interpretation which is circular. This age is obliged to pass again where it has already passed, which on the whole makes that the only danger which interpretation really runs; but it is a supreme danger, for it is paradoxically the signs which make it run the risk. The death of interpretation is to believe that there are signs, signs that exist primarily, originally, actually, like coherent, pertinent, and systematic marks.

The life of interpretation, on the contrary, is to believe that there is nothing but interpretations. It seems to me that one must understand well that which many of our contemporaries forget, that *hermeneutics and semiology are two ferocious enemies.* A hermeneutic that in fact winds itself around a semiology, believing in the absolute existence of signs, gives up the violence, the incompleteness, the infinity of interpretations, so as to create a reign of terror where the mark rules [*régner la terreur de l'indice*] and suspects language—we recognize here Marxism after Marx. On the other hand, a hermeneutic that envelopes around itself this intermediate region of madness and pure language enters into the domain of languages that never stop implicating themselves—it is there that we recognize Nietzsche.

Translated by Alan D. Schrift

Notes

*Originally published as "Nietzsche, Freud, Marx," In *Nietzsche, Cahiérs du Royaumont* (Paris: Les Éditions du Minuit, 1964), pp. 183–92.—ED.

1. The "round table" Foucault refers to was a discussion held during the Seventh International Philosophical Colloquium at Royaumont, July 4–8, 1964. At the Colloquium on Nietzsche, papers were presented by Foucault, Jean Beaufret, Henri Birault, Giorgio Colli and Mazzino Montinari, Gilles Deleuze, Edouard Gaéde, Danko Grlic, Pierre Klossowski, Karl Löwith, Gabriel Marcel, Herbert W. Reichert, Boris de Schloezer, Gianni Vattimo, and Jean Wahl.—TRANS.

2. Cf. Friedrich Nietzsche, *Daybreak,* Section 446.

3. The reference to Perseus appears in the preface to the first German edition of *Capital.*—TRANS.

4. Cf. Friedrich Nietzsche, *Beyond Good and Evil,* Section 39. [The German text, which reads *"ja es könnte selbst zur Grundbeschaffenheit des Daseins gehören, dass man an seiner völligen Erkenntnis zugrunde ginge,"* is quoted by Foucault from the French translation as *"périr par la connaissance absolue pourrait bien faire partie du fondement de l'être."*—TRANS.]

5. Cf. Friedrich Nietzsche, *On the Genealogy of Morals,* Essay One, Sections 4 and 5.

6. Gilles Deleuze, *Nietzsche et la philosophie* (Paris: Presses Universitaires de France, 1962). English translation: *Nietzsche and Philosophy,* translated by Hugh Tomlinson (New York: Columbia University Press, 1984).—TRANS.

7. See, for example, the definition of "psychology" as "morphology and *the doctrine of the development of the will to power*" in *Beyond Good and Evil,* Section 23.—TRANS.

3

Interpreting Texts With and Without Nietzsche

Eric Blondel

In the likeness of its subject, the title of this essay carries a double meaning, in that it offers itself precisely as something which must be interpreted. Why? Because the title does not possess only one meaning, as it ought; but it possesses two meanings: that is to say, it is ambiguous, ambivalent, uncertain, at the same time multiple and mysterious, obscure—like the Sphinx, who proposed riddles to be interpreted that only Oedipus could manage to unravel.

By means of an analogy, at the level of superficial grammatical structures, "interpreting texts" signifies both the "interpretation of texts" ["*interpréter des textes*"] and also "texts which interpret" ["*les textes interprétant*"]. I would like to illustrate and to explicate this rich ambiguity by interpreting—precisely—two texts which themselves interpret. Thus, we have the question of interpretation placed at two different levels: one of commentary on the text and one of the text itself which practices interpretation by assuming [*en posant*] its own subject as interpretive. Two texts will be used here—from Balzac and from Proust—as parables of interpretation *on* the text and *in* the text. The interpretation of these two interpretive texts will allow for posing, in the second place, the theoretical problem of interpretation. Third, it will evoke the conception of interpretation that Nietzsche proposes.

I. Two Interpretive Texts

The first text is dated 1834. It is taken from a novel by Honoré de Balzac, *Father Goriot,* and offers us the introduction of an important character in that work, Vautrin, in the form of a portrait. This portrait, which belongs to a classic genre of the novel in general and, above all, in nineteenth century French literature—heir of the seventeenth and eighteenth century moralists and memorialists like Retz and Saint-Simon—takes the place of other portraits of individuals composing the regular clientele of the boardinghouse directed by the widow Vauquer.

Between these two characters and the others, Vautrin, the forty-year old man with painted whiskers, was the transition. He was one of those of whom the lower class say, "Here is a fine strappling!" He was broad-shouldered, boasted a protruding breast, showing sinews, thick square hands, with tufts of thickly growing hair of a glowing russet tinge between the knuckles. His face, which was marked with premature wrinkles, afforded signs of hardness which his lithesome, winning manners belied. His bass baritone voice, at one with his coarse cheerfulness, was not offensive. He was an obliging man, prompt to laugh. Should some lock be out of order, he would straight-away take it to pieces, tinker it up, oil it, file and put it into order again, saying "I am the man for locks." Besides, he was conversant with everything—ships, the sea, France and foreign lands, business, man, events, laws, hotels, and prisons too. Should anyone complain too much, he readily proffered his help. Many times had he lent money to Madame Vauquer and some boarders; but his debtors would rather have died than not return it, so much overawed were they, de-spite his good-humored air, by a certain deep determined look of his. By the very way he spat, he showed imperturbable cold blood which would not make him wince before murder to get clear of a dubious position. Like a stern judge, his eye seemed to probe deep into all questions, all consciences, all feelings. He was wont to leave after lunch, come home for dinner, disappear for the whole evening and return by midnight, thanks to a latch-key which Madame Vauquer had entrusted to him. He of all others benefited by this privilege. There-fore, he was on good terms with the widow whom he called "Mama" while holding her by the waist, a compliment hardly under-stood! The old wife fancied that it was still easy to do, whereas only Vautrin had arms long enough to press this ponderous circumference. One of his characteristic features was to pay a generous fifteen francs for the "gloria" he treated himself with for a dessert. Less superficial folk than these youngsters were, carried away with the whirlwind of Parisian life, or these old people, blind to what did not directly affect them, would not have heeded the shady impressions Vautrin made on them. He knew or he guessed the business of those around him while no one could enter into his thoughts or avocations. Although he had thrown his seeming good-humoredness, unimpaired cheerfulness and affability as a barrier between others and himself, he would often allow one a glimpse into the dreadful depth of his character. Often a sally of his, worthy of some Juvenal, by means of which he seemed to relish flouting the laws, to whip high society, to convince them of their lack of logic with themselves, might have suggested that he bore a grudge towards the social condition and that there lay a carefully hidden mystery in the very depth of his life.[1]

An interpretation will have to follow this text step by step to throw into relief progressively the meaning, the process [*la démarche*], and the effect. Because of a lack of space, we must be satisfied with summarizing what a detailed and consistent analysis of the text will allow to be established. Generally speaking, the portrait is destined to show, to describe; it has in view the character, the nature, and the personality of an individual in his or her psychological, social, and practical truthfulness, and so forth. The portrait wishes to reach the truth: it seeks, by diverse means, to invest or to outline what will be called, abstractly speaking, the *concept* of some human being. Certainly, it provides very diverse means of *revelation* at the service of the author, who, in the classic eighteenth and nineteenth century novel, is supposed to be, by his acute penetration of the character, equal to an all-powerful God and, above all, insightful and omniscient. But the author needs all of these opportunities in developing the portrait, since it is incumbent upon him, as a human and superhuman demiurge—like his reader and his divine model—to reveal the truth of a being, such as God can fathom it, from the signs that the reader's simply human point of view can furnish. A classic in this sense, Balzac overcomes the specific difficulty of a descriptive—in reality, purely interpretive—portrait, binding interior and exterior according to a code which is his own: the material context (places, disguises, tics, habits, furnishings, manners, physiognomy, etc.) directly signifies a psychology. The description focuses little by little, proceeding from the town, the house, the furniture, the attire, the face, to end with a similarly significant detailed account of the eyes, the skin, or behavior, which indicates a mentality, a personality, a soul. It is known that Balzac, for himself, believed in the phrenology of Gall,[2] which inferred psychological and spiritual characteristics from the outward appearance—the anatomy (the head, limbs, body . . .)—of an individual. These marks, strictly coded, signify, *a contrario*, that the portrait maker wants to assure himself against the uncertainty and precariousness of an apparently descriptive and intuitive—in reality, strictly *interpretive*—enterprise (which rests on the belief that one is able ''to see'' the underlying being in its very concept). To produce a portrait is to interpret a being according to those signs and from those indices which, as it is said in the splendid fragment from Heraclitus, "do not show, but (solely) indicate" (Diels-Kranz, *Fragmente des vorsokratiker,* §93). In our text, phrases such as "one of his characteristic features," "by the very way he spat, he showed . . . ," "the shady impressions made on them," even the precise detail about "his face," "his voice," "his shoulders," "he was . . . ," "like a stern judge . . . ," leave it understood that one can define a being, know what characteristics outline it.

But the interest of this text, apparently so well coded and certain of its investigative means that it might appear to be simplistic and to make use of a parascientific and almost "racist" method of characterization (its idea is that the type of a man can be disclosed surely by his outward appearance), is, in fact, how it decodes, disarranges, and obscures the portrait. Indeed, the text insists no less on the mystery and uncertainty of the proposed portrait than on the infallible rules of the code. Better still: it accomplishes the tour de force in presenting a nondescriptive portrait, a nonportrait, an antiportrait. The description of Vautrin does not capture [*décrit:* depict] him: his definition renders him indefinable; the detailed accounts allude to his ambiguity. The portrait is a mask. The more precise Balzac is, the more the uncertainty and blurred image are extended: "seeming good-humoredness," "hidden mystery," "allow one a glimpse," "he seemed," "a barrier," "suggested." Paradoxically, this portrait-text, with a descriptive and explicative intention, reveals and insists upon its conjectural and interpretive character. The portrait-text dismantles the procedural apparatus and makes it apparent in its interpretive uncertainty: "there lay a carefully hidden mystery in the very depth of his life." Thus, we are both duped and discreetly informed that we are not to trust any appearances, any signs, in truth not even this discourse which wishes to be truthful. Returning to this portrait after having read the rest of the novel, which reveals that Vautrin is a convict, we will understand why this portrait was an interpretation and why it was not one. But the portrait itself leaves it understood without saying it explicitly.

On the other hand, the following text by Marcel Proust expressly thematizes the ambiguity and interpretive character of the portrait, indeed of all imaginary portraits, in which we are tempted to capture a character or a person. Thus, Proust considers the novel, "literature," as the object that he takes as a theme at the same time that he is practicing it. The portrait, literature, is here, explicitly, both a practice [*une pratique:* a method] and a representative placement in the abyss of this practice ["*en abyme*"],[3] as Gide said, a "theme": interpretation, conscious of itself, takes for its object interpreting (interpretation) itself.

But first, let us read before interpreting this interpretation of interpretation.

Madame Swann at the Bois de Boulogne

I had given pride of place to plainness in the scale of aest
and worldly greatness, when I caught sight of Madame
foot, in a woollen polonaise with a small toque bedecked w
of a lophophore on her head, a nosegay of violets pinne
blouse, in a hurry, cutting across the Accacia Avenue as
it were the shortest way home, winking an answer to the ge
in their carriages who, as they made out her silhouette from
would bow to her and say to themselves that no one was as
However, instead of plainness, it was display which I set highest
once I had compelled Francoise who was dog-tired and said her l
were collapsing "beneath her," to mark time for an hour, at last
saw, coming out of the Avenue from Porte Dauphine—for me a pic
ture of royal prestige, a majestic arrival, such as no real queen later
could ever afford me the impression, because I harbored a less uncertain and more actual notion of their power—carried away by the
flight of two mettlesome horses as slender and as sophisticated as can
be seen on the drawings of Constantin Guys, with a bulky coachman
settled on the box, provided with furs in the Cossack fashion, by the
side of a puny groom reminding one of the "tiger" of "late
Baudenord,"[4] I saw—or rather felt the imprint of its shape in my
heart with a clean and wearying wound—a peerless Victoria, purposely slightly too high on its wheels, and allowing, through its up to
date smartness, hints to older forms, in the depth of which Madame
Swann leisurely lay, her hair now turned fair with just one grey wisp,
girt with a headband of flowers, mostly violets, from which flowed
long veils, with a mauve sunshade in her hands, an ambiguous smile
on her lips, in which I only saw the benevolence of a Majesty and in
which there was above all the provocative look of a "cocotte,"[5] and
which she turned gently towards those who greeted her. Such a smile,
in reality, suggested to some, "I do remember very well, it was
lovely," to others, "How much I should have liked that! It was too
bad," and to others still, "But, if you are willing! I shall still follow
the lane for a while and shall cut across as soon as I can." Whenever
unknown folk passed by she still allowed an idle smile to float around
her lips, as though addressed towards the expectation or the memory
of some friend and which made them say, "How beautiful she is!"
And only for certain men she cut a bitter, strained, shy and frigid
smile which suggested, "Yes, you rascal, I know you have a viper's
tongue, and that you can't help chatting! Do I, for one, bother about
you?"[6]

73

¹emand a very long interpretive
.ily in overly general terms.
.of the narrator *à propos* a central
.as given her name to the title of the
.. He begins with two long sentences
pressions that conjure the image of Ma-
récy, about whom the reader knows already
.aot know: she is a demi-monde, that is to say,
society. As for himself, the narrator, who will
.ce of naiveté and jealousy with the daughter of the
vidence of the first impressions of a young, innocent
. jealousy and the gossip (the tales about Madame
.irectly in the realm of interpretation. The narrator (as a
.ɔ novelist distinct from and confounded with the character)
.old observation: (a) the simple and brute reality—an elegant
.cribed as such; (b) an interpretation of exterior signs directed
.e sublimity of the character [*dans le sens de la majesté du person-*
-is it a metaphor or a simple metonymy creating the illusion?; and
actual reality in its striking and demystifying contrast with the euphe-
.istic and flattering interpretation: "Such a smile, in reality, suggested . . . " (taken in the form of a theatrical dialogue).

On the whole, the text informs us of reality's ambiguity and shows us
how interpretation, to which reality must be committed because of its enigmatic character, is precarious, illusory, subject to error, to overemphasis,
grandiloquence, and confusion. Thus, this text offers a reflection on the
sign, the necessity of which—as a moralist and man about town—Proust
emphasizes in the absence of a revelation of what it signifies. He also
stresses what the deceptive, unreliable type [*caractère*][7] signifies—in a rhetorical framework. Are the objects and amazing environment which surround Madame Swann valuable for comparison, for definition (metaphor),
or are they associated with the definition of this character only by contingent liaison (metonymy)? Is Madame Swann comparable to a queen or is
she only a pretentious whore seeking to create an illusion by gathering
round herself a royal show? Such is the question of interpretation the moralist poses, who, in "fashionable society," has learned to be suspicious of
exterior signs, and thus recognizes the lesson of Jean-Jacques Rousseau, the
moralists (La Rochefoucauld, La Bruyère, etc.), and the memorialists of the
court of Louis XIVth (Saint-Simon). It is indeed a question of interpretation, since the interpretive error concerning signs is here discovered, de-
tected as such: reality is only an ensemble of signs, which only gives an
interpretive knowledge [*connaissance:* understanding], never objective and
explicative certainty. Every portrait, in the broadest sense of the term, is

only an interpretive conjecture *à propos* ambiguous signs—a choice among the multiple meanings which man must give to each phenomenon in the world.

Thus, we have read—and interpreted—two texts: the first, by Balzac, works out a riddle, the interpretation of which it begins, while the other text by Proust, less classical and more "literary" by its secondary reflection, thematizes the very problem of interpretation. From these two examples, we can see what is the philosophically problematic structure of interpretation.

II. The Problem of Interpretation

As we have seen already, though in an obscure fashion, the concept of interpretation, the implications of which I would like now to develop philosophically, implies that one is inscribed in an ambiguous situation. Our examples have shown this, with differences, in both cases with the portraits of Vautrin/Jacques Collin (the convict) and Madame Swann/Odette de Crécy (the "prostitute"). To produce a portrait is to interpret, making use of *ambiguous signs,* of that which does not fail to appear—if the individuals themselves are supposed to have an ambiguous nature or situation. This ambiguity, or equivocation (the corresponding epithet, in its double meaning, manifests the moral value attached to duplicity), indeed this ambivalence, constitutes the nature and proper status of the object. Consequently, it cannot be simply shown, explicated, but must give/conceal itself at the risk of an interpretation. The risk of interpretation, then, creates the relations with the riddle, the mystery, soothsaying. The romantic value and status of this interpretive situation—characteristic of the nineteenth and also twentieth century novel—are patent in a short story by Balzac entitled *Sarrasine* (1830),[8] of which Roland Barthes has offered a very expanded and very interesting commentary in his book *S/Z*. *S/Z* underlines the reader's uncertainty regarding the identity of the principal character (man/woman, S/Z), uncertainty generalized and produced throughout the novel, a novel of ambiguity and equivocation (social, sexual, literary, grammatical, and interpretive). In his *Proust et le Monde sensible,*[9] the critic Jean-Pierre Richard underlines the "duplicity" of Gilberte, the daughter of Madame Swann, duplicity "that, in some regards, resembles the erotic equivocation of cunning."[10] It can be added that Gilles Deleuze, in *Proust and Signs*, insists on all sorts of Proustian ambiguities, confirming that the world of signs is one of ambiguity requiring an apprenticeship of interpretation: "At the end of the Search [*Recherche*], the interpreter understands what had escaped him . . . "[11]

In the second place, interpretation supposes that we enter into the field of *plurality*. "To interpret a text," says Barthes, "is not to give (more or less justified, more or less free) meaning, but on the contrary to appreciate what *plural* constitutes it. Let us first posit the image of a triumphant plural, unimpoverished by any constraint of representation (of intuition)."[12] More precisely, I would add that interpretation implies the plurality, indeed, the *indetermination of the code:* perhaps even its *latency*, in the sense that the code is implicit, hidden by the plurality or by the unconsciousness, a failure to recognize: indeed, where the code is hidden by the text. The image which appears to me revealing here, in this instance, is one Shakespeare uses at the time of choosing the three caskets [*coffrets*] by the three suitors of Portia in *The Merchant of Venice* (Act III, Scene ii). Freud has offered a magnificent rendering of this situation that is exemplary of interpretation.[13] There is interpretation because there are several caskets, and also because the code permitting the apt choice is hidden, dissembled, dissimulated [*dissimulé*]. Portia alone has fixed the code secretly and only she knows the code (the role of the *plainness* of the modest metal that is lead), and the sign for recognizing a good interpretation, the portrait, is concealed in one of the closed caskets. Latency and plurality: it is the indeterminacy of the code which is, at once, in a certain manner, outside the text; or if in the text, it remains latent. In this respect, if what is called "structuralism" characterizes itself by the privilege given to the internal relations that constitute the text, interpretation is nonstructuralist at first. It finds itself, by its status outside the text, or, in every case, in an outside [*l'extériorité*] defined by latency and mystery. In order to have interpretation, it is necessary that the text not give itself, evidently, its own code, but that the text expose itself to its outside, the environment which in fact makes it an *irresponsible toy* (which cannot respond only by itself or answer for itself). The text is not *the author* (*auctor:* guarantor) of interpretation; the text submits to it. This situation of submission, indeed of alienation, of guardianship, leads us to confirm and to return to the image forged by Plato, in the *Phaedrus* (275 d-e), in order to speak about the reading that takes hold of the text in spite of itself and in spite of the intentions of its author. The text, says Plato, is like an orphaned infant for whom its father can no longer provide support, since he is absent. Just as writing is a murder of the father and reading takes advantage of the infant, on account of its weaknesses, the interpretation violates the text in a certain sense, corrupts it, imposes itself on the text from the outside, without any guarantees purely intrinsic to and acknowledged by the text. And, for that, it is necessary that it have a virtual multiplicity of latent, indeterminate codes, and that it says something about the context, an outside of the text, which can charge and then alter the meaning of the text.

Third, this latency-plurality-indeterminacy of the code(s) is implied at three levels:

(a) the possibility for *proliferation* of interpretations, the *plurality* of possible points of view on a text, or at least the virtual pluralism of perspectives according to how they can envisage the texts. To make these three remarks more explicit: the *proliferation* of interpretations is the security of the text's fecundity, of its richness—it situates the text as a space of singularity and plurality, the intersection of the singular and the plural. In this respect, we can speak of a kind of Bergsonianism, of negative-entropy [*néguentropie*], as opposed to total conceptual austerity, to all Jansenism-Malthusianism which would individualize, limit, and emasculate the text. Further, the *plurality* signifies that the text does not distinguish itself expressly from interpretations given to it, and that it is, first of all, not so much definition as expansion, but an overture for perspectives and multiplicity. Finally, and we are going to return to this, *pluralism,* in the sense of the tolerance of the multiple and different, indeed, contradictory opinions, makes the text a place for confrontation: all at once polemic and pacific, a kind of democratic space *par excellence*—one should not fail to bear in mind, in opposition, all the sorts of fundamentalisms and "*intégrismes*" [the groups fightening for the wholeness and purity of Roman Catholic fundamentalism in France] which disfigure the texts without pluralizing them;

(b) as we have come to see, abandoning all dogmatic, unilateral authority seeking to impose a true unique meaning on the text, interpretation opens the space, liberates, increases its breadth, and reaches for open, high seas, as Nietzsche said in a beautiful metaphor [*Gay Science,* section 363; see end of 289]. It puts an end to the oppression of a supposed oneness of "the" truth; and

(c) perspectivism: rendering the truth more collective than individual, absolute in its partiality or bias, interpretation places generality in relation with the singular perspective, the universal into relation with the ego. To return to an expression of Stendhal's philosophically reworked by Jean Granier,[14] there is an egotism of interpretive truth. Egotism signifies a relation to the ego or the self, not as a self-sufficiency [*autarcie*] nor a privilege of the singular, concrete ego. And it recalls that in this respect, the truth is interpretive because evaluation and pathos are categories for the truth about being. Thus, *always related to a value* [*valorielle:* valuing, the fact that interpretation gives values] and *pathetic,*[15] interpretive truth places itself at the articulation of the singular, the ego and the universalizable (I have in mind Kierkegaard). In this sense, as suggested in some lofty lines regarding this problem, borrowed from Granier,[16] the truth is perhaps only interpretive. Or, in order to say it like Nietzsche, each truth is, perhaps, simply only an interpretation even when dressed in colors of the most objective, universal neutrality [*Beyond Good and Evil*, section 22].

Fourth point: it is an obvious point rarely emphasized. Interpretation implies an object on which it works, a point of departure, material. As an object of interpretation, every text is marked by its inevitable, unforgettable material character. A text: it is an ensemble of signs, traces, marks, differences inscribed in a stubborn, resistant, material, obvious by its firmness, its permanence, and even by its brute, sometimes disconcerting and untimely presence. The text is there, massively; it constrains because it contradicts, modifies, runs counter to interpretation! "So ist es" ["that is how it is"], as Hegel would say. One wishes to add that the text would say, like Luther, "Ich kann nicht anders," "I can't do otherwise" [in English in original—TRANS.], I cannot refrain from being there. This remark places the text in a situation opposing interpretation, which sometimes, unconstrained, makes short work of it, forgets its, effaces it, abuses it. But it is necessary, immediately, to recall that the text—as that which must be read, received, comprised—cannot be distinguished from its reception by the reader-interpreter. There is, then, as Nietzsche recalls so often, a strict distinction *and* necessary confusion between the text and its interpretation. A text not interpreted is a dead text; but interpretation free from the text, outside the text or against the text, is *not* the text, as Nietzsche says. This antinomy—that Nietzsche presents as that of philosophy (over interpretation) and philology understood as "*ephexis* [suspension of judgment] in interpretation" (*Antichrist*, section 52), of philosophy as infinitely free interpretation, and of philology as "the art of reading *well*," as the capacity for "meditating a half-hour on six lines" [KGW IV, 2: 19[1]]—this antinomy introduces two questions intimately tied to interpretation as such:

(a) According to what standard does the text exist outside its singular or plural interpretations? We have seen the dilemma without ever resolving it: interpretation is mistaken and accurate, justice and injustice, truth and violence, blindness and partiality, but gives value to the text. Indeed, the text must be distinguished from interpretation: but according to what standard is the text not dead and incomplete without the interpretation of the reader—its finality which one can never pretend to eliminate?

(b) Is it not *abuse* (*Missbrauch* [misuse] as Nietzsche, philologist and attentive reader of the *sacred* text of the Bible, says) to confound interpretation and text, notably in the case, very frequently, where the risk incurred is not of multiplying the text, but of limiting it, cutting it off according to the castrating and dogmatic singularity or oneness of a point of view, a narrow perspective, a *mansarde* [*On the Genealogy of Morals*, Third Essay, section 18], a weak partiality? From the richness of plurality, at the border of identity or identification, to fall into the human, all-too-human, singular, is that not to fail in interpretation?

From these questions, one can infer a fifth and last remark concerning the problem of interpretation. Setting out from the text, and withdrawing from it, central or eccentric (in the double sense of that epithet), interpretation is simultaneously other than and the same as the text. Philosophically speaking, interpretation and the text are homogenous, whereas the concept—exterior and imported—decenters the text with regards to its place, to its intent, and to its own nature. The concept empties the text of itself and locates it, with respect to itself, in a field forcefully marked and traversed by the dualism. Concept and text are two, heterogeneous, whereas interpretation situates itself *in* the text, in the internal play of the text with which it is coextensive. Interpretation cuts away from the dualist slash [*coupe à la coupure dualiste*]—sensible/intelligible, concept/sensible. Interpretation remains close to the text, instead of imposing its abstracted, ideal externality.

III. Nietzsche and Interpretation

The issue at stake in interpretation, for Nietzsche, is not simply epistemological. For him the interest is an interpretation of being, an interpretation of ontological significance, where being is interpreted as an interpreting-interpreted text. It is not by chance that Nietzsche uses the German word *Auslegung,* which signifies exegesis of texts (notably biblical texts), rather than *Interpretation,* which he reserves to designate that which, whether fact or text, is more about the order of variation, indeed, the embellished or romantic fantasy about reality taken as a pretext. From a philosophical point of view, and given this image of philological-exegetical origin, in the work of Nietzsche interpretation is directly related to the death of God. If God is dead, the absolute foundation of truth—like the veracious God of Descartes—collapses so that we have but the unwarranted *signs* of truth, and things no longer have any value in themselves but are what we make them by our interpretations. With the death of God the interpretation of signs is born, where meaning is present and absent, value made and dissipated. Here I will be able to propose only an-all-too brief sketch of the Nietzschean philosophical and philological problem of interpretation that I have explained (and interpreted!) in my book, *Nietzsche, le Corps et la Culture.*[17]

A. Being

(1) One of Nietzsche's fundamental ideas is the enigmatic character of life as the being of that which is according to the principle of the will to power. Life, frequently represented with the aid of feminine metaphors (*vita femina,* as it is said in *The Gay Science,* [section 339]),[18] is always an

enigma. One of the consequences of this is that signs—we have only signs, necessarily ambiguous and always misleading, above all for philosophers—can speak of being, of life, only indirectly. This situation necessitates a particular interpretive discipline called "genealogy" which attempts to relate every expression, every sign, to its hidden or remote origin in the body, in a certain will, life, in active drives [*pulsions*]. It is significant that, in order to define genealogy interpretively, Nietzsche uses metaphors, which is to say interpretations, rather than conceptual explications, dependent on the senses of hearing and smelling—faculties of "knowledge" used indirectly when the authentic object of the phenomenon is hidden, latent, ambiguous: odor and sound present the body *in absentia.*

(2) Being, for Nietzsche, is not constituted in advance, preexisting on the whole; it is not a foundation that knowledge will discover through an extrinsic revelation. On the contrary, being *is as* interpreted [*l'être est comme interprété*]; it is constituted in and through interpretation. In this case, it is, as explained by Granier in *Le Discours du monde,* "sketched."[19] It is, then, play more than "truth," evolving and practical rather than theoretical. But this conception implies that being has no foundation, since the interpretation which composes being is always the interpretation of an interpretation, unless one could come to an end or *re*present (trace it back to) a pure, ultimate being, a founder. The groundwork of being, its foundation, is an interpretation in its turn [*tour:* turning, circuit, place, order]. Or, again, one can say that being is "fundamentally" interpretation. An ultimate, "solid" ground is never attained. Thus, being is unfathomable, according to Nietzsche. Nietzsche's ontology breaks with Platonist ontology in a way that it is a kind of negative "theology," where being is quite other rather than the same (as itself).

(3) This conception of being as interpreted leads to the corollary that being is equal to an ensemble of *signs.* Being *is* not; it designates, it signifies. This character of the sign has four consequences essential to Nietzsche's conception of Being as it relates to the question of interpretation:

(i) The sign makes reference; it refers to what it is and what it is not, since it is a related but irrelevant substitute for what it replaces and signifies. In this respect, the arbitrariness of the sign marks an alterity of being by the reference to itself which necessitates interpretation.

(ii) The sign places unity and plurality in relation on the basis of alterity and difference. In interpretation, being is at the same time singular, unique, and plural. Through the sign, interpretation renders plural that which is univocal and, inversely, abridged and simple what is multiple. Thus, to take up again an expression used by *The Gay Science* [section 344] in its designation of Homer's Ulysses, being is *polytropos;* it has a thousand aspects, a thousand turns and ruses, but is, also, singular. Thus, Nietzsche opens being to multiplicity, but he insists, also, on philology to draw together the interpretations and to enclose the unity in the infinite diversity of possible significations.

(iii) If being is sign(s), it does not comprise things but symbols: the world is not; it symbolizes itself, that is to say, it multiplies itself through reference to itself; it becomes thicker and deeper. *"Die Welt ist tief, Und tiefer als der Tag gedacht,"* as it is said in *Thus Spoke Zarathustra* ["Before Sunrise"—TRANS.]: the world is profound and more profound than the day thought. As for himself, Nietzsche augments this profundity by the terms he uses to define his philosophy and genealogy, which refer to disciplines implicating reference, symbolism: symptomatology, semiotic (the science of the signs of diseases) [*Twilight of the Idols,* "The 'Improvers' of Mankind," sections 1–2]. He returns, equally to his own advantage, to a term Goethe uses in *Faust II* to reuse it, parody it, and transform it: all that is transitory is only symbol (*Alles Verg ängliche Ist nur ein Gleichnis*) [see *The Gay Science,* "Songs of Prince Vogelfrei" ("To Goethe"); *Thus Spoke Zarathustra,* "Upon the Blessed Isles" and "On Poets"—TRANS.]. The transcendence of the world is that it is to itself its own symbol, as an efflorescence of signs.

(iv) Finally, being—as sign(s)—is mystery: as a text of Nietzsche says at the outset of his career, "nature has lost the key" ["On Truth and Falsity in Their Extramoral Sense" (1873), section I—TRANS.]. We advance, then, in "a forest of symbols" (Baudelaire). Being is to be interpreted; it does not offer itself in a "theoretical" (contemplative) luminous obviousness, but in the uncertain work on references, liaisons (sym-bols), of which the code, if it ever existed, exists no longer because God is dead. Thus, liberation opens the boundless and uncharted seas of signification celebrated by Nietzsche in so many texts. This emancipation of meaning, the infinite fecundity of the text, has for a counterpart obscurity, wandering [*l'errance*], uncertainty. If, as Nietzsche writes, there is an infinity of possible interpretations [*The Gay Science,* section 374—TRANS.], in return, being remains [*demeure:* lives, resides, continues] multiple, "undulating," uncertain and "diverse."[20] We are wandering in the riddle of being. It is no longer Oedipus and his glorious, victorious liberty; it is the Sphinx, "inexorable as my curiosity,"[21] the risk of straying and death.

B. Interpretation

(1) Interpretation, in the writings of Nietzsche, assumes an importance of ontological rather than epistemological order. As it has been seen already, interpretation is a philological metaphor of philosophical-metaphysical scope. According to this metaphor, the world is a text, and being is deciphered [*déchiffré*: unraveled). But who "writes"? Who interprets? Our active drives. Interpretation binds the text of the world, of being, to the *body,* that is to say, the body-mind totality that represents the active drives and their hierarchy in the "self," *Selbst,* that "great reason" [*Thus Spoke Zarathustra,* "On The Despisers of the Body"]. From this point of view two remarks must be made:

(i) Nietzsche *never* gives *the concept* of interpretation, *only metaphors* of interpretation, generally corporeal (bodily) and physiological. In order to sum up very briefly the analysis of my book, *Nietzsche, le Corps et la Culture,* I would like to point out that Nietzsche uses the metaphors of digestion-incorporation, politics and government, and, finally, philology. Each one in this metaphoric series respectively assists the interpretation of the one preceding it. The interpretive play of active desires, like the mind, resembles the stomach; it combines like a political collective, a configuration of relations of force, according to unity and multiplicity; and the body interprets, chooses, simplifies, and abridges like a philological reader.

(ii) So to interpret is to digest and to control like the body. We do not find the concept of the body either in Nietzsche's work, but a philological interpretation of the body as an ensemble of signs, as a text to be deciphered without a fixed nature but represented figuratively as a multiple center of forces in movement. As interpretation is interpreted through bodily metaphors, so the body is interpreted according to the image of the text and signs.

In every case, one always returns to a kind of circle: interpretation cannot be defined, coded; it can only be interpreted—otherwise there would be contradiction, and one would fall back into an objective and metaphysical explicative ontology. This circle, which is more like an open spiral, is a movement of metaphoric displacement (*meta-phor* signifies dis-placement), and I call the interpretive relation of interpretive metaphors by the name *linkage-transfer* [*enchaînement-report*]. Interpretation is both free and bound; it is enchained and slipping forward.

Nietzsche is, then, consistent with his principles when he interprets metaphorically the notion of interpretation.

(2) Nietzsche is wedged between the (philological) necessity and the (''philosophical'') freedom of interpretation, between interpretive plurality and the insistent reminder of the reality/truth of the text. A text does not say simply, ''This is not the text, it is an interpretation'' [*Beyond Good and Evil*, section 22], but it does not speak only a sole signification; it is ordered plurality. This regulated wandering is due to the fact that Nietzsche places the text in relation with the plurality of the body, sending philosophy outside philosophy, returning philosophy to the body which decenters and pluralizes it. Only an abstract philosophy reads the text univocally: the thought of the body displaces and multiplies being and interpretation. Hence, genealogy is itself pulled between liberty and reality in interpretation, between physiology and philology.[22]

(3) Given the fact that the text is placed in relation with the body, Nietzschean interpretation is at the same time immanently internal, structuralist, and referential, extrinsic. On the one hand, indeed, the interpreter Nietzsche wants to consider the *text as text* (*einen Text als Text zu lesen*) [see *The Will to Power*, section 479— TRANS.], without any other consideration than the text itself—that is how the philologist ''meditates a half-hour on six lines''! On the other hand, he refers to the text, to its reader and its author, *as body:* the best examples of this are aphorisms 246 and 247 in *Beyond Good and Evil*, which treat the specific bodily character of classical style in relation to the modern style of the Germans (breath, rhythm, ''a *great* period''). Thus, we can establish in Nietzsche's writing two different and yet interconnected antinomies: one between text as reality and interpretation as liberty and fantasy; and the second, which is not confounded entirely with the first, between the internal structure of the text and the external reference to the body. Given this sketch, I would like to say that Nietzsche is one who refashions the question of *meaning:* since the text ceases to be closed, stable, and unique, thanks to the body, he liberates and dissolves meaning all at once, relating the body with the text in order that the text multiplies and ''lives dangerously'' [*The Gay Science,* section 283].

(4) From this union with the body, which completes the ''sketch'' of being's meaning, follows the idea [*trait*], already raised, that interpretation cannot be suspended as an exterior supplement to a supposed fundamental being. Interpretation is being: being *is* interpretation itself at its ''foundation'' entirely, so that being/to be is to interpret and being has to be interpreted. On this point I refer the reader to several interesting remarks made by Johann Figl in his book on Nietzsche, *Interpretation als philosophisches*

Prinzip.[23] Figl emphasizes that interpretation, in this respect, is both sub-jective and objective: interpretation *of* being (as object) and interpretation of (*by*) being (of itself as subject).

(5) Interpretation, writes Nietzsche, consists in "rendering oneself master of a text" [KGW, VIII, 1, 2 [168] or *Will to Power,* Section 643; cf. Blondel, *Nietzsche, le Corps et la Culture,* p. 324ff—TRANS.]. But who is the interpreter? The active drives in a plural configuration of forces, which can be called, in spite of its fluctuation, an ego, me, the self, *Selbst.* As emphasized in the Platonic image of the orphan already cited, the text is thus subject, by interpretation, to an ensemble of exterior forces:

—to the powers which subdue it, dominate it, seize it, dissimulate it, incorporate it, and dissolve it;

—to a body;

—that is to say, to a perspectivism, which marks both singularity, the particular point of view, and spatial exteriority: reading is *hic et nunc* indi-vidual, particular, historic, and removable, all of which situates the text outside itself;

—as one can see, to a subjectivism, a particularity that values, that is pathetic, concrete, egotistical: there is no general, abstract, universal interpretation. And what passes itself off as such, that is, scientific "expla-nation" [*Erklärung*], challenged by Nietzsche, is only a form of interpre-tation where the singularity of an active configuration prevails over the perspectival plurality of active drives in their varied and variable ensemble. Explanation, on the contrary, is static, unembodied, abstract, no-where [*sans lieu*] (Utopian), "objective" by a feeble neutrality, whereas interpre-tation is the real singularity of a possible bodily plurality. Indeed, the per-spectives are plural or many only formerly or *in abstracto:* each one is real as a singularity, and only passes from one to the other by meta-phor, by linkage-transfer, by slipping and lack of equivalence [*inadéquation*]. One could explicate this connection as it is referred to by Leibniz, who singu-larizes the monads to the extreme, so that Nietzschean perspectivism is a monadology without God to unify and to reconcile the points of view. Or else, it is, again, a Spinozism, where the modes would not be unified in God/Nature. And, finally, one can envision the world of Berkeley, where the ideas-things are universalized and made consistent and compatible by recourse to God, who is missing in Nietzsche's writings since he is dead. Interpretation passes from one singular perspective to another by metaphor. In this regard, I would like to say, like Paul Ricoeur, that interpretation is linked to metaphor as an imaginative power, not to describe, but to *rede-scribe* the world.[24] For all that, as the imaginative, metaphorical faculty, interpretation, inasmuch as it is bound again to the body and to its plural singularity, is the horizontal transcendence of the world, in Nietzsche. It is the body which, as will to power, hence overcoming, assumes and renders possible this *self-overcoming* [*Selbstüberwindung*], that I would like to interpret as *overcoming* of the *self* [*Überwindung des Selbst*], of the Same. Or, in order to speak like Kant, whom Nietzsche follows here without realizing it, the schematism, which first permits us to transcend empirical singularity without the aid of a concept, is (in Nietzsche's work) ensured by the will to power of the body, according to a sequence which could be followed in this manner: body–perspectivism–metaphor–linkage–transfer–imagination–schematism–interpretation–transcendence–death of God. Displaced by the body, metaphorical interpretation constitutes the text of the world by redescribing it.

(6) We have seen that, according to Nietzsche, the world—being—is enigma, and that it is the body that "shakes concepts," as Nietzsche writes (*Untimely Meditations II* [*The Use and Advantages of History for Life*, chapter 10—TRANS.]). One can consider that, for Nietzsche, it is life which is linked to interpretation as passage, body, fecundity, plurality, whereas knowledge is always linked, in its univocal abstraction, to death. It is not by chance that the Nietzschean philosophy of interpretation is at the same time a thought about the affirmation of life, the body, plurality, fecundity, the riddle, the symbolic and becoming.

(7) In the Nietzschean philosophy of interpretation, the singular becomes, by interpretive metaphor, universalizable plurality, multiple expression; fact becomes meaning. The sensible object, which is the whole appearance of being as opposed to dead and theoretical abstraction, insofar as it is interpretable, surpasses itself and signifies itself through itself, without passing through the exteriority of the concept. Interpretation makes being be, makes being pass from brute facticity to signification, makes manifest what the sensible is in itself symbolically and provides meaning. It goes beyond *itself* (becomes *itself*) by signifying *itself*. This is a philosophy of interpretation which constitutes an ontology of the immanent transcendence of the sensible-real. Thus, interpretation is, in Nietzsche's writings, the symbol of *Überwindung,* overcoming [*dépassement*]—of life as fecundity and overcoming. The overman creates because he is not in a world which is, but reads the text of the world and of being by creating it through interpretive metaphor which constitutes it and overcomes it.

Translated by Gayle L. Ormiston

Notes

1. Honoré de Balzac, *Le Père Goriot* (Paris: Société d'Éditions Littéraires et Artistiques, 1900), pp. 17–19. The passage was cited in French and English by

Blondel; it was translated by Jacques Blondel. Cf. *Father Goriot and Other Stories*, translated by Ellen Marriage and Clara Bell (Philadelphia: The Gebbie Publishing Company, 1899), pp. 15–16.—TRANS.

2. Franz Josef Gall (1757–1828) was a German physician who believed that a correlation existed between mental abilities and the formation of the skull. In effect, Gall believed that skull formation determined personality and behavior.—TRANS.

3. When written with a *y*, *abyme* (a term of heraldry meaning the center of a blazon), here *en abyme*, designates the practice or technique of representation by which, for instance, the act of representing is represented in the representation itself as a design is included in a blazon of armorial bearings: there is the story within the story, the representation within representation, interpretation within interpretation (a portrait). Van Eyck's "J. Arnolfini and His Wife," Velasquez's "Las Meninas," and the theatre scene in *Hamlet* are examples of *abyme*. André Gide first used the term expressly as a literary theme in his novel *The Counterfeiters*, a novel about the creation of a novel.

4. A hint to a short novel by Balzac, *Les Secrets de la Princesse de Cadignan* [*Oeuvres Complètes*, volume 24 (Paris: Ancienne Maison Michel Lévy Frères, 1896)—TRANS.]

5. A professional, a "hooker."

6. Marcel Proust, *A La Recherche du Temps perdu I:Du Côté de Chez Swann I, Oeuvres de Marcel Proust* (Paris: Gallimard, 1919), pp. 288–89. The passage cited was translated by Jacques Blondel. Cf. *Remembrance of Things Past: Swann's Way*, volume 1, translated by C. K. Scott Moncrieff (New York: Random House, 1934), pp. 319–20.—TRANS.

7. Given Blondel's discussion of the ambiguity of signs in parts II and III, it should be noted that *caractère* not only carries the designation for personality or character, but it also signifies "character" as letter, mark, type. Here the ambiguity turns not only on the deceptive nature of Madame Swann's personality but on Proust's (the narrator's) description and interpretation.—TRANS.

8. Honoré de Balzac, *Sarrasine, Oeuvres Complètes*, volume 24; English translation by Richard Miller in appendix I to Roland Barthes, *S/Z* (New York: Hill and Wang, 1974), pp. 222–54.—TRANS.

9. Jean-Pierre Richard, *Proust et le Monde sensible* (Paris: Éditions du Seuil, 1974) [see pp. 134ff., 155ff., 214ff.—TRANS.]

10. *Ibid.*, p. 134.

11. Gilles Deleuze, *Proust and Signs*, translated by Richard Howard (New York: George Braziller, 1972), p. 13; cf. "Apprenticeship," pp. 25–27.—TRANS.

12. Barthes, *S/Z*, p. 5.

13. See Sigmund Freud, "The Theme of Three Caskets" (1913), translated by James Strachey, in *The Standard Edition of the Complete Psychological Works of Sigmund Freud*, Vol. 12 (London: The Hogarth Press, 1958), pp. 291–301; see also *A General Introduction to Psychoanalysis*, translated by Joan Riviere (New York: Simon and Schuster, 1963), pp. 35–37.—TRANS.

14. Jean Granier, *Le Discours du monde* (Paris: Éditions du Seuil, 1977)[see p. 136ff.—TRANS.].

15 *Ibid.*, pp. 156ff. and 262ff.

16. *Ibid.*, pp. 42–52; cf. *Le Désir du moi* (Paris: Presses Universitaires de France, 1983), chapter VI, p. 125ff

17. Eric Blondel, *Nietzsche, le Corps et la Culture* (Paris: Presses Universitaires de France, 1986). [See especially the chapters entitled "Nietzsche et la généalogie de la culture, le *Versuch*," "Nietzsche et la philologie généalogique," "Critique du discours métaphysique: la généalogie philologique et la *misologie*," "Le corps et la métaphores," and "La philosophie: analyse généalogique de la culture."—TRANS.]

18. See my "Nietzsche: Life as Metaphor," in *The New Nietzsche: Contemporary Styles of Interpretation*, edited by David Allison (Cambridge: MIT Press, 1985), pp. 150–75.

19. Granier, *Le Discours du monde*, particularly pp. 237–40.

20. Montaigne, *Essais*, I, 1. [Montaigne, *The Complete Works of Montaigne: Essays, Travel Journal, and Letters*, translated by Donald M. Frame (Stanford: Stanford University Press, 1948); see especially *Essays*, book I, "By Diverse Means We Arrive at the Same End," pp. 3–5.—TRANS.]

21. This line is from "The Sphinx," a poem written by Nietzsche. It appears in *Nietzsches Gesammelte Werke (Musarionausgabe)*, volume 20, p. 226, and in the new edition (KGW): *Dithyrambs of Dionysus*. For a more developed commentary and interpretation of the riddle (and the poem), see Blondel, *Nietzsche, le Corps et la Culture*, p. 8ff.—TRANS.

22. Cf. my "Guillemets de Nietzsche," in *Nietzsche aujourd'hui*, volume II (Paris: Union générale d'Édition "10/18", 1973), pp. 153–78, as well as "Nietzsche et la philologie" by H. Wismann (pp. 325–35) and "Règles philologiques pour une lecture de Nietzsche" by Richard Roos (pp. 303–18) in the same volume. The tension between the sophistic and the philosophic in Nietzsche's work is presented in a remarkable fashion by Reinhard Low in *Nietzsche Sophist und Erzieher* (Weinheim: Acta Humaniora, 1984).

23. Johann Figl, *Interpretation als philosophisches Prinzip* (New York and Berlin: Walter de Guyter, 1982)

24. Paul Ricoeur, *The Rule of Metaphor*, translated by Robert Czerny (Toronto: University of Toronto Press, 1977), cf. pp.7, 173–225, and 239–46. See also Paul Ricoeur, *Du Texte à l'Action: Essais d'herméneutique, II* (Paris: Éditions du Seuil, 1986), a collection of essays that deal specifically with the question of interpretation and the general problem of hermeneutics.—TRANS.

4

Psychoanalysis and the Polis*

Julia Kristeva

Up until now philosophers have only interpreted the world. The point now is
to change it.

—Karl Marx and Friedrich Engels, *Theses on Feuerbach*

The delusions [*Wahnbildungen*] of patients appear to me to be the
equivalents of the [interpretive] constructions which we build up in the
course of an analytic treatment—attempts at explanation and cure.

—Sigmund Freud, "Constructions in Analysis"

. . . Academic discourse, and perhaps American university discourse
in particular, possesses an extraordinary ability to absorb, digest, and neu-
tralize all of the key, radical, or dramatic moments of thought, particularly,
a fortiori, of contemporary thought. Marxism in the United States, though
marginalized, remains deafly dominant and exercises a fascination that we
have not seen in Europe since the Russian *Proletkult* of the 1930s. Post-
Heideggerian "deconstructivism," though esoteric, is welcomed in the
United States as an antidote to analytic philosophy or, rather, as a way to
valorize, through contrast, that philosophy. Only one theoretical breakthrough seems consistently to *mobilize* resistances, rejections, and deafness:
psychoanalysis—not as the "plague" allowed by Freud to implant itself in
America as a "commerce in couches" but rather as that which, with Freud
and after him, has led the psychoanalytic decentering of the speaking subject to the very foundations of language. It is this latter direction that I will
be exploring here, with no other hope than to awaken the resistances and,
perhaps, the attention of a concerned few, after the event [*après coup*].

For I have the impression that the "professionalism" [. . .] is never
as strong as when professionals denounce it. In fact, the same preanalytic
rationality unites them all, "conservatives" and "revolutionaries"—in all

cases, jealous guardians of their academic "chairs" whose very existence, I am sure, is thrown into question and put into jeopardy by psychoanalytic discourse. I would therefore schematically summarize what is to follow in this way:

1. There are political implications inherent in the act of interpretation itself, whatever meaning that interpretation bestows. What is the meaning, interest, and benefit of the interpretive position itself, a position from which I wish to give meaning to an enigma? To give a political meaning to something is perhaps only the ultimate consequence of the epistemological attitude which consists, simply, of the desire *to give meaning*. This attitude is not innocent but, rather, is rooted in the speaking subject's need to reassure himself of his image and his identity faced with an object. Political interpretation is thus the apogee of the obsessive quest for A Meaning.

2. The psychoanalytic intervention within Western knowledge has a fundamentally deceptive effect. Psychoanalysis, critical and dissolvant, cuts through political illusions, fantasies, and beliefs to the extent that they consist in providing only one meaning, an uncriticizable ultimate Meaning, to human behavior. If such a situation can lead to despair within the polis, we must not forget that it is also a source of lucidity and ethics. The psychoanalytic intervention is, from this point of view, a counterweight, an antidote, to political discourse which, without it, is free to become our modern religion: the final explanation.

3. The political interpretations of our century have produced two powerful and totalitarian results: fascism and Stalinism. Parallel to the socioeconomic reasons for these phenomena, there exists as well another, more intrinsic reason: the simple desire to give a meaning, to explain, to provide the answer, to interpret. In that context I will briefly discuss Louis Ferdinand Céline's texts insofar as the ideological interpretations given by him are an example of political delirium in avant-garde writing.

I would say that interpretation as an epistemological and ethical attitude began with the Stoics. In other words, it should not be confused with *theory* in the Platonic sense, which assumes a prior knowledge of the ideal Forms to which all action or creation is subordinate. Man, says Epictetus, is "born to contemplate God and his works, and not only to contemplate them but also to interpret them [*kai ou monon teatin, ala kai exegetin auton*]." "To interpret" in this context, and I think always, means "to make a connection." Thus the birth of interpretation is considered the birth of semiology, since the semiological sciences relate a sign (an event-sign) to a signified in order to *act* accordingly, consistently, consequently.[1]

Much has been made of the circularity of this connection which, throughout the history of interpretive disciplines up to hermeneutics, consists in enclosing the enigmatic (interpretable) object within the interpretive theory's preexistent system. Instead of creating an object, however, this process merely produces what the interpretive theory had preselected as an object within the enclosure of its own system. Thus it seems that one does not interpret something outside theory but rather that theory harbors its object within its own logic. Theory merely projects that object onto a theoretical place at a distance, outside its grasp, thereby eliciting the very possibility of interrogation (Heidegger's *Sachverhalt*).

We could argue at length about whether interpretation is a circle or a spiral: in other words, whether the interpretable object it assigns itself is simply constituted by the interpretation's own logic or whether it is recreated, enriched, and thus raised to a higher level of knowledge through the unfolding of interpretive discourse. Prestigious work in philosophy and logic is engaged in this investigation. I will not pursue it here. Such a question, finally, seems to me closer to a Platonic idea of interpretation (i.e., theorization) than it does to the true innovation of the Stoics' undertaking. This innovation is the reduction, indeed the elimination, of the distance between theory and action as well as between model and copy. What permits this elimination of the distance between nature (which the Stoics considered interpretable) and the interpreter is the extraordinary opening of the field of subjectivity. The person who does the interpretation, the subject who makes the connection between the sign and the signified, is the Stoic sage displaying, on the one hand, the extraordinary architectonics of his *will* and, on the other, his mastery of *time* (both momentary and infinite).

I merely want to allude to this Stoic notion of the primordial interdependence of *interpretation, subjective will,* and mastery of *time*. For my own interest is in contemporary thought which has rediscovered, in its own way, that even if interpretation does no more than establish a simply logical connection, it is nevertheless played out on the scene of speaking subjectivity and the moment of speech. Two great intellectual ventures of our time, those of Marx and Freud, have broken through the hermeneutic tautology to make of it a *revolution* in one instance and, in the other, a *cure*. We must recognize that all contemporary political thought which does not deal with technocratic administration—although technocratic purity is perhaps only a dream—uses interpretation in Marx's and Freud's sense: as transformation and as cure. Whatever *object* one selects (a patient's discourse, a literary or journalistic text, or certain sociopolitical behavior), its interpretation reaches its full power, so as to tip the object toward the *unknown* of the interpretive theory or, more simply, toward the theory's *intentions*, only when the interpreter *confronts* the interpretable object.

It is within this field of confrontation between the object and the subject of interpretation that I want to pursue my investigation. I assume that at its resolution there are two major outcomes. First, the object may succumb to the interpretive intentions of the interpreter, and then we have the whole range of domination from suggestion to propaganda to revolution. Or second, the object may reveal to the interpreter the unknown of his theory and permit the constitution of a new theory. Discourse in this case is renewed; it can begin again; it forms a new object and a new interpretation in this reciprocal transference.

Before going any further, however, I would like to suggest that another path, posthermeneutic and perhaps even postinterpretive, opens up for us within the lucidity of contemporary discourse. Not satisfied to stay within the interpretive place which is, essentially, that of the Stoic sage, the contemporary interpreter renounces the game of *indebtedness, proximity,* and *presence* hidden within the connotations of the concept of interpretation. (*Interpretare* means ''to be mutually indebted''; *prêt:* from popular Latin *praestus,* from the classical adverb *praesto,* meaning ''close at hand,'' ''nearby''; *praesto esse:* ''to be present, attend''; *praestare:* ''to furnish, to present [as an object, e.g., money].'') The modern interpreter avoids the presentness of subjects to themselves and to things. For in this presentness a strange object appears to speaking subjects, a kind of currency they grant themselves—interpretation—to make certain that they are really there, close by, within reach. Breaking out of the enclosure of the presentness of meaning, the *new* ''interpreter'' no longer interprets: he speaks, he ''associates,'' because there is no longer an object to interpret; there is, instead, the setting off of semantic, logical, phantasmatic, and indeterminable sequences. As a result, a fiction, an uncentered discourse, a subjective polytopia come about, canceling the metalinguistic status of the discourses currently governing the postanalytic fate of interpretation.

The Freudian position on interpretation has the immense advantage of being midway between a classic interpretive attitude—that of providing meaning through the connection of two terms from a stable place and theory—and the questioning of the subjective and theoretical stability of the interpretant which, in the act of interpretation itself, establishes the theory and the interpreter himself as interpretable objects. The dimension of *desire,* appearing for the first time in the citadel of interpretive will, steals the platform from the Stoic sage, but at the same time it opens up time, suspends Stoic suicide, and confers not only an interpretive power but also a transforming power to these new, unpredictable signifying effects which must be called *an imaginary.* I would suggest that the wise interpreter give way to delirium so that, out of his desire, the imaginary may join interpretive closure, thus producing a perpetual interpretive creative force.

1. What Is Delirium?

Delirium is a discourse which has supposedly strayed from a presumed reality. The speaking subject is presumed to have known an object, a relationship, an experience that he is henceforth incapable of reconstituting accurately. Why? Because the knowing subject is also a *desiring* subject, and the paths of desire ensnarl the paths of knowledge.

Repressed desire pushes against the repression barrier in order to impose its contents on consciousness. Yet the resistance offered by consciousness, on the one hand, and the pressure of desire, on the other, leads to a displacement and deformation of that which otherwise could be reconstituted unaltered. This dynamic of delirium recalls the constitution of the dream or the phantasm. Two of its most important moments are especially noteworthy here.

First, we normally assume the opposite of delirium to be an objective reality, objectively perceptible and objectively knowable, as if the speaking subject were only a simple knowing subject. Yet we must admit that, given the cleavage of the subject (conscious/unconscious) and given that the subject is also a subject of desire, perceptual and knowing apprehension of the original object is only a theoretical, albeit undoubtedly indispensable, hypothesis. More importantly, the system Freud calls perception-knowledge (subsequently an object of interpretation or delirium) is always already marked by a *lack:* for it shelters within its very being the nonsignifiable, the nonsymbolized. This "minus factor," by which, even in perception-knowledge, the subject signifies himself as subject of the desire of the Other, is what provokes, through its insistence on acceding to further significations, those deformations and displacements which characterize delirium. Within the nucleus of delirious construction, we must retain this hollow, this void, this "minus 1," as the instinctual drive's insistence, as the unsymbolizable condition of the desire to speak and to know.

Yet delirium holds; it asserts itself to the point of procuring for the subject both *jouissance* and stability which, without that adhesive of delirium, would disintegrate rapidly into a somatic symptom, indeed, into the unleashing of the death drive. It can do so, however, only because the discourse of delirium "owes its convincing power to the element of historical truth which it inserts in the place of the rejected reality."[2] In other words, delirium masks reality or spares itself from a reality while at the same time saying a truth about it. More true? Less true? Does delirium know a truth which is true in a different way than objective reality because it speaks a certain subjective truth, instead of a presumed objective truth? Because it presents the state of the subject's desire? This "mad truth" (*folle vérité*) of delirium is not evoked here to introduce some kind of relativism or epistemological skepticism.[3] I am insisting on the part played by truth in delirium to indicate, rather, that since the displacement and deformation peculiar to delirium are moved by desire, they are not foreign to the passion for knowledge, that is, the subject's subjugation to the desire to know. Desire and the desire to know are not strangers to each other, up to a certain point. What is that point?

Desire, the discourse of desire, moves toward its object through a connection, by displacement and deformation. The discourse of desire becomes a discourse of delirium when it forecloses its object, which is always already marked by that "minus factor" mentioned earlier, and when it establishes itself as the complete locus of *jouissance* (full and without exteriority). In other words, no other exists, no object survives in its irreducible alterity. On the contrary, he who speaks, Daniel Schreber, for example, identifies himself with the very place of alterity, he merges with the Other, experiencing *jouissance* in and through the place of otherness. Thus in delirium the subject himself is so to speak the Phallus, which implies that he has obliterated the primordial object of desire—the mother—either because he has foreclosed the mother, whom he finds lacking, or because he has submerged himself in her, exaggerating the totality thus formed, as if it were the Phallus. Delirium's structure thus constitutes the foreclosure of the paternal function because of the place it reserves for the material—but also feminine—object which serves to exclude, moreover, any other consideration of objectality.

By contrast, if it is true that the discourse of knowledge leads its enigmatic preobject, that which solicits interpretation—its *Sachverhalt*—inside its own circle and as such brings about a certain hesitation of objectness, it does not take itself for the Phallus but rather places the Phallus outside itself in what is to be known: object, nature, destiny. That is why the person through whom knowledge comes about is not mad, but (as the Stoics have indicated) he is (subject to) death. The time of accurate interpretation, that is, an interpretation in accordance with destiny (or the Other's Phallus), is a moment that includes and completes eternity; interpretation is consequently both happiness and death of time and of the subject: suicide. The transformation of sexual desire into the desire to know an object deprives the subject of this desire and abandons him or reveals him as subject to death. Interpretation, in its felicitous accuracy, expurgating passion and desire, reveals the interpreter as master of his will but at the same time as slave of death. Stoicism is, and I'll return to this point, the last great pagan ideology, tributary of nature as mother, raised to the phallic rank of Destiny to be interpreted.

2. Analytic Interpretation

Like the delirious subject, the psychoanalyst builds, by way of interpretation, a construction which is true only if it triggers other associations

on the part of the analysand, thus expanding the boundaries of the analyzable. In other words, this analytic interpretation is only, in the best of
cases, *partially true*, and its truth, even though it operates with the past, is
demonstrable only by its *effects in the present*.

In a strictly Stoic sense, analytic interpretation aims to correspond to
a (repressed) event or sign in order to *act*. In the same sense, it is a *connection* between disparate terms of the patient's discourse, thereby reestab-
lishing the causes and effects of desire; but it is especially a connection of
the signifiers peculiar to the analyst with those of the analysand. This second circulation, dependent on the analyst's desire and operative only with
him, departs from interpretive mastery and opens the field to suggestion as
well as to projection and indeterminable drifts. In this way, the analyst approaches the vertigo of delirium and, with it, the phallic *jouissance* of a
subject subsumed in the dyadic, narcissistic construction of a discourse in
which the *Same* mistakes itself for the *Other*. It is, however, only by detach-
ing himself from such a vertigo that the analyst derives both his *jouissance*
and his efficacy.

Thus far, we have seen that analytic interpretation resembles delirium
in that it introduces desire into discourse. It does so by giving narcissistic
satisfaction to the subject (the analyst or the analysand), who, at the risk of
foreclosing any true object, derives phallic jubilation from being the author/
actor of a connection that leaves room for desire or for death in discourse.

Yet the analytic position also has counterweights that make delirium
work on behalf of analytic truth. The most obvious, the most often cited, of
these is the *suspension* of interpretation: silence as frustration of meaning
reveals the ex-centricity of desire with regard to meaning. Madness/mean-
inglessness *exists*—this is what interpretive silence suggests. Second, the
analyst, constantly tracking his own desire, never stops analyzing not only
his patients' discourse but also his own attitude toward it which is his own
countertransference. He is not fixed in the position of the classical interpreter, who interprets by virtue of stable meanings derived from a solid
system or morality or who at least tries to restrict the range of his delirium
through a stable theoretical counterweight. This is not to say that analytic
theory does not exist but rather that, all things considered, its consistency is
rudimentary when compared to the countertransferential operation which is
always specific and which sets the interpretive machine in motion differently every time. If I know that my desire can make me delirious in my
interpretive constructions, my return to this delirium allows me to dissolve
its meaning, to displace by one or more notches the quest for meaning
which I suppose to be *one* and *one only* but which I can *only* indefinitely
approach. *There is meaning, and I am supposed to know it to the extent that
it escapes me.*

Finally, there is what I call the *unnameable:* that which is necessarily enclosed in every questionable, interpretable, enigmatic object. The analyst does not exclude the unnameable. He knows that every interpretation will float over that shadowy point which Freud in *The Interpretation of Dreams* calls the dreams' "umbilical." The analyst knows that delirium, in its phallic ambition, consists precisely in the belief that light can rule everywhere, without a shadow. Yet the analyst can sight and hear the unnameable, which he preserves as the condition of interpretation, *only if he sees it as a phantasm.* As origin and condition of the interpretable, the unnameable is, perhaps, the primordial phantasm. What analysis reveals is that the human being does not speak and that, a fortiori, he does not interpret *without* the phantasm of a return to the origin, without the hypothesis of an unnameable, of a *Sachverhalt.*

Furthermore, analysis reveals that interpretive speech, like all speech which is concerned with an object, is acted upon by the desire to return to the archaic mother who is resistant to meaning. Interpretive speech does this so as to place the archaic mother within the order of language—where the subject of desire, insofar as he is a speaking subject, is immediately displaced and yet, henceforth, situated. The return to the unnameable mother may take the form of narcissistic and masochistic delirium, in which the subject merely confronts an idealized petrification of himself in the form of an interpretive Verb, interpretation becoming, in this case, Everything, subject and object. This is what analytic interpretation confronts, undergoes, and, also, displaces.

For, in short, the analyst-interpreter or the interpreter turned analyst derives the originality of his position from his capacity for displacement, from his mobility, from his polytopia. From past to present, from frustration to desire, from the parameter of pleasure to the parameter of death, and so on—he dazes the analysand with the unexpectedness of his interpretation; even so, however, the unexpectedness of the analysis is in any case sustained by a constant: the desire for the Other. ("If you want me to interpret, you are bound in my desire.")

Since Edward Glover's *Technique of Psychoanalysis* (1928), a highly regarded work in its time, analytic theory has appreciably refined its notion of interpretation.[4] The criteria for sound interpretation may undoubtedly vary: "good adaptation" of the analysand, "progress," appearance of remote childhood memories, encounter with the analyst's transference, and so on. Or criteria for a sound interpretation may even disappear, leaving only the need for a temporary sanction (which may be on the order of the parameters already outlined) within an essentially open interpretive process. In this process, *one* meaning and *one meaning alone* is always specifiable for a particular moment of transference; but, given the vast storehouse of the unknown from which analytic interpretation proceeds, this meaning must be transformed.

If it seems that analytic interpretation, like all interpretation in the strong sense of the word, is therefore an action, can we say that this interpretation aims to change the analysand? Two extreme practices exist. In one, the analysis suggests interpretations; in the other, it assumes a purist attitude: by refusing to interpret, the analysis leaves the patient, faced with the absolute silence of the interpreter, dependent on his own capacity for listening, interpreting, and eventually changing. Faced with these excesses, one could argue that in the vast majority of analyses a psychotherapeutic moment occurs which consists in compensating for previous traumatic situations and allowing the analysand to construct another transference, another meaning of his relationship to the Other, the analyst. In the analytic interpretation, however, such a therapeutic moment has, ultimately, no other function than to effect a transference which would otherwise remain doubtful. Only from that moment does true analytic work (i.e., *dissolving*) begin. Basically, this work involves removing obvious, immediate, realistic meaning from discourse so that the meaninglessness/madness of desire may appear and, beyond that, so that every phantasm is revealed as an attempt to return to the unnameable.

I interpret, the analyst seems to say, because Meaning exists. But my interpretation is infinite because Meaning is made infinite by desire. I am not therefore a dead subject, a wise interpreter, happy and self-annihilated in a uniform totality. I am subject to Meaning, a non-Total Meaning, which escapes me.

Analytic interpretation finally leads the analyst to a fundamental problem which I believe underlies all theory and practice of interpretation: the heterogeneous in meaning, the limitation of meaning, its incompleteness. Psychoanalysis, the only modern interpretive theory to hypothesize the heterogeneous in meaning, nevertheless makes that heterogeneity so interdependent with language and thought as to be its very condition, indeed, its driving force. Furthermore, psychoanalysis gives heterogeneity an operative and analyzable status by designating it as sexual desire and/or as death wish.

3. Can Political Interpretation Be True?

The efficacy of interpretation is a function of its transferential truth: this is what political man learns from the analyst, or in any case shares with him. Consider, for example, those political discourses which are said to reflect the desires of a social group or even of large masses. There is always a moment in history when those discourses obtain a general consensus not so much because they interpret the situation correctly (i.e., in accordance with the exigencies of the moment and developments dictated by the needs of the majority) but rather because they correspond to the essentially utopian desires of that majority. Such political interpretation interprets *desires;* even if it lacks reality, it contains the truth of desires. It is, for that very reason, utopian and ideological.

Yet, as in analysis, such an interpretation can be a powerful factor in the mobilization of energies that can lead social groups and masses beyond a sadomasochistic ascesis to change real conditions. Such a mobilizing interpretation can be called revolution or demagogy. By contrast, a more objective, neutral, and technocratic interpretation would only solidify or very slowly modify the real conditions.

All political discourse that wants to be and is efficacious shares that dynamic. Unlike the analytic dynamic, however, the dynamic of political interpretation does not lead its subjects to an elucidation of their own (and its own) truth. For, as I pointed out earlier, analytic interpretation uses desire and transference, but only to lead the subject, faced with the erosion of meaning, to the economy of his own speaking. It does so by deflating the subject's phantasms and by showing that all phantasms, like any attempt to give meaning, come from the phallic *jouissance* obtained by usurping that unnameable object, that *Sachverhalt,* which is the archaic mother.

Of course, no political discourse can pass into nonmeaning. Its goal, Marx stated explicitly, is to reach the goal of interpretation: interpreting the world in order to transform it according to our needs and desires. Now, from the position of the post-Freudian, post-phenomenological analyst—a position which is really an untenable locus of rationality, a close proximity of meaning and nonmeaning—it is clear that there is no World (or that the World is not all there is) and that *to transform* it is only one of the circles of the interpretation—be it Marxist—which refuses to perceive that it winds around a *void.*

Given this constant factor of the human psyche confirmed by the semiotician and the psychoanalyst when they analyze that ordeal of discourse which is the discourse of delirium, what becomes of interpretive discourse? Indeed, what happens to interpretive discourse in view of the void which is integral to meaning and which we find, for example, in the "arbitrariness of the sign" (the unmotivated relation between signifier and signified in Saussure), in the "mirror stage" (where the subject perceives his own image as essentially split, foreign, other), or in the various forms of psychic alienation? Clearly, interpretive discourse cannot be merely a hermeneutics or a politics. Different variants of sacred discourse assume the function of interpretation at this point.

Our cultural orb is centered around the axiom that "the Word became flesh." Two thousand years after a tireless exploration of the comings and goings between discourse and the object to be named or interpreted, an object which is the solicitor of interrogation, we have finally achieved a discourse on discourse, an interpretation of interpretation. For the psycho-analyst, this vertigo in abstraction is, nevertheless, a means of protecting us from a masochistic and jubilatory fall into nature, into the full and pagan mother, a fall which is a tempting and crushing enigma for anyone who has not gained some distance from it with the help of an interpretive device. However, and this is the second step post-phenomenological analytic ratio-nality has taken, we have also perceived the incompleteness of interpreta-tion itself, the incompleteness characteristic of all language, sign, discourse. This perception prevents the closure of our interpretation as a self-sufficient totality, which resembles delirium, and at the same time this perception of interpretation constitutes the true life of interpretations (in the plural).

4. Literature as Interpretation: The Text

Philosophical interpretation as well as literary criticism therefore and henceforth both have a tendency to be written as *texts*. They openly assume their status as fiction without, however, abandoning their goal of stating One meaning, The True Meaning, of the discourse they interpret.

The fate of interpretation has allowed it to leave behind the protective enclosure of a metalanguage and to approach the imaginary, without neces-sarily confusing the two. I would now like to evoke some specifics and some dangers of openly fictional interpretation in literary discourse itself. So as not to simplify the task, I will take as my example a modern French novelist, Louis Ferdinand Céline (1894–1961), whose popular and musical style represents the height of twentieth-century French literature and whose anti-Semitic and para-Nazi pamphlets reveal one of the blackest aspects of contemporary history.

I consider all fiction (poetic language or narrative) already an inter-pretation in the broad sense of the speaking subject's implication in a trans-position (connection) of a presupposed object. If it is impossible to assign to a literary text a preexisting "objective reality," the critic (the interpreter) can nevertheless find the mark of the interpretive function of writing in the transformation which that writing inflicts on the language of everyday com-munication. In other words, *style* is the mark of interpretation in literature. To quote Céline, "I am not a man of ideas. I am a man of style. . . . This involves taking sentences, I was telling you, and unhinging them."[5] Such an interpretive strategy is clearly an enunciative strategy, and, in Célinian language, it uses two fundamental techniques: *segmentation* of the sentence, characteristic of the first novels; and the more or less recuperable *syntactical ellipses* which appear in the late novels.

The peculiar segmentation of the Célinian phrase, which is considered colloquial, is a cutting up of the syntactic unit by the projected or rejected displacement of one of its components. As a result, the normally descending modulation of the phrasal melody becomes an intonation with two centers. Thus: "I had just discovered war in its entirety. . . . Have to be almost in front of it, like I was then, to really see it, the bitch, face on and in profile."[6]

An analysis of this utterance, not as a syntactic structure but as a *message* in the process of enunciation between a speaking subject and his addressee, would show that the aim of this ejection is to *thematize* the displaced element, which then acquires the status not merely of a theme but of an emphatic theme. "La vache" ("the bitch") is the vehicle for the primary information, the essential message which the speaker emphasizes. From this perspective, the ejected element is desyntacticized, but it is charged with supplementary semantic value, bearing the speaker's emotive attitude and his moral judgment. Thus, the ejection emphasizes the information kernel at the expense of the syntactic structure and makes the logic of the message (theme/rheme, support/apport, topic/comment, presupposed/posed) dominate over the logic of syntax (verb-object); in other words, the logic of enunciation dominates over that of the enunciated. In fact, the terminal intonational contour of the rheme (along two modalities: assertive and interrogative) indicates the very point at which the modality of enunciation is most profoundly revealed. The notable preponderance of this contour with the bipartition theme/rheme in children's acquisition of syntax or in the emotive or relaxed speech of popular or everyday discourse is added proof that it is a *deeper* organizer of the utterance than syntactic structures.

This "binary shape" in Céline's first novels has been interpreted as an indication of his uncertainty about self-narration in front of the Other. Awareness of the Other's existence would be what determines the phenomena of recall and excessive clarity, which then produces segmentation. In this type of sentence, then, the speaking subject would occupy two places: that of his own identity (when he goes straight to the information, to the rheme) and that of objective expression, for the Other (when he goes back, recalls, clarifies). Given the prevalence of this type of construction in the first phases of children's acquisition of syntax, we can state that this binomial, which is both intonational and logical, coincides with a fundamental stage in the constitution of the speaking subject: his autonomization with respect to the Other, the constitution of his own identity.

To Freud's and René Spitz's insistence that "no" is the mark of man's access to the symbolic and the founding of a distinction between the pleasure principle and the reality principle, one could add that the "binarism" of the message (theme/rheme and vice versa) is another step, a fundamental step, in the symbolic integration of negativism, rejection, and the death drive. It is even a decisive step: with the binarism of the message and before the constitution of syntax, the subject not only differentiates pleasure from reality—a painful and ultimately impossible distinction—but he also distinguishes between the statements: "I say by presupposing" and "I say by making explicit," that is, "I say what matters to me" versus "I say to be clear" or even, "I say what I like" versus "I say for you, for us, so that we can understand each other." In this way, the binary message effects a slippage from the I as the pole of pleasure to the *you* as addressee and to the impersonal *one,* he, which is necessary to establish a true universal syntax. This is how the subject of enunciation is born. And it is in remembering this path that the subject rediscovers, if not his origin, at least his originality. The "spoken" writing of Céline achieves just such a remembering.

In addition, in Céline's last novels, *D'un château l'autre, Nord,* and *Rigodon,* he repeatedly uses the famous "three dots" (suspension points) and the exclamations which sometimes indicate an ellipsis in the clause but serve more fundamentally to make the clause overflow into the larger whole of the message. This technique produces a kind of long syntactic period, covering a half-page, a full page, or more. In contrast to Proustian fluctuation, it avoids subordinations, is not given as a logical-syntactic unit, and proceeds by brief utterances: clauses pronounceable in one breath which cut, chop, and give rhythm. Laconism (nominal sentences), exclamations, and the predominance of intonation over syntax reecho (like segmentation but in another way) the archaic phases of the subject of enunciation. On the one hand, these techniques, because of the influx of nonmeaning, arouse the nonsemanticized emotion of the reader. On the other hand, they give an infrasyntactical, intonational inscription of that same emotion which transverses syntax but integrates the message (theme/rheme and subject-addressee).[7]

From this brief linguistico-stylistic discussion, I would like to stress the following: style is interpretation in the sense that it is a connection between the logic of utterance and the logic of enunciation, between syntax and message and their two corresponding subjective structures. The unobjectifiable, unnameable "object" which is thereby caught in the text is what Céline calls an *emotion.* "Drive," and its most radical component, the death drive, is perhaps an even better term for it. "You know, in Scriptures, it is written: 'In the beginning was the Word.' No! In the beginning was emotion. The Word came afterwards to replace emotion as the trot replaced the gallop."[8] And again: "Slang is a language of hatred that knocks the reader over for you . . . annihilates him! . . . at your mercy! . . . he sits there like an ass."[9]

It is as if Céline's stylistic adventure were an aspect of the eternal return to a place which escapes naming and which can be named only if one plays on the whole register of language (syntax, but also message, intonation, etc.). This locus of emotion, of instinctual drive, of nonsemanticized hatred, resistant to logico-syntactic naming, appears in Céline's work, as in other great literary texts, as a locus of the ab-ject. The abject, not yet object, is anterior to the distinction between subject and object in normative language. But the abject is also the nonobjectality of the archaic mother, the locus of needs, of attraction and repulsion, from which an object of forbidden desire arises. And finally, abject can be understood in the sense of the horrible and fascinating abomination which is connoted in all cultures by the feminine or, more indirectly, by every partial object which is related to the state of abjection (in the sense of the nonseparation subject/object). It becomes what culture, the *sacred*, must purge, separate, and banish so that it may establish itself as such in the universal logic of catharsis.

Is the abject, the ultimate object of style, the archetype of the *Sachverhalt*, of what solicits interpretation? Is it the archi-interpretable? This is, as I said earlier, something analytic interpretation can argue. Meaning, and the interpretation which both posits and lives off meaning, are sustained by that *elsewhere* which goes beyond them and which fiction, style (other variants of interpretation), never stops approaching—and dissolving.

For this is in fact the central issue in Céline as in the great writers of all times. By their themes (evil, idiocy, infamy, the feminine, etc.) and their styles, they immerse us in the ab-ject (the unnameable, the *Sachverhalt*), not in order to name, reify, or objectify them once and for all but to dissolve them and to displace us. In what direction? Into the harmony of the Word and into the fundamental incompleteness of discourse constituted by a cleavage, a void: an effervescent and dangerous beauty, the fragile obverse of a radical nihilism that can only fade away in "those sparkling depths which [say] that nothing exists any more."[10]

Yet this pulverization of the abject, the ultimate case of interpretation by style, remains fragile. Because it does not always satisfy desire, the writer is tempted to give one interpretation and one only to the outer limit of the nameable. The *Sachverhalt*, the abject, is then embodied in the figure of a maleficent agent, both feminine and phallic, miserable and all-powerful, victim and satrap, idiot and genius, bestial and wily. What once defied discourse now becomes the ultimate object of one and only one interpretation, the source and acme of a polymorphous *jouissance* in which

the interpreter, this time in his delirium, is finally reunited with what denies, exceeds, and excites him. He blends into this abject and its feminine-
maternal resonance which threatens identity itself. This interpretive
delirium—writing's weak moment—found in Céline the Jew as its privileged object in the context of Hitlerism. The historical and social causes of
Céline's anti-Semitism can be sought in monotheism, or, rather, in its deni-
als, and in the history of France and the reality of the Second World War.
His anti-Semitism also has a more subtle foundation, more intrinsically
linked to the psychic instability of the writer and the speaking subject in
general: it is the fascination with the wandering and elusive other, who attracts, repels, puts one literally beside oneself. This other, before being another subject, is an object of discourse, a nonobject, an abject. This abject
awakens in the one who speaks archaic conflicts with his own improper
objects, his ab-jects, at the edge of meaning, at the limits of the interpretable. And it arouses the paranoid rage to dominate those objects, to transform them, to exterminate them.

I do not presume to elucidate in this brief presentation the many
causes and aspects of Céline's anti-Semitism. A lengthier consideration of
the subject can be found in my *Pouvoirs de l'horreur.* I have broached this
difficult and complex subject here to indicate by a *paroxysm,* which we
could take as a *hyperbole,* the dangerous paths of interpretive passion, fascinated by an enigma that is beyond discourse. For the psychoanalyst, it
recalls a desiring indebtedness to the maternal continent.

I would like the above remarks to be taken both as a "free association" and as the consequence of a certain position. I would want them to
be considered not only an epistemological discussion but also a personal
involvement (need I say one of desire?) in the dramas of thought, personality, and contemporary politics. Such a vast theme ("the politics of interpretation") cannot help but involve a multiplicity of questions. If their
conjunction in my paper seems chaotic, inelegant, and nonscientific to a
positivist rationality, this conjunction is precisely what defines for me the
originality and the difficulty of psychoanalytic interpretation. The task is
not to make an interpretive summa in the name of a system of truths—for
that attitude has always made interpretation a rather poor cousin of theology. The task is, instead, to record the *crisis* of modern interpretive systems without smoothing it over, to affirm that this crisis is inherent in the
symbolic function itself, and to perceive as symptoms all constructions, including totalizing interpretation, which try to deny this crisis: to dissolve,
to displace indefinitely, in Kafka's words, "temporarily and for a lifetime."

Perhaps nothing of the wise Stoic interpreter remains in the analyst
except his function as *actor:* he accepts the text and puts all his effort and

desire, his passion and personal virtuosity, into reciting it, while remaining indifferent to the events that he enacts. This "indifference," called "benevolent neutrality," is the modest toga with which we cover our interpretive desire. Yet by shedding it, by implicating ourselves, we bring to life, to meaning, the dead discourses of patients which summon us. The ambiguity of such an interpretive position is both untenable and pleasurable. Knowing this, knowing that he is constantly in abjection and in neutrality, in desire and in indifference, the analyst builds a strong ethics, not normative but directed, which no transcendence guarantees. That is where, it seems to me, the modern version of liberty is being played out, threatened as much by a single, total, and totalitarian Meaning as it is by delirium.

Translated by Margaret Waller

Notes

Translator's note.—I would like to thank Domna Stanton and Alice Jardine for their help on an earlier version of this translation.

1. See Victor Goldschmidt, *Le Système stoïcien et l'idée de temps* (Paris, 1953).

2. Sigmund Freud, "Constructions in Analysis," *The Standard Edition of the Complete Psychological Works of Sigmund Freud,* translated and edited by James Strachey, 24 vols. (London, 1953–74), 23:268.

3. See in my *Folle vérité* (Paris, 1979) the texts presented in my seminar at l'Hôpital de la Cité Universitaire, Service de psychiatrie.

4. See esp. Jacques Lacan, "De l'interpretation au transfert," *Le Séminaire de Jacques Lacan,* vol. 11, *Les Quatre Concepts fondamentaux de la psychoanalyse* (Paris, 1973), pp. 221 ff.

5. Louis Ferdinand Céline, "Louis Ferdinand Céline vous parle," *Oeuvres complètes,* 2 vols. (Paris, 1966–69), 2:934.

6. "Je venais de découvrir la guerre toute entière. . . . Faut être à peu près devant elle comme je l'étais à ce moment-là pour bien la voir, *la vache,* en face et de profil" (Céline, *Voyage au bout de la nuit, Oeuvres complètes,* 1:8).

7. For a lengthier discussion of Céline's style and its interpretation, see my *Pouvoirs de l'horreur: Essai sur l'abjection* (Paris, 1980). [*Powers of Horror: An Essay in Abjection,* translated by Leon Roudiez (New York: Columbia University Press, 1982)—ED.]

8. Céline, ''Céline vous parle,'' p. 933.

9. Céline, *Entretiens avec le professeur Y* (1955; Paris, 1976), p. 72.

10. Céline, *Rigodon, Oeuvres complètes,* 2:927.

5

Sending: On Representation

Jacques Derrida

At the beginning of this century, in 1901, the French philosopher Henri Bergson made a remark about what he called "our word representation," our French word representation: "Our word representation is an equivocal word which ought never, according to its etymology, to designate an intellectual object presented to the mind for the first time. It ought to be reserved . . . " etc.

For the moment I leave aside this remark of Bergson's. I shall let it wait on the threshold of an introduction which I propose to entitle simply "Sending," in the singular.

Imagine that French were a dead language.

I could just as well have said: Represent that to yourselves, French, a dead language.

And in some archive of paper or stone, on some roll of microfilm, we could read a sentence. I read it here, let it be the opening sentence of this introductory address, for example this: "One might say that we represent something [*nous sommes en représentation*]."

Are we sure we know what this means, today? Let us not be too quick to believe it.

I have begun intentionally by allowing the word "representation" to appear already inserted in an idiom. Its translation into another idiom would remain problematic, which is another way of saying it could not be done without remainder. I shall not analyze all the dimensions of this problem but shall limit myself to what it most obviously points to.

What do we ourselves know when we pronounce or listen to the sentence I just read? What do we know of this French idiom?

Now what we already know is that if we are here in Strasbourg as representing, then this event bears an essential relation to a double body [*corps*], understanding this word in the sense of "body of work" [*corpus*] or "organized body" [*corporation*]. I think on the one hand of the body of philosophy which can itself be considered a corpus of discursive acts or of texts but also as the body or corporation of subjects, of institutions and of philosophical societies. We are mandated, in one way or another, under some form or degree of legitimacy, to represent these societies here. We may be considered more or less explicitly instructed representatives, delegates, ambassadors, emissaries, I prefer to say envoys. But on the other hand this representation maintains also an essential relation to the body or corpus of the French language. The agreement that authorizes this congress was made in French between philosophical societies whose very constitution alludes to their belonging to a linguistic domain, to a linguistic difference that does not coincide with a national difference.

What in this connection refers philosophical or philosophico-institutional acts back to language, to the supposed constitutive factor of a language or group of languages known as "Latin," obviously cannot be excluded from our discussion, all the more because the chosen theme, *representation*, allows itself less than most to be detached or dissociated from its linguistic embodiment, its lexical and above all nominal embodiment, or as others would be quick to say from its nominal representation. I will return to this point.

The sentence with which such a discourse might have begun ("One might say that we represent something"), all of whose idiomatic resources, as I said, will not be analyzed here, suggests at least this in addition: the sentence evokes the more or less representative representatives, the envoys we are mandated to be, under the aspect and in the highly regulated time of a kind of spectacle, of exhibition, of discursive if not oratorical performance, in the course of ceremonious, coded, ritualized exchanges. This event is a consecrated gathering, a feast or ritual destined to renew the pact, the contract or the symbol. Allow me to salute with some insistence the place of what is taking place here. The event takes place, thanks to the hospitality of one of our societies, in a city which, while it does not, as it once very symbolically did, lie outside of France, is nevertheless not just any French city. This frontier city is a place of passage and of translation, a buffer zone, a privileged site for encounter or competition between two immense linguistic territories, two also among the most densely populated worlds of philosophical discourse. And it turns out (an idiom hesitating between chance and necessity) that in dealing with representation we shall not, as philosophers, be able to restrict ourselves to Latinity. It will be neither possible nor legitimate to overlook the enormous historical stake in this question of Latino-Germanic translation, of the relation between *repraesentatio* and the *Stellen* of *Vorstellung* or *Darstellung*. For some centuries it has been the case that as soon as a philosopher, of no matter what linguistic habits, engaged in an inquiry into *repraesentatio, Vor-* or

Darstellen, he finds himself, on both sides of the frontier, on both banks of the Rhine, taken, surprised, preceded, anticipated by the close co-destination, the strange co-habitation, the contamination and the enigmatic co-translation of these two vocabularies. The philosophical—and it is *philo-sophical* societies that send us here as their representatives—can no longer, in this case, allow itself to be enclosed in a single idiom, at the risk of floating, neutral and disembodied, remote from every body of language. It is just that the philosophical turns out in advance to be engaged in a mul-tiplicity, a linguistic duality, or duel, in the region of a bilingualism that it cannot suppress without suppressing itself. And one of the numerous sup-plementary involutions of this enigma follows the line of this translation—and of this translator's task. We do not "represent something" only as representatives, as delegates or officeholders sent to an assembly which is to discuss representation; the problem of translatability that we shall not be able to avoid will also be a problem of representation. Is translation of the same order as representation? Does it consist in representing a sense, the same semantic content, by a different word of a different language? If so is it a question of the substitution of one representative structure for another? And as a privileged example, both supplementary and deep, do *Vorstellung* and *Darstellung* play the role of German representations of French (or more generally Latin) representation or vice versa, is "representation" the perti-nent representative of *Vorstellung*, indeed of *Darstellung*? Or does the so-called relation of translation or of substitution already escape the orbit of representation, and in that case how should we interpret representation? I shall come back to this exemplary question but I am satisfied just to situate it at the moment.

Let us suppose that French is a dead language. We think we can dis-tinguish a dead language from a living one and use for this a set of rela-tively rigorous criteria. Confident in this very naive presumption, represent to yourselves now the following scene of deciphering: Some philologists occupied with a written corpus, with a library or a silent archive, have not only to reconstitute the French language but at the same time to fix the sense of certain words, to establish a dictionary or at least some entries for a dictionary. Without any other context than that of written documents, in the absence of living informants to intervene in this context, the lexicologist would have to elaborate a dictionary of words (you are aware that dictio-naries of words and dictionaries of things are differentiated—more or less as Freud differentiated representations of words [*Wortvorstellungen*] and representations of things [*Sach-* or *Dingvorstellungen*]). Confident in the unity of the word and in the double articulation of language, such a lexicon should classify the different items of the word "representation" by their meanings and their use in a certain state of the language and taking account of a certain richness or diversity of corpuses, codes, and contexts. So one should presuppose a profound unity of these different meanings, and that a law will come to regulate this multiplicity. A minimum and shared semantic kernel would justify upon each occasion the choice of the "same" word "representation" and would allow itself, precisely, "to represent" by means of it, in the most different contexts. In the political domain, we can speak of parliamentary, diplomatic, or union representation. In the aesthetic domain, we can speak of representation in the sense of mimetic substitution, notably in the so-called plastic arts, but, in a more problematic manner, of a theatrical representation in a sense which is not necessarily or uniquely reproductive or repetitive but in order to name in this case a presentation [*Darstellung*], an exhibition, a performance. I have just evoked two codes, the political and the aesthetic, leaving for the moment in suspense the other categories (metaphysical, historic, religious, epistemological) which are inscribed in the program of our meeting. But there are also all sorts of subcontexts and subcodes, all sorts of *uses* of the word "representation," which seems then to mean image, perhaps nonrepresentative, nonreproductive, nonrepetitive, simply presented and placed before our eyes, before our imaginative or mental gaze, according to the traditional metaphor which can also be interpreted and overdetermined as a representation of representation. More broadly, we can also look for what there is in common between the nominal occurrences of the word "representation" and so many idiomatic locutions in which the verb "to represent," indeed "to represent oneself," does not appear simply to modulate, in the mode of the "verb," a semantic kernel which one could identify according to the nominal model of "representation." If the noun "representation," the adjectives "representing," "representable," "representative," the verbs "represent" or "represent oneself" are not only the grammatical modulations of a single and identical meaning, if kernels of different meanings are present, at work in or produced by these grammatical modes of the idiom, then the lexicologist, the semanticist, indeed the philosopher who would try to classify different varieties of "representation" and of "representing," to give account of the variables or the divergences from the identity of an invariant meaning, is going to have a rough time of it.

The hypothesis of the dead language is useful to me only as a heuristic. It draws attention to a situation in which a context is never able to be saturated for the determination and *identification* of a sense. Now in this respect the so-called living language is structurally in the same situation. The two conditions for fixing the meaning of a word or overcoming the polysemy of a name—namely, the existence of an invariant under the diversity of semantic transformations on one hand, the possibility of determining a context which would saturate the meaning on the other hand—these two conditions seem to me in any case as problematic for a living language as for a dead one.

And this is more or less, here and now, our situation, we who represent something. Whether or not one lays claim to a philosophic use of so-called natural language, the word *"représentation"* does not have the same semantic field and the same mode of functioning as an apparently identical word (*"representation"* in English, *"Repräsentation"* in German) or as the different words that people take to be its equivalents in current translations (once again, and I shall return to this point, *Vorstellung* is not just one example here among others). If we want to understand each other, to know what we are talking about in relation to a theme which is truly common to us, we have before us two types of great problematic. We can on the one hand ask ourselves what discourse based on representation means in our common language. And then we shall have to do a job which is not fundamentally different from that of the semantic lexicologist who is projecting a dictionary of words. But on the other hand, presupposing an implicit and practical knowledge on this subject, basing ourselves on a living contract or consensus, believing that in the end all subjects competent in the *franca lingua* understand each other about this word, that the variations are only contextual and that no essential obscurity will obfuscate discourse about representation, we shall try to give an account, as they say, of representation today, the thing or the things named *"representations"* rather than the words themselves. We would have in mind a sort of philosophical *"dictionnaire raisonné"* of things rather than words. We would presuppose that there could be no irremediable misunderstanding as to the content and the destination of the message or the sending named *"representation."* In a *"natural"* situation (as we also say a natural language), one could always correct the indeterminacy or the misunderstanding; and it is at bottom by philosophy that one would correct philosophy, I mean the bad effects of philosophy. These would follow from a practice that is current and apparently profoundly philosophical: to think what a concept means in itself, to think what representation is, the essence of representation in general. This philosophical practice first pushes the word to its very greatest obscurity, in a highly artificial way, in abstracting it from every context and every use value, as if a word were to regulate itself on a concept independently of any contextualized function, and in the limit independently of any sentence. You will recognize in this a type of objection (let us call it roughly "Wittgensteinian," and if we wish to develop it during the colloquium let us not forget that it was accompanied for Wittgenstein, at a given stage of his career, by a theory of representation in language, a picture theory which should be significant to us here, at least as regards what is "problematic" about it). In this situation, philosophical common usage always tries to stop the philosophic vertigo which catches it up by its language, and to do that by a movement of which I was saying just a moment ago that it was philosophical (philosophy against philosophy) but which is also prephilosophical, because in it one behaves as if one knew what "representation" meant and as if one had only to adjust this knowledge to a present historical situation, to distribute the articles, the types or the problems of representation in different regions but belonging to the same space. A gesture at once very philosophical and prephilosophical. We can understand the legitimate concern of the organizers of this congress, who in order to avoid "too great a dispersion" proposed Sections for the orderly distribution of themes (Aesthetics, Politics, Metaphysics, History, Religion, Epistemology). "To avoid too great a dispersion": this accepts a certain polysemy provided that it is not too excessive and lends itself to a rule, that it allows itself to be measured and governed in this list of six categories or in this encyclopedia as a circle of six circles or six jurisdictions. Nothing more legitimate, in theory and in practice, than this concern of the Program Committee. Nevertheless, this list of six categories remains problematic, as everyone knows. They cannot be spread out upon the same table, as if one did not imply or never overlapped another, as if everything were homogeneous inside each of the categories or as if this list were *a priori* exhaustive. And you must imagine Socrates arriving in the early dawn of this Symposium, tipsy, late, and asking: "You tell me there is aesthetic, political, metaphysical, historic, religious and epistemological representation, as if each were one among others, but in the end, aside from the fact that you are probably enumerating too many or too few, you have not answered the question: what is representation in itself and in general? What makes all these representations called by the same name? What is the eidos of representation, the being-representation of representation?" As for this well-known schema of the Socratic question, what limits the possibility of this fiction is that for essential reasons, questions of language which do not allow of being assigned to a simple and limited place, Socrates would never have been able to ask this kind of question about the word "representation," and I think we must begin with the hypothesis that the word "representation" translates no Greek word in any obvious way, leaving nothing aside, unless it is reinterpreted and reinscribed deeply into history. This is not one problem of translation among others, it is the problem of translation itself and its supplementary complication of which I spoke just now. Before knowing how and what to translate by "representation," we must interrogate the concept of translation and of language which is so often dominated by the concept of representation, whether it be a matter of interlinguistic transla-

tion, or intralinguistic (within a single language), or even, to revert for convenience to Jakobson's tripartite distinction, intersemiotic translation
(between discursive and nondiscursive languages, art for example). Each
time we would find the presupposition or the desire for an invariable identity of sense already present behind all the usages and regulating all the
variations, all the correspondences, all the interexpressive relations (I use
this Leibnizian language deliberately, what Leibniz calls the "representative
nature" of the monad constituting this constant and regulated relation of
interexpressivity). Such a representative relation would organize not only
the translation of a natural or a philosophic language into another but also
the translatability of all regions, for example also of all the contents distrib-
uted in the sections allowed for by the Program Committee. And the unity
of this list of sections would be assured by the representative structure of
the table itself.

   This hypothesis or this desire would be precisely that of representation, of a representative language whose object would be to represent something (to represent in all the senses of the delegation of presence, of
reiteration rendering present once again, in substituting a presentation for
another *in absentia* and so on); such a language would represent something,
a sense, an object, a referent, indeed even another representation in whatever sense, which would be anterior and exterior to it. Under the diversity
of words from diverse languages, under the diversity of the uses of the same
word, under the diversity of contexts or of syntactic systems, the same
sense or the same referent, the same representative content would keep its
inviolable identity. Language, every language, would be representative, a
system of representatives, but the content represented, what is represented
by this representation (meaning, a thing, and so on) would be a presence
and not a representation. What is represented would not have the structure
of representation, the representative structure of the representative. Language would be a system of representatives or also of signifiers, of place-
holders [*lieu-tenants*], substituted for what they say, signify, or represent,
and the equivocal diversity of the representatives would not affect the unity,
the identity, indeed even the ultimate simplicity of the represented. Now it
is only starting with these premises—that is to say, a language as a system
of representation—that the problematic in which we are caught up would
be set in place. But to determine language as representation is not the effect
of an accidental prejudice, a theoretical fault or a manner of thinking, a
limit or a closure among others, a form of representation, precisely, which
came about one day and of which we could rid ourselves by a decision
when the time comes. Today there is a great deal of thought against representation. In a more or less articulated or rigorous way, this judgment is
easily arrived at: representation is bad. And this without being able to as-

sign, in the final analysis, the place and the necessity of that evaluation. We should ask ourselves what is this place and above all what may be the various risks (in particular political ones) of such a prevalent evaluation, prevalent in the world at large but also among the most diverse fields, from aesthetics to metaphysics (to return to the distinctions of our program) by way of politics, where the parliamentary ideal, to which the structure of representation is so often attached, is no longer very inspiring in the best of cases. And yet, whatever the strength and the obscurity of this dominant current, the authority of representation constrains us, imposing itself on our thought through a whole dense, enigmatic, and heavily stratified history. It programs us and precedes us and warns us too severely for us to make a mere object of it, a representation, an object of representation confronting us, before us like a theme. It is even difficult enough to pose a systematic and historical question on the topic (a question of the type: "What is the system and the history of representation?") now that our concepts of system and of history are essentially marked by the structure and the closure of representation.

When one tries today to think what is occurring with representation, at once the extension of its domain and its being called in question, it is impossible to avoid (whatever conclusions one may come to about it) this central motif of Heideggerian meditation when it attempts to determine an epoch of representation in the destiny of Being, a post-Hellenic epoch in which relations to Being would have to come to a halt as *repraesentatio* and *Vorstellung,* in the equivalence of one to the other. Among the numerous texts of Heidegger that ought to be read in this connection I must limit myself to a passage in *Die Zeit des Weltbildes* ("The Epoch of World-views") in *Holzwege.* Heidegger there inquires about what best expresses itself, the sense [*Bedeutung*] which comes best to expression [*Ausdruck*] in the word *repraesentatio* as in the word *Vorstellung.*[1] This text dates from 1938, and I would like first to draw your attention to one of the peculiarly contemporary features of this meditation. It has to do with publicity and publication, the media, the accelerating pace at which intellectual and philosophical production is becoming technical (is in short becoming a product), in a word everything that could be included today under the heading of a producing society, of representation, of spectacle, with all the responsibilities that implies. Heidegger initiates in this same place an analysis of the institution of research, of the university and of publication in connection with the dominant position of representation thought, of the determination of appearance or presence as an image-before-one or the determination of the image itself as an object installed before [*vorgestallt*] a subject. I reduce and over-simplify a train of thought which engages itself on the side of the determination of what-is as object and of the world as a field of objectivity for a subject [*subjectité*], the institutionalization of knowledge being unthinkable without this objective setting of representation [*cette mise en réprésentation objective*]. In passing Heidegger evokes furthermore the life of the intellectual who has become a "researcher" and has to participate in the programs of congresses, of the researcher tied to the "instructions of publishers, who decide nowadays what books should be written or not written." Heidegger adds here a note that I want to read because of its date and because it belongs by right to our reflection on the epoch of representation:

> The growing importance of the reign of the publisher finds its explanation not only in the fact that publishers (through the book trade, for example) acquire a better sense of the needs of the public or master the commercial side of the matter better than authors. It is rather that their own work takes on the form of a procedure which is planned in advance and, constantly reorganizing itself, is oriented towards the question of knowing how, by the commissioned and group publication of books and writings, it is possible to gain and maintain an entree into the world under the aspect of publicity [*ins Bild der Öffentlichkeit*]. The preponderance of collections, series, journals and pocket editions is already a consequence of this effort on the part of publishers, which in its turn agrees with the intentions of the researchers, who in this way not only make themselves known and noticed more easily and quickly in series and collections but have ready access, on a more developed front, to efficient organization.

Here now is the most palpable articulation, which I lift out of a long and difficult development that I cannot reconstitute here. If we follow Heidegger, the Greek world did not have a relation to what-is as to a conceived image or a representation (here *Bild*). There what-is is presence; and this did not, at first, derive from the fact that man would look at what-is and have what we call a representation [*Vorstellung*] of it as the mode of perception of a subject. In a similar way, in another age (and it is about this sequence of ages or epochs, *Zeitalter,* arranged to be sure in a nonteleological fashion but grouped under the unity of a destiny of Being as fate [*envoi*], *Geschick,* that I would like to raise a question later on), the Middle Ages relates itself essentially to what-is as to an *ens creatum*. "To be something that-is" ["*être-un-étant*"] means to belong to the created order; this thus corresponds to God according to the analogy of what-is [*analogia entis*], but, says Heidegger, the being of what-is never consists in an object [*Gegenstand*] brought before man, fixed, stopped, available for the human subject who would possess a representation of it. This will be the mark of modernity. "That what-is should become what-is in representation (literally in the being-represented, *in der Vorgestelltheit*), this is what makes the epoch [*Zeitalter*] which gets to this point a new epoch in relation to the preceding one." It is thus only in the modern period (Cartesian or post-Cartesian) that what-is is determined as an ob-ject present *before* and *for* a subject in the form of *repraesentatio* or *Vorstellen*. So Heidegger analyzes the *Vorgestelltheit des Seienden*. What do *Stellen and Vorstellen* mean? I translate, or rather for essential reasons I couple the languages:

> It is something entirely different that, in contrast to Greek understanding, signifies [*meint*] modern representation [*das neuzeitliche Vorstellen*], whose signification [*Bedeutung*] reaches its best expression [*Ausdruck*] in the word *repraesentatio*. *Vorstellen bedeutet hier,* representation signifies here: *das Vorhandene als ein Entgegenstehendes vor sich bringen, auf sich, den Vorstellenden zu, beziehen und in diesen zu sich als das massegebenden Bereich zurückzwingen,* to make the existent (which is already before one: *Vorhandene*) come before one as a standing-over-against, to relate it to the self who represents it and in this way to force it back to the self as a determining field.

It is the self, here the human subject, which is the field in this relation, the domain and the measure of objects as representations, its own representations. I interrupt my citation for a moment.

Heidegger thus uses the Latin word *repraesentatio* and settles at once into the equivalence between *repraesentatio* and *Vorstellung*. This is not illegitimate, on the contrary, but it does require explanation. As "representation," in the philosophical code or in ordinary language, *Vorstellung* seems not to imply immediately the meaning that is carried in the *re-* of *repraesentatio*. *Vorstellung* seems to mean simply, as Heidegger emphasizes, to place, to dispose before oneself, a sort of theme or thesis. But this sense or value of being-before is already at work in "*pre*sent." *Praesentatio* signifies the fact of presenting and *re-praesentatio* that of *rendering* present, of a summoning as a power-of-bringing-back-to-presence. And this power-of-bringing-back, in a repetitive way, is marked simultaneously by the re- of representation *and* in this positionality, this power-of-placing, disposing, putting, that is to be read in *Stellen* and which at the same time refers back to the self, that is to the power of a subject who can bring back to presence and make present, make something present to itself, indeed just make itself present. This making-present can be understood in two senses at least; this duplicity is at work in the term representation. On the one hand, to render present would be to bring to presence, into presence, cause or allow to come in presenting. On the other hand, but this second sense is implicit in the first, causing or allowing to come, implying the possibility of causing or allowing to return, to render present, like all "rendering," all restitution, would be to repeat, to be able to repeat. Whence the idea of repetition and return which resides in the very meaning of representation. I will say of a word that to my knowledge is never used thematically in this context that it is the "render" that is split, meaning *sometimes,* as in "to render present," just to present, to allow or cause to come to presence, into presentation, *sometimes* to cause or allow to return, to restore for the second time to presence, perhaps in effigy, by sign or symbol, what was not or was no longer present, this *not* or *no-longer* having a very great diversity of possible modes. Now what is the source, in philosophical or more or less scientific language, of the semantic determination of *repraesentatio* as something that takes place in and for mind, within the subject and over against it, in it and for it, object for a subject? In other words, how could this meaning of *repraesentatio* be contemporary, as Heidegger says it is, with the Cartesian or Cartesian-Hegelian epoch of the *subjectum*? In representation, the present, the presentation of what is presented comes back, returns as a double effigy, an image, a copy, an idea as a picture of the thing henceforth at hand, in the absence of the thing, available, disposed and put forward for, by, and in the subject. *For, by* and *in,* the system of these prepositions (puttings-forth) marks the place of representation or of the *Vorstellung.* The prefix *re-* marks the repetition in, for, and by the subject, *a parte subjecti,* of a presence which otherwise would present itself to the subject without depending upon it or without having it in its own place. Doubtless the present which returns thus had already the form of what is for and before the subject but was not at its disposition in this preposition itself. Whence the possibility of translating *repraesentatio* by *Vorstellung,* a word which, in its literality and here as a metaphor, we could say somewhat hastily (but I am reserving this problem) marks the gesture which consists of placing, of causing to stand before one, of installing in front of oneself as available, of localizing ready at hand, within the availability of the preposition. And the ideality of the idea as a copy in the mind is precisely what is most readily available, most repeatable, apparently most docile to the reproductive spontaneity of the mind. The value "*pre-,*" "being-before," was certainly already present in "present"; it is only the rendering available of the human subject that makes representation happen, and this rendering available is exactly that which constitutes the subject as a subject. The subject is what can or believes it can offer itself representations, disposing them and disposing of them. When I say offer itself representations, I could just as easily say, scarcely changing context, offer itself representatives (political ones for instance) or even, and I will come to this, offer itself to itself in representation or as a representative. We see this positional initiative—which will always be in relation with a certain highly determined concept of freedom—marked within the *Stellen* of *Vorstellung*. And I must content myself with situating here the precise place of the necessity of the whole Heideggerian meditation on the *Gestell* and the modern essence of technique.

If *rendering present* is taken to mean the repetition which restitutes thanks to a substitute, we come back to the continuum or the semantic coherence between representation as an idea in the mind pointing to the thing (for instance as the "objective reality" of the idea), as the picture in place of the thing itself, in the Cartesian sense or in the sense of the empiricists and on the other hand aesthetic representation (theatrical, poetic, literary, or visual) and finally political.

The fact that *there should be* representation or *Vorstellung* is not, according to Heidegger, a recent phenomenon, characteristic of the modern epoch of science, of technique and of subjectness [*subjectité*] of a Cartesian-Hegelian type. But what would be characteristic of this epoch is rather authority, the dominant generality of representation. It is the interpretation of the essence of what is as an object of representation. Everything which becomes present, everything which happens or presents itself is apprehended without the form of representation. *Representation* becomes the most general category to determine the apprehension of whatever it is that is of concern or interest in any relation at all. All of post-Cartesian and even post-Hegelian discourse, if not in fact the whole of modern discourse, has recourse to this category to designate all the modifications of the subject in its relationship with an object. The great question, the generative question, thus becomes, for this epoch, that of the *value* of representation, of its truth or its adequacy to what it represents. And even the criticism of representation or at least its delimitation and its most systematic excesses—at least in Hegel—seem not to call again into question the very determination of experience as subjective, that is to say, representational. I think this could be shown in Hegel, who nevertheless reminds us regularly of the limits of representation insofar as it is unilateral, only on the side of the subject ("as yet it is only a representation," he always says in the moment of proposing a new *Aufhebung;* I shall come back to this in a moment). *Mutatis mutandis*, Heidegger would say the same of Nietzsche, who however was strongly opposed to representation. Would he have said the same of Freud, in whom the concepts of representation, of *Vorstellung, Repräsentanz*, and even *Vorstellungsrepräsentanz* play such a particular and organizing role in the obscure problematics of impulse and of repression, and in whom by the most roundabout ways the work of mourning (introjection, incorporation, interiorization, idealization, so many modes of *Vorstellung* and of *Erinnerung*), the notions of phantasm and of fetish retain a close relationship with a logic of representation or of representativeness? Again I keep this question aside for the moment.

Of course, Heidegger does not interpret this reign of representation as an accident, still less as a misfortune in the face of which we must retract shivering. The end of *Die Zeit des Weltbildes* is very clear in this respect, at the point where Heidegger evokes a modern world which is beginning to remove itself from the space of representation and of the calculable. We might say in another language that a criticism or a deconstruction of representation would remain feeble, vain, and irrelevant if it were to lead to some rehabilitation of immediacy, of original simplicity, of presence without repetition or delegation, if it were to induce a criticism of calculable objectivity, of criticism, of science, of technique, or of political representation. The worst regressions can put themselves at the service of this antirepresentative prejudice. Reverting to the Heideggerian position itself, let me make this point, which will prepare far in advance a question in its turn on Heidegger's path or undertaking: so as not to be the accident of a faux-pas, this reign of representation should have been fated, predestined, *geschickte,* that is to say, literally sent, dispensed, assigned by a fate as a summary of a history (*Geschick, Geschichte*). The advent of representation must have been prepared, prescribed, announced from far off, emitted, I will say signaled at a distance [*télésigné*] in a world, the Greek world, where however representation, the *Vorstellung* or the *Vorgestelltheit des Seienden* had no dominion. How can this have happened? Representation is to be sure an image, or an idea as an image in and for the subject, an affection of the subject in the form of a relationship to the object which is in it as a copy, a painting or a scene (an idea, if you prefer, more in a Cartesian sense than a Spinozoistic one, which gives rise to a question in passing: that is no doubt why Heidegger always refers to Descartes without naming Spinoza—or perhaps others—in designating this epoch). Representation is not merely this image, but to the extent that it is this supposes that the world is previously constituted as visible. Now if for the Greeks, according to Heidegger, the world is not essentially a *Bild,* an available image, a spectacular form offered to the gaze or to the perception of a subject; if the world was first of all presence [*Anwesen*] which seizes man or attaches itself to him rather than being seen, intuited [*angeschaut*] by him; if it is rather man who is taken over and regarded by what-is, it was nevertheless necessary for the world as *Bild,* and then as representation, to declare itself among the Greeks, and this was nothing less than Platonism. The determination of the being of what is as *eidos* is not yet its determination as *Bild,* but the *eidos* (aspect, look, visible figure) would be the distant condition, the presupposition, the secret mediation which would one day permit the world to become representation. Everything happens as if the world of Platonism (and in saying the world of Platonism I also reject the idea that something like Platonist philosophy might have produced a world or that inversely it might have been the simple representation, as reflection or as symptom, of a world that sustains it) had prepared, dispensed, destined, sent, put on its way and on its path the world of representation—as far as our own time, by way of positions or outlooks of Cartesian, Hegelian, Schopenhauerian, even Nietzschean types, and so on, that is to say the whole of the history of metaphysics in its presumed unity as the indivisible unity of a sending.

In any case, for Heidegger no doubt Greek man before Plato did not inhabit a world dominated by representation; and it is with the world of Platonism that the determination of the world as *Bild* announces itself and is sent on its way, a determination that will itself prescribe predominance of representation and send it on its way.

> On the other hand while for Plato the being-what-is of what-is [*die Seiendheit des Seienden*] is determined as *eidos* (aspect, sight, *Aussehen, Anblick*), here we find the presupposition laid down well in advance [sent: *die weit voraus geschickte Voraussetzung*], from long ago mediately, in a hidden way, dominant [ruling: *lang in Verborgenen mittelbar waltende Voraussetzung*] so that the world could become image [*Bild*].

The world of Platonism would thus have given the send-off for the reign of representation, it would have destined it without itself being subjected to it. It would have been at the limit of this sending, as the origin of philosophy. Already and not yet. But this already-not-yet should not be the dialectical already-not-yet which organizes the whole Hegelian teleology of history and in particular the moment of representation [*Vorstellung*] which is already what it is not yet, its own overflowing. The *Geschick,* the *Schicken,* and the *Geschichte* of which Heidegger speaks are not sendings of the representative type. The historiality they constitute is not a representative or representable process, and in order to think it we need a history of being, of the sending of being on its way, no longer regulated or centered on representation.

It remains here then to think out a history which would no longer be of a Hegelian type or dialectic in general. For Hegelian, even neo-Hegelian, criticism of representation [*Vorstellung*] seems always to have been an *Aufhebung* [*relève*] of representation, keeping the latter in the center of becoming, as the form itself, the most general formal structure of passing from one moment to the next, and that in the present form of the already-not-yet. Thus—but these examples could be multiplied—between aesthetic and revealed religion, between revealed religion and philosophy as absolute knowledge, it is always the *Vorstellung* which marks the limit to be transcended [*à relever*]. The typical syntagma is thus the following: it is *as yet* only a representation, it is *already* the following stage but that remains *still* in the form of the *Vorstellung*, it is only the subjective unilaterality of a representation. But the "representative" form of this subjectness is taken up [*relevée*], it continues to inform the relationship to being after its disappearance. It is in this sense and following this interpretation of Hegelianism—at once strong and classical—that the latter would belong to the epoch of subjectness and of representationality [*Vorgestelltheit*] of the Cartesian world. What I retain from the two last points I have just too superficially evoked is that in order to begin to think out the multiple bearings of the word "representation" and the history, if there is one which really is one, of *Vorgestelltheit*, the minimal condition would be to bring up two presuppositions, that of a language of representative or representational structure, and that of a history as a process scanned according to the form or rhythm of *Vorstellung*. We should no longer try to represent to ourselves the essence of representation, *Vorgestelltheit*. The essence of representation is not a representation, it is not representable, there is no representation of representation. *Vorgestelltheit* is not just *Vorstellung*. Nor does it lend itself to this. It is in any case by a gesture of this type that Heidegger interrupts or disqualifies, in different domains, specular reiteration or infinite regress [*renvoi à l'infini*].

This move on Heidegger's part does not only lead us to think of representation as having become the model of all thought of the subject, of every idea, of all affection, of everything that happens to the subject and modifies it in its relation to the object. The subject is no longer defined only in its essence as the place and the placing of its representations; it is also, as a subject and in its structure as *subjectum*, itself apprehended *as a representative*. Man, determined first and above all as a subject, as being-subject, finds himself interpreted throughout according to the structure of representation. And in this respect he is not only a subject represented (I open up here in the direction in which one can still say of the subject today, in one way or another, that it is represented, for example by a signifier for another signifier: "the signifier," says Lacan, "is what represents a subject for another signifier"[2] and all the Lacanian logic of the signifier works also with this structuration of the subject by and as representation): an "entirely calculable" subject, says Lacan, as soon as it is "reduced to the formula of a matrix of significant combinations."[3] What thus brings the reign of representation into accord with the reign of the calculable is precisely Heidegger's theme; he insists on the fact that only calculability [*Berechenbarkeit*] guarantees the certainty in advance of what is *to be represented* [*der Vorstellender*] and it is toward the *incalculable* that the limits of representation can be transcended. Structured by representation, the represented subject is also a representing subject. A representative of what is and thus also an object, *Gegenstand*. The trajectory which follows upon this point would be roughly the following. By a "modern" *Vorstellung* or *repraesentatio* the subject brings what-is back before itself. The prefix *re-* which does not have necessarily the value of repetition signifies at least the availability of the causing-to-come or to-become-present as what-is-there, in front, placed-before [*pré-posé*]. The *Stellen* translates the *re-* insofar as it designates the making available or the putting in place, whereas the *vor* translates the *prae* of *praesens*. Neither *Vorstellung* nor *repraesentatio* would be able to translate a Greek thought without diverting it elsewhere, which, moreover, all translation does. It has happened for example in French that *phantasia* or *phantasma* has been translated by representation; a lexicon of Plato does this, for instance, and the *phantasia kataleptikē* of the Stoics is frequently translated "comprehensive representation." But this would suppose anachronistically that the *subjectum* and the *repraesentatio* are possible and thinkable for the Greeks. Heidegger challenges this and in appendix 8 of *Die Zeit des Weltbildes* tends to demonstrate that subjectivism was unknown in the Greek world, even to the Sophists; being would have been understood there as presence, it would appear in presence and not in representation. *Phantasia* names a mode of this appearing which is not representative. "In the uncovering [*Unverborgenheit*], *ereignet sich die Phantasia, phantasia* comes into its own, that is to say the coming-to-appearance [*das zum Erscheinen-Kommen*] of the present as such [*des Anwesenden als eines solchen*] for the man who for his part is present for what appears." This Greek thought of *phantasia* (whose fate we should follow here in all its displacements, up to the allegedly modern problematic of "fiction" and "phantasm") addresses itself only to presence, the presence of what is for the presence of man, its sense unmarked by the values of representative reproduction or of the imaginary object (produced or reproduced by man as representations). The enormous philosophical question of the imaginary, of the productive or reproductive imagination, even when it assumes once more, for example in Hegel, the Greek name of phantasy, does not belong to the Greek world but comes up later, at the epoch of representations and of man as a representing subject: "*Der Mensch als das vorstellende Subjekt jedoch phantasiert.*" Man as a representing subject, on the other hand, gives himself over to fantasy, that is to say, moves about in the *imaginatio* (the Latin word always marks the access to the world of representation), to the extent that its representation [*sein Vorstellen*] imagines what-is as the objective in the world insofar as it is a conceived image (the German is still indispensable: *insofern sein Vorstellen das Seiende als das Gegenständliche in die Welt als Bild einbildet*).

How is man, having become a representative in the sense of *Vorstellend*, also and at the same time a representative in the sense of *Repräsentant*, in other words, not only someone who has representations, who represents himself, but also someone who himself represents something or someone? Not only someone who sends himself or gives himself objects but who is sent [*est l'envoyé de*] by something else or by the other? When he has representations, when he determines everything that is as representable in a *Vorstellung*, man fixes himself in giving himself an image of what is, he makes of it an idea for himself, he translates for himself what is or gives himself its translation into an image (*Der Mensch setzt über das Seiende sich ins Bild*, says Heidegger). From that point on he puts himself on stage, says Heidegger literally, *setzt er sich selbst in die Szene*, that is to say, in the open circle of the representable, of shared and public representation. And in the following sentence, the expression of staging [*mise-en-scène*] is displaced or folded into itself; and, as in the translation, *Übersetzen*, the placing [*mise, Setzen*] is no less important than the stage. Putting himself forward or putting himself on stage, man poses, represents himself as the scene of representation (*Damit setzt sich der Mensch selbst als die Szene, in der das Seiende fortan sich vor-stellen, präsentieren, d.h. Bild sein muss:* in that way, a man puts himself forward as the stage on which what-is must from now on re-present itself, present itself, that is to say, be an image). And Heidegger concludes: "Man becomes the representative [this time *Repräsentant*, with all the ambiguity of the Latin word] of what is in the sense of ob-ject [*im Sinne des Gegenständigen*]."

In this way we can reconstitute the chain of consequences that sends us back from representation as idea or as the objective reality of the idea (relation to the object), to representation as delegation, perhaps political, thus to the substitution of subjects identifiable with one another and the more replaceable as they are objectifiable (and here we have the other side of the democratic and parliamentary ethics of representation, that is to say, the horror of calculable subjectivities, innumerable but which can be numbered, computed, the crowds in concentration camps or in the police computers or those of other agencies, the world of the masses and of the mass media which would be also a world of calculable and representable subjectivity, the world of semiotics and of information theory and of communications). The same chain, if we assume that it hangs together and if we follow the development of the Heideggerian motif, traverses a certain system of pictorial, theatrical, or aesthetic representation in general.

Some of you may perhaps consider that this reverential reference to Heidegger is excessive, and particularly that German is becoming rather invasive for the opening of a Congress of philosophy in the French language. Before concluding with an attempt to suggest some types of question

for the debates which are about to begin, I would like to justify this recourse to Heidegger and to the German of Heidegger in three ways.

First justification. The problematic opened up by Heidegger is to my
knowledge the only one today to treat representation as a whole [*dans son
ensemble*]. And already I must go beyond even this formula: the undertaking or the stepping forward, the path of thought called Heideggerian is here
more than a problematic (a problematic or a *Fragestellung* still owing too
much to representative pre-positionality, it is the very quality of being a
problem which draws attention to itself in this case). It is not concerned
with the whole or the gathering only as *system* or as *structure;* this path of
thought is unique in referring the gathering of representation back to the
world of language and of languages (Greek, Latin, and Germanic) in which
it opened out, and in making of languages a question, a question not predetermined by representation. What I shall try to suggest presently is that
the force of this gathering in the path of Heideggerian thought opens another type of problem and still leaves scope for thought, but I think it is not
possible today to circumvent, as is too often done in Francophone philosophic institutions, the space cleared by Heidegger.

Second justification. If in pointing out—and I have not been able to
do more—the necessity of referring to Heidegger, I have often spoken German, it is because, in addressing the question of representation, French-
speaking philosophers must feel the philosophic necessity of emerging from
latinity in order to think the event of thought which takes place under the
word *repraesentatio*. Not emerging just to emerge, or to disqualify a language or to go into exile, but in order to think out the relationship to one's
own language. To indicate only this point, an essential one to be sure, what
Heidegger situates "in front," so to speak, the *repraesentatio* or the *Vorstellung,* is neither a presence, nor a simple *praesentatio* nor *praesentatio*
and nothing more. A word that is often translated by "presence" in this
context is *Anwesen, Anwesenheit,* whose prefix *in this context* (I must insist
on this point) announced a coming to disclosure, to appearance, to patency,
to phenomenality rather than the prepositionality of an objective being-
before. And we know how since *Being and Time* the questioning concerning
the presence of Being is referred back radically to that of temporality, a
movement that the latinate problematic of representation, let us say to deal
with the matter much too quickly here, no doubt inhibited for essential reason. It is not enough to say that Heidegger does not recall us to the nostalgia of a presentation hidden under representation—and anyway if there is
nostalgia it does not lead us back to presentation. Not even, I will add, to
the presumed simplicity of *Anwesenheit. Anwesenheit* is not simple, it is
already divided and differentiated, it marks the place of a cut, of a division,
of a dissension [*Zwiespalt*]. Involved *in* the opening-up of this dissension,

and above all *by* it, under its assignation, man is watched by what-is, says Heidegger, and such is taken to be the essence [*Wesen*] of man "during the great Greek epoch." Man thus seeks to gather in saying [*legein*] and to save, to keep [*sozein, bewahren*] while at the same time remaining exposed to the chaos of dissension. The theatre or the tragedy of this dissension is not yet seen as belonging either to the scenic space of presentation [*Darstellung*] nor to that of representation, but the habit of dissension is seen as opening up, announcing, and forwarding everything that will come afterwards to fix itself as *mimēsis,* and then imitation, representation, with all the parade of oppositional couples that will form philosophical theory: production/reproduction, presentation/representation, original/derivative, etc. "Before" all these pairs, if one may so put it, there will never have been presentative simplicity but another twist, another difference, unpresentable, unrepresentable, one might say *non-jective, a-jective,* neither objective, nor subjective, nor projective. What of the unpresentable or the unrepresentable? How to think it? That is the question now, I will come back to it in a moment.

Third justification. This one really floats on the Rhine. I had thought at first, for this congress of societies of philosophy in the French language in Strasbourg on the theme of representation, to take the European measure of the event by referring to what happened 80 years ago, at the turn of the century, at the time when Alsace was on the other side of the frontier, if I may so put it; I had first thought of referring to what happened and what was said about representation at [the meeting of] the French Society of Philosophy. You will see that the linguistic altercation with the other-as-cousin led there to a whole debate to stabilize French philosophical vocabulary, and that a proposal was even made there on the one hand to exclude, to destroy the French word "representation," to strike it from our vocabulary, no more and no less, to put it out of service because it was only the translation of a word which came from beyond the blue line of the Vosges; or on the other hand, if absolutely necessary and putting on a brave face against historic misfortune, to "tolerate" the use of this word which is, it was said at the time with some xenophobic resentment, "hardly French." I have given up the idea of exploring with you the thrilling corpus of this gallocentric discussion. Its record is to be found in the *Bulletin de la Société française de Philosophie* for 1901, to which what is rightly called the *Vocabulaire technique et critique de la philosophie* [*Technical and Critical Vocabulary of Philosophy*] of Lalande refers back. But I have not given up the idea of citing some representative extracts from it. In the very rich article on the word "presentation" a proposal of double banishment, both of the word *presentation* and of the word *representation,* can be seen in process of formation. During the discussion which took place at the Society of

Philosophy on May 29th 1901, on the subject of the word "presentation," Bergson had said this: "Our word representation is an equivocal word which ought never, according to its etymology, to designate an intellectual object presented to the mind for the first time. It ought to be reserved for ideas or images which bear the mark of prior *work* carried out by the mind. There would then be grounds for introducing the word presentation (also used by English psychology to designate in a general way all that is purely and simply presented to the intelligence)." This proposal of Bergson's recommending the authorization and the official legitimation of the word *presentation* evoked two kinds of objection of the greatest interest. I read: "I have no objection to the use of this word [*présentation*]; but it seems to me very doubtful that the prefix *re*, in the French word *représentation*, should have originally had a duplicative value. This prefix has many other uses, for example, in *recover, retire, reveal, require, recourse,* etc. Is not its true role, in *representation*, rather to mark the *opposition* of subject and object, as in the words *revolt, resistance, repugnance, repulsion,* etc.?" (This last question seems to me at once aberrant and hyper-lucid, ingenuously inspired.) And here M. Abauzit rejects, as Lachelier will later, Bergson's proposal, the introduction of the word *presentation* in place of the word *representation*. He disputes the view that the *re* of representation implies a duplication. If there is duplication, it is not, he says, in the sense that Bergson indicates (repetition of a prior mental state) but "the reflection, in the mind, of an object conceived as existing in itself." Conclusion: "Presentation is therefore not justified." As for Lachelier, he recommends a return to French and thus purely and simply the abandonment of the philosophical use of the word *representation:* "It seems to me that *representation* was not originally a philosophical term in French, and that it became one only when a translation was wanted for *Vorstellung* [here Lachelier seems at least to overlook, even if he is not altogether wrong at a certain level, the fact that *Vorstellung* too was a translation of the Latin *repraesentatio*]. But people certainly said *represent* something *to oneself* and I think that the particle *re*, in this expression, indicated, according to its ordinary sense, a reproduction of what had been antecedently given, but perhaps without one's having paid attention to it. . . . M. Bergson's criticism is therefore, strictly speaking, justified; but one ought not to be so strict about etymology. The best thing would be not to talk at all in philosophy of *representations* and to be content with the verb *to represent to oneself;* but if there is really a need for a substantive, *representation* in a sense already consecrated by usage is better than *presentation* which evokes, in French, ideas of a wholly different order." There would be much to say about the considerations that lead to this conclusion, on the necessary distinction, according to Lachelier, between current usage and philosophical usage, about the mistrust of etymologizing, about the transformation of sense and the philosophical development of sense when we pass from an idiomatic verbal form to a nominal form, about the need to do philosophy in one's own language and to mistrust the violence done to it by translation, about the respect, nevertheless, due to established usages which are better than neologisms or the artifice of a new usage dictated by philosophy, etc. I do not have the time to dwell on all this but I would only like to indicate that this truly xenophobic mistrust with respect to philosophical importations into ways of talking is not only concerned, in Lachelier's symptomatic text, with the invasion of French by German, but in a more general and more domestic fashion with the violent contamination, the graft that takes badly and which in truth ought to be rejected, of philosophical language on to the body of natural and ordinary language. For it is not only in French, and coming from German philosophy, that these unhappy traces have been left. The trouble has already begun within the body of the German language, in the relation of German to itself, in Germanic German. And one can see Lachelier dreaming of a therapeutics of language which would not only avert French problems coming from Germany but which would be exported in the form of a European council of languages. For, he murmurs, our German friends themselves have perhaps suffered the effects of philosophical style, they have perhaps been "shocked" by the philosophical use of the word *Vorstellung*. I will content myself with citing this passage: " . . . In the ordinary sense, *take the place of . . .* , this prefix [*re*] seems rather to express the idea of a second presence, of an imperfect repetition of the primitive and real presence. It has been applied to a person who acts in the name of another, and to a simple image which makes present to us in its way an absent person or thing. From this comes the sense of *representing to oneself* [*se représenter*] internally a person or a thing by imagining them, from which point we have finally arrived at the philosophical sense of *representation*. But this passage seems to me to involve something violent and illegitimate. It ought to have been possible to say *representation-to-oneself* [*se-représentation*], and not being able to do this the word should have been renounced. Also it seems to me likely that we did not ourselves derive *representation* from *represent to oneself* but simply copied *Vorstellung* in order to translate it. We are certainly obliged, today, to tolerate this use of the word; but it seems to me hardly French." And after some interesting allusions to Hamelin, Leibniz and Descartes with respect to the use they nevertheless made of the same word Lachelier concludes in this way, and this is the point that matters to me: "There would be grounds for inquiring whether *Vorstellung* was not derived from *sich etwas vorstellen* (to represent something to oneself), and whether the Germans themselves were not shocked when people began to use it in philosophical style." (I note in passing the interest of this insistence on the *self* of *represent to oneself* [*sur le se de représenter*] as well as on the *sich* of *sich vorstellen*. It indicates to what degree Lachelier is rightly sensitive to this auto-affective dimension which is undoubtedly the essential factor in representation and what is more clearly marked in the reflexive verb than in the noun. In representation it matters above all that a subject gives himself room, procures himself, makes room for himself and in front of him for objects: he represents them to himself and sends them to himself, and it is thus that he has them at his disposal).

. . . . .

The reflections I have been presenting to you, if I think of them as expected (or less expected), are expected questions and not conclusions. Here then, to conclude nevertheless, a certain number of questions that I would like to submit to you in their most economical formulation, indeed in the telegraphic form suitable to such a dispatch.

First question. This touches on the history of philosophy, of language and of French philosophical language. Is there such a language, and is it a single language? And what has happened to it or at its borders since the debate of 1901 on the terms *presentation* and *representation* in the *Société française de Philosophie*? What does the development of this question presuppose?

Second question. This relates to the very legitimacy of a general interrogation on the essence of representation, in other words, the use of the name and title "representation" in a colloquium in general. This is my main question, and although I must leave it in a minimally schematic state I should explain it a little more than the preceding one, the more so because it may perhaps lead me to outline another relation to Heidegger. It is still a question of language and translation. One might object, and I take this objection seriously, that in ordinary situations of ordinary language (if there are such things, as we ordinarily think) the question of knowing what we envision under the name of representation is very unlikely to arise, and if it arises it does not last a second. It is adequate in this way to a context which is not saturated but reasonably well determined, as it precisely is in what we call ordinary experience. If I read, if I hear on the radio that the diplomatic or parliamentary representatives [*la représentation diplomatique ou parlementaire*] of some country have been received by the Chief of State, that representatives [*représentants*] of striking workers or the parents of schoolchildren have gone to the Ministry in a delegation, if I read in the paper that this evening there will be a representation of some play, or that such and such a painting represents this or that, etc., I understand without the least equivocation and I do not put my head into my hands to take in what it means. It is clearly enough for me to have the competence usually required in a certain state of society and of its educational system. . . . Given that words always function in an (assumed) context destined to assure in the normal way the normality of their functioning, to ask what they can mean before and outside every such determined context is to study (it might perhaps be said) a pathology or a linguistic dysfunction. The schema is well known. Philosophical questioning about the name and the essence of "representation" before and outside of every particular context would be the very paradigm of this dysfunction. It would necessarily lead to insoluble problems or to pointless language games, or rather to language games which the philosopher would take seriously without perceiving what, in the functioning of language, makes the game possible. In this perspective it would not be a question of excluding philosophical styles or models from ordinary language but of acknowledging their place among others. What we have made of the word "representation" as philosophers in the last centuries or decades would come to be integrated, more or less well, into the ensemble of codes and usages. This also would be a contextual possibility among others.

This type of problematic—of which I indicate only the most rudimentary opening moves—can give rise, as we know, to the most diverse developments, for example on the side of a pragmatics of language; and it is significant that these developments should have found a favorable cultural terrain outside the duel or dialogue of the Gallo-Germanic *Auseinandersetzung* within which I have somewhat confined myself up to now. However it may be with its more or less Anglo-Saxon representatives, from Peirce (with his problematic of the represented as, already, *representamen*), or from Wittgenstein, if he was English, to the most diverse champions of analytic philosophy or speech act theory, is there not in all this a decentering in relation to the *Auseinandersetzung,* which we too readily consider a point of absolute convergence? And in this decentering, even if we do not necessarily follow it along the Anglo-Saxon tracks I have referred to, even if we suspect them of being still too philosophizing in the hegemonic sense of the term, and if in truth they had their first defenders in Central Europe, will there perhaps be found the incitement to a problematic of a different style? It would not be a question simply of submitting so-called philosophical language to ordinary law and making it answer before this last contextual court of appeal, but of asking whether, in the very interior of what offers itself as the philosophical or merely theoretical usage of the word representation, the unity of some semantic center, which would give order to a whole multiplicity of modifications and derivations, is to be presumed. Is not this eminently philosophical presumption precisely of a representative type, in the central sense claimed for the term, in that a single self-same presence delegates itself in it, sends [*envoie*], assembles, and finally recognizes? This interpretation of representation would presuppose a representational pre-interpretation of representation, it would still be a representation of representation. Is not this presumption (unifying, bringing together, derivationist) at work in Heidegger all the way up to his strongest and most necessary displacements? Do we not find an indication of this in the fact that the epoch of representation or *Vorstellung*, or more generally *Gestell*, appears there as an epoch in the destiny or the *Geschick* of being? Although this epoch is neither a mode nor, in the strict sense, a modification of something that is, or of a substantial sense, although no more is it a moment or a determination in the Hegelian sense, it is certainly announced by an *envoi* of being which first of all uncovers itself as presence, more rigorously as *Anwesenheit*, as we have seen. In order for the epoch of representation to have its sense and its unity as an epoch, it must belong to the grouping [*rassemblement*] of a more original [*originaire*] and more powerful *envoi*. And if there had not been the grouping of this *envoi*, the *Geschick* of being, if this *Geschick* had not announced itself from the start as the *Anwesenheit* of being, no interpretation of the epoch of representation would come to order it in the unity of a history of metaphysics. . . . This grouping is the condition, the being-together of what offers itself to thought in order for an epochal figure—here that of representation—to detach itself in its contour and order itself in its rhythm in the unity of a destination, or rather of a "destinality," of being. No doubt the being-together of the *Geschick*, and in it of the *Gestell*, is neither that of a totality, nor that of a system, nor that of an identity comparable to any other. No doubt we should take the same precautions with respect to the grouping of every epochal figure. Nevertheless the question remains: if in a sense that is neither chronological, nor logical, nor intrahistorical in the current sense, all interpretation according to destiny or history [*toute interprétation historiale ou destinale*] prescribes for the epoch of representation (in other words modernity, and in the same text Heidegger translates: the era of the subjectum, of objectivism and subjectivism, of anthropology, of aestheticomoral humanism, etc.) an original *envoi* of being as *Anwesenheit*, which itself translates as presence and then as representation according to translations which are so many mutations in the same, in the being-together of the same *envoi*, then the being-together of the original *envoi* arrives reflexively in a way at itself, the most closely to itself, in *Anwesenheit*. Even if there is dissension [*Zwiespalt*] in what Heidegger calls the great Greek epoch and the experience of *Anwesenheit*, this dissension groups itself in the *legein*, escapes, preserves itself and thus assures a sort of indivisibility of what is destined [*du destinal*]. It is in basing itself on this grouped indivisibility of the *envoi* that Heidegger's reading can single out [*détacher*] epochs, including the most powerful, the longest, and also the most dangerous of all, the epoch of representation in modern times. Since this is not an epoch among others, and since it is *singled out,* in its privilege, in a very particular way, might one not be tempted to say that it is itself detached, sent, delegated, taking the place of what in it dissembles itself, suspends itself, reserves itself, retreats and retires there, namely *Anwesenheit* or even presence? Several types of this detachment will be found (metaphor, metonymy, mode, determination, moment, etc.), they will all be unsatisfactory for essential reasons. But it will be difficult to avoid the question whether the relationship of the epoch of representation to the great Greek epoch is not still interpreted by Heidegger in a representative mode, as if the couple *Anwesenheit/repraesentatio* still dictated the law of its own interpretation, which does no more than to redouble and recognize itself in the historical text it claims to decipher. Behind or under the epoch of representation there would be, drawn back, what it dissembles, covers over, forgets as the very *envoi* of what it still represents, presence or *Anwesenheit* in its grouping in the Greek *legein* which will have saved it, first of all from dislocation. My question then is the following, and I formulate it too quickly: Wherever this being-together or with itself of the *envoi* of being divides itself, defies the *legein,* frustrates the destination of the *envoi,* is not the whole schema of Heidegger's reading challengeable in principle, deconstructed from a historical point of view? If there has been representation, it is perhaps (and Heidegger would recognize this) just because the *envoi* of being was originally menaced in its being-together, in its *Geschick,* by divisibility or dissension (what I would call dissemination). Can we not then conclude that if there has been representation, the epochal reading that Heidegger proposes for it becomes, in virtue of this fact, problematic from the beginning, at least as a normative reading (and it wishes to be this also), if not as an open questioning of what offers itself to thought beyond the problematic, and even beyond the question as a question of being, of a grouped destiny or of the *envoi* of being?

What I have just suggested concerns not only the reading of Heidegger, the one he makes of the destination of representation or the one we would make of his own reading. What I have just suggested concerns not only the whole ordering of epochs or periods in the presumed unity of a history of metaphysics or of the West. What I have just suggested concerns the very credit we would wish, as philosophers, to accord to a centered and centralized organization of all the fields or of all the sections of representation, grouped around a sustaining sense, of a fundamental interpretation. If there has been representation, as I said a moment ago, it is that the division will have been stronger, strong enough to have as a consequence that this sustaining sense no longer keeps, saves, or guarantees anything in a sufficiently rigorous fashion.

So the problematics or metamorphoses of representation that are called "modern" would no longer at all be representations of the same, diffractions of a unique sense starting from a single crossroads, a single place of meeting or passing for convergent enterprises, a single coming together or a single congress.

If I had not been afraid of abusing your time and your patience, I would perhaps have tried to put to the test such a difference of representation, a difference that would no longer, in contrast to *Anwesenheit,* organize itself according to presence or as presence, a difference that would no longer represent the same or the reflexivity of the destiny of being, a difference that would not be recoverable in the sending of the self, a difference as a sending that would not be one, and not a sending of the self but sendings of the other, of others. I would have tried this proof not in proposing some demonstration cutting across the different sections proposed by our Program Committee, across different types of problematic of representation itself: rather and preferably in going over to the side of what *is not represented* in our program. Two examples of what is thus not represented and I will have finished.

First example. In the various sections anticipated, is there at least a virtual *topos* for what, under the name of psychoanalysis and under the signature of Freud, has left to us such a strange body [of texts] so strangely charged with "representation" in all languages? To put this another way, does the vocabulary of *Vorstellung,* of the *Vorstellungsrepräsentanz,* in its abundance, its complexity, the prolix difficulties of the discourse that carries it, manifest a determinate and complete episode of the epoch of representation, as if, without thinking them as such, Freud was arguing confusedly with himself under the implacable constraints of a conceptual program and heritage? The very concept of drive and the "destiny of the drive" [*Triebschicksal*], which Freud situates at the frontier or the limit between the somatic and the psychic, seems not to be constructible without having recourse to a representative scheme, in the sense first of all of delegation. Similarly the concept of repression (primary or secondary, strictly speaking) is constructed on a concept of representation: repression bears essentially on representations or representatives, delegates. This emphasis on delegation, if we follow Laplanche and Pontalis here in their concern for systematization, would give rise to two interpretations or two formulations on Freud's part. Sometimes the drive itself is considered a "psychic representative" [*psychische Repräsentanz* or *psychischer Repräsentant*] of somatic excitations; sometimes the drive is considered the somatic process of excitation itself, and the latter represented by what Freud calls "representatives of the drive" [*Triebrepräsentanz* or *Triebrepräsentant*] which in their turn are envisaged either—principally—as representatives in the form of representation in the sense of *Vorstellung* [*Vorstellungsrepräsentanz* or *-repräsentant*], with a greater insistence on the ideational aspect, or under the aspect of the quantum of affect of which Freud came to say that it was more important in the representative of the drive than the representational aspect (intellectual or ideational). Laplanche and Pontalis propose to surmount Freud's apparent contradictions or oscillations in what they call his "formulations" by recalling that nevertheless, and I quote, "One idea remains always present: the *relation* of the somatic to the psychic is conceived neither in the mode of parallelism nor in that of a causal link; it has to be understood in comparison to the relation that holds between a delegate and the person he represents," adding in a note: "We know that, in such a case, the delegate, while he is in principle no more than the 'proxy' of the one he represents, enters into a new system of relations which runs the risk of modifying his perspective and of influencing the instructions that have been given him." What Laplanche and Pontalis call a *comparison* bears the whole weight of the problem. If this comparison with the structure of delegation is to be something on the basis of which we are to interpret matters as weighty as the relations between soul and body, the destiny of drives, repression, etc., the object of the comparison must no longer be considered as self-evident. What does it mean to charge or delegate someone, if we do not allow this movement to be derived from, interpreted as, or compared with anything else? What is a mission or a sending? This type of question can be justified on the basis of other parts of Freudian discourse, and more narrowly of other appeals to the word or the concept of representation (for example the representation of a goal [*Zielvorstellung*] or above all the distinction between representations of words and representations of things [*Wort-* and *Sach-* or *Dingvorstellung*] with respect to which we know the role Freud assigned to it between the primary and secondary processes or in the structure of schizophrenia). One might wonder if, as Laplanche and Pontalis suggest in a slightly embarrassed way on several occasions, the translation of representation or representative by "signifier" lends itself to a clarification of Freudian difficulties. That obviously is what Freud's Lacanian heritage is basically betting on today. Here I can only point out the stake it has in this question, which I have tried to situate in other writings. And the question I pose about Freud (in his relation to the epoch of representation) can in principle apply also to Lacan. At all events, when Laplanche and Pontalis say about the word *Vorstellung* that "its meaning [*acception*] is not modified by Freud at the beginning but the use he makes of it is original," this distinction between meaning and use is precisely where the problem lies. Can we distinguish between the semantic content (ultimately stable, continuous, self-identical) and the diversity of uses, functions, and contextual surrounds while assuming that these latter cannot displace, indeed totally deconstruct, the identity of the former? In other words, are so-called "modern" developments—like Freudian psychoanalysis, but we could cite others—thinkable only by reference to a fundamental semantic tradition, or again to a unifying epochal determination of representation, which they can still be considered to represent? or on the other hand should we find in them an incitement leading us to look altogether differently at changes of direction in domains of thought [*la diffraction des champs*]? Are we justified in saying, for example, that the Lacanian theorization of *Vorstellungs-repräsentanz* in terms of a binary signifier producing the disappearance, the *aphanisis* of the subject, is wholly self-contained within what Heidegger calls the epoch of representation? I can do no more here than point out the setting of this problem, which cannot admit of a simple response. I do so in referring chiefly to two chapters of the Seminar on *The Four Fundamental Concepts of Psycho-Analysis* ("Tuché and Automaton" on the one hand, "Aphanisis" on the other). It is highly significant that, in these chapters in particular, Lacan should define his relation to the Cartesian "I think" and to Hegelian dialectic, that is to say to the two most powerful organizing moments that Heidegger assigns to the reign of representation. The structural elements of the problematic to which I refer here have been recognized and fundamentally interpreted for the first time in the works of Lacoue-Labarthe and Nancy, from *Le titre de la lettre,* their joint work, to their latest publications, respectively *Le sujet de la philosophie* and *Ego sum.*

The *second* and last *example* promised concerns the limit-question of the unrepresentable. To think the limit of representation is to think the unrepresented or the unrepresentable. There are very many ways of placing the emphasis here; and this displacement of emphasis can effect powerful swerves. If to think the unrepresentable is to think beyond representation in order to think representation from its limit, that can be understood as a tautology. And that is a first answer, which could well be that of Hegel or that of Heidegger. Both of them think of thought, that of which representation is afraid (according to the remark of Heidegger who wonders simply if we are not afraid of thinking), as something that crosses the boundary or takes a step beyond or to the hither side of representation. This is even the definition of thought for Hegel: *Vorstellung* is a mediation, a mean [*Mitte*] between the unfree intellect and the free intellect, in other words thought. This is a double and differentiated way of thinking thought as the beyond of representation. But it is the form of this passage, the *Aufhebung* of representation, that Heidegger still interprets as something that belongs to the epoch of representation. Nevertheless, although Heidegger and Hegel are not thinking thought as the beyond of representation in the same way here, a certain possibility of a relation to the unrepresentable seems to me to bring Hegel and Heidegger together (bring together at least what these proper names refer to if not what they represent). This possibility would concern the unrepresentable not only as that which is foreign to the very structure of representation, as what one *cannot* represent, but rather and also what one *must not* represent, whether or not this has the structure of the representable. I mention here the immense problem of the *prohibited* that bears on representation, on what it has been possible to translate more or less legitimately (another extraordinary problem) from a Jewish or Islamic world as "representation." Now I would not say that this immense problem, whether it concerns objectifying representation, mimetic representation or even simple presentation, or yet indeed simple naming, is just overlooked by thoughts of a Hegelian or Heideggerian type. But it seems to me in principle relegated to a secondary or derivative place in Heidegger (in any case it does not to my knowledge form the object of any specific attention). And as for Hegel, who speaks of it more than once, in particular in his *Lectures on Aesthetics,* it is perhaps not unwarranted to say that the interpretation of this prohibition is found derived and reinscribed in a procedure of much wider scope, dialectical in structure, in the course of which the prohibition does not constitute an absolute event that comes from a wholly-other which would quite break up or asymmetrically reverse the progress of a dialectizable procedure. This does not necessarily mean that the essential traits of the prohibition are misunderstood or distorted in it. For example the disproportion between the infinity of God and the limits of human representation are taken into account and thus the wholly-other can be seen to declare itself [in Hegel's treatment]. Conversely, if one argued to some dialectical effacement of the cutting edge of the prohibition, this would not imply that any taking into account of this cutting edge (for example in a psychoanalytic discourse) would not eventually lead to an analogous result, that is to a re-inscribing of the origin and significance of the prohibition upon representation in an intelligible and wider process in which the unrepresentable would disappear again like the wholly-other. But is not disappearance, non-phenomenality, the destiny of the wholly-other and of the unrepresentable, indeed of the unpresentable? Here again I can only indicate (by mentioning work that has been carried out during the whole of this year with students and colleagues) the beginning and the necessity of an interrogation for which nothing is in the slightest degree certain, above all what is calmly translated as prohibition or as representation.

To what, to whom, to what destination have I been ceaselessly referring in the course of this introduction, at once insistently and elliptically? I will venture to say: to back-references [*renvois*] and references which would no longer be representative. Beyond a closure of representation whose form could no longer be linear, indivisible, circular, encyclopedic, or totalizing, I have tried to retrace a path opened on a thought of the *envoi* which, while (like the *Geschick des Seins* of which Heidegger speaks) of a structure as yet innocent of representation, did not as yet gather itself to itself as an *envoi* of being through *Anwesenheit,* presence and then representation. This *envoi* is as it were pre-ontological, because it does not gather itself together or because it gathers itself only in dividing itself, in differentiating [*différant*] itself, because it is not original or originally a sending-from [*envoi-de*] (the *envoi* of something-that-is or of a present which would precede it, still less of a subject, or of an object by and for a subject), because it is not single and does not begin with itself although nothing present precedes it; and it issues forth only in already sending back: it issues forth only on the basis of the other, the other in itself without itself. Everything begins by referring back [*par le renvoi*], that is to say, does not begin; and once this breaking open or this partition divides, from the very start, every *renvoi,* there is not a single *renvoi* but from then on, always, a multiplicity of *renvois,* so many different traces referring back to other traces and to traces of others. This divisibility of the *envoi* has nothing negative about it, it is not a lack, it is altogether different from subject, from signifier, or that letter of which Lacan says that it does not withstand partition and that it always reaches its destination. This divisibility or this *différance* is the condition for there being an *envoi,* possibly an *envoi* of being, a dispensation or a gift of being and time, of the present and of representation. These *renvois* of traces or these traces of *renvois* do not have the structure of representatives or of representation, nor of signifiers, nor of symbols, nor of metaphors, nor of metonymies, etc. But as these *renvois* from the other and to the other, these traces of *différance,* are not original and transcendental conditions on the basis of which philosophy traditionally tries to derive effects, subdeterminations, or even epochs, it cannot be said for example that representative (or signifying or symbolic, etc.) structure *befalls* them; we shall not be able to assign periods or have some epoch of representation follow upon these *renvois.* As soon as there are *renvois,* and it is always already, something like representation no longer waits and we must perhaps arrange to tell this story differently, from *renvois* of *renvois* to *renvois* of *renvois,* in a destiny which is never certain of gathering itself up, of identifying itself, or of determining itself (I do not know if this can be said with or without Heidegger, and it does not matter). This is the only chance—but it is only chance—for there to be history, meaning, presence, truth, language, theme, thesis, and colloquium. Still we have to suppose that the chance is given us—and the law of this chance, the question remaining open as to whether, to say it in classical language, the irrepresentable of *envois* is what produces the law (for example, the prohibition of representation) or whether it is the law which produces the irrepresentable by prohibiting representation. Whatever the necessity of this question of the relationship between law and traces (or the *renvois* of traces, the *renvois* as traces), it exhausts itself perhaps when we cease representing law to ourselves, apprehending law itself under the species of the representable. Perhaps law itself outreaches any representation, perhaps it is never before us, as what posits itself in a figure or composes a figure for itself. (The guardian of the law and the man from the country are "before the law," *Vor dem Gesetz,* says Kafka's title, only at the cost of never coming to see it, never being able to arrive at it. It is neither presentable nor representable, and the "entry" into it, according to an order which the man from the country interiorizes and gives himself, is put off until death.) The law has often been considered as that which puts things in place, posits itself and gathers itself up in composition (thesis, *Gesetz,* in other words what governs the order of representation), and autonomy in this respect always presupposes representation, as thematization, becoming-theme. But perhaps the law itself manages to do no more than transgress the figure of all possible representation. Which is difficult to conceive, as it is difficult to conceive anything at all beyond representation, but commits us perhaps to thinking altogether differently.

Translated by Peter and Mary Ann Caws

Notes

*Derrida's French title is *"Envoi,"* which has a literary as well as a literal sense; in certain poetic forms the envoi served as a dedication, a signing-off, a summary, something with which the poem was as it were "sent off" to the prince, perhaps, for whom it was written. *"Envoyer"* means just "to send," and since Derrida's own text was the opening address to a congress of French-speaking philosophical societies (whose members had been "sent" to Strasbourg, where it was held—another significant fact in the context of the paper—as "representing" their respective philosophical constituencies) his title has also the sense of a "send-off" for the work of the congress. A further sense of *"envoi"* as "dispatch," something sent with urgency and in telegraphic language, is also sometimes in play in this text.

As the text proceeds, however, the force of the term becomes more metaphysical. The German equivalent of *"envoyer"* is *"schicken,"* and in Heidegger the term *"Geschick"* (often translated "destiny") occurs in connection with the emergence of the idea of Being, which is as it were "sent out" from some origin as "destined." This origin is clearly not accessible directly; if it is, in Derrida's language, the "original *envoi*" (and in this part of the text I have tended to leave the term in French), it can be approached only by means of a *"renvoi"* or "sending-back.'' But "*renvoi*" brings its own complexities, since it is also the term used for "reference" in the scholarly sense (to footnotes, to earlier works, etc.). The problems of translation thus posed are considerable and have sometimes been solved in this case also by simply not translating at all.

The phrase that Derrida takes as a starting-point of his meditation: *On dirait alors que nous sommes en représentation,* I have translated as "One might say that we represent something," exploiting the sense of *en représentation* that conveys the responsibilities of a class or office to be seen as standing for something, as maintaining standards. But of course it means all the other things he suggests as well. Finally, the singular title "*Envoi*" echoes the plural "*Envois*" that Derrida uses as the title of the first part of *La Carte postale.*—TRANS. (PC) [Jacques Derrida, *La Carte postale: de Socrate à Freud et au-delà* (Paris: Aubier-Flammarion, 1980), English translation by Alan Bass, *The Post Card: From Socrates to Freud and Beyond* (Chicago: University of Chicago Press, 1987).—ED.]

1. Martin Heidegger, *Holzwege* (Frankfurt: Klostermann, 1950), p. 84.

2. Jacques Lacan, *Écrits* (Paris: Seuil, 1966), p. 835.

3. *Ibid.,* p. 860.

6

Derrida on Representation: A Postscript

Peter Caws

Like so much of the rest of his writing, Derrida's essay *Envoi*, translated here as "Sending: On Representation" (a note on the senses of the title is appended to the translation), is an occasional text, one produced in response to a contingent event, something that happened or befell as it were in the writer's path ("occasion" being from *ob* with *cadere* "to fall"), in this case an invitation to open a congress of French-speaking philosophical societies devoted to the topic of representation. Occasions can serve as touchstones for a writer's preoccupations and methods, and on this one Derrida was obviously both on form and in character; the result is a text that is exemplary both in its strengths and in its idiosyncrasies. In reading it we can learn a great deal, not only about Derrida but about the ambiguous reputation he has come to enjoy among philosophers in the English-speaking world.

The strengths of the text, as of Derridean texts in general, are its philosophical scholarship and its philosophical imagination. Derrida works (or plays) along a philological axis that extends from Greek via Latin to German, and he knows intimately its languages and its literature, from the pre-Socratics to Heidegger. Especially Heidegger. French thought, he thinks, is hampered by its Latinity; when it comes to representation, with its *re*, its *prae*, its *esse*, the intricate burden of this Latinity needs to be lightened by some Teutonic directness: *Vorstellung*. But just what is stood before us? Presumably existing things themselves, and indeed once, Derrida suggests, for the Greeks perhaps, consciousness could face the world without the interposition of representation. By now, though, he seems to think, we are irremediably involved with layer upon layer of representation; even the bluntness of the German becomes indirect, complicated by reflection, corrupted by Latinity: *Anwesenheit, Vorstellungsrepräsentanz*.

"Sending" is a meditation on language, on translation, on congresses of philosophy, on the organization of the discipline of philosophy, on the history of the long slide from immediacy to insulation, from Being to the whole series of stand-ins for Being. It is a meditation that follows a tortuous path, spontaneously, we may sometimes feel perversely, a path strewn with linguistic allusions and rhetorical questions, whole series of them, a *long* path which, like the *Holzwege* that Heidegger took as an image for some of his own excursions, leads one is not quite sure where. Some philosophical texts begin with a difficulty and show us how to think differently about the issue; Derrida's ends with a difficulty (of conceiving anything at all beyond representation) and with a call for thinking differently—how, he doesn't say.

In spite of the classical, Socratic nature of this aggravation of the problem (and we must remember, to do him justice, that Derrida's communication was at the *opening* of the congress) we are nevertheless tempted to feel a certain Anglo-Saxon impatience with it. Can't we still get at the unrepresented things? Not in the Husserlian mode of *Zu den Sachen selbst* but in the down-to-earth mode of physicalism, for example (which it is true, as Derrida shows himself to be aware, the Anglo-Saxons, or Anglo-Americans, got from Vienna)? So as not to start a chain of unanswered rhetorical questions of my own let me say that I do not, myself, think that the debate is closed on the metaphysics of presence, nor that the transparent anchoring of discourse in reference is as hopeless as Derrida or his local allies (I think, for example, of Rorty) claim it is. If there were a way of cutting through to a primordial observer-world relationship, then a lot of what Derrida does here would, from a certain point of view, be *mere* scholarship. It would not thereby be deprived of philosophical interest, but we could leave it safely aside as we got on with other things.

But one has to be circumspect all the same in trying any abrupt dismissal of Derrida by means of down-to-earth cutting-through. It was another Derridean text, prepared for another congress in the same series, in Montreal rather than (as in this case) in Strasbourg, and devoted to the topic of communication,[1] whose treatment in this way by Searle[2] provoked Derrida's prolonged and sarcastic rebuttal in "Limited Inc a b c . . . "[3] In spite of its word-play (calculated perhaps to produce more dismissive Anglo-American impatience, if not downright embarrassment) "Limited Inc" does succeed in showing the *complication* of Derrida's thought, a feature of it that he admittedly enjoys and that is not addressed by the relative straightforwardness of Searle's comment.

One might ask of this complication whether it is baroque or Byzantine—whether it is indulged in for aesthetic effect, or contrived for political effect. This is a hard question, the answer to which depends on beliefs and intentions not made plain on the surface of the text. As a strategy Derrida's style might be a fending-off; his texts are dauntingly long in relation to the intrinsic interest of their subject-matter ("Limited Inc" is in fact longer than Austin's *How To Do Things With Words,* which is the pretext for its latter half). But it might also be a send-*up.*

In the case of "On Representation" there is certainly a political undertone, having to do with an old xenophobia in French thought, with the permeability of the French-German border, linguistic and philosophical if not cultural and juridical. But a different kind of politics, the philosophical politics of Europe and of the English-speaking world, may also be in play. In "Signature Event Context" and "Limited Inc" Derrida manifests an almost obsessive concern with "linguistic" philosophy; the length and passion of his treatment of Searle & Co. betray an involvement that runs very deep. The first *Envois* of *La Carte postale* to which the singular *Envoi* of "Sending" consciously refers were *sent* from Oxford (the *carte postale* mainly in question is a representation of Socrates writing, prodded from behind by Plato—Plato metonymically compelling Socrates to be his mouthpiece, a bit of deception at the beginning of Western metaphysics, just as Heidegger always said).

Derrida feels rather dépaysé, rather off center, in Oxford, the headquarters as it were of linguistic philosophy. "Since the beginning of this trip I have the impression . . . that everything looks like everything else, myself first of all, in a postcard, the postcard—that I am. There is only that, this reproduction of a reproduction of which I am dying . . . "[4] In "Sending" he is at home again, and although the topic is conceptual he sometimes seems to be saying: this too is linguistic philosophy, on *our* territory, and a more scholarly, more intricate, more subtle linguistic philosophy than that of Austin or Searle. It is certainly philosophizing about language and about its limitations, the lack of a "semantic center" for terms as laden with history as "representation"; there is something Socratic about that too, and it is consciously invoked by Derrida in his engaging image of the tipsy Socrates arriving at dawn and asking what all cases of representation have in common.

But is Derrida's (rhetorical) questioning really Socratic? Socrates, it seems to me, tended to use his interrogations to establish that people didn't know what they were talking about, hadn't thought their positions through—and yet were willing to let heavy consequences hang on their thoughtlessness: the conduct of the state or the health of the soul. Derrida on the other hand shows that we know quite well, for the most part, what we are talking about, it is just that our ways of doing so, of saying exactly what we mean (or of knowing exactly what linguistic expressions mean) have become problematic because of the ramifications and accretions of language. At the same time the issues that hang on *these* uncertainties often seem less than urgent. It is true that Heidegger writes as if they were of tremendous moment, but the truth is that to many of us representation just doesn't seem that portentous.

This remark may bring us as close to the essence of the Derrida problem as we are likely to get. A great deal of philosophy in the English-speaking world, since Moore, say, has been devoted to the *dissolution* (or as I am almost tempted to say the "deconstruction" *avant la lettre*) of linguistic tangles, to the cure of bad philosophical habits acquired in imitation of pretentious Germanic scholarship, to the re-opening of basic questions stripped of their inherited baggage, "in plain English" as it were. Is there an expression "in plain French"?—I think not. (The trouble may lie there!) At the same time the Viennese tributary to the English-speaking mainstream brought a direct confrontation with empirical evidence, and seemed to restore the immediacy of the as-yet-unrepresented. There turned out to be plenty to say about language, but just not the sort of thing, in this tradition, that Derrida says.

So there is a basic lack of common philosophical purpose, not so much between Anglo-American and Continental *philosophy* (that, as I keep saying in the hope that it will turn out to be true, is a dead issue) as between the analytic habits of their respective philosophers of language—for if Derrida isn't a philosopher of language I don't know what he is. Derridean philosophy of language delights in pointing out all the connections we haven't thought of in a text or way of speaking, all the tricky ways in which the linguistic complexities we have unconsciously internalized may be leading us (or our interlocutors) down false trails, all the conceptual and historical intricacies language conceals, all the worn and used associations it drags along with it, all the marks of wear and use it carries in itself, openly or under the surface. But none of this need affect the main frame, as it were, the working structure that carries the burden of everyday commerce with the world—it seems peripheral, about as relevant to basic questions of grammar or semantics as Old Church Slavonic to the revolution.

It is just the central working features of language, the indexicals and performatives, the markers and transformations, the levels of use and mention, the opacity of reference and the indeterminacy of translation (and these in principle, with examples, rather than in practice, with cases), that preoccupy Anglo-American philosophy of language. Derrida knows some of this but speaks of it with a certain Gallic mockery: "It's the ' "Fido"-Fido' problem (you know, Ryle, Russell etc., and the question of knowing whether I call my dog or mention the name he bears, whether I use or name his name. I adore these theorizings, often Oxfordian moreover, their extraordinary and necessary subtlety as much as their imperturbable naivete, psychoanalytically speaking; they will always trust in the law of quotation marks. . . .)."[5]

Again the issue is as much between English and French as between Anglo-American and continental philosophy. Derrida finds English rebarbative: "How do they manage to avoid the plural? Their grammar is very dubious. I wouldn't have been able to love you in English, you are (*tu es*) untranslatable."[6] How in fact do we manage to do philosophy in English? That seems to be the underlying question, and I will devote some closing remarks to it. For English is in fact the confluence of the two linguistic traditions that confront one another across the Rhine in "Sending"; and whether it was the cold air of the North Sea or the wind and sky of the frontier or the westward vista over the Pacific (as seen, for example, from Berkeley), something in the history of this bastard language, by the Germanic out of the Latin, seems to have opened it up and lightened it and developed habits of plain speech.

Seen from the crowded center of European sophistication these may indeed have an appearance of naivete, but they seem to work, not only for grasping the empirical more or less transparently but also for laying down relatively simple hypotheses about language itself which nevertheless show themselves to be capable of generating the complexities of its actual uses. This strategy of approaching the complex through the straightforward used to be recommended by Descartes, but these days some of the least Cartesian thinkers in the world are French. The point is that although it is certainly quite all right to be baroque or even Byzantine there is no need to be if one isn't so inclined; at the same time mutual recriminations between those who are and aren't seem fairly pointless.

It is partly a matter of character, and perhaps less national than personal. How do *I* stand with respect to representation? Am I troubled by the veils that lie between me and the world, even perhaps between me and myself? In one of the "sendings" of *La Carte postale* Derrida encloses a picture of himself, taken in a "photomaton" at Paddington: "When I have nothing to do in a public place I photograph myself and usually I burn myself [*je me brule*]."[7] It is hardly necessary to point out that it is the picture that is burned, yet the assimilation of the subject to its representation is typical.

We can lose ourselves in the play of representations—or we can try to think the world beyond it and ourselves as it were on this side of it. Between them, even so, the play, if we let it, will expand to fill the available philosophical space. It may even come to seem that the play and its law— for this is a serious matter, as Derrida in all non-seriousness is prepared to admit—are all there is. On this point however even Derrida, finally, is not so sure. There may be a limit to representation, he thinks, in the endless backward reference of history; there may be a limit in the law of the unrepresentable. There may be one, we might still want unregenerately to add, in the immediacy of existence. Perhaps all three.

Notes

1. Jacques Derrida, "Signature, Event, Context," *Glyph* 1, 1977: 172–177.

2. *Ibid.*, pp. 198–208.

3. Jacques Derrida, "Limited Inc a b c . . . ," *Glyph* 2, 1977: 162–254.

4. Jacques Derrida, *La Carte postale* (Paris: Flammarion, 1980), p. 41. [*The Postcard: From Socrates to Freud and Beyond*, translated by Alan Bass (Chicago: University of Chicago Press, 1987), p. 35—ED.]

5. *Ibid.*, p. 108; "psychoanalytically speaking" is in English in the original. [English translation, p. 98.—ED.]

6. *Ibid.*, p. 124. [English translation, p. 113.—ED.]

7. *Ibid.*, p. 42. [English translation, p. 37.—ED.]

7

The Interpretation of a Text

Manfred Frank

Translator's Introduction

Manfred Frank begins "The Interpretation of a Text" [*"Textausle-gung,"* 1974] by supporting a premise that he attributes to Schleiermacher: "Nothing is perfectly clear, everything demands the work of interpretation." The interpreter, moreover, looks for rules: rules "that determine the grammar of a given text," grammar being "the totality of an epoch's socio-cultural codes"; and rules by which the text is a unique expression of that grammar.

But what is a text? Frank answers that it is "a discourse [*Rede*] that is fixed in writing, cohesive [*zusammenhängende*], and for the most part literary." And because it is written it has qualities that distinguish it from a speech-act. The latter "reveals a certain aspect of the world" in which it takes place, whereas the former has no such limitations, and can refer to any world, even one that has vanished. Understanding the latter leads to the intentions of the speaker, but a written text is "in a certain sense independent of the intentions of its creator."

With this distinction in view, Frank criticizes the interpretation theory of E. D. Hirsch, Jr., because of the central position it accords authorial intention. According to Frank, "writing detaches that which is written from the meaning [*Sinn*] that [the author] gives his words." It is, he maintains, "in the understanding of its readers that the text, even the biographical text, gains a reference [*Bedeutung*] that surpasses the memory of its origin." In this way, interpretation is "creative reading": it imputes meaning.

Frank argues that there is generally more to a text than the fact that it is written: it has aesthetic qualities; interpretation is often and "rightly associated with the interpretation of poetic (or sacred) texts." To understand such a text "entails enjoying it as a work of art." In this connection, Frank presents Derrida's objection to a hermeneutics like Ricouer's that "takes poetic expression for the small detour that (immaterial) meaning pursues in order to become (materially) identifiable.'' Frank presents Derrida as having concluded that this is "the legacy of Plato and Aristotle, namely the idea that truth . . . may be fragmented in appearance, but that the philosopher or text interpreter gathers in once again that which has been scattered about.'' This Platonic conception fails to recognize in the text an individual "expression" that "is the condition of the possibility of (the text's) meaning.'' It fails, that is, to come to terms with the text aesthetically.

Regarding the coherence that characterizes a text, Frank contends that "the unity of the text (especially of the poetic one) is not a function of its grammar but of the intellectual mobility of its reader whose . . . creative power, through interpretation, makes up for the absence of a textual unity.''

Text Analysis and Text Hermeneutics

A. Three Characteristics of the Text-as-Work

If we find hardly satisfactory the information that textual linguistics puts in our hands regarding the criteria of a text's coherence, we will not deny that something like order or structurization reigns in the "polyfunctional" or "disseminal" language forms [*Sprachgebilden*] of the avant garde. Even if the semantic interpretation leaves us in the lurch, we do not cease to conceive of these language forms as the deposits of purposefully creative and order-giving activities: as *works* [*Werke*].

Unfortunately, the signification of this expression—"work"—is hardly less disputed than that of "text." Andras Sandor has recently suggested that we only speak of a text when the "material structure of expression" ["*materielle Ausdrucksgefüge*"] is meant (S. J. Schmidt speaks of the "text form to be filled out" ["*Textformular*"]), but of the work as the totality of its conversions into discourse, interpretation or presentation [*Aufführung*]. According to this, the written text displays itself in "work manifestations" the ideal unity of which is constituted by "*the* work."[1] Thus Wolfgang Iser writes: "The work is the being-constituted [*Konstituiertsein*] of the text in the consciousness of the reader."[2] He too uses, if not consistently, "text" in the sense of an "objective-material structure of expression that is not concretized, a text form to be filled out.''

Now apart from the fact that the etymology of both *work* and *text* points back to the reference of "basketwork" ["*Flechtwerk*"], and that the term "work" also functions in modern aesthetics (e.g., for Adorno) as a criterion of delimitation for premodern artistic creations, Iser and Sandor have committed this term to a reference that is not confirmed by our use of language. It seems reasonable, therefore, to hold to the well-tested philological definition given by Schleiermacher. In his lectures on hermeneutics he distinguished three characteristics in the content of the work,[3] for which he also uses the expression "deed-thing" [*Tat-sache:* without the hyphen "fact"]. By this he understands—literally—a meaningful *thing* that owes its existence to the *deed* of an individual who creates meaning. As a fact the work is "structured" (incidentally he introduced the concept of structurization—*Strukturiertheit*—into the terminology of our field, as J. Wach has already emphasized[4]).

Then "the work" is subsumed under a certain "genre" (discourse), a conventionalized "pattern of style (language use)." Schleiermacher speaks also of a "type fixed in the language" or of the "power of a form already fixed":[5] for example, it is a systematic scholarly work, a letter, a section in a handbook or a lyric poem. The genre does not want to be overlooked: only those who identify it can establish where the author follows a convention and where he proceeds beyond it. Thus, for example, in Thomas Mann's *Doktor Faustus* an imitation of the powerfully traditional genre of the lives of saints was long held to be the willful style of the chronicler Zeitblom. Yet of course every work—this is the third characteristic—contains more or less prominent marks of an *individual composition*. It has an unmistakable *style* that it shares with no other work and that to this extent evades the rules of codification. The style is the irreducible particularity [*Nicht-Allgemeine*] of the work.

Of these three characteristics of the work—structurization, membership in a genre and style—it clearly is style alone, the individual use of discourse, that we can bring into harmony with the definition of the text attempted at the outset. For only style—whether written or spoken—is a characteristic of discourse, and texts were up to this point, of course, determined to be written discourses.

B. Outlines of a Structural Text Analysis

One could also have arrived at this conclusion through reflection on the related references of the terms "structure" and "text." To be structurized entails two things for a work: (1) the expressive substances of the individual signs must clearly be distinct from all others of their kind at their own level of constitution; and (2) they must assume a quite particular position relative to the entire meaning within a hierarchy of levels of constitution. At the same time that would be a somewhat too broadly undertaken etymological interpretation of the Latin word *structura*. It is widely known that the so-called structuralists have analyzed the system of language according to this model. Already with Schleiermacher the point of the concept of structure was that the "language values" [*"sprachliche Werte"*], as he calls them—in other words the references of the signs distinguished and interwoven in a system—cannot be conceived of as subsequent additions to the work of expressive articulation. The significance (of the sign) is rather the work of arrangement and segmentation (of the expression) itself. Thus it does not precede the sign in the sense that subsequently it is only named by the expression. Rather the significance of the signs is at first formed at the intersection of the sliding levels of expression [*signifiant*] and meaning [*signifié*]. That is, one and the same movement are synthesized with each other and in the process are determined, distinguished, and established for what they are.

This is—in broad outlines—the basic insight of linguistic structuralism. Before its transferability into the domain of texts is examined, it is important to indicate the semantic proximity, grasped in this way, of the concept of *structure* to the concept of the text. The current *metaphor of interweaving* points to this already. In texts, says Husserl (in section 124 of *Ideas*), "strata" of expressions and references are "interwoven." If the stratum of expression is already based in itself, one could pull it aside and lay bare the equally independent stratum of cuts that create meaning beneath it. But that's not the way it works. For its part the "upper stratum" is embedded in the "lower stratum," and warp and woof cannot be separated from each other without undoing the entire fabric. "This forces us to replace the geological metaphor of layers with what in an actual sense is textual (in other words, handwoven) pictoriality."[6] Fabrics are texts [*texta sunt*]. They relate the discursive (the meaning) to the non-discursive (the expression); the linguistic layer is "interwoven" with the pre-linguistic layer according to a regulated system of the kind of text.

From this parallel between *structure* and *text* the following becomes immediately clear: although texts are written discourses (and thus in Saussure's distinction of *langue*—language system—and *parole*—language use—belong to the structural level of *parole*), one can describe them in an analogous way to the procedures of linguists insofar as texts are not only actions [*Tathandlungen*] but also works [*Tatsachen*]. It is well-known that this was the methodological basis of operations for the *structuralist analysis of texts* as it gradually grew out of the philological practice of "grammatical interpretation" under the influence above all of Saussure, the Russian formalists and the structural mythology of Claude Lévi-Strauss and as it in our own time was continued and differentiated by Émile Benveniste, A. Julien Greimas, Roland Barthes, and Julia Kristeva. The first postulate of this theory demands to extend structural methods, which at first were tried in phonology and lexical semantics on smaller units of language than those of the sentence (phonemes, morphemes, syntagmas), to discourse—thus to chains of so-called "large units" (sentences and intentionally interpreted expressions).[7] This postulate merely returns, as we see, in textual linguistics.

Being composed systematically is thus no privilege of language; it equally characterizes ensembles of significance at higher stages, such as the discourse of an epoch, of a myth, of an ideology, of a genre, of a single piece of writing, as far as their "language elements" are systematically connected as different complexes of significance through the unity of a view that has been taken [*Hinsichtnahme*] (of that which "the author had in mind"). Further, in order to describe those ensembles of significance in this way their "language elements" need to be distinguished clearly from each other according to the law of determination through antithesis,[8] and also to be arranged hierarchically on different levels of constitution.

This in any case is the viewpoint of the "*structure* of a piece of writing,"[9] as Schleiermacher's "grammatical interpretation" openly elucidated and tried it for what was likely the first time in the history of hermeneutics. In the process of text structurization two levels of arrangement are to be distinguished: the vertical relations, in which the linguistic or textual-linguistic orders approach one another (the phonetic, phonological, morphological, syntactic, contextual, pragmatic, isotopic, and so on—E. Benveniste speaks of *integrative* relations); and the horizontal relations, which sustain the elements of a homogenous order with each other, in other words the rules on *one* particular level of constitution that decide their *distribution* (for example, the order of words in the sentence, of sentences in the paragraph, of paragraphs in the text, of the text in the "complete language area" of its epoch and in intertextuality, and so on: here the different steps of the hermeneutic spiral become visible, as Schleiermacher conceives of them in his speech to the Academy of 1828[10]). Schleiermacher already had in mind this double arrangement of every piece of writing, explicitly considered by Benveniste and applied by Greimas to texts,[11] when he distinguished relations of *coordination* from those of the *subordination* of the units of signification ("elements") with regard to the whole meaning of a piece.[12]

What he labeled *grammatical interpretation* anticipates, as Peter Szondi first observed,[13] in outline form the working hypothesis of structurization as it—no doubt at an advanced level of the operation of linguistics—has been developed and in part practiced in our own day above all by A. J. Greimas and R. Barthes.[14] Its advantage is to make the work of understanding the meaning not, of course, dispensable (the setting up of the structural semantics or syntax of a text is always the result of interpretive conjectures and plans), but still to hold it in the bounds of what can be intersubjectively regulated. This side of interpretation is called "grammatical" or "structural" for the precise reason that it regards every particular "language value" as an element in a system,[15] within which its signification comes to it "through opposition within unity."[16] As an element in a synchronic structure every signification is delimited in a particular way by its immediate surroundings and ultimately by the entirety of the text. (Schleiermacher distinguishes contrast-relations—"qualitative contrasts"— from "transitions," in other words, "quantitative differences."[17]) Neither a dissenting declaration of meaning by the author nor an individual prejudice of the interpreter can change this. The so-called "main ideas" of a text (namely, the textual analogues to the "language values" of grammar) cannot, as soon as the structure is determined, any longer be regarded simply as products of an extratextual invention of the interpreting subject. To this extent Schleiermacher can plainly say that the reconstruction of the fabric of signs—at least for a logically composed piece of writing—presents "no further difficulties" methodologically.[18]

C. Two Examples of Classical Textual Analysis

Before beginning with textual analysis on the basis of these premises, one must of course consider a number of additional points. First, the choice of the term "text" in the program of textual analysis is merely an act of economy: one saves a more exact specification of the sort of text being thought of concretely. A grammar of *the* text would doubtlessly unearth such generality as to be useless to the practice of interpretations. Of course, poetics could profit from this. Thus T. Todorov wants to explore the poetic universals whose manifestation is the individual poetic work.[19] All scholarly disciplines, he explains, proceed to the general: there could be no science of bodies, but at most physics, chemistry, geometry. Correspondingly, there could be no science of Kafka's novel *The Trial,* only one of its "literariness": poetics.[20]

Roland Barthes does not go so far. In one of his most forceful essays, the *Introduction à l'analyse structurale des récits,*[21] he attempts to give the laws of formation not of creative writing generally, but of one genre: the story. This sort of text is also something conventional indeed: it has its rules and universals that must be formulated as such. This initial methodological decision is characteristic of the classical conception of structuralist textual analysis: it first proves itself not in the field of specific interpretation, but in the framework of that which one traditionally calls genre poetics.

At the beginning is the thought that, like every semiological system, the story can also be regarded as a net of distributional and integrative relations (in the sense given above) among elementary units of content. Barthes labels these units *functions* because they are not semantically loaded in their being-for-itself but only in their relation to all others. One can divide these elementary functional units, according to whether they appear among elements of the same or of different textual levels, into distributional functions (*functions* in the more narrow sense) or "functions" of integrating nature (so-called *Indices*). As expected, functions appear more in the syntagmatic realm (horizontal), indices more on the level of paradigmatic relations between units of the story. Here metonymy and there metaphor finds its place.

That sounds rather abstract, but still examples can easily be produced. Take any story with a repeating symbol, for example, a spot that—who knows?—points to an entanglement in guilt. That, according to Barthes' division, would be a typical *index;* for it does not join units of the story horizontally, but sticks in the story's body like a spear: as a leitmotif it goes "right through" and "integrates" sequences of the story that apparently are attempting to pull apart from each other. For example, someone opens a door and actually the way into a room should open up. But then the eyes of the actor fall onto a rusty red spot on the door, which makes his hair stand on end and his blood stand still. By contrast, a function of the story would be the unit opening-the-door, for this function is syntagmatically chained to the view into a room into which the horrified actor, who just saw the spot, now steps. This stepping in, or rather the sequence of sentences that deal with it, would be the next function. Everything that is regulated in a neighborly way between story sequences has the character of a function of the story.

Barthes' division into functions and indices corresponds exactly, by the way, to both of the basic rules on which Schleiermacher builds grammatical integration. Schleiermacher distinguishes between two possibilities for determining the unit of references in texts. On the one hand, he says, the references are set by their belonging to a certain national language, and within this once again as bounded off from certain nearby references: horse, workhorse, mare, nag, sorrel, and so on would be, for example, such a paradigmatic chain. On the other hand, however, references are also determined horizontally by their "surroundings," thus, as we say today, by their context: for example, only the syntagmatic context makes clear that the "sorrel" [*Fuchs,* or fox] designates a reddish brown horse and not an animal of the species of dogs.[22]

Barthes divides the functions further into those whose existence is essential for the course of the story and the connection of actions (these he calls *fonctions cardinales* or *noyaux,* similar to Schleiermacher's "main ideas") and into those that have the function more or less of padding, serving as catalysts bridging together the action (he calls them catalytic functions, approximately corresponding to the "secondary ideas" of which Schleiermacher speaks). The *cardinal* functions create internal (logical) relations; the *catalytic* functions create external ones. An illustration of this immediately comes to mind from the story of Bluebeard. The knight Bluebeard, who is already indicated as a strange and extraordinary being by his blue beard, marries seven women one after the other and slaughters them all, because all fail to resist their curiosity to enter the forbidden slaughter-house with a key that has been given to them purposely to spur their desire to do so. The seventh woman is named (in Tieck's version) Agnes and when, after a long time thinking it over both this way and that, she finally opens the room, this sequence of action (opening) is obviously cardinal. By contrast, the fact that she pushes down the latch is unimportant or more "*complétif*" (catalytic).

For the *Indices* too Barthes makes yet a further, analogous division: there are units of the story as *Indices* in the strict sense—and as *informa-tion.* Barthes also calls the indices "parameters"; they run like a thread through the entire story and provide hand signs as to the correct assessment of a character (such as the blue-beardedness of the knight Bluebeard and his frivolous game with human curiosity), or also indicators for certain condi-tions of feeling, moods, world views. The grim tone of the entire Blue-beard story would be a typical index, as would the directedness of the characters into the future: for curiosity is indeed only a particular way for the actors to realize their opening into the future. As *information,* by con-trast, Barthes designates signals that only help determine time, place and external accompanying circumstances. In Tieck's version of *The Knight Bluebeard* there is a certain Simon, a brother of Agnes, who broods con-stantly about time and futurity, and that seems to be a narrative index. By contrast, Agnes' observation—she makes it directly before the dramatic de-cision: "How nicely the sun has risen!"—seems merely to contribute infor-mation concerning the time.

It is important that Barthes emphasizes—again exactly like Schleier-macher—that these functions are able continually to pass into each other: the catalytic can become essential, as can that which seems essential be revealed as unimportant by the course of the story. And likewise a seem-ingly secondary piece of information can prove to determine the action. Again two examples of this. Earlier we established that it is important that Agnes does not resist her curiosity and enters the forbidden room. That she uses a key for this seems merely catalytic, a bridge over the action. Now the opposite turns out to be the case: the key has from this moment on a spot of blood that cannot be cleaned off; in other words, its function grows into that of a cardinal characteristic and even into that of an index, insofar as the spot (like the key itself) becomes a sexual symbol whose "dissemi-nal" appearance at several points of the tale assumes a function of integrat-ing meaning, of a leitmotiv. And another example: the remark of Agnes' on the day when she herself is to be slaughtered, which seems only to contain information as to the time—"How nicely the sun has risen!"—proves to be an indicator: for the text's reader knows, that the sunrise "announces" ["*an-zeigt*"] Agnes' impending rescue; for brother Simon's permanent brooding over the future has finally so infected the other brother Anton that he too begins to worry about his sister and undertakes a night ride to Blue-beard's castle. The brothers arrive precisely at "sunrise," and the reader senses or now knows that when Agnes says the sun has risen, the brothers cannot tarry much longer.

The further course of the story's analysis can be summarized more briefly; it already shows traces of rendering into dogma the procedures of text-structurization.

Barthes took the smallest elements of the story as functions. The next higher level of integration would be that on which they are joined. Analo-gous to linguistics, Barthes speaks of a *syntax of narrative functions*. But in analogy to the linguists' procedure, he takes this talk of a syntax seriously; in other words, he looks for an "atemporal matrix" of syntagmatic rules of connection. One must see what this signifies: it expressly does not have to do with the real sequence of individual sentences, but with the syntax of their connection. That could already be observed in Lévi-Strauss' analysis of the Oedipus myth (in a famous text from *Structural Anthropology*): Lévi-Strauss makes four thematic headings and watches how the contents of the columns relate to each other.[23] And these relations are dealt with in a strictly logical way: *a* is to *b* as *c* is to *d*. It does not matter how in the real Oedipus tale the sentences follow each other, motivate each other stylisti-cally, and move away from each other. Through this methodological deci-sion, what is transitory in the course of the story is, so to speak, turned to stone. It is wrong still to speak of *sequences* at all; for all sequences are inscribed in a stem-like schema, in other words, in a little tree of structure.

Schleiermacher, incidentally, regards such a procedure as possible only in the case of "systematic scholarly" works ("Here," he says, "one idea is a direct form of the whole and of the same apart that integrates everything particular"[24]). By contrast, if a lyrical, dramatic or epic poem is to be interpreted, it must be tested how the cardinal characteristics are influenced by "means of representation" specific to the genre and by seemingly secondary ideas—effects that cannot be brought into view from a standpoint that is fixated exclusively on the syntactic moment. Schleier-macher hints at the conclusion that "here the hermeneutic interpretation reaches onto the psychological side."[25]

It is not to be feared that in structural analysis the logic of this in-scription in little trees of structure would forcibly assert itself ("this has to do, it must be observed, with a hierarchy that remains in the interior of the level of functions"; Schleiermacher too handles the syntactic units, as far as possible, as functional schemata in changing contexts and at different levels of integration). That is not what is dubious, but rather that for the sake of this procedure every consideration of the concrete connection of the story, of the story's style, and so on, is suppressed. Barthes is indeed committed to the dream of "écriture without style."[26]

With that a methodological decision is reached that leads to still more inevitable consequences at the higher levels of integration. Style indicates a subject working uniquely with language. Barthes, of course, has no use for anything of the kind. Nor are "actions" considered, unless under the condition that it is clearly stated that *actions* are to designate autonomous sequences of the story, fully abstracted from acting subjects. Each of these subjects can be treated as a grammatic subject; and this is how it happens. As linguists speak of two- or three-place verbs, without needing to refer back to an individual using the verb, so Roland Barthes says that every sequence generally implies two actants [*Aktanten*]. An example: the unit of action "to cheat someone" is intentional deceit for one partner and for the other it is "a dirty trick" (*Fraude-Duperie*). An exhaustive grammatical inventory of actions would have to record the corpus of all conceivable configurations and interactions between those who act and submit them to a list of rules. (Todorov names two: *derivations*, if it has to do with explaining other relationships than those that have been set, and *actions*, when it has to do with describing changes of the same that vary according to context.)

Operations of this kind call for decisional procedures that can only be used with a preview of the highest level of the story: namely, of the entire semantic-syntactic undertaking of "narration." As those who act were, so to speak, derived from the syntax of action sequences (as the grammatical subjects between whom the sequences mediate), so the interaction of the author and the reader (the literary message's transmitter-receiver couple) is dealt with. If the author says, for example, "This, my dear reader, I ask you particularly to observe," the address itself is only a sign in the semiotic system of the story: in no case are empirical persons meant. Barthes gives a few noteworthy indications of the way one can identify, immanent in the text, the narrative stance of the author. This all ultimately entails, of course, a cleansing of pragmatic aspects out of the story. One can—this is Barthes' basic idea—reformulate every sentence that points to a situation, an intention or a subject in such a way that it becomes a descriptive expression: in this way, the text is hermeneutically neutralized; and this applies also to the way in which Barthes in one last spiral wants to surmount the historical and socioeconomic dimension of the text, which is in the same manner reduced to a reference between sign systems of different extension ("*intertextualité*").

With Barthes' *Introduction à l'analyse structurale des récits* one has
the impression that the textual analysis, after brief and fruitful contact with
the text itself, takes off so steeply into matters of general principle that the
gain in scholarly rigor is paid for with an enormous impoverishment in the
understanding of the meaning. Indeed, soon French literary scholarship in
part left the path of almost servile orientation around the taxonomic model
of the text—in analogy to the taxonomy model of linguistic structure— and
in part proceeded in much looser fashion. The experiences of May 1968
surely formed the breaking point between the structuralist and the so-called
poststructuralist approaches to textual analysis.[27] Times of revolutionary
sentiment are interested more in changing orders than in producing or de-
fending them. The structuralist textual analysis of the early 1960s was able
to secure its scholarliness only by either laying bare the rules of literariness
behind texts themselves or attempting to do so for a particular kind of text
(for example, the story). There is since greater interest in the structure and
construction of *individual* texts; and again Roland Barthes was one of the
first to pursue the new tendency. His great Balzac interpretation, entitled
S/Z, is a roadsign in his intellectual biography and a milestone within the
development of structural analysis of texts. Barthes devoted a two-year seminar at the École Pratique des Hautes Études (1968 and 1969) to Balzac's
story *Sarrasine* (1830) and thereafter published the results.[28]

What makes *S/Z* attractive for the methodology of textual interpretation is simultaneously that which alienates this attempt from the orthodox
structuralist tradition. (Derrida has spoken mockingly of this tradition as
''ultrastructuralism.''[29]) Barthes breaks in this book not only with genre
poetics, but generally with the prejudices of taxonomism, according to
which a text's elementary units of meaning can be derived in monocausal
fashion from a story-code, isolated in itself and ''atemporal.''[30]

That signifies at the same time, of course, a rejection of scientific
methodologism, following which the analysis of a text has to proceed according to trans-subjective ''discovery procedures'' and may not tolerate
irresolvable ambiguities. The idea that the text is a fabric of units of meaning, forced by a ''transcendental'' cardinal meaning into a certain arrangement, is dismissed in *S/Z* as ''metaphysical.'' The ''transcendental
meaning,'' if there is one, would organize all other signs according to its
plan, rather like a magnet ordering iron splinters on a piece of paper, or like
a genome laying out particular bits of hereditary information in the code of
a living organism—or also, one is reminded by the adjective ''transcendental,'' like in Kantian philosophy pure consciousness stamping its order on
the mass of material. In the meantime this view is unacceptable to Barthes,
because it fails at meeting the claim made in the Bataille quotation that

serves as the work's motto: to acknowledge the text as a form of multiple meanings. *S/Z* attempts to take this into account by regarding the text as the intersection of codes often crossing and communicating with each other. Their basically open interaction is not determined by any rule that has been taken out of play. Every single seme, in other words, every smallest unit of meaning, can and should become the seed of an immense plurality of meaning effects [*Sinneffekten*], with each shooting up, so to speak, as a different row of connotatively created branch lines.

To elucidate: one notices immediately that this is not at all an economic procedure. If an axiom of scholarly procedure is to reduce the multiplicity of phenomenal nature to the lowest number of fundamental laws conceivable; and if literary scholarship *as scholarship* is to explain the multiplicity and variety of conceivable meaning in terms of the fewest structures of signification conceivable; then poststructuralist textual analysis wants, so to speak, to multiply textual meaning. It has the meaning "explode," it supports the text's ambiguity by uncovering it as such. That does not imply, of course, that it pours additional obscurity into the text; but it implies that it uncovers the textual (poetic, rhetorical, "technical") modes of operation at work in the text's obscure reaches, which would be suppressed if through interpretation the story were reduced like a column of figures to its sum. For what distinguishes literature from riddles, charades, and arithmetic problems, is that interpretation does not replace and, as it were, solve the piece of writing.

Instead of committing the elementary semic [or semantic] units to a certain center of meaning, to be pronounced as the sum total, *S/Z* wants to separate them "in the manner of a minor earthquake"[31]; instead of reducing their dispersion, *S/Z* wants to multiply it. How does that appear in concrete terms? Well, Barthes calls for carving up the text into all its units of action. These units of action he also calls units of reading ("Lexias"). This call is to be taken literally. One is, so to speak, supposed to take a pencil and continually write onto the printed text numbers in parentheses before the individual blocks of action and meaning, in the course of which, one lexia corresponds exactly to that which Barthes earlier called a function. Barthes arrives at 561 lexias for this thirty-odd-page story. And his book is constructed so that the lexias are completely cited under their respective numbers and then commented upon.

This commentary is not at all arbitrary; there is no warrant for the subjective streams of every association conceivable happening to come to the reader's mind. "Interpretation is not open to *every* meaning,[. . .]; it is signified and can be wrong"; thus there is "an authentic interpretation."[32] The control to which Barthes submits consists in his observing each lexia by the standard of a set of "codes." Is this not in contradiction to the issuance of a linguistic system model? Not necessarily: Barthes still operates, to be sure, with the structuralist category of the code, the system and the "systematic mark"[33]: but he multiplies the codes and works no longer with only one. Every code signifies a systematic investigation within which every sequence of the story can be examined. "Under the hermeneutic code, we list the various (formal) terms by which an enigma can be distinguished, suggested, formulated, held in suspense, and finally disclosed."[34] The application of this is indicated in the analysis at the end of the lexia concerned, under initials, such as HER (hermeneutic code), for example, after the title that provokes a question, appeals to a puzzle and its solution: who or what is this Sarrasine?

Barthes calls the second code the "semic," the code that controls the order of significations: that which is said and into which semantic frame it is inserted. It is characteristic that Barthes, as in the *Introduction,* forbids assigning the semes to particular persons or subjects: they are supposed to be only thematically noted, in infinitive form. "We allow them," he says, "the instability, the dispersion, characteristic of motes of dust, flickers of meaning."[35] (This limitation does not in fact keep Barthes from characterizing this code occasionally as the "personal code.")

This is especially pertinent to the elements of the third or so-called "symbolic code." It takes effect for the first time in the second lexia; "I was sunk in one of these reveries" and so on, with which a symbolic field is opened up that points ahead to all kinds of mysterious occurrences, like masculinity-femininity, castration, coldness-warmth, stones and flesh and so forth.

Fourth, there is the "proairetic code," signifying the resolution, the decision through which I put a state of indecision behind me, by deciding between two or more possibilities (also, depending on the case, the priority that I give a thing or an action). For Barthes the term means quite simply the "code of action" or the structure of action in the story: for example, the pieces of information that I assemble under one name; the modes of behavior that I observe in the actors and that make me fear, anticipate, overlook or in terror leave certain things.

Finally, there is the "cultural or reference code" (initials: REF) that concerns "citations from the store of knowledge and wisdom," for example, when an Adonis painting by a particular painter is being dealt with, when Pygmalion and the cardinals in Rome are spoken of. To summarize: whenever the text itself lets us see that it is "inter-text," that it is woven into social and cultural "co-texts" to which it refers and from which it allows itself to suffer visitations continually: for example, from the code of the Parisian bourgeoisie with its money hunger, its tightly controlled aggressiveness and vitality, its taboos, and so on.

If—in the final appraisal—Barthes' revision of classical structuralism may be welcomed as the bridge in the direction of a hermeneutics of understanding meaning and if one hopes that his attempt will have followers, nevertheless one should not overlook the fact that Barthes in the final analysis does not break with the code model of understanding. To be sure, he corrects the most glaring deficiencies; yet a report that is codified in multiple ways is still capable of being systematically decoded. The "plural text" is "multiple": open to interpretation it is not. That corresponds to Barthes' fade-out of reading as a process of the uncontrollable discovery and assignment of meaning. The text itself assumes the role of the hermeneutic subject: "In operational terms, the meanings I find are established not by 'me' or by others, but by their *systematic* mark: there is no other proof of a reading than the quality and endurance of the systematics; in other words: than its functioning."[36] The heuristic side of this finding remains as little worked over as in the design of an objective interpretation according to E. D. Hirsch. Its claim of objectivity was also limited, of course, to the testing of already completed interpretations. The motives behind an interpretation, how the interpretation settles into a work and whether there are rules around which it is oriented: in both cases this remains in the obscurity of that on which "scholarship" fails to express itself.[37]

D. The Limits of the Code Model for Analyzing Texts
   and the Task of Understanding Style

The problem of textual interpretation seemed to have found an answer in the structuralism of the 1960s. But does structuralism really give an answer to what we conceive of as the concretization of a piece of creative literature? Had we not called upon the interpreter of literary texts to pursue the flow of the story's meaning and thereby to proceed beyond what the structuralists, following information theory, call "decoding"? Decoding is possible for those and only those systems of signs that give each expression a lasting and quite particular interpretation. One masters the system in question through being able to pass beyond its expressions to their significations while conforming to the rules, in other words, to recognize these expressions *as* signs. Now the example of a piece of writing instructs us that the allocations of significance to particular expressions (can) slip away from obligatory rules in the course of the story (of the text-reader communication) and consequently appeal to the reader's collaboration in the creation of meaning. This is, as Schleiermacher assures us, the point at which "the hermeneutic operation extends to the psychological side."[38] Thus one can—and essentially the grammatical or structural interpretation does this—treat the text "on the one side" as a form without a world, abstracted from situations, and without an author. The "other side" of interpretation is entered as soon as the text's connection to living communication, which the piece of writing interrupted, is reestablished: then one no longer analyzes but interprets the text; textual analysis becomes textual hermeneutics. Now our contact with literature has taught us that two different acts of reading do not leave the original significations intact.

In order to take this knowledge into account, we must separate ourselves from the code model of structuralist textual analysis. Indeed structuralism falls short as soon as it takes the leap from a proven procedure of textual analysis to a global thesis concerning the mode in which texts exist, an alternative to the concept of the work, which, as we saw, includes *style* besides the decodable characteristics of structure and genre.

Style is a characteristic not of language but of discourse. It effects not only a selection and arrangement, in each instance unique, of the given word material; it also shifts the boundaries of linguistic normality that had been in effect until then. For this reason one must deal with it as that which is inexplicable, non-conventional, in the text; and it will be difficult, if not impossible, to subject it to scholarly analysis like the grammatical-structuralistic one that dreams of "writing without style."[39] By contrast, what Schleiermacher called the "other side" of textual interpretation appeals to the productivity of the subject; for this reason he also calls it "psychological" or "technical" (in other words, art-like, inventive) interpretation. Its *"entire purpose,"* he says, *"can be designated as complete understanding of style,"*[40] with "style" meaning "an author's individual mode of combination" and not the combination of words according to the standard of a syntactic rule or a *genus dicendi*.[41] The sentence or the discourse or the mode of discourse, considered as cases of the application of universal regularities, are "objects of grammatical interpretation" and appeal only to "language as a general concept," in other words, to the mechanism that produces all "necessary forms for subject, predicate and syntax."[42] But these, Schleiermacher continues, "are not positive means of explaining" the individual selection and linkage of words, "but only negative means, because whatever contradicts them . . . cannot be understood at all."[43] The uniqueness of a style "cannot be constructed *a priori*." Indeed, "in grammatical terms, individuality cannot be summarized in a concept.[. . .] No style fits into a concept."[44] In retrospect—above all, when the culture (for example, in the course of critical interpretation) reconquers the stylistic excesses for normal language[45]—we can perhaps generally characterize and thereupon "know" the technique of *this* style; before that it is necessary to "guess."

Only the general is known or recognized in the end; and a text's style could become an object of knowledge only to the degree that it is not a single piece but, for example, reproduces the discourse of its epoch, its class, its stratum, its occupation and so on (a so-called stylistic *stratum:* simple style, developed style, elevated style, poetic style, and so on), or also the discourse of a certain type of language *use* that has been established among several language participants (a so-called stylistic *type:* situational style, functional style, the style of a sort of text, and so on).[46] In all of these examples style is not something individual, but rather common to several speakers. And only through the selection of individual facts does a scholarly description arrive at their generalizability. That is ensured by the rule according to which what is many-sided and variable in the (textual) material can be dealt with as having *one* characteristic and in this way be brought together under one concept. We could call this condition *the criterion of uniform and like-meaning repeatability.* It dominates the entire field of the (so-called "semiological") disciplines that are oriented around the concept of the sign, thus also the procedures of structural analysis of texts.

However, the individual, for example, style, is in the real sense of the word indivisible and thus incommunicable: not in the sense of the classical model of atoms as the indivisibility of an infinitesimally small substance that "only" enters relations with itself, but as that which exists without an internal double and without relation, that which consequently and in a literal sense is without equal and *thus evades the criterion of like-meaning repeatability.* To record an individual expression and re-produce it in the act of reading (in other words, re-create it) does not then signify (and this is decisive) *articulating the same linguistic sequence again and indeed with like meaning,* but rather *undertaking another articulation of the same linguistic sequence.* For, says August Boeckh (one of the great forgotten practitioners of method in our field from the first half of the last century), "one can never produce the same thing again. . . ."[47]

Humboldt had shown why this is: in every situation of understanding through language, even in the special cases of self-understanding [*Selbstverständigung*] and of understanding texts, two modes of perception crash into one another, of which only the conventional part is covered [*zur Deckung kommt*], while "*the more individual rises above.*"[48] There can be no complete congruence "in one indivisible point," for every sign- or text-mediated understanding creates an historically unstable union of the general with an individual *view* of the general that could not again become general. The effort at understanding would reach objectivity only under the condition that one could oversee the meaning from an Archimedean point outside of language; but we are caught in the happenings of language, also when we interpret texts. "Every day and every speaker," says Sartre, "change the references *for everyone*. Indeed the others twist my words around."⁴⁹ For that reason every articulation is not only re-productive (in other words, re-appearing or rigid convention), but rather inventive in a systematically uncontrollable way. Individual style always jolts the sign synthesis that joins writing and meaning, it always shifts the boundaries of normality that had been in effect. For that reason the decision about the "true meaning" of a literal expression has fundamentally the character of a conjecture.

Thus every interpretation remains *in the final analysis* hypothetical. Sartre speaks of a "hypothesis of understanding" (*une hypothèse compréhensive, notre compréhension conjecturale*) that one must propose in order nonetheless to understand that which is not disclosed through the convention of discourse and of words, that which is radically "new" in an expression. Of course, "the truth of this reconstruction cannot be proven, nor can its probability be measured."⁵⁰ This irreducibly hypothetical character of understanding is what distinguishes textual interpretation from the methodological and deductive procedures of scientism. For this reason we cannot simply derive the meaning of an expression put in the form of a text from a book of grammar and the dictionary: because whatever has meaning is not caused but motivated. *Motivated* means actions that can be produced and also understood only through the mediation of a (Peircean) interpreter. The enrollment of a cause (of the motive or incentive) that is supposed to "explain" the action in retrospect and derive it from prerequisites is only a repetition on a reflective plane of the interpretation—before all reflection—that the action itself, from its own situation in preview of a particular future, had already given this situation.⁵¹ The grammar that a speaker or an author internalizes in order to be a competent participant in the contemporary conventions of linguistic action never operates with the certainty of a machine responding to the *input* of certain expressions with the *output* of significations firmly attached to them. For every signification of a language must first prove itself in and for the situation to which the author—*acting with language*—applies it. Language *motivates* him to this degree (he cannot simply say what he wants), but it does not condition his use of language (he can always say something more and something other than that foreseen by the rules of grammar and of the dictionary that have been codified to that point). This relates directly to the fact that language first attains its ultimate significance in the act of expressing itself [*des Sich-Äusserns*] and in this self-expression [*Entäusserung:* self-renunciation] assumes a distance necessarily and uncontrollably from the meaning-term syntheses that previous language usage had maintained generally as conventions. In order not to fall short of this (possible) innovation of meaning, the interpreter must proceed through surmise and the formation of hypotheses beyond the deductive system of a linguistic-pragmatic code; and precisely this crossing of boundaries leads, where it is successful, to *understanding [Verstehen]*. The understanding *[Verständnis]* of a text is, as Schleiermacher already emphasized, inexhaustible (for the process of communication continually accumulates new meaning, in other words, it also shifts the designs of concretization that until then had been undertaken by the community of receivers).[52] "A thousand possibilities will always remain open even if one understands something in this phrase that makes sense."[53] And "as long as only one such possibility has not been entirely rejected, we cannot speak of any necessary insight."[54] Derrida ridicules the scientistic option of followers of an "objective interpretation" by using the metaphor of "a few wolves of the type of 'indecidability'" that break into the sheepfold of codifying and hinder the shepherd of generative textual grammar from counting his sheep and determining where the boundaries of text and concretization lie.[55]

What is significant for a theory of textual interpretation in Derrida's criticism of hermeneutic objectivism and of the model of generative grammar is that he does not assert his argument *against* the minimal consensus concerning the nature of a system of understanding, but to the contrary derives his argument from this consensus. To this extent he also corrects the scientistic option of classical structuralism itself.

This minimal consensus is based upon the view that semiotic systems intersubjectively impart significance to their elements by articulating directly the available graphic or phonic material of expression, in other words, by making certain cuts each time at the same places into what previously had been the unarticulated and insignificant material of signifiers; through these cuts the individual blocks are broken off from each other and thus given a profile, an outline, singularity and in brief "differential characteristics." Only after the work of making distinctions and of the formation of intervals between the "full and positive terms" is finished can the "distinctiveness" of the signs be complete.[56] Saussure has designated the differences between the terms of an already constituted language as "oppositions."[57] The concept of constituted language (and by analogy of the already composed text) suggests a situation of completeness and immutability in the system. The model on which structural theories of language and of the text are based is for good reason the crystal lattice in which, at a sufficiently low temperature, all molecules are fixed in their places and rendered immobile, both distinguished from and connected to all others. In contrast to the world of elements, the historical-cultural world cannot be cooled down to an absolute freezing point; language thrives only in a certain warmth. Texts, Derrida says, are always transformations of other, earlier texts, as signs are always new articulations of other signs that had been used before. For the concept of differentiality makes it immediately clear that no sign is present for itself in an unmediated and atemporal manner, as the model of "opposition" would have it. The idea of differentiality states indeed: if a sign obtains its particular meaning only by distinguishing itself from all others, then it clearly does not refer in the first instance to *itself.* It has no original identity, but rather first obtains one, before returning to itself, by taking the detour by way of all other signs (the French *"différer"* means both to postpone something and to be distinguished from . . .). If one accepts this and in addition recognizes that this course leads through infinity, one has given notice to the scientistic idea of an original and time-less presence or familiarity of at least *one* meaning for and with itself, a meaning to which I return with certainty by all the paths I travel to and beyond signs. Such a meaning, extracted from the play of structure, would be the *principle* of structure: Derrida is given to calling it "transcendental meaning." But the unity of this Archimedean point is always lost to begin with; none of the paths I follow through the text's fabric of relationships, in order to determine the wealth of its oppositions/references and its entire meaning, is reliable in leading me back to the point of departure. The par-adigm of re-flection (of the speculative return to the point of departure) fails to stand up to the experience that semantic oppositions constitute an economy of no limits.[58]

This does not somehow signify that in consequence anarchy would break out in the system of signs (and in textual interpretation). Saussure's insight, that the "differentiation of a certain *value* for a term x" takes place "through the formation of associative sequences of 'oppositions'," can indeed be formulated as a strict, universal law. But this rule leaves entirely open which and how many oppositions I write onto the list of as-sociations. This has the result that the addition of a new differentiation (that shifts the references of the oppositions constituted to that point)—and something of the kind happens in every textual interpretation that penetrates more deeply, as in every productive conversation—is unpredictable. As soon as one introduces the concept of process—and thus of time—into the textual system, its boundaries are blurred, to the displeasure of the scholar who as a consequence cannot assume the completeness [*Geschlossenheit*] of the semantic economy and thus guarantee any longer the recursiveness of the linguistic types and the uniformity [*Gleichsinnigkeit*] of their use.

So as not only to assert abstractly that this constant slippage of mean-ing beneath the writing occurs, but to demonstrate it as an event of the literary text itself, let me refer to the example of Kafka's story *The Hunter Gracchus.* Like the Flying Dutchman and like Coleridge's *Ancient Mariner,* Gracchus is punished for the crime of daring boldly to violate a border (in the geographical as in the religious sense) because of his curiosity about the world. This costs him his celestial home and forces him, living and dead for an eternity as he navigates the earthly waters, to consider what is unwish-able in his hunt and his misdeed.[59] What makes the story special is, of course, that in it the aimlessly drifting ship begins the cruise that leads nowhere on the tides of poetic discourse itself. That the ship is called "bark" (a Mediterranean fishing vessel) suggests indeed a quotation from the metaphorical tradition of the "ingenii barca," of poetry as navigation and cruise. Moreover, Kafka does not miss his opportunity to ascribe to the bark's course the artistic qualities (already exhibited in the story of *Odradek*) of fickleness and uncommitted signification, in which there is an after-effect of the curse of Cain: "A fugitive and a vagabond shalt thou be . . . " ("now up, now down, now right, now left, always in motion. The hunter was transformed into a butterfly"). But the bark [*Barke*] also receives identity from the similarity of sound between it and "*Bahre*" [*bier*] as the symbol of the writer. Indeed, Coleridge's *Ancient Mariner*, known to Kafka, in the end atones for his sacrilegious slaying of the holy beast through his insatiable urge to communicate, which carries him—neither really living nor dead—into the imaginary realm of poetry: "I pass like night from land to land;/I have strange power of speech."[60] Just like Kafka's writer. He is, as it is put in the journal entry, "dead while alive and the real survivor."[61] Finally Kafka has the hunter, as it were, leap out of the text and present himself as its author: "No one," he says, "will read what I write here." Thus the "misery" of the loss of this heavenly place, where man in fact is at home, affects the process of writing itself, a process elsewhere characterized by Kafka as a loss, as a questionable violation of a threshold, indeed, as a "hunt," in other words, as a "storming of the (last earthly) boundary."[62] In the instability of the literary production of meaning, the infinity of this lost cruise becomes its own figure of warning: as a case of sin out of the innocence of signification, the innocence that only lights up in the "silence" of child-like "knowledge."[63]

Recent French literary theory gives this expression through the discourse of the infinite text, the "*texte général.*" While Odysseus (re-) discovers his Ithaca, for a boundary violator like the Hunter Gracchus there is no longer any home. Nor is there still a home-like meaning, from which the fabric of references in the modern text would arise and to which—through interpretation—it would be restored. Derrida spoke of the elimination of limits [*Entgrenzung*] in the textual economy, which takes from every sign its identity and "tears it out of control into the whirlpool of writing."[64] Meaning has no anchor—in other words, no definitive, no certain interpretation—in the infinite text; it attests, as Derrida says, to "an irreducible and *creative* multiplicity."[65]

E. The Inadequacy of a Pragmatics of Understanding Style

One will perhaps object that recent linguistic and literary scholarship has overcome its orientation around the code model as well as its presumptions concerning the unequivocality of a statement. For several years, so-called linguistic *pragmatics* have instructed us not only to pay attention to the grammatical correctness and the significance of sentences, but to inquire into the intention behind their use.[66] One and the same sentence content (for instance, "I will refute you") can be interpreted as a threat, as irony, as a promise, as boasting, as a program, indeed (under certain circumstances), as flirtation. Now, one could believe that style also (as the *mode* of language *use*) is the expression of an intentional action and can be investigated in as scholarly a fashion as Austin's and Searle's so-called "illocutionary" or "speech acts."

Doubts are in order for this extension of the text model to linguistic actions and also to style. For the pragmatist "to understand an intention" never means "to understand an individual," but rather to master a convention with which the individual encodes his intentions. Conventions are essentially ordered by rules and hence, as Searle says,[67] repeatable with the same meaning. (Not the wolves of indeterminability: the pragmatic shepherd has them all under control, to take up Derrida's image again.)

Under this condition the style of a text would be nothing but a case in which a universally (or at least regionally) valid rule had been applied. The pragmatic conception of style finds inspiration in Austin's and Searle's theory of language acts, in which the action character of speaking as much as the "net of circumstances and social conventions"[68] receives consideration. One must see, of course, that with this the field of that which Saussure called "*acte de la parole*," the field that as a field of possibilities for individual choice and innovations was opposite the field of linguistic social behavior [*Sozialität*] ("la langue"), now is subject to a kind of pragmatic grammar, the system of rules for context and action. It is easy to admit the existence of such rules, without thereby surrendering Saussure's insight that *in the final analysis* it is always the *individual* speech act—and not the intersubjective norm that motivates but never compels—that decides on the pragmatic meaning of an expression (without the decision binding *understanding* of the expression): "Thus in *langue* [language]," writes Saussure, "there are always two sides in correspondence with each other. The *langue* is social/individual. . . . If one attempts to set aside one of these two aspects, it can only be for the purposes of abstraction. There is social and individual *langue*. Forms and grammars exist only socially. But the changes proceed from an individual."[69]

The conception of a "pragmatic stylistics" has gone in the meantime so far as to ascertain that the particular possibility of choice ("stylistic choice") is only the way in which the author realizes a linguistic action (or the intersubjective convention inscribed in that action). There is no provision for deviating from or transforming the rule, precisely because a deviation or a transformation would no longer have the capacity to be decoded as the rule's specific case. This scientistic premise defines the boundaries of the pragmatic concept of style.

Each case is the particular of a generality. However, it is not permissible to confuse the individual with the particular. The particular can always be exposed as one element in an order filled with other elements of the same kind; the individual must be *guessed* in its uniqueness. Yet guessing does not mean bringing out what is already inherent or assumed to be the significance in something. For there is, following Peirce's insight, no significance inherent in the sign by the strength of a role, but only fallible conclusions drawn from interpretations given earlier.[70] Accordingly, there can be no grammar of style, and thus no grammar of the text, although some representatives of the blossoming textual linguistics in the structuralistic succession (above all, Barthes' and Todorov's) assert this. (Barthes himself and Todorov also have since corrected this original view of theirs.)

Through its unrepeatability, in other words, its untranslatability, the "individual addition"[71] bursts through the synthesis, formed true to convention, of the speech act type, in which an intention and a proposition coexist. And only because of this, "habent sua fata libelli," in other words, do the books have their destinies of meaning and take part in the processes of transforming language and shifting meaning, processes that hold no interest for pragmatics or textual linguistics, indeed, for which they know no explanation. This distinguishes them from a literary relationship that proceeds from the experience "that every (poetic) work of art represents not only an unmediated, but indeed a never entirely repeatable, unconsignable, individual and actually anarchic lived experience" [*Erlebnis*] that continually extends the boundary "of everything said to that point." Every experience [*Erfahrung*] exists in unstable unity with the concept through whose help it took place, but every new one "bursts through the formula of what has been acquired to that point. [. . .] What we call our intellectual existence is located without interruption in this process of extension and return. In it art has the task inexplicably to transform and renew the picture of— and action in—the world, bursting with its lived experiences [*Erlebnisse*] through the formula of learned experience [*Erfahrung*]."[72]

F. Foundation for a Model of "Technical Interpretation"

Even if textual *pragmatics* gives no satisfactory answer to the question of what it means to understand a literary text, one must look around in other realms of the formation of theory. True, contemporary models of interpretation are numerous, but they do not possess, with one exception, any sufficient criterion for the description of a stylistic expression. And only this last, as Schleiermacher already emphasized, completes the business of textual interpretation—*technical interpretation.*[73]

This one exception is Sartre: his *Questions de méthode* with its, by claim and format, equally powerful "application to a person and a work," the *Idiot de la famille.* Above all, this *chef-d'oeuvre* may stand in passing as the state's witness for the enduring relevance of that which Schleiermacher had called the "technical interpretation: the complete understanding of style."

Man, says Sartre (and this is correspondingly valid for Sartre's concept of the text as well), is a *"universel singulier,"*[74] an *individual generality.*[75] He is *general* insofar as in the way he connects words and sentences he manifests not only the drama of an individual socialization, but rather through that, the entirety of the rules of his epoch at all layers of language, as can be comprehended by a patient structural analysis (for example, following Barthes). Past that, however, the text is *individual,* insofar as it internalizes, applies, interprets and thereby steps over this given entirety of rules, with all its semiological varieties, in a way unique to itself. No element of a symbolic order (for instance, a linguistic order or one pertaining to the poetry of a genre) is indeed lord of its own application-in-a-situation, and precisely because the order—the social code—does not itself appear as such on the level of the *use* of symbols. The universals of even a generously defined grammar reach their impassable limit with that which is *not* general, the individual and its style. If one calls the order of codified signs and types of expression the "sayable," style would be the "unsayable" (*l'indisable,* as Flaubert calls it),[76] the potential for meaning that exists in the language system as it is but that has not or has not yet been expressed, the potential that the creativity of the speaking-writing individual is able to articulate in the system. Sartre speaks of a "hermeneutics of silence";[77] it is this that designates the real accomplishment of textual interpretation. This *silence,* of course, is only a heuristic and passing moment of interpretation: "Temporarily moving through non-communication one comes to an expression and to communication that is so much more intensive, and in this way the capacities of language are activated."[78]

Under this condition the interpreter's work will consist in discovering the "individual addition" in each structural moment of the text and, from the other side, in identifying traces of the suspended [*aufgehobenen*] symbolic order in the author's individual style.[79] Schleiermacher called this the objective-subjective, historical *and* divining method of interpretation,[80] with "divination" meaning the attempt to guess at the original act by which the author discovered meaning [*den Akt der ursprünglichen Sinnfindung*], on the near side of linguistic convention.[81]

No one guarantees the interpreter that he actually has touched the author's individual style (or, put more cautiously, the textual subject's), or even that he has spanned the distance of time separating his world from the world of his text. Jürgen Kreft has shown very nicely how problematic the maxim is that the interpreter has to become like the "original reader" by absorbing, for example, all of the information that he can presume was known to a contemporary of the text as a participant in a social system.[82] The "ideal reader" is a scientistic fiction in which it is ignored that the "objective spirit" of an epoch comes into play irregularly in an unforseeably complex [*verzweigten*] communicative field, indeed, in a heterogeneous fashion, and that it appears broken into as many facets as there are individuals to appropriate or transform it in a particular way. Who, for example, is the "intended or primary receiver" for Sophocles' drama *Oedipus the King*? The spectators of Sophocles' tragedies? Hardly, for they were the receivers of the tragedies of Sophocles' predecessor, Aeschylus, into whose dramatic performances those of Sophocles were supposed to be tied without further preparation. "If Sophocles, who was like the other dramatists in being a creative theologian, reinterprets being, then this would mean that his dramatic texts would first have to create for themselves the adequate reader."[83] And this "adequate reader" we can be as well as (or, following Schleiermacher, even "better than") the Athenian public of the 5th Century B.C.

Putting-oneself-into-the-Zeitgeist of the author is an exertion not to be confused with that of "divination." Even when the interpreter has studied or appropriated the structure of an epoch as minutely as Sartre did for that of Flaubert's day, he still has obtained no understanding for Gustave Flaubert's special way of writing: he knows (or senses) the general; the individual is closed to him.

To guess the "individual," a "differential interpretation" is needed.[84] Through it the distance between two simultaneous "sections" or "layers" of historical "objectivity" is supposed to be made visible: that which L. Spitzer called "stylistic deviation."[85] *Regressive analysis* deals in the division of labor with the text's comparatively universal moment, while *progressive synthesis* "guesses (divines)" whether and to what extent the text has gone beyond its given structure. "It is really," Sartre explains, "the difference between *the points in common* (*communs*) and the idea or the concrete attitude of the person investigated, the enrichment of these points, their type of concretization, their transformations, and so forth, that above all else give us *clarity* regarding our object."[86] With the difference found by "comparison" and "distinction," the textual fact that has been drawn out in this way can, by "conjectures" and "hypotheses of understanding,"[87] be made transparent for the outline in its singularity. And it can receive an inquiry as to how far it has changed, maintained or reorganized a certain layer of the social code relative to the initial situation ("progressive synthesis").

All of these aspects and procedures can arise, respectively, from a predominant interest in structure—insofar as it is structure that serves the outline as a basis and insofar as every outline must realize itself in a (new) case of structure—or in individuality—insofar as the individual absorbs the structure in a unique way and removes itself from the general. Here in the latter we confront again the multiplicity of aspects registered in Schleiermacher's "positive formula" of hermeneutics.[88]

This multiplicity also unfolds for Sartre, always on two planes that are superimposed on each other: to be examined on the first is the relationship of epochal circumstances to the living totality of the author (biography), on the second the relationship of his "fundamental project" (*projet fondamental, intuition embryonnaire*)[89] to the totality of his particular outlines (documents, testimonies of his life, works, and so on). For both cases the interpretive accent lies on the break, the difference, by which the individual proceeds beyond the given, in other words, on his *style*. And just as style, an author's characteristic mode of combination, points back directly to a certain world view (*conception du monde*) and indirectly to a life story,[90] so for its part does the life story point to more comprehensive social structures of the epoch, from which it at the same time must be contrasted through a distinction that comes from understanding [*durch verstehende Unterscheidung*]: this is needed in order that the unique drama of a childhood and finally of an entire life can become visible behind the generality constituted by the stage in the development of intellectual and material productive forces, or of energies for creating meaning, or of forms of interaction in the society or in families that are peculiar to this exact epoch. "Il nous faut *deviner à la fois* des structures sociales [. . .] et une drame *unique* de l'enfance."[91] Motivated by questions that the work puts to the life, the regressive analysis seeks in continually extending the horizon of its questions to reveal the *situation* in which the universal comes to terms with the individual.

Between the individual expressions and the general conditions that they indicate, therefore, there arises—without there always being full correspondence, for the work can be silent about its motivations or overdetermine them, interpreting them somehow in any case—there arises in this way a kind of "back and forth." And this latter stretches through several planes that are hierarchically superimposed on each other and in the end, "by coming near" the object of investigation, "permits an assessment" of it, the man and his aims "in their full historical depth."[92]

Sartre teaches the interpreter of the text to compare his assignment with the attitude opposed to ethical appeal: no one forces him "to guess the individual moment." Nor can it be objectified through theoretical demonstration. By its style the work puts questions to the life and to the time, in other words, it puts them in question. Poetry calls the reader or interpreter to creative collaboration by reminding him, as though it were his task, of his ability to move beyond constituted structures of meaning, by reminding him of the fact of freedom. Not the piece of writing, but *we* ourselves are responsible for meaning.

Another lesson pointing beyond the field of literary scholarship is contained in the appeal for understanding: namely, to commit oneself to the rights of the individual in all of his irreplaceability and singularity. It is more convenient, of course, to overlook the "individual addition" (Boeckh) and be tied to what the easily scrutinized scholarly procedures of textual analysis bring up: "writing without style."[93] Judged by the methodological ideal of the exact natural sciences, the idea of the individual's irreducibility to the structure appears trivial or sentimental: the world will continue to exist without him. It is still easier for it—Sartre reminded us of this[94]—to continue to exist without human beings at all.

Translated by Robert E. Sackett

Notes

What follows is a translation of the second half of "Textauslegung," in *Erkenntnis und Literatur,* D. Harth and P. Gebhardt, eds. (Stuttgart: J. B. Metzlersche Verlagsbuchhandlung, 1982), pp. 141–60—ED.

1. A. Sandor, "Text und Werke: Forschungslage und Versuch eines literaturwissenschaftlichen Modells," *Deutsche Vierteljahrshefte* 53 (1979): 478–511.

2. Wolfgang Iser, *Der Akt des Lesens. Theorie ästhetischer Wirkung* (Munich: W. Fink, 1976), p. 39 [*The Act of Reading: A Theory of Aesthetic Response* (Baltimore and London: The Johns Hopkins University Press, 1978), p. 19.—ED.].

3. Friedrich D. E. Schleiermacher, *Hermeneutik und Kritik,* edited by Manfred Frank (Frankfurt: Suhrkamp, 1977), cf. pp.167–70, *passim.* [See "*The Hermeneutics:* Outlines of the 1819 Lectures," in *The Hermeneutic Tradition: From Ast to Ricoeur,* edited by Gayle L. Ormiston and Alan D. Schrift (Albany: State University of New York Press, 1990), pp. 97–98. Hereafter HT—ED.]

4. J. Wach, *Das Verstehen. Grundzüge einer Geschichte der hermeneutischen Theorie im 19. Jahrhundret,* vol. I: *Die grossen Systeme* (Tübingen, 1926), p. 133f.

5. Schleiermacher, *Hermeneutik und Kritik,* pp. 132, 169, 321f. [HT, pp. 97–98.—ED.]

6. Jacques Derrida, *Marges de la philosophie* (Paris: Les Éditions de Minuit, 1972), p.191 [cf. *Margins of Philosophy,* translated by Alan Bass (Chicago: University of Chicago Press, 1982), p. 160.—ED].

7. Roland Barthes, "Introduction à l'analyse structurale des récits," *Communications* 8 (1966): 3 [see "Introduction to the Structural Analysis of Narratives," in *Image—Music—Text,* translated by Stephen Heath (New York: Hill and Wang, 1977), p. 81ff.—ED.].

8. J. G. Fichte, *Nachgelassene Schriften,* edited by H. Jacob, vol. II (Berlin, 1937), p. 355.

9. Schleiermacher, *Hermeneutik und Kritik,* pp. 139, 230, *passim* [see HT, p. 87.—ED.].

10. *Ibid.,* p. 329ff,; see also Manfred Frank, *Das individuelle Allgemeine. Textstrukturierung und interpretation nach Schleiermacher* (Frankfurt: Suhrkamp, 1977), p. 305ff.

11. Cf. A. J. Greimas, *Sémantique Structurale* (Paris: Larousse, 1966); Paul Ricoeur, *La métaphore vive* (Paris: Les Éditions du Seuil, 1975), p. 88ff. [*The Rule of Metaphor,* translated by Robert Czerny (Toronto: University of Toronto Press, 1977), pp. 66ff.—ED.].

12. Schleiermacher, *Hermeneutik und Kritik,* p. 139 [see HT, p. 86 and "The Aphorisms on Hermeneutics from 1805 and 1809/10," p. 71.—ED.].

13. Peter Szondi, *Einführung in die literarische Hermeneutik* (Frankfurt: Suhrkamp, 1975), p. 14.

14. Frank, *Das individuelle Allgemeine,* p. 262ff.

15. Schleiermacher, *Hermeneutik und Kritik,* p. 139f, [see HT, pp. 87–88.—ED.].

16. *Ibid.,* p. 144 [HT, p. 98.—ED.].

17. *Ibid.,* p. 144ff. [HT, pp. 92–93.—ED.].

18. *Ibid.,* p. 139 [HT, p. 87.—ED.].

19. Tzvetan Todorov, "Poetik," in *Einführung in dem Strukturalismus,* edited by F. Wahl (Frankfurt: Suhrkamp, 1977), pp. 108 and 111.

20. *Ibid.,* p. 110.

21. Barthes, "Introduction à l'analyse structurale des récits," pp. 1–27 ["Introduction to the Structural Analysis of Narratives," pp. 79–124—ED.].

22. Schleiermacher, *Hermeneutik und Kritik,* p. 101ff. [see HT, pp. 77 and 86–87.—ED.].

23. Claude Lévi-Strauss, *Anthropologie structurale*, vol. I (Paris: Les Éditions du Seuil, 1958 and 1974), p. 236.

24. Schleiermacher, *Hermeneutik und Kritik*, p. 138 [see HT, pp. 95–96.— ED.].

25. *Ibid.*, p. 142.

26. Roland Barthes, *S/Z*, (Paris: Les Éditions du Seuil, 1970) German translation: *S/Z*, translated by Jürgen Hoch (Frankfurt: Suhrkamp, 1976), p. 9 [*S/Z*, translated by Richard Miller (New York: Hill and Wang, 1974), pp. 10–11—ED.].

27. Cf. R. Brutting, *'Texte' und 'Ériture' in den französischen Literaturwissenschaften nach dem Struckturalismus* (Bonn, 1976).

28. Barthes, *S/Z*.

29. Jacques Derrida, *L'écriture et la différence* (Paris: Les Éditions du Seuil, 1967), p. 42 [*Writing and Difference*, translated by Alan Bass (Chicago: University of Chicago Press, 1980), p. 26—ED.].

30. Barthes, *S/Z*, p. 10ff. [English translation, p. 3ff.—ED.].

31. *Ibid.*, p. 17 [English translation, p. 13—ED.].

32. Jacques Lacan, *Les quatre concepts fondementaux de la psychanalyse* (Paris: Les Éditions du Seuil, 1973), p. 225f.; and *Écrits* (Paris: Les Éditions du Seuil, 1966), p. 353.

33. Barthes, *S/Z*, p. 15 [English translation p. 11—ED.].

34. *Ibid.*, p. 23 [English translation, p. 19—ED.].

35. *Ibid.*, p. 24 [English translation, p. 19—ED.].

36. *Ibid.*, p. 15 [English translation, p. 11—ED.].

37. Richard Palmer, *Hermeneutics: Interpretation Theory in Schleiermacher, Dilthey, Heidegger, and Gadamer* (Evanston: Northwestern University Press, 1969), pp. 62–63.

38. Schleiermacher, *Hermeneutik und Kritik*, p. 142 [see HT, p. 98.—ED.].

39. Barthes, *S/Z*, p. 9 [English translation, p. 5—ED.].

40. Schleiermacher, *Hermeneutik und Kritik*, p. 168 [see HT, p. 97.—ED.].

41. *Ibid.*, p. 171 [pp. 96–97; see also p. 79.—ED.].

42. *Ibid.*

43. *Ibid.*

44. *Ibid.*, p. 172 [see HT, p. 97.—ED.].

45. J. Starobinski, *L'Oeil Vivant II: La relation critique* (Paris: Éditions Gallimard, 1970), p. 25.

46. W. Sanders, *Linguistische Stiltheorie* (Göttingen, 1973), p. 93ff.

47. August Boeckh, *Enzyklop die und Methodologie der philologischen Wissenschaften*, edited by E. Bratuschek (Darmstadt, 1966), p. 126.

48. Wilhelm von Humbolt, *Gesammelte Schriften*, edited by A. Leitzmann (Darmstadt, 1968), Bd. 5, p. 418.

49. Jean-Paul Sartre, *Critique de la raison dialectique, précédé de 'Questions de méthode'*, tome I, *Theorie des ensembles practiques* (Paris: Éditions Gallimard, 1960), p. 180 [*Search for a Method*, translated by Hazel Barnes (New York: Alfred A. Knopf, 1968), p. 90—ED.].

50. Jean-Paul Sartre, *L'Idiot de la famille. Gustave Flaubert de 1821 à 1857*, tome I (Paris: Éditions Gallimard, 1971), p. 56 [*The Family Idiot*, vol. I, translated by Carol Cosman (Chicago: University of Chicago Press, 1981), p. 45—ED.].

51. Frank, *Das individuelle Allgemeine*, p. 322ff.; Frank, *Das Sagbare und das Unsagbare. Studien zur neuesten französischen Hermeneutik und Texttheorie* (Frankfurt: Suhrkamp, 1980), p. 66ff.

52. Schleiermacher, *Hermeneutik und Kritik*, pp. 80f., 94, 196, *passim* [see HT, p. 97.—ED.].

53. Jacques Derrida, "LIMITED INC a b c . . . ," translated by Samuel Weber, *Glyph 2: Johns Hopkins Textual Studies* (1977): 201.

54. Schleiermacher, *Hermeneutik und Kritik*, p. 317 [cf. HT, p. 95.—ED.].

55. Derrida, "LIMITED INC a b c . . . ," p. 216.

56. Ferdinand de Saussure, *Cours de linguistique générale*, Édition critique préparée par T. de Mauro (Paris: 1972), p. 155f. [see *Course in General Linguistics*, translated by Wade Baskin (New York: McGraw Hill, 1966), p. 117ff.—ED.].

57. *Ibid.*, pp. 166–168 [English translation, p. 118—ED.].

58. Derrida, *L'écriture et la différence*, p. 422ff. [*Writing and Difference*, p. 290ff.;—ED.]; see also "LIMITED INC a b c . . . ," p. 183ff.

59. Franz Kafka, *Sämtliche Erzählungen*, edited by P. Raabe (Frankfurt: 1970), p. 285ff.

60. Cf. Manfred Frank, *Die unendliche Fahrt. Ein Motiv und sein Text* (Frankfurt: Suhrkamp, 1979).

61. Franz Kafka, *Tagebücher 1910–1923*, edited by M. Brod (Frankfurt: Suhrkamp, 1973), p. 340.

62. *Ibid.*, pp. 345, 347.

63. Cf. G. Kurz, *Traum-Schrecken. Kafkas Literarische Existenzanalyse* (Stuttgart: 1980).

64. Jacques Derrida, "Le *retrait* de la métaphore," *Poésie* 7 (1978): 105 [see "The *Retrait* of Metaphor," *enclitic* (1978): 7–8—ED.].

65. Derrida, *Positions* (Paris: Les Éditions de Minuit, 1972), p. 62, cf. p. 82 [*Positions*, translated by Alan Bass (Chicago: University of Chicago Press, 1981), p. 45, cf. p. 60—ED.].

66. Cf. S. J. Schmidt, *Texttheorie* (Munich: 1973); K. Steirle, *Text als Handhing* (Munich, 1975).

67. John Searle, "Reiterating the Differences: A Reply to Derrida," *Glyph 2: Johns Hopkins Textual Studies* (1977): 207.

68. Sanders, *Linguistische Stiltheorie*, p. 123.

69. Ferdinand de Saussure, *Cours de linguistique générale*, Édition critique par R. Engler, 2 vols. (Wiesbaden: 1968), p. 28 [see *Course in General Linguistics*, p. 13—ED.].

70. Samuel Weber, "Das linke Zeichen. Zur Semiologie Peirces und Saussures," *Fugen. Deutsch-franzosisches Jahrbuch fur Text-analytik* (1980): 61.

71. Boeckh, *Enzyklopä die und Methodologie der philologischen Wissenschaften*, p. 83.

72. R. Musil, *Gesammelte Werke in 9 Bänden*, edited by A. Frisé (Reinbek: 1978), Bd. 8, pp. 1151–1152.

73. Schleiermacher, *Hermeneutik und Kritik*, p. 168, cf. p. 170ff. [see HT pp. 96–99.—ED.].

74. Sartre, *L'Idiot de la Famille*, tome I, p. 7 [*The Family Idiot*, p. ix—ED.].

75. Sartre, *L'Idiot de la Famille*, tome III, p. 432.

76. Jean-Paul Sartre, *Situations IX, mélanges* (Paris: Éditions Gallimard, 1972), p. 111f.

77. Sartre, *L'Idiot de la Famille*, tome III, p. 29.

78. Starobinski, *L'Oeil Vivant II: La relation critique*, p. 56.

79. Sartre, *Critique de la raison dialectique*, pp. 85–86ff. [*Search for a Method*, pp. 132–133—ED.]; cf. Frank, *Das individuelle Allgemeine*, p. 293ff.; and *Das Sagbare und das Unsagbare*, p. 36ff.

80. Schleiermacher, *Hermeneutik und Kritik*, p. 93ff. [cf. HT, p. 98.—ED.].

81. *Ibid.*, p. 169f., *passim* [see HT p. 97.—ED.].

82. J. Kreft, *Grundproblem der Literaturdidatik. Eine Fachdidaktik im Konzept sozialer und individueller Entwicklung und Geschichte* (Heidelberg: 1977), p. 133ff.

83. *Ibid.*, p. 140f.

84. Schleiermacher, *Hermeneutik und Kritik*, p. 92 [cf. HT, p. 98.—ED.]; see also Sartre, *Critique de la raison dialectique*, pp. 88 [*Search for a Method*, p. 137—ED.].

85. Cf. L. Spitzer, *Stilstudien*, 2 volumes (Munich: 1928; Darstadt: 1961).

86. Sartre, *Critique de la raison dialectique*, p. 88 [*Search for a Method*, p. 137—ED.].

87. Sartre, *L'Idiot de la Famille*, tome I, p. 56 [*The Family Idiot*, vol. I, p. 45—ED.].

88. Frank, *Das individuelle Allgemeine*, p. 289ff.

89. Sartre, *L'Idiot de la Famille*, tome II, p. 1490.

90. Schleiermacher, *Hermeneutik und Kritik*, p. 168 [see HT, p. 97.—ED.]; see also Sartre, *Critique de la raison dialectique*, p. 90 [*Search for a Method*, p. 140—ED.].

91. Sartre, *Critique de la raison dialectique*, p. 91 [*Search for a Method*, p. 143: "They lead us to suspect at once both social structures . . . and a *unique* childhood domain."—ED.].

92. *Ibid.*, p. 92 [English translation, p. 146—ED.].

93. Barthes, *S/Z*, p. 9 [English translation, p. 5—ED.].

94. Jean-Paul Sartre, *Situations II: Qu'est-ce que la littérature?* (Paris: Éditions Gallimard, 1948), p. 316 [*What is Literature?* translated by Bernard Frechtman (Secaucus, N.J.: Citadel Press, 1949), pp. 150–151—ED.].

8

Hermeneutic Ellipses:
Writing the Hermeneutical Circle in Schleiermacher*

Werner Hamacher

What a catastrophe! Then there will be readers who can read.

—Friedrich Schlegel, *On Incomprehensibility*

I.

There's a strange logic by which witnesses for the prosecution can, against their own will, strengthen the defendant's case when brought before the court's bench. Similarly, the pacesetters for the universalization of hermeneutics, as a part of a larger process of its emancipation from the doctrines of inspiration and rationalism, have not been able to stop speaking, implicitly or manifestly, for the other side. Against the positions of a hermeneutics which was supposed to secure the apparently tightly sealed doctrinal building of theological dogmatics and the canonical systems of rationalism, the most complete attacks—and, thanks to their disputational skill in argumentation, the most effective ones—were delivered by Friedrich Schleiermacher in conjunction with the transcendental turn of Kantian critical philosophy and its further developments by theorists among the romantics. Hermeneutics had long understood itself largely as an appendix to the individual disciplines of theology and philology, or else to formal logic, and had contented itself with the establishment of a heuristic canon that served the interpretation of "obscure passages," be they from the Bible or from Greek or Roman classics. By contrast, it was with Schleiermacher's hermeneutics that for the first time the conditions of understanding in general were systematically called into question. Through the methodical reflection upon its transcendental and historical conditions, he meant to liberate hermeneutics from the "nook of a parentheses"[1] in theological and philological treatises, and to be able to "secure [for it] another place"[2]: a

177

place which, "as the *Wissenschaft* of the unity of knowledge" within the system of dialectics, it would be entitled to occupy alongside ethics as the "*Wissenschaft* of history," and physics as the doctrine of the "natural" side of human experience.[3] Now Schleiermacher's emancipation of hermeneutics from its placement in the corner, in the shadows of accredited philosophic disciplines, operates with arguments that are borrowed from the arsenal of the opponent's side, and in its formulation of the concept of a general hermeneutics, these arguments constitute residues of the very representationalism he criticized—and in both cases this is not accidental, nor by reason of some strategic error, but rather occurs under the coercion that issues from its transcendental questioning itself and thus from the very instrument of its emancipation. In the history of its influence, the distortions of Schleiermacher's doctrine of interpretation, such as they appear in a particularly crass manner in its reception by Dilthey and Gadamer, have been able to claim a certain plausibility only through the appeal to just those moments in his theory in which the tradition of universally valid and historically invariable truths of reason lives on. For the elaboration of not only a universal hermeneutics, but also and especially a *literary* hermeneutics— and the relationship of one to the other cannot itself remain unexamined—it is therefore especially important to grasp these residues as precisely as possible: to define their function in the economy of a new hermeneutics that at once claims to be a hermeneutics of the new, and in this manner to undo a series of limitations that oppose, from the side of classical transcendental philosophies, the analysis of processes of understanding and the development of a usable *organon* of philological *Wissenschaften*.

II

In his "Fundamentals of Grammatics, Hermeneutics and Criticism" [*Grundlinien der Grammatik, Hermeneutik und Kritik*, Landshut, 1808],[4] the Schelling student Friedrich Ast writes that "hermeneutics is the art of discovering, with necessary insight, the thoughts of a writer from out of his discourse." In his lectures "On the Concept of Hermeneutics, with Reference to F. A. Wolf's Indications and Ast's Primer" [*Über den Begriff der Hermeneutik mit Bezug auf F. A. Wolfs Andeutungen und Asts Lehrbuch*],[5] Schleiermacher emphasizes in relation to this definition that it is to its advantage no longer to reserve the field of the hermeneutic operation exclusively for classical authors and for the Bible, but to open it to texts from one's own language and from the immediate present—be these a matter of newspaper articles, scientific and scholarly discussions, or "advertisements"—and to open it to that in them which, as "something foreign,"[6] opposes the unmediated understanding. But together with the praise for the expansion of hermeneutics' field of objects such as it is announced—in however deeply unpronounced a manner—in Ast's definition, a twofold reproach also appears. On the one hand Schleiermacher finds fault with the still restrictive treatment of spoken discourse, and the subordination implied thereby of the difficulties which it, too, may present for understanding. On the other, he protests against the expression, "that the thoughts of the author ought to be discovered with necessary insight"[7]: the process of literary-scholarly understanding does not proceed according to the logic of deduction or dialectical synthesis, and it leads to a certainty that does not correspond to that of mathematical solution. Neither the sheer "reproducing or copying [*Nachbilden*] of that which is already shaped [*Gebildeten*],"[8] nor the positivistic "collection and weighing of minute historical moments"[9] (still widely practiced today) may appropriately grasp the stylistic peculiarity of a text. For that mimetic "copying" of a literary production—which Schleiermacher, together with Ast (but on different grounds), nonetheless holds to be indispensable—must first make a solid historical-grammatical basis for itself in this "collection" in order not to fall into sheer arbitrariness. But this "collection" is, by itself alone, not in a position to reconstruct the "individual combinatory mode of an author, which, disposed differently in the same historical position and form of discourse—that is, with the same initial historical, linguistic and generic conditions—"would have yielded a different result."[10] The web of the communicative net tied by language and history, and reconstructed by the linguistic and historical *Wissenschaft,* is never so tight that the individuality of an author couldn't succeed in slipping through it. What presents itself as the strength of language, namely, that it is not only a universally valid, codified *system* of language, but also—through its individual speakers and their always specific *employment* of language—always an "original productivity,"[11] must turn out to be the weakness of hermeneutics—so long as hermeneutics is not prepared to set alongside its historical archives and grammatical inventories of rules a form of understanding that is complementary to the productivity which founds language. Schleiermacher names this form of understanding "divinatory procedure." This operation of "guessing" [*Erraten*],[12] which wholly concerns the irreducible individuality of a text and its composition, and which for its part demands the engagement of the interpreter's individuality, does not allow for methodical regulation. But since it belongs to the "complete" interpretation of each and every work, and even prescribes the interest of interrogation and the "way of posing the question"[13] for grammatical interpretation (that is, that kind of interpretation that seeks to structure a system of language that has become foreign, and to translate it into a system that is contemporary to the interpreter and his "cognitive community" [*Erkenntnisgemeinschaft*][14]), no hermeneutic operation may, in principle, have the character of "necessary insight." Its field is not that of necessity, but rather that of the realization of possibilities, none of which can make a claim for the sufficient representation of truth: "so long as even just one such possibility has not been totally eliminated, one can't speak of a necessary insight."[15]

Now the point of Schleiermacher's critique of Ast's postulate of necessity lies in the fact that it is a critique of his dissolution of the hermeneutic circle. The fundamental principle of hermeneutics consists of the postulate "that, just as certainly as the whole is understood from out of the part, so too may the part only be understood out of the whole."[16] But this circle may only be viewed as closed where the totality of a language system, in each and every one of its moments and each and every one of its actualizations in the employment of the language, is present completely and without remainder. Ast could maintain such a seamless continuity between the whole and its parts only by way of his construction of a "hermeneutics of the spirit," in which the "hermeneutics of the letter" (which relates to the explanation to words and content) and the "hermeneutics of meaning" (which relates to the intention of an author in the context of his time) are bound together into a tensionless whole.[17] But the factical aporias that set in with the construction of the circle are papered over with this kind of speculative spiritual hermeneutics propagated by Ast.

It is here that a first connection appears between Schleiermacher's critique of the exclusion of "living discourse" [*lebendige Rede*] from out of hermeneutics' realm of objects, and his critique of the subordination of practical aporias within the theory of the hermeneutic circle. In an "intimate conversation" with a "friend," his way of living and way of thinking are familiar to the conversational partner, and are at all times *more* familiar than the linguistic and historical conditions under which a text, from Greek antiquity for example, arose, and which can be reconstructed only with great effort. But when even under such circumstances, in which the totality of linguistic, historical and personal factors is "given," difficulties of understanding nonetheless arise, then this fact gives the lie to the thesis that all particulars can be completely explained through a given whole. A segment breaks from the formation of a given horizon of agreement and thereby betrays the consensus between the speakers, itself oriented toward an ideal of a preestablished harmony, of ping-pong-like mechanics (Schleiermacher speaks of the "almost unmental [*geistlosen*] and entirely mechanical" activity, in which "discourse is, like a ball, regularly received and returned"[18]). But this segment is, once again, the "individual combinatory mode" of a speaker: "I very often catch myself, in the middle of an intimate conversation, performing hermeneutic operations, when I'm not satisfied with a normal level of understanding, but rather seek to discover how the friend probably made the transition from one thought to another, or when I track down the probable context of opinions, judgment and endeavors that would have him express himself on an object being discussed just so, and not otherwise."[19] The individual mode of an expression, and the specific "just so and not otherwise" of its combination can not be firmly inscribed in any body of rules of any language community; and they thus need, for their hermeneutic explanation just as for their production of spontaneous individuality, an effort of the "divinatory faculty" that certainly reflects upon rules but is not fixed by them. From the context of Schleiermacher's reference to the speech situation, at least two things are sufficiently clear: "that the living expression [in the] immediate presence of the speaker"[20] is nearer to that free productivity at the foundation of language use than the written expression can ever be; and that writing favors the forgetting of its genesis, the amnesia of "free self-determination"[21] in the use of signs, and thereby introduces the development of the mechanistic concept of the hermeneutic operation's circular character. And yet the extraordinarily complex connection between this fundamental principle of hermeneutics—which Schleiermacher seeks to hold on to, while opposed to its mechanistic treatment by Ast—and the problem of writing's character—the solution of which has to be a pressing task for any *literary* hermeneutics—needs to be given a profile through a still closer examination.

For the sake of expanding the field of hermeneutic operations beyond the limits of the canon of theological and rationalist writing, and beyond the realm of that which is fixed in writing, Schleiermacher appeals to the very old priority of living discourse over writing, something ambiguously postulated by Plato and rarely put into question even today. In order to depose an old tradition of hermeneutics as a regional *Wissenschaft*, he mobilizes the older and more powerful one of philosophy as the universal and fundamental *Wissenschaft*. In order to make hermeneutic techniques capable of a finer differentiation, one exploring even the nuances of a person's individual stylistic gesture, he submits the admitted differentiation between written and oral language uses to a blunt hierarchization. Primacy and privilege remain reserved for the spoken word: up to and including Gadamer who, in his "Fundamentals of a Philosophic Hermeneutics" under the title *Truth and Method* [*Wahrheit und Methode: Grundzüge einer philosophischen Hermeneutik*], ceaselessly hypostasizes the conversation into the model of the "hermeneutic phenomenon,"[22] and leaves no doubt that he also wants to have the act of reading understood according to precisely this model. "Written transmission . . . , to the extent that it's decoded, is pure spirit [*reiner Geist*] to such a degree that it speaks to us as if it were present."[23] The peculiar semanticism in this conception of hermeneutics, which for its part can only rest upon an apodictically maintained representation of speech and its object within the historical continuum of meaning, has as its consequence the postulate that "the real hermeneutic task" is the "retransformation" of writing into speech.[24] Such a "retransformation" is possible only under the condition that—disregarding all historical and empirical determinants—writing be construed as the ideational form of abstraction of phonetic speech, the conceptual character of which offers the guarantee for a further return, itself not in need of mediation, to its meaning. The conversation is not only the model, it is also the matrix of all other verbal articulations, as especially that of writing: "The sign-language of writing indeed refers back to the real [eigentliche] language of speech."[25] Nowhere more strikingly, nor more ironically, than in his characterization of writing does one of Gadamer's main theses manifest itself in his book (a thesis arising out of misunderstandings of Heidegger): that of the pre-judgmental structure [Vorurteilsstruktur] of understanding which effectuates itself across history. Really, only speech is language, writing is signs, and as the derivative of the former, it refers to the "real language," and not to that which is itself the object of this language of speech. Writing is a secondary sign, a sign of a sign; or as Aristotle, in his Peri Hermēneias, decisively formulates it for the history of theories of writing up to Gadamer: "Thus there are the sounds to which the voice is formed, signs of the representations called forth in the soul, and writing is then a sign of the sounds."[26] Aristotle's concept of writing and Plato's comparable concept, proposed in his "Phaedrus" dialogue, are given in Gadamer's hermeneutics a reedition—abbreviated, but only that much more affirmative—under the sign of continuity, instead of submitting them to an analysis of their often controversial function in connection with their ontologies. But contrary to the suggestion which Gadamer's representation gives, these concepts are not at all simply carried forward continuously in the history of theories of language and hermeneutics, but rather undergo striking changes, above all during the period of their transcendental turn.

However much Schleiermacher accents the homogeneity of speech and writing within their sign-character, and however powerfully the Platonic-Aristotelian tradition still lives on in his definition of writing, this definition nonetheless also distinguishes itself from that tradition through decisive differences. His formulation of "the state of speech fixed for the eye through writing"[27] pushes the homogenization of speech and writing so far that writing is no longer characterized for him as a subordinated sign, but rather as a special state of speech. Writing is arrested speech, fixed and held speech, in which it no longer becomes objectified for the ear as a course of sound, but rather becomes objectified as image and shape for another organ of sensuousness, for the eye. By way of this opening of the traditional boundary between speech and writing, the hermeneutic principles that have been acquired in association with the former—and these are especially the conception of language as "act" and "a moment of life bursting forth," and the divinatory attention to its stylistic singularity—can legitimately also be claimed for the appropriate understanding of the latter, of writing. Thus Schleiermacher's pressing advice to the

> editors of written works, to practice industriously the interpretation of the more significant conversation. For the immediate presence of the speaker, the living expression which announces the participation of his whole spiritual being, the way in which here the thoughts develop out of the life common to all, this all leads—much more than the solitary observation of a wholly isolated text—to understanding a series of thoughts as at once a moment of life bursting forth, as an act connected to many other acts, even of other kinds, and it is precisely this side that is most often postponed, indeed for the most part thoroughly neglected, with the explanation of writers.[28]

The *function* of the expansion of the realm of hermeneutic objects and of the redefinition of the relation between writing and speech steps forth here with all of its pregnant meaning: it serves the attempt to model the interpretation of wholly isolated and inanimate writing according to the paradigm of the interpretation of the socially delivered and "living expression" of speech, and in this way to secure for the interpretation of texts as well the understanding of the central point at which all perspectives on language converge—the understanding of the "moment of life bursting forth" or of the "conception-decision [*Konzeptionsentschluss*],"[29] the activity of the speaking subject that actually founds meaning. But with corresponding clarity a *consequence* of this expansion and redefinition also steps forth: when writing is characterized as a state of speech, this speech—however much it might be distinguished as living, immediately present, social—must also itself bear the mark of the negatively valorized attribute of writing, and be affected by absence, death, isolation. To the generalization of the hermeneutic operation under the sign of phonocentrism and logocentrism, there corresponds as its flip-side the decentering emergence of a graphematics [*Graphematik*], which withdraws from the regime of logocentrism. With this, it's not just that the historical continuum of the master role of the paradigm of speech is once again interrupted; this paradigm itself comes apart at the joints. The "living moment" of speech "bursting forth" shows itself as traversed by the trace of a mortifying writing.

The conflict becomes virulent between the paradigm of living speech and that of isolated and exterior writing when Schleiermacher, in the detailed discussion of the problems issuing from the fundamental principle of the hermeneutic circle, once again affirms their essential indifference. The hinge between both forms of language's articulation is formed by memory [*Gedächtnis*], in which the characteristics of speech and writing are mixed together into an impermeable amalgam. Memory, like writing, is given the task of "fixing" the particular, so that one might be able to return to it from out of the series of all the other particulars of a given whole that are grasped in the course of understanding. Understanding thus is achieved *ex definitione*—that is, insofar as it is defined as the understanding of the particulars from out of the whole and of the whole from out of its particulars—only in the doubled run-through of the series of particular elements of the text or speech: in a preliminary understanding, only those significations can be actualized which are deposited in the general repertoire of a language, the syntactic and semantic system of rules of which can contain no information whatsoever concerning the particular composition of this specific whole, which is not preformed in the system. Only the possibility provided by memory and writing, of a return from the preliminary and incomplete understanding of the whole, oriented toward the register of linguistic conventions, to its particular component parts, allows for the appropriate grasping of their specific function within the composition of a discourse which, at the limit, is independent of the rules. To this extent, every divinatory act—which seeks to delimit the irreducibly individual gesture of a speech, a textual series or a period—is referred *a priori* to the fixing of speech in the medium of memory or writing as the condition of its possibility. Without the possibility of a return from the whole to its parts, neither the specificity of the whole nor that of its moments could be understood; without the trace of remembering in memory or the trace of writing on the paper, there's no understanding, but rather only preunderstanding which remains within the bounds of inanimate linguistic conventions.

In view of the function of the *fixing* of discourses, which is to found meaning, the double deficiency of writing and memory noted by Schleiermacher—even if merely parenthetically, as it were—appears as a danger for the entire hermeneutic project. Schleiermacher puts it clearly:

> There must therefore certainly be an understanding of the whole given . . . merely through the particular, but this particular will necessarily only be an incomplete one if memory has not held fast to the particular, and if we, after the whole has been given, cannot return to the particular in order then to understand it more exactly and completely from out of the whole. With this there once again disappears altogether the distinction between that which is only aurally perceived, and that which we have before us in writing, in that for the former we also, through memory, seize upon all the advantages

which appear to belong exclusively to the latter—so that, as Plato also already said, the utility of writing consists only in remedying the lack in memory, but ambiguously so, since it is grounded in the decay of memory and also reencourages precisely this decay.[30]

In Plato's (written) dialogue *Phaedrus,* the Egyptian myth of the origin of writing recounted by Socrates in fact leaves no doubt about writing's fatal infirmity. Its inventor Theuth, the god of the underworld, of the dead, is told by Ammon the sun god:

> This invention will infuse much more forgetfulness into the souls of the learners, out of neglect of remembering, for, trusting in writing, they will remember only from the outside, by way of foreign signs, and will not remember inwardly, immediately and on their own. Thus you have not invented a medium for actual remembering [*mnēmes, die Erinnerung*], but only for the faculty of reminding [*upomnēseos, das Erinnern*], and of wisdom you contribute to your students only its appearance, and not the thing itself. (274a)[31]

A remedy and aid to memory, writing, "ambiguous" as it is, contributes to memory's illness, to its decay, to its loss. Nonetheless, Schleiermacher cannot, no more than Plato, contest its necessity. For memory is finite and limited, however much it might, as the faculty of representation, oppose itself to the successive loss of presence in the passing of time. Its deficiency is in need of the remedy, if something like understanding is to be at all possible: the re-presenting of something become absent, the re-remembering of something forgotten, the guessing of something foreign, the reanimation of something dead. This remedy is guaranteed to understanding only by writing and the exterior forms of archivizing [*Archivierung*] the living. "Speech has to become writing,"[32] wherever the reach of memory does not suffice to guarantee mutual understanding and, with it, homogeneity within the community and continuity within the course of history. Yet irreducibly, this indispensable supplemental gift [*Beigabe*], this necessary aid which is even the telos of the living organism of speech understanding itself—the telos, for otherwise Schleiermacher couldn't speak of speech "having to become writing"—is also always at the same time a poison, a decomposition and dissociation of this organism. What ought to tend toward rendering the life of the spirit infinite and, at any rate, toward its totalization, is at the same stroke its radical finitization, its depravation, and its disintegration. Writing is thus at once the condition of possibility and the ground of impossibility for the authentic self-understanding of speaking subjects; the foundation for the comprehending reconstitution of the speech of the other in the context of its inventoried grammatical and semantic language conventions, and, at "one" with this, the destruction of any and every form of the constitution of meaning and thus of any and every hermeneutics. It's not surprising, then, that Schleiermacher, in his talk on the concept of hermeneutics, doesn't want to risk this very concept, and that he seeks to banish the infection that threatens his entire hermeneutic undertaking with the ambiguity of writing, by supporting himself with the citation from Plato's text, disarming the function and power of writing, and limiting the utility of writing to consisting precisely *only* in its remedying of the deficiency of memory. And it's also understandable that, having defined memory and writing as the constituents of communication and, furthermore, of historical and social life, he remarks in a marginal note to the "Sketches of a System of Moral Doctrine" [*Entwürfe zu einem System der Sittenlehre*]: "But communication through writing alone, without living dialogics, always becomes dead."[33]

III

The possibility of understanding and the possibility of hermeneutics prove to be, in Schleiermacher's attempt at their foundation, systematically bound up with their own failure. The unstoppable quavering of their ground appears in a yet harsher light when one considers that not only they, but also, with them, the flanking theories of language and the subject must forfeit their steady stance due to the necessary eruption of writing's destruction of meaning. Schleiermacher proceeds—in this, a precursor of Saussure[34]—from the double character of language: it is a grammatical-semantic system, which "conditions the thought of all individuals . . . if one [considers] individual people only as a place for language,"[35] as well as language usage, "having arisen from each and every act of speech and returning to the individual."[36] Now, under language usage, one should not understand a merely mechanical and repetitive actualization of the grammatical system and the rules of social relations (invariable only in appearance) laid down in it, rules through which a "cognitive community" defines itself. Language usage admittedly does not manage without this mechanical side of the realization of pregiven schemata. Through it, each speaking individual incessantly renders present his objective social determinants. But with the rubric "language usage,"[37] Schleiermacher's theory of language nonetheless accents the predominance of the generative aspect of each discursive action and thereby the general language- and meaning-constituting power of self-socializing individuals. The two aspects of language, its being both the system of language and the act of language,

consequently do not relate to one another symmetrically: if under the one
the speaker represents himself as the product of a pregiven language, under
the other he represents himself as its producer. But how language is generated, and how an already given one is modified and transformed, constitute
the main interest for the perspective of a hermeneutics which has to do with
the *differentia specifica* of each individual act of language. The hermeneutic
technique belonging to this realm of knowledge goes by the name, in
Schleiermacher, of "psychological interpretation," and therefore allows one
to forget only all too easily that it has to make do with constructs that owe
their existence to the—by virtue of the *natural* determination of finite reason—"untranslatable peculiarity [*unübertragbaren Eigentümlichkeit*]"[38] of
verbal productions. Schleiermacher's concept of psychological interpretation has nothing in common with a psychology, however conditioned, not
even with a *psychologia rationalis:* it means nothing other than the logic of
the production of language and literary works and is thereby no less close
to the side of physis than to that of psychic process, through which the
naturally conditioned particularity of a verbal utterance—however untranslatable it might be—produces the reason [*Vernunft*] that is identical for all
speaking beings.

Every verbal production, which is more than the mechanical imitation
and execution of pregiven socio-grammatical rules—and there is none that
would not be more than this,—presents itself as the "differential" between
physis and psyche, between exteriorization and interiorization [*Entäusserung und Verinnerung*], between "inner speaking," from which cognition
arises, and outward discourse, which orients itself toward others.[39] As this
differential which founds language and cognition, it realizes a "determinate
identity of the transcendental with the empirical"[40]—that is, an identity of
the schema valid for all, according to which the most general concepts are
formed and in which individual speakers have the guarantee of mutual understanding, and the condition of one's being influenced [*Affektion*]—
uniquely for each different individual—by the multiple circumstances in
which one becomes active. But if the transcendental is supposed to become
sense experience—as is demanded by the concept of its identity with the
empirical—then there must be within the process of semiosis an instance
that works toward the identical schematism against the background of the
empirical. For everything general needs its positing within the empirical
and is nothing at all without its positing, just as each individual thing has to
produce the general from out of itself in order to find in it the guarantor of
its determination. That instance in which the transcendental and the empirical—and with them, nature and spirit, individual and society, inner and
outer—mediate one another into a determinate identity—and that means
their mutual self-production—is, once again, memory.

It is in memory, which cannot exist without language and thus remains a secondary phenomenon despite its mediating status, that language
is constitutive of both subject and society. Memory alone, and not the spontaneously produced verbal gesture, "is the necessary condition of communication [*Mitteilung*] outside of oneself and within oneself."[41] In order to
be able to relate to oneself *as* oneself—and it is this alone that "communication within oneself," strictly understood, can mean—the I needs a
bond that on the one hand is not immediately it itself (for then it wouldn't
be able to become aware of itself in the mode of the *as*), but on the other
hand also doesn't advance against it as sheer exteriority (for then it couldn't
gain any access to itself as *self*)—and yet which nonetheless joins it with
itself. Memory puts such a bond at the I's disposal—but only at the cost of
having the self, in irrecuperable supplementarity [*in uneinholbarer Nachträ-
glichkeit*], always only *thinking of* its self, slip away from itself. In memory
the I, however deeply its trace might have imprinted itself upon it, is already no longer present to itself, and it is only in the de-presenting distance [*depräsentierenden Distanz*] that the I finds the prop—perpetually
withdrawing itself, but never completely withdrawn from it—for its awareness of itself *as self*. Self-consciousness and self-accord are thereby characterized as inconclusive hermeneutic events, in which a still-indeterminate I
places itself [and disregards itself, *sich hinwegsetzt*] on the far side of the
temporal difference opened up by its fixing in the memory trace, through
the positing of an equivalence with this very fixed or established verbal
shape, and experiences itself determined as self by this shape. This process
is inconclusive because every act of self-accord brings with it a temporal
index that indicates to it not only that its positing of equivalence is a positive of equivalence *with* the inequivalent, but also that it itself takes place in
the *medium* of the inequivalent. The hermeneutics of the self, the hermeneutics of the "communication . . . within itself" [*"Mitteilung in sich"*] is
that of its inconclusive partition [*Teilung*] within itself; the hermeneutics of
a self that is not its own ground; a hermeneutics of the interruption of
hermeneutics. Through its mnemonic linguisticality, self-consciousness is
distinguished as a radically finite self-consciousness, as one which cannot
consolidate itself in any conclusive figure—such as was aimed at by reflection theory in its speculative variety. The intrinsic ambiguity of self-
relation—that the I, as a verbal and memory trace, can certainly become
relatively objective to itself, but at no time can become present to itself
and, with this, become an indubitable self—marks a fundamental deficiency within the concept of subjectivity itself. Schleiermacher interprets
this (and supplements it at the time) as the result of "absolute
dependency"[42] upon an instance transcendent of subjectivity, upon an other
(understood theologically by him) that must be positioned outside of the

self-relation and that therefore holds and checks the latter in relation to its unsublatable ambiguity. But it is clear that Schleiermacher's theological *interpretation* of the heterogeneity within the phenomenon of self-relation only exports a moment out of its doubled structure which his *description* had uncovered and that this moment—irreducible exteriority—itself only receives its cogent explanation from out of the intrinsic tensional relation between I and I. Whoever would not reproduce Schleiermacher's hermeneutics of self-accord—his hermeneutics *itself*—in its theological orientation, but rather would understand it, will have to derive the hypostasis of an altogether Other from out of the intrinsic heterogeneity of the self, and think it as the attempt at a release from the immanent tensions of its self-relation.[43] It is only as the memory of God that memory is the secured place for the safekeeping of the self and guarantor of its understanding; as finite memory, as writing, it is the place of possible forgetting still *within* the self—and still includes in this the forgetting of God.

Memory is the "necessary condition" for "communication outside of oneself" as well, since every conversation between two different persons excludes simultaneity—no differently than does the self-conversation from which Schleiermacher conceives subjectivity. One's own speech must be made independent of the time of its production, must be countermanded and held back—in memory—so long as the other is still speaking. Thus memory, which forms the foundation for the linguistic combination of words into sentences, also becomes the foundation for the social "combination"—in Schleiermacher's language, the ethical "combination"[44]—within which the two different speakers gather themselves. It posits at the origin of one's speech the acknowledgment of the other—just as self-accord, in advance of every empirical otherness, had posited the acknowledgment of the alterity of the self in itself—and yet thereby economizes his otherness in such a way that it does not evaporate into abstract disparity. The unsublatable non-simultaneity which installs itself with memory is thus the necessary condition for every form of verbal, self-referential and social relation. It is only in its medium that the "identity of the transcendental with the empirical" can realize itself, but for this very reason also only as a "determinate"—that is, in the form of a precarious, untranslatable—individuality.[45]

The identity which Schleiermacher treats and which is indispensable for every form of self-accord and understanding of the other as other, does not have the conclusive, synthetic shape of the *result* such as is attributed to it by speculative dialectics. It achieves itself rather more as a movement *between* the transcendental and the empirical, for which Hegel surely would not have spared the polemical formulation of "bad infinity." And yet it ought to achieve itself within their frame and according to the regularities that they impose upon it. Schleiermacher's concept for the delicate relationship between the general and the individual, within which all verbal and language-generative acts manifest themselves, is called the "schema of oscillation between the general and the particular."[46] It is not without reason that the title of "oscillation" claims an emphatic status in Schleiermacher's texts. A relation between the particular and the general in which the former would not turn out to be a mere particle of the latter which subsumes it or from which it could be deduced, can only be adequately grasped—and then admittedly only also at the cost of a refusal of the logic of the concept—as a quantitative relationship and under the form of a metaphor which accordingly cannot appear in the repertoire of logics of subsumption: as a swaying, hovering and pendulating between the two related terms. Along with this sense of swinging and—as if weaving, textualizing—shuttling to and fro, a further sense might have been called to mind for the classical philologist Schleiermacher with the choice of the term "oscillation," and one which entertains a closer connection to language: *oscillum* is in fact a derivation of *os,* mouth, face, and thus means little mouth, little face and mask. Oscillation, understood in its etymological context, would indicate that "originary" movement of language in which it is allotted to something or someone, which has neither language nor face, is neither intuition nor concept.[47] Every word, every utterance "is an oscillation between the determinacy [*Bestimmtheit*] of the particular and the indeterminacy [*Unbestimmtheit*] of the general image. . . .The identity of the particular and the genus [*Gattung*] is posited in this oscillation."[48] Conceptual generalities, such as they are indispensable for communicative acts, allow themselves to be won from the chaos of individualities exclusively through an abstraction which is injurious to the determinacy and thereby the communicability of the individual; thus the process of abstraction needs, for its correction, a supplementary individual which is given to it within the subject of abstraction and which makes a priori each generalization into the individual one of a linguistic and cognitive community or of a determinate speaker. But with the determination of the speaker, something incommunicable is posited in each abstraction—which, as closed off, would no longer be communicable: "we can never express something individual through language."[49] Between these two poles, the individual and the general, which no longer belong to the realm of the verbal in the strict sense, language oscillates and constitutes itself in the interval between their two impossibilities—labile, paradoxical, and always incomplete—*as* oscillation; as oscillation between terms that only experience their determination *from* this oscillation and *in* it. If, namely, general concepts are not at all *given* in memory, but rather it must first of all *generate* them qua abstraction—as Schleiermacher so impressively demonstrates in his "Dialectic" lecture on general schematism and language;[50] if, therefore, inscription in memory is the operation constitutive of language and understanding *kat' exochen*, then Schleiermacher's description of the emergence of language must lead—counter to his idealistic tendency which seeks to claim the general as a concept of autonomous power[51]—to the conclusion that there cannot be a general, historically and culturally invariable schematism of signification which would not always already be tinged by individual historical and social conditions. Schleiermacher himself emphasizes the impossibility of a purely individual verbal gesture which could shape itself without the instance of an other—be it even that other in which the I knows itself as being determined as self. Memory, as language-forming schematism, neither submits to the rules of a code, nor behaves idiomatically in its generative acts; thus the traces of remembering which it fixes can be neither utterly undecodable, nor universally transparent. The functional mode of memory withdraws from these polar concepts not because they, oxymorically, amalgamate within it, but because they take their leave from it. The "schema of oscillation between the general and the particular" is thus not one that allows itself to be characterized as a movement of mediation between given quantities; it is much more the case that it produces these for the first time through the oscillation as their ever-varying, vibrating margins. General and individual, transcendental and empirical, are functions of the oscillation, and that which is incommunicable in them as abstract structures coats and overdraws [*überzieht*] the interpolar realm of oscillation as well, in ever-varying shadings with its incomprehensibility.

IV

It has become clear that the difficulties which are set out for hermeneutics by the fact that it has to refer to writing when it is a matter of grasping more comprehensive verbal structures, or those that have become historical—that these difficulties have in no way been eliminated even through Schleiermacher's theorems from the philosophy of subjectivity and of language, which allow themselves to be read as the complement to his hermeneutics and which can in particular serve to render more precise the process of language formation and, thereby, the object of psychological-technical interpretation. On the contrary: what at first glance appeared as the difficulty of a special hermeneutics, of literary hermeneutics, shows itself to be a problem of much broader reach once one has looked at the general conditions under which language and, with it, social interaction can arise. Every hermeneutics that refers to language-formed structures is struck by this problem—whether it is a matter of the fact of self-consciousness, of linguistic phenomena such as semantic or referential orderings, of graphic or plastic representations, of codes of behavior or other "symbolic systems"—as, for example, ethics. None of these hermeneutics— and they must be differentiated from one another, if they are to take account of the diversity of the realms of their objects—can disregard the minimal conditions for the constitution of their objects, which are at once also their own conditions: "memory," the "necessary conditions of communication outside oneself and within oneself,"[52] the temporal difference posited with this, and the possibility of forgetting. And none of these hermeneutics— Schleiermacher makes this clear in all of his considerations of dialogics, ethics and aesthetics—can disregard the fact that the constitutive defect in the structure of their objects and in their own modes of procedure only allows itself to be supplemented through a problematic means of assistance: through writing or a fixing substitutable for it.

Writing in its broadest—if one wishes, "metaphorical"—sense has the advantage of elevating the act of language creation, otherwise merely subjective and bound to momentary spontaneity, to the rank of objectivity. In this manner alone can the language of the I (or of an other, more complexly structured language-instituter) encounter himself and others as a relative whole: maintain its specificity and at the same time be the object of rule-governed observation. "Inner speaking is the language of memory, writing is the memory and the tradition of language, through which it first becomes fully objective and communication is posited independent of the time of production."[53] With this advantage of the graphic supplement,[54] which distinguishes it as the instance of establishing the "determinate identity of the transcendental and the empirical" and as the "schema of the oscillation between the general and the particular," its aggravating disadvantage nonetheless remains indissolubly connected: that it effects the decay of the memory which it itself empowers, the decay of the identity— realized in memory and in the supplement itself—of the general and the particular, of the transcendental and the empirical, the decay of the possibility of understanding and, with this, of life. "Communication through writing alone, without living dialogics, always becomes dead."[55] Now against the ruinous double function of writing in the production of sign and meaning, it can be argued—and this has happened insistently and with considerable persuasive power—that writing is, according to Schleiermacher's striking formulation, precisely only a "necessary" condition for the unification of the general and the particular, but not their *causa per quam*. But this qualification, however obvious it must appear to be in the context of the rhetoric of distinctions pertaining to metaphysical philosophizing, in no way withstands the description that Schleiermacher provides for the function and effect of writing. Living dialogics itself owes itself only to the fixing of a combination of traces of remembering within memory, and in order to remain a "living" one and to totalize itself within history, it is referred and exiled [*verwiesen*] to material graphesis and its province— which is not immediately subject to the demand of the intellectual function. The intellectual spontaneity in the act of founding sign and meaning, which is the only one that could, if need be, have attributed to it the function of a *causa per quam,* cannot receive the status of a sufficient condition. Every *causa* of this sort becomes traversed by the aporetic stroke of the *conditiones sine quibus non:* the necessary conditions provided by writing and its implications. What is living in sign systems thus enters unforeseeably into a position that is diametrically opposed to that provided it by Schleiermacher: dialogics becomes the supplement, arising out of writing, of a deficit in writing, which yet for its part was supposed to be merely the supplement of speech. Such a radical inversion with the positional framework of the functions of primary and derivative, the instituting and the instituted of meaning, of inner and outer, life and death is possible, however, only out of the common ground provided by the fact that both opposites—and, to be sure, as incomplete in themselves and with one another—are originally alloyed within the status of writing. Within it meaning *is* no longer and not yet again, there is not life and yet not death, not the power of a positing purely from out of itself alone and also not the passivity of the merely posited— but rather always both at once and none altogether. No verbal or verbally mediated praxis and no hermeneutic operation can blinker itself from this indetermination or overdetermination of its medium and object, without becoming blind to its own conditions.

From the irreducibly double effect of writing in all sign systems and in all operations lying within the breadth of its reach, at least three consequences for a hermeneutic theory may now be drawn.

The status and the functional mode of graphic articulations can no longer be understood according to the model of "living" speech as soon as it is recognized that its validity is subverted by the necessary intervention of writing. Writing can claim a relative autonomy with respect to speech not only insofar as it withdraws from the logic of self-presentation—and even identifies and banishes [*ausweist*] this logic as a mere effect of its ambiguity—but also with a view to its material shape. As far as I can see, Schleiermacher is, along with Hamann, one of the first theorists of language who proclaimed writing's right to its own history: "To this is added that, for criticism, writing also is, outside of language, something for itself, and has its positive element which, if we abstract from writing, does not appear in speech. . . . Writing has its own history. Alterations appear in it independent from the alterations in speech. But such alterations are nonetheless essential moments in the totality of the history of language."[56] If one thinks of baroque pattern poetry, of Mallarmé's *Coup de dés,* of Hölderlin's "Look, dear sir, a comma!" ["*Sehen Sie, gnädiger Herr, ein Komma!*"], and of the value which an author like Francis Ponge is able to give to the punctuation and the typefaces of his texts, then it is clear what a large role the material aspect of written articulation would have to play in a specifically *literary* hermeneutics—and yet still, to this day, doesn't play. The imagistic character of writing admittedly doesn't make the business of interpretation and its theories any easier. To be sure, it's less easy to abstract from the materiality of the graphic sign than from that of the phonetic one. And yet it, too, is transparent to the eye—for Schleiermacher, the "schema of all sensuous activities"[57]—only by way of the interference of the "intellectual function" *as* sign and in reference to its significance. More resistantly than any other sign-complex, writing opposes itself to the idealizing pressures of reason and must therefore, in a boundary region between an "organic" and an "intellectual function," remain in a strange half-opacity, a scandal for every hermeneutic effort.[58]

Although *literary* hermeneutics is a regional one, it yet may claim, on the grounds of the specific realm of its object—and this would be the second of the consequences alluded to—a special status within the sphere of both a general as well as a fundamental hermeneutics. If, as Schleiermacher's descriptions indicate, writing functions as the problematic instituting and necessary condition of every sign-system, even of the molecular one of the self-relation of the subject, then a hermeneutics which directs itself toward the literal constitution of texts, and whose themes are the specific forms of fictionality of verbal constructs, can raise the ironic claim of staking out the foundation for every fundamental hermeneutics and, as a regional one, the field for every general hermeneutics. This is to say that it would be able, in a distinctive manner, to indicate scripturality [*Schriftlichkeit*] as the perpetually self-decentering structure of every thinkable form of articulation and experience. This claim would be ironic because in its activity such a hermeneutics would carry out the permanent dismantling of the hermeneutic paradigm of (self-)presentation and of living speech, without being able to replace it by another. In accordance with Schleiermacher's argument that the experience of a universal can only be achieved in the unceasing approximation by way of the particular, this is a critique of the principled insufficiency of principles and paradigms of understanding. Where it pretends to perceive its specific potentials, a literary hermeneutics that draws from Schleiermacher operates on the edge between regional hermeneutics and metahermeneutics. Oscillating between both, it uncovers as the latter the general conditions of understanding, as the former the particular, material and historical modifications which traverse every pretension toward universal validity.

In the course of the transcendental turn which hermeneutics accomplishes with Schleiermacher's reflections, it bumps up, in the instance of writing, against a figure—this is the third consequence—upon which the project of transcendentalism founders. What is asked for are the most universal forms, valid for all time, under whose rules the development of signsystems and their corresponding acts of understanding are possible. The answer is found in a medium that indeed joins the transhistorical universals with sensuous representations—and to that extent perceives those tasks which the Kantian critique of reason had relegated to transcendental schematism—but that can carry out this business of mediation only at the cost of a radical historicization of its promise of universality, and consequently of a break therewith. The trace of remembering and graphic fixing are— always at "once"—the condition of possibility of transcendental schematization, and the condition of its impossibility. Writing, the organon of transcendence, detranscendentalizes. With this it is not only said that no speaker and no interpreter can ever be certain of the truth of the spoken or the interpreted because their joining within transcendental schematism is necessarily marked by the irregular break of writing. Truth itself becomes, under the aspect of its appointment by writing, something finite, passing, instituted, a fiction of possibilities of significance, which is not foreign to determinate empirical constellations of power alone and which, within the frame of their economy, can at all times be relieved by others.[59] As the instituting of the "schema of oscillation between the general and the particular," writing jumps the tracks not only of their dichotomy, but also of every other one: between life and death, addition and removal, communication and untranslatability, nature and culture, sensibility and intelligibility, inner and outer, truth and fiction, remembering and forgetting, unity and difference . . . Between the individual opposites and within them, writing marks a difference out of which they spring, but by which they are always at the same time struck with the mark of incompletion. Writing (de)generates the series of oppositions—including also that between writing and spoken speech. Neither the logic of opposition, nor that of a dialectical synthesis (indissolubly indebted to the former) can serve as the plumbline for hermeneutic operations which seek to do justice to the differential function of the graphic supplement. Hermeneutics is not to orient itself by the logic of the concept, the derivative character of which Schleiermacher never tired of accenting with all emphasis, despite his own inclinations deriving from the philosophy of identity. Rather, it is to orient itself by a logic—if it still is a logic—of those verbal forms which withdraw from the regime of the concept and its inventory of rules. As necessary as the methodical reflection upon the transcendental conditions of understanding in general is for any interpretive *Wissenschaft* that would not run aground in crude positivism, it is just as indispensable for it that there be the systematic analysis of the genesis and the paradoxical function of those conditions (of which here, with the example of writing, only an abstract sketch could be given). With the phrase, "Interpretation is art,"[60] Schleiermacher himself drew a consequence from out of the loosening of the transcendental obligation to which hermeneutic theory was bound up until his time, a consequence which can serve as a hint toward that logic which hermeneutics—and especially literary hermeneutics—would have to work out.

Interpretation is art because none of the rules entered in the register of grammatics can simultaneously contain the rule for their application within language *usage;* thus, neither a complete knowledge of the language system, nor a complete knowledge of the individual combinatory mode of a writer is possible. Both can be gained only under the presupposition that a transcendental grammatics could extend its mastery into the finest offshoots of its various actualizations. Into the breach that opens up between language system and usage, an understanding has to leap, one that for its part can follow neither the grammatical calculus, nor the sheer subjectivism of the interpreter, but rather must mobilize those moments that were effective in the process of language's rise and of self-understanding. "The whole business of hermeneutics should be viewed as a work of art, but not as if the execution ended in a work of art, but rather so that the activity only bears the character of art in itself, since the application is not also given along with the rules, i.e., cannot be mechanized."[61] The activity to which Schleiermacher here attributes the character of art—and does so not just in the sense of technique, but also in that of artistry—is the same that is at work in the act of original self-agreement. Schleiermacher characterizes it as a rhetorical one: "Thinking becomes complete through inner speech, and to that extent speech is only thought itself that has come about. But where one who is thinking finds it necessary to fix the thoughts for himself, there an art of speech also arises, transformation of the original [speech], and henceforth, interpretation also becomes necessary."[62] This "art of speech," rhetoric, is that form of language through which a thought "fixes" itself for its combination with other thoughts, for the self-understanding of the one who thinks, and for its communication to potential interpreters. Both the mnemotechnical function of this fixing as well as the effect of the alteration of the "originally" thought through the medium of rhetorical or grammatical tropes makes rhetoric into a functional equivalent of writing. Rhetoric has additionally in common with writing that, brought in for the sake of understanding, it precisely hinders understanding and needs a special theory of the art [*Kunstlehre*], indeed, hermeneutics, for the elucidation of its "obscurities." The twisting and estrangement that is done to the literal meaning through the violence of rhetoric and writing thus ought to be undone through an inverse movement on the part of the art of understanding—and indeed in such a manner that the specific form of displacement can thereby be brought under control as a moment of that "literal" meaning. Schleiermacher's concept of the relation between rhetoric and hermeneutics can draw support on this point from their late-classical and Protestant tradition: "The correlation of hermeneutics and rhetoric consists in this, that every act of understanding is the reversal of an act of speech, in that the thought which lay at the basis of speech must come into consciousness."[63] If one meanwhile takes Schleiermacher's thesis about the artistic character of hermeneutics seriously, then rhetoric does not only belong within its sphere of objects, but is an integral component of the hermeneutic operation itself. Every step in an interpretation is bound to correspond with a rhetorical—or grammatical—figure. And the same ought to hold for the universal rules (or, as Schleiermacher prefers to write: pieces of advice) which are given out by hermeneutics. Only by virtue of the close alliance between hermeneutic and rhetorical operations does *literary* hermeneutics legitimate its title: as a theory of the *art* of understanding which methodically reflects the structure and function of the *scripturality* as well as of the *rhetoricity* of its objects and of its own procedure.

V.

The rhetoricity of hermeneutic operations is not immediately thematized in Schleiermacher's texts. But it manifests itself from out of the systematic connection within which he localizes rhetoric and hermeneutics, and out of the context of his descriptions. It comes forth in the most undisguised manner in the discussion which Schleiermacher devotes to the most intractable problem of hermeneutic practice: the fundamental principle of the hermeneutic circle, "that, just as certainly as the whole is understood from out of the parts, so too can the part only be understood from out of the whole."[64] Now Schleiermacher rarely neglects to designate that figure which emerges from the mutual presupposition of whole and part as a merely "apparent" circle in understanding, and not because he finds in it deductive and inductive procedures mixed in an inadmissible manner (on the contrary, he only holds such knowledge to be scientific and scholarly, to be *wissenschaftlich*, which is gained from out of the synthesis of these two operations[65]). Rather, he so designates it because he maintains that there are two readings of a work, structurally different from one another, that do not stand in circular dependency upon one another and thus do not allow the circle to become a vicious one. The task of the "cursory reading" of a work is to mediate a pre-understanding of the whole only on its grammatical level and in its rough main features. The concern of a second reading is then to grasp, according to the standard of the grammatical pre-understanding, the relation of the parts to the whole, the individual compositional gesture, and the determinate meaning that emerges from out of the relation of all the details to one another and to the whole of the text. This second reading can be brought to a successful conclusion only on the condition that, in it, the analysis of the compositional technique is constantly accompanied by the divination of the individual logic of the production of the text.

Just how problematic in principle the assumption of such a naive first reading is, which would not yet proceed synthetically and would be disinterested in the law of composition, becomes evident in Schleiermacher's advice for the cursory structuring of the grammatical "outside" of literary works. It should proceed, so he informs us, according to a schema of substitution that allows the reader to formulate an overarching concept for a closed sequence of sentences, under which concept all the elements of this sequence are thought to be contained. Such a substitution is executed on all the sentences of a text which hang together with one another, and indeed in such a manner that after the structuring of the whole text according to the model of substitution one has gained not an incoherent series of abstract overarching concepts, but rather a whole of the sort of a completed sentence. In Schleiermacher's formulation:

> For every articulation of sentences that hangs together more precisely . . . there is in some manner . . . a main concept which dominates it or—as we might also express ourselves—is the word for it; and this word can, just like the individual word in the individual sentence, receive its fully determined meaning correctly only if it is read in context with the other similar words, i.e. every articulation of sentences, be it larger or smaller, can only be understood correctly from out of the whole to which it belongs.[66]

The substitution for a segment of a text by its main concept is thus one of the two fundamental hermeneutic operations; together with the second, the combination of the substitutions into a sequence having the form of a sentence, it represents the condition for the construction of the whole of the text from out of its parts and for the understanding of the parts from out of their whole. But both fundamental operations of such hermeneutics follow rhetorical models: the substitution achieves itself according to the pattern of selecting a concept from a given syntagmatic chain, thus representing a *pars pro toto*, a metonymy that functions as metaphor; the combination of the individual conceptual paradigms into a new syntagmatic series inverts

the first model and may be described most economically as the metony-
mization of metaphoric substitutions. The hermeneutic syntagm earned
through both operations then relates for its part to the text which it tran-
scribes as a metonymy that is to fulfill the function of a metaphor.[67] Each
reading would be the synecdoche of the text read.

   The rhetoricity of these fundamental hermeneutic operations corresponds with that rhetorical procedure which Schleiermacher saw at work in
the origin of language. The interpretive reference to texts is not in principle
different from the verbal reference to objects of the world of experience. It
only represents an elongation of the rhetorical interpretation of the world
and the self into the sphere of the historical and philological *Wissenschaften*. On the ground of Schleiermacher's concept of language-
constitution—later on more developed by Nietzsche—stands the
assumption that no historically invariable categories prescribe the rule to
the relation of language to objects, but rather that all forms of verbal articulation—within the bounds set up by the ''schema of oscillation''—spring
from an always particular intuition and its rhetorical transformation. It is
only from the standpoint of the ''logic of the concept''[68] that it can be
maintained that the ''literal'' meaning is also the original one. From the
standpoint of a doctrine of schematism which accentuates the initiative of
the individual, it is ''crazy to posit a literal meaning temporally before the
tropaic one—[as in the case of] white and snow-white.''[69] On the contrary,
one should proceed in the reverse sense, that ''the tropaic meaning dissolves itself in the literal one,''[70] and that in the language of the concept its
origin from out of the rhetorical transformation of intuitions is forgotten.
The examples which Schleiermacher notes for such transformations in the
drafts for his hermeneutics are metaphor and metonymy. On the theme of
the origination of language, he considers the following: ''That one looks
upon a particular case, just because it is the familiar one, as the whole
circumference of the original meaning. This is often the case with metaphor
and everywhere the case with metagony,[71] i.e., a) movement and shape are
identical for language where it can pursue the shape genetically, *planto,
serpens*.''[72] As in the case of *serpens*, which only designates a self-
entangling, the movement is substituted for the whole shape; from the syntagmatic axis of combination, a dominant trait is projected upon the
paradigmatic axis of similarity and functions there as ''representative'' of
the whole shape. It is no different in the second example given by Schleiermacher: ''That the content of intuition is limited for a specific sphere already given by the context. Here there belongs . . . what with respect to the
speech-act falls under the formula of *continuo pro contento*. The sphere in
which the connection of the *continuo* with the *contento* falls is already
given and the whole is only to be viewed as an ellipsis of that in the part

which is already presupposed in the whole as known."[73] In the case of this metonymy as well, a part is selected from out of a whole and used in the "speech-act" as an index of the whole.

But all language-constitutive figures which proceed according to the model of selection and distribution receive their meaningfulness only at the expense of the eclipsing of at least one element that may indeed be given in the immediate context (and there also only problematically), but that in the further course of the tradition of language, as Schleiermacher points out, falls thoroughly into forgetfulness and can no longer be actualizable. The ellipsis effects this elimination of at least one element from out of a given chain of signifiers in order to make the word's representation gained thereby combinable into a totality of thought with other words' representations. Ellipsis thus lies at the bottom of both of the language-founding rhetorical-grammatical figures and, with them, at the bottom of the fundamental hermeneutic operations. Ellipsis is the rhetorical equivalent of writing: it de-completes, in order to make ideational totalities possible—but each whole gained with its assistance remains imprinted with the trace of the original elimination.[74] At the same time it also withdraws, like writing, from every alternative of presence and absence, whole and part, proper and foreign, because it is only on its—perpetually self-hollowing—ground that such conceptual oppositions can develop: it withdraws from its own proper concept. Ellipsis eclipses (itself). It is the "figure" of figuration: the area no figure can contain.

The totality which can be construed with the help of the two rhetorical-hermeneutic operations of substitution and combination is a priori de-completed by the ellipsis that prescribes the course for both. But it is not only in its rhetorical foundation that the "fundamental principle" of the hermeneutic circle proves itself to be fractured—it is so also in its practical consequences for interpretation. It is only with great difficulty that Schleiermacher can overtrump his problematic in the course of his attempt to argue plausibly the necessity of an explanation of the part from out of the whole: "And as, then, each smaller part is thus conditioned through a larger one that is itself once again a smaller part, it thus clearly follows that even the part can only be perfectly understood through the whole."[75] Progressing from a smaller part to an ever greater one, the hermeneutic operation grasps the word in the sentence, the sentence in the discourse, the discourse in the genre, this in its history and in the history of other literary productions, the literary history in connection with the social history, both of them in relation to the interpreter and his "cognitive community" . . . and in this way, in increasingly wide connections, dissolves that strict relation of the always relative whole to its parts which, as a concrete relation to be reconstructed, was to be the central concern of the interpretation. But in the progressive dilution of the bond between the part and the whole which enters in with the progression toward ever greater unities, it is only the consequential outcome of the merely loose joining of the parts of a text to larger organizations that displays itself: "for the explanation depends only upon the clear view that this part of a text is really also a whole in relation to the present word . . . To the extent, however, that this is not certain, the application will also be uncertain."[76] Neither the application of the fundamental hermeneutic principle, nor this principle itself can be made secure because the mutual coherence of different elements of a text within a common whole may be displayed only through the comparison of the elements, while the result of this comparison itself needs legitimation through further attempts at comparison. The "comparative procedure"[77] which Schleiermacher introduces in support of the grammatical one leads to an infinite regress which, incapable of restituting the originally eclipsed textual element, is also incapable of constituting that totality which would allow one to understand with certainty the part as part of a specific whole, and the whole from out of its specific parts.

Since, to approximate more nearly the ideal of perfect understanding, hermeneutics' grammatical procedure perpetually has to transgress the syntagmatic linkages of substitutive overarching concepts which it itself produced, it becomes clear that both the category of substitution (for each substitution is based upon an abstraction that has to prove itself in connection with other substitutes of text-segments) as well as the category of the syntagm (for each sentence-like connection has to legitimate itself through its connection with others) remain insufficient—because of the two conditioning ellipses—to give adequate contours to the relation between whole and part, general and particular. The hermeneutic operation thus succumbs to a movement of displacement that is in principle unstoppable, that can check itself through nothing other than a merely provisional last term. This movement traverses the two most important hermeneutic operations, selection and combination, their corresponding concepts of part and whole, and, with them, the ideal of an adequate representation of a text in its interpretation. There is no ultimate court of appeal before which the partiality of the part and the totality of the whole could prove themselves which would not for its part be in need of legitimation and, at the limit, incapable of legitimation. The part is never demonstrably part of *its* whole, the whole never the whole of *its* parts. The hermeneutic circle opens itself, and makes every closure into a heuristic hermeneutic fiction—admittedly employable, economizing the deficit of understanding, and yet one that can neither accommodate itself to the ideal of perfect understanding, nor eliminate the loss, constitutive of language and understanding, which the ellipses bring with them. Understanding cannot remain within the limits of the economy of the circle, within the limits of the whole, for this whole is itself the result of rhetorical-grammatical tropes and as such the subcode of a language game that for its part is not codifiable. The tropes imprint it with the mark of a linguistic difference that does not allow itself to be filled out via any epistemological labor. Every hermeneutic operation carries out the proliferation of ellipses and multiplies its exhaustion of resources in the production of meaning, its fragmentation in the production of totalities.

Schleiermacher didn't conceal to himself the fundamental deficit of the grammatical procedure of interpretation. The opening in the hermeneutic circle designates for him that gap in the repertoire of the *language system*'s syntactic-semantic rules which indicates its derivation from the free initiative of speaking subjects and keeps open the free space both for verbal innovations as well as for the always individual hermeneutic achievement of divination. Just as "a perfect knowledge of language" is unattainable for the grammatical procedure of hermeneutics, so too is "a complete knowledge of man" unattainable for the technical-psychological procedure;[78] and yet, in Schleiermacher's presentation, it is to be reserved for the latter to fill—in however revocable a manner—the gaps in the stock of positive knowledge with the means of divination—itself ungovernable and yet founding of meaning. Divination is that method which provides the questions for the grammatical procedure of comparison and thereby condemns it to inconclusiveness; but at the same time it is supposed to be that court of appeal before which the phenomenon of the new—that which par excellence is in need of interpretation—solves its puzzle.

> For what do we want to do whenever we come upon a passage where an ingenious author uses a formulation or a combination for the first time in the language? Here there is no other procedure than to depart divinatorily from the state of thought-production in which the author was seized, and to ascertain how the needs of the moment could have worked upon the fund of language actively at hand for the author in just this and no other manner; to imitate [*nachzubilden*] that creative act, and here as well, once again, there will be no certainty without application of a comparative procedure on the psychological side.[79]

Even the divinatory mimesis of the logic of production of a text—a further kind of play of substitution—is insufficient to establish securely the interpretation of a use of language that has not yet been entered into the register of the language system. The advice offered by Schleiermacher—that both procedures, the divinatory and the grammatical-comparative one, should supplement one another, so that "the procedure of interpretation appropriate to the art might perfectly attain its goal"[80]—disregards the fact that both procedures are incapable of a "perfect knowledge" of their respective objects. The divinatory substitution of the productivity of the interpreter for that of the interpreted—the most seductive and most unmediated one that Schleiermacher accepted into the catalog of hermeneutic operations—admittedly rests upon the grammatical comparison, in order to proceed with assurance that it is the substitution of precisely this *specific* interpreted; but the grammatical comparison, a mechanical calculus, is in no position to give an account of the *novum* of a use of language, and thus can in no case assist the divinatory metaphor to certainty and completeness. The category of the new, which Schleiermacher employed with an emphasis unlike that of scarcely anyone before him, is—like writing and like the ellipsis—a scandal for understanding. Divination as well is not invulnerable to the impertinence of the new. Just like the cursory first reading, so does the second reading, which has to do with the irreducibly individual moment of a composition, remain referred to rhetorical figures whose conflict forbids completeness and certainty to an interpretation.

Schleiermacher sought to accommodate the inconsistency of the hermeneutic "fundamental principle" in that he corrected the thesis of the circle, itself aimed at absolute synthesis, through the thesis of hermeneutic approximation. Understanding accordingly accomplishes itself—and not only in the comparative procedure, with respect to which Schleiermacher was explicit—in such a manner that "we always bring a related element, already understood, closer to that which is not yet understood, and thus enclose the non-understanding within ever narrower boundaries."[81] The "still" foreign and new is thus supposed to be joined with the "already" understood, so that within the understood the motive for the still non-understood, and thereby at the same time the ground of its incomprehensibility, appears. The hermeneutics of approximation offers not only "to find out the concealed addition of, as it were, lost indications,"[82] it seeks to understand the concealed *as* concealed, the foreign *as* foreign: the other as other. Its result can meanwhile only be ambiguous.

Divination displays a necessary failure in that the "appropriation"[83] of the other which is accomplished by it under the sign of substitution, falsifies this other into something identical and, in its translation, betrays to the language system the "untranslatability" of the individual production. From this failure the hermeneutics of approximation draws the consequence that the other can only be maintained and "given back"[84] *as* other in its interpretation in that it is lacking as *other*. Were it to remain purely outside of the system of rules of grammatical operations, then it would be altogether unknowable and would not be understood as their modification; but were it to be translated into the register of already known uses of language, then its untranslatable alterity would be sacrificed and once again not understood as the modification of that register. The foreign can be understood *as* other if it is lacking as *other;* it only becomes understandable as *other* when it is not understood *as* other. It is thus necessarily only understood as other when it is understood otherwise than as it is and when the rules of understanding about this themselves become otherwise [*sich . . . selber verändern*]. The foreign, the other is not at all graspable by an understanding that proceeds according to the logic of the oppositions of alterity and identity, according to the rhetoric of substitution and combination. It becomes accessible only to a process of interpretation which brings about active interpretation and, as such, also always brings about alteration of the other and, beyond this, unprogrammable alteration of the rules of understanding themselves.

The hermeneutics of approximation follows, paradoxically, a logic of distancing [*Ent-Fernung*]: with each motion toward the other, it steps back into greater distance, and each step that leads away from it draws it nearer. Only that hermeneutics which resists the seduction of dissolving the other into the same does not proceed in a reductive manner; and only that one which disdains hypostasizing the other into the altogether Other, into a theological *negativum*, does not proceed mystically. Between both forms of reductionism, in the interval between the same of the other and the other of the same, there operates an understanding that mobilizes dissent in the production of consensus, that alters with every iteration, preserves displacement within understanding, and reads a hermetics of the new within hermeneutics. This hermeneutics works within the doctrine of correct understanding as the agent of incomprehensibility. Schleiermacher's friend Friedrich Schlegel wrote its ironic laudatio. It is only in such a manner that hermeneutics accommodates itself to the fact which Schleiermacher expressed as follows: "Non-understanding will never altogether dissolve itself";[85] but it can do this only at the cost of acknowledging its attempt at self-foundation as failed, and, from out of the doctrine of the art of an understanding that does not self-evidently understand itself [*das sich nicht von selbst versteht*], becoming an understanding that, at the limit, does not itself understand [*das sich, a limine, selbst nicht versteht*].

Schleiermacher was not the Schleiermacher (the veil-maker) as Nietzsche, his most significant successor in the theory of interpretation, had apostrophied him.[86] His attempt to formulate the conditions and rules of understanding is one of the few to have energetically criticized and successfully avoided an unreflected grammaticism as well as the syntheticism of speculative provenance. At a time when in questions of hermeneutics, it is almost exclusively still a matter of the banal alternatives of scientistic formalism and journalistic semanticism, it is precisely Schleiermacher's hermeneutics that could teach us to show them both the door. That it is itself in need of a critical paratheory in which the effects of the scripturality and the rhetoricity of not only its objects, but also of understanding itself are discussed, lies in the consequence of Schleiermacher's insights. Criticism and amendment are functions of the elliptical paraphrase in which every understanding of its object and of itself sacrifices something, in order to "give back"—it—itself—otherwise.

Translated by Timothy Bahti

Notes

This text was written in early 1979 and published in German in the same year. [In *Texthermeneutik: Geschichte, Aktualität, Kritik,* edited by Ulrich Nassen (Paderborn: Verlag Ferdinand Schöningh KG, 1979), pp. 115–148—ED.]. For the English version, several sentences have been added and several deleted.

1. The Schleiermacher texts are cited according to the edition of *Hermeneutik und Kritik* edited by Manfred Frank (Frankfurt: Suhrkamp, 1977). The first citation is from p. 313. Henceforth citations from this edition will be given by page number only.

2. p. 311.

3. pp. 76, 77.

4. Landshut, 1808; partially reprinted in Hans-Georg Gadamer and Gerhard Boehm, ed., *Seminar: Philosophische Hermeneutik* (Frankfurt: Suhrkamp, 1976), pp. 111–130. See *The Hermeneutic Tradition: From Ast to Ricoeur,* edited by Gayle L. Ormiston and Alan D. Schrift (Albany: State University of New York Press, 1990), pp. 39–56. Hereafter HT.—ED.]

5. In *Hermeneutik und Kritik,* pp. 309–346.

6. pp. 313, 314.

7. p. 317.

8. Ast, sec. 80; [see HT, p. 46.—ED.].

9. p. 318.

10. p. 318.

11. p. 326.

12. p. 318.

13. p. 375.

14. p. 341.

15. p. 317.

16. p. 329.

17. Ast, sec. 81 [see HT, pp. 46–47.—ED.].

18. p. 309.

19. p. 315.

20. p. 316.

21. p. 184.

22. Hans-Georg Gadamer, *Wahrheit und Methode,* 2nd ed. (Tübingen: Mohr, 1965), p. 360 [see *Truth and Method,* translated by Garrett Barden and John Cumming (New York: Seabury Press, 1975), 2nd edition pp. 340–341—ED.].

23. *Ibid.,* p. 156 [*ibid.,* p. 145—ED.].

24. *Ibid.,* p. 371 [*ibid.,* pp. 354–355—ED.].

25. *Ibid.,* p. 370 [*ibid.,* p. 354—ED.].

26. Aristotle, *Lehre vom Satz,* in *Kategorien—Lehre vom Satz,* unaltered reprint of the 1958 reedition of the 1925 2nd edition (Hamburg: Meiner, 1974) [Philosophische Bibliothek, vols. 8/9].

27. p. 315.

28. p. 316.

29. p. 184.

30. p. 333.

31. Plato, *Phaedrus,* cited according to Schleiermacher's translation of vol. 4 of the collected works (Hamburg: Meiner, 1967). Cf. for the interpretation of this text Jacques Derrida, "La pharmacie de Platon," *La Dissémination* (Paris: Seuil, 1972) ["Plato's Pharmacy," in *Dissemination,* translated by Barbara Johnson (Chicago: University of Chicago Press, 1981)—ED.].

32. p. 98.

33. p. 386.

34. Peter Szondi was the first to call attention to this, in "Schleiermachers Hermeneutik heute," in Szondi, *Schriften* II (Frankfurt: Suhrkamp, 1978), p. 118 [translated by Harvey Mendelsohn in Peter Szondi, *On Textual Understanding and Other Essays* (Minneapolis: University of Minnesota Press, 1986), pp. 95–113—ED.].

35. pp. 78, 79.

36. p. 80.

37. Friedrich Schleiermacher, *Hermeneutik,* edited by Heinz Kimmerle (Heidelberg, 1959), p. 39 [see "The Aphorisms on Hermeneutics from 1805 and 1809/10," HT, p. 58.—ED.].

38. p. 372 (in context).

39. p. 376.

40. p. 381.

41. p. 385. Cf. the author's *"Pleroma*—zu Genesis und Struktur einer dialektischen Hermeneutik," in G. W. F. Hegel, *"Der Geist des Christentums." Schriften 1796–1800,* edited by Werner Hamacher (Berlin: Ullstein, 1978), passim.

42. Friedrich Schleiermacher, *Glaubenslehre,* sections 3–5.

43. This hypostasis of the other into the altogether Other which Schleiermacher accomplishes is only affirmed in Manfred Frank's interpretation of Schleiermacher (in his *Das individuelle Allgemeine. Textstrukturierung und interpretation nach Schleiermacher* [Frankfurt: Suhrkamp, 1977], and in the introduction to his edition of Schleiermacher's *Hermeneutik und Kritik*) when he writes that the Other is the "transcendental" ground from which the subject experiences its "imprinting" and thereby finds access to itself. The fact of the imprinting can certainly not be denied. But within the subject the possibility of such an imprinting must already be given. This, though, is unthinkable if the "immediate self-cognition" gathers itself around the point of "feeling," as in several of Schleiermacher's considerations, or in immediate self-possession. It is only in its *mark* of imprinting, for which the structure of subjectivity must offer at least a prop, that the Other could become real *as* Other: its transcendental status is thus conditioned through the structure of the subject, i.e., the structure of the *work* that certainly is not of immediacy. But under such circumstances there can no longer be any talk of one sided "dependency." This would reduce the instance of the other to a moment within a hierarchical bipolar structure and take from it the meaning of an opening and initiating of self-understanding: a model for anything but a "protestant" hermeneutics, and certainly not for any hermeneutics of singularity.

44. p. 381 (sec. 187).

45. p. 381. It is almost unnecessary to note that Schleiermacher's concepts "transcendental" and "empirical" certainly derive from the Kantian vocabulary,

but that their usage remains non-Kantian throughout, as with the talk of the "*identity* of the transcendental and the empirical."

46. p. 374. [cf. HT, pp. 79 and 94, 98.—ED.].

47. Cf. on the meaning of the word, the fascinating study by K. Meuli, *Altrömischer Maskenbrauch* (in his *Schriften* I, especially pp. 261–264). There he writes: "Linguistically the word is clear: *oscillum* goes back via *osculum* to *os*, 'mouth,' 'face' . . . *oscillum* thus means 'little mouth,' 'little face'; the glosses translate *stomation, prōsopon, prosopeion*, 'mask.' But here one should not think of face masks; the *oscilla* are rather much more *pilae*, little round balls of woolen shreds or threads . . . ; Macrobius strikingly names them *capita*, 'heads': one also used onions or poppy buds for them. . . . They had to be scary in order to ward off evil; according to Varro, one hung out *oscilla* where someone had hanged himself. Hanged persons are, like all who died a violent death, dangerous returners, and the *oscilla* here evidently have, according to widespread practice, the task, as *apotropaion, probaskanion*, to keep distant from the dwelling of the living the unwanted uncanny. . . . " (*ibid., pp. 262, 263*).

48. p. 458.

49. p. 466.

50. p. 458.

51. Cf. as one example among many, the defense of the correspondence theory of truth and of the "system of innate concepts" against the possibility of a "difference in the intellectual function" (p. 462).

52. p. 385.

53. p. 382.

54. The term comes from Jacques Derrida. Manfred Frank has also attempted to point out and reconstruct the concept of the supplement, which Derrida develops from texts of Rousseau and Plato, in Schleiermacher (in *Das individuelle Allgemeine*, pp. 119, 120), albeit by being more faithful to Schleiermacher than Derrida was, and essentialistically alleviating the tensions he had noted.

55. p. 386.

56. p. 262ff., cf. p. 267.

57. p. 445.

58. p. 459ff. and p. 465 (in context).

59. With this interpretation we have only drawn out the line to which Schleiermacher's texts contain, so to speak, the mathematical equivalent.

60. p. 80.

61. p. 81.

62. p. 76.

63. p. 76.

64. p. 329.

65. p. 95.

66. p. 331.

67. This attempt at structuring orients itself according to the model of the two axes of language put forward by Roman Jakobson; cf. Jakobson, *Poetik. Ausgewählte Aufsätze 1921–1971*, edited by E. Holenstein and T. Schelbert (Frankfurt: Suhrkamp, 1979).

68. *Hermeneutik*, Kimmerle edition, p. 58 [cf. *Hermeneutics: The Handwritten Manuscripts*, translated by James Duke and Jack Forstman (Missoula, Mont.: Scholars Press, 1977), p. 71—ED.].

69. *Ibid.*, p. 35 [*ibid.*, p. 72—ED.].

70. *Ibid.*, p. 39 [*ibid.*, p. 76—ED.].

71. A photocopy of Schleiermacher's manuscript makes it appear probable to me that everywhere where Kimmerle reads "metagonie," it should be "metonymy."

72. *Ibid.*, p. 58. [*Ibid.*, p. 72—ED.]. In his essay "Über Wahrheit und Lüge in aussermoralischen Sinn," Nietzsche refers to the same figure and the same example in order to exemplify the rhetoricity of language: "We speak of a 'snake': the designation concerns nothing but the self-entwining, and thus could also be attributed to the worm" (Nietzsche, *Werke*, edited by Karl Schlechta [Munich: Hanser, 1954]), III, 312. Nietzsche admittedly radicalizes the consequences of his observation to the point of the ironic sacrifice of the concept of truth.

73. *Hermeneutik*, Kimmerle edition, p. 58ff. (in context) *Hermeneutics*, p. 72—ED.].

74. In order to be precise here about the standard set by the reach and intent of this essay, one would need an exact presentation of Schleiermacher's concept of the sentence and especially an analysis of his "dynamic" concept of the copula; even this element of the sentence, a combinatory one in the strictest sense, may be understood as ellipsis. Cf. *ibid.*, p. 41f. and *Hermeneutik und Kritik*, pp. 120–123. [cf. HT, p. 65. Schleiermacher writes: "Ellipses are signs of a developing life."—ED.].

75. p. 331.

76. p. 329f.

77. pp. 325, 341.

78. p. 81.

79. p. 325.

80. p. 326.

81. p. 324.

82. p. 317.

83. p. 320.

84. p. 466.

85. p. 328.

86. Nietzsche, *Werke,* II, 1149 [*Ecce Homo,* "Why I Write Such Good Books—The Case of Wagner," section 3. Here Hamacher refers to Nietzsche's remark, "In the history of the quest of knowledge . . . "—ED.].

9

Sharing Voices*

Jean-Luc Nancy

Introduction

First of all, it is a question of interpretation. It is a question of asking oneself, now, what delimits this concept and, with it, the entire "hermeneutic" problematic, as well as the entire thematic of interpretation as the modern substitute for "truth." It is a question of showing that everything submitted to the motif of *interpretation,* insofar as it defines a kind of fundamental tonality of our modernity, according to diverse accounts, remains caught in an interpretation of what "interpretation" itself gives to thought.[1]

For that reason, at first it will be necessary to give an account of the hermeneutic motif in its modern form, in the philosophical space from which it is supposed to proceed: that is to say, the "hermeneutics" appropriated by Heidegger to characterize the access, beyond the "metaphysical," to the thought of being as being. It will turn out that this thought can be called neither a method nor a preliminary hermeneutic (it dismisses hermeneutics as such), but that the *being* in question gives itself and is given only in a *hermēneia*[2]—"the most primordial" [*originel:* primitive, authentic] meaning of which will have to be elucidated. Further, *being* is not anything for which the *meaning* will be reached by hermeneutic means, but *hermēneia* is the "meaning" of this being that we are—"men," "interpreters" of *logos.* No "philosophy of interpretation" is the measure of this "humanity."

But beyond Heidegger himself, and although on account of him, it will be necessary to take up once again the most ancient philosophical document concerning *hermēneia,* Plato's *Ion:* that is to say, as will be seen, it will be necessary once more to take up the sharing and the dialogue of philosophy and poetry, such that in traversing itself, it is finally in the dialogue in general, or in "communication," that being will emerge necessarily. Confronted by "understanding the discourse of the other," and to the extent that it unites the presupposed essentials of a philosophy of interpretation, no "philosophy of communication" is the measure of what will be required, henceforth, in the society of man—"communication," "dialogue," and, consequently, "community."[3]

This essay explores what one can risk calling the modern misinterpretation of interpretation and, therefore, it has only one end: to serve as a preamble, to incite a reevaluation of our relations, insofar as we are interpreters of that dialogue which distributes our "human" scene to us, and thus which provides us with our being or our "destination."—It explores what would be, inseparably, nothing other than another *poetical* and another *political* sharing of our voices.

I

I am interested, therefore, at first, in the gesture by which Heidegger was able to articulate the motif of interpretation as it pertains to a "most primordial" *hermēneia*, or else—if it is fairer to say it in this way—that gesture by which he disarticulates [*désarticulé:* to separate at the joints] hermeneutics in order to open it towards an entirely different dimension of *hermēneuein*. What is involved in this gesture is nothing other than the famous *hermeneutic circle*—not so much as a simple characteristic special to hermeneutics (of which the circle will be either the privileged resource or particular aporia), but, indeed, with all the value of a constitutive principle of hermeneutics, or interpretation as such and in general.

As one knows, the enterprise of *Being and Time*[4] finds its inaugural possibility in a certain—indissolubly "methodological" and "ontological"—treatment of the hermeneutic circle. According to this heading, moreover, the thought of Heidegger, that is to say, the thought that interrogates the *closure of metaphysics*,[5] cannot be separated from a fundamental explication with hermeneutics (an *Auseinandersetzung* [altercation; discussion] as the Germans say: a debate or contention in order to implicate and to exclude each other reciprocally). There is no chance of that: hermeneutics is implicated in an essential way in metaphysics. This implication belongs to the hermeneutic circle. The closure is, therefore, that of the circle, and like the circle—according to what remains to be seen—it closes and it opens itself, it divides [or multiplies—TRANS.] itself in the text of philosophy.

Before examining the treatment of the circle by Heidegger, let us consider it in its classic form (for which it is necessary to understand the usage it receives *after* Heidegger). Ricoeur has given the most direct statement of it, and, thus he qualifies it himself, the most "brutal": "It is necessary to understand in order to believe, but it is necessary to believe in order to understand."[6] Without a doubt this statement brings in, with "belief," an element seemingly foreign to philosophy. Here Ricoeur's hermeneutics addresses the "sacred." But it is not the "sacred" that determines by itself a regimen of "belief": the "sacred" is no less than another object, an object of philosophy, and Ricoeur does not carry us away surreptitiously into the realm of faith.[7] The belief in question designates quite well its ordinary notion: the adherence to a meaning (which is not necessarily "sacred") absent in immediate evidence and demonstrative discourse. In effect, this notion responds to, in what would be the "brutal" manner, a strictly philosophical requirement of the hermeneutic circle. And with that, one can or cannot take into consideration the ultimate Christian request for Ricoeur's purpose, or one can or cannot consider the principal role played by the exegesis of holy books in the history of hermeneutics. Or else, in a more appropriate fashion: one can consider this role, but that would not signify what philosophical hermeneutics would have to have to be differentiated from or purged of religious hermeneutics. The exegesis of holy texts signifies, on the contrary, that this last theme, from the Greek fathers up to Schleiermacher and after that Bultmann, has been possible only in the space of philosophy, and according to a fundamental hermeneutic determination of philosophy.[8]

The philosophical requirement of hermeneutics is, thus, one that concerns preliminary belief, that is to say, a precomprehensive anticipation of that very thing which is the question to be comprehended, or the question which comprehension must finally command. For Ricoeur, who designates this motif also as one of a "participation in meaning," this anticipated participation addresses itself to the sacred. It forms the devotion minimally necessary to orient the investigation, so that it can furnish its own question and its own "in view of which" [*"en vue de quoi"*: object at which it is aimed]. Thus oriented and directed, hermeneutic practice will permit an immediate adherence to the sacred, lost in the modern world. This belief is constituted by this practice in the form of a "sacred innocence" or "critical innocence" which will come to substitute itself as the "first innocence." Thus, the hermeneutic circle has the nature and the function of a double substitution: the anticipated belief itself is substituted already for the lost, former belief (for a primitive adherence to meaning, or for a primitive adherence of meaning), and the belief mediated by the critical interpretation substitutes itself in order to bring to an end this lost belief and the anticipated belief. On the whole, this lost substitution presents traces of a dialectical *recovery* [*relève:* negation and recuperation]: the immediacy of the participation in meaning is cancelled and conserved in the final product of the hermeneutic process. According to this last point, the circle thus supposes three determining traits: an originary (lost) immediacy, the intervention of a substitute for that originary state, and the negation and conservation [*relève*] of that substitute.

In this way, the hermeneutic circle is suspended in the supposition or the presupposition of an origin: both the origin of meaning and the possibility of participating in it, the infinite origin of the circle in which the interpreter is caught always already. The circle can be nothing other than the movement of an origin, lost and recovered by the mediation of its substitute. Insofar as it renders possible the right direction for interpretive research, this substitute implies a mode for the conservation and preservation of the origin up to and through its loss. Hermeneutics requires—very profoundly, very obscurely perhaps—that the "participation in meaning" is unaware of the absolute interruption. On account of this profound continuity, hermeneutics represents the process of a historicity which is valued both as suspension and as revival of the continuity. It designates in the most accentuated fashion the *history* of a *permanence* and a *remanence*,[9] that is to say, the possibility of returning from (or to) an origin.

This possibility—experienced as a necessity—has haunted the romantic idealism in which modern philosophy is born, and it has perhaps even constituted its idealism as such: as the thought of returning to the origin. It has determined in particular an idea of hermeneutics of which Schleiermacher is the principal representative.[10] Schleiermacher's hermeneutics has its source in the exigency of returning from or to the origin. This return simultaneously takes the strict form, issued from the domain of aesthetics, of the reconstruction of the original significance of a work,[11] and the more complex form, issued from the domain of religion, of the comprehension of symbols that are religious representations: in effect, in the comprehension of the symbol it is the primordial [*originel*] (and original [*original*]) element of religious *sentiment* which expands. But this sentiment is primordial in particular because, fundamentally, it is not anything other than the immediate consciousness, that is to say, the *subject* according to Schleiermacher.[12]

In its act of birth, modern hermeneutics is the operation—mediated by a history and as history—of the recovery or the reappropriation of a subject, of a subject of meaning and of the meaning of a subject.[13] In playing with the two broad, traditional sides of Christian interpretation (which are themselves retaken, transformed, and recovered in modern hermeneutics), one could say that the allegorical interpretation of meaning always gives the subject, and the grammatical interpretation of the subject always gives the meaning . . .

The hermeneutic circle is the process of this double interpretation, of which the condition is formed then by the presupposition of meaning, or by that of the subject, according to the side or the moment one would like to privilege. Hermeneutic *belief* in general is not anything other than that presupposition which can assume alternatively—or, moreover, simultaneously—the philosophic figure of the couple, meaning and the subject, the religious figure of the gift of revelation in the symbol, the aesthetic figure of the original work and its tradition.

*

*   *

If interpretation is to be defined as a movement towards the comprehension of a meaning, its fundamental rule is, thus, that meaning must be given in advance to the interpreter—in the manner of an anticipation, an "in view of which" (a *Woraufhin*) or a "participation." The meaning must be *pre-given*, which is perhaps only a very general condition of *meaning* as such. (How could there be meaning without a meaning, of meaning itself, preliminary to the meaning which can comprehend the semantic as well as the controlling meaning of the word "meaning"?) But perhaps that excludes the possibility that meaning will be *given* purely and simply—in all the rigor of the idea of a *gift* [*don:* present], which fits neither anticipation nor premonition. It will be necessary to return to this point. Let us say, for the moment, that the most general condition of hermeneutics, insofar as it is the process [*procès:* production] of meaning and the subject, is the circular condition of a *pre-understanding.*

Thanks to the intermediary role of Bultmann's theological hermeneutics, the motif of *preunderstanding* is that by which the general problematic of contemporary hermeneutics is engaged.[14] Bultmann inherited the motif from Heidegger. It is here that we are at a crossroads [the parting of ways—TRANS.]. In the transmission of the modern hermeneutic tradition to Heidegger and in the transmission from Heidegger to Bultmann (or in the *interpretations* of hermeneutics by Heidegger and of Heidegger by Bultmann), the philosophical destiny of interpretation is confronted—or moreover, the philosophical interpretation of hermeneutics is confronted.

In *Being and Time,* Heidegger summons the hermeneutic motif in consideration of the concept of preunderstanding which he develops. Nevertheless, is it a question of an anticipation of a primordial meaning (subject), lost and recovered?—such is the whole question.

By their nature, two indications of this question engender doubt regarding the existence of a simple correspondence between the hermeneutic circle and Heideggerian preunderstanding—and engender doubt, consequently, regarding the hermeneutic interpretation (Bultmannian or Gadamerian) of Heidegger. The first indication is met with in the complex treatment which Heidegger gives to the hermeneutic circle as such, and in the distance which it marks very distinctly vis-à-vis this circle. The second indication is related to the abandonment, after *Being and Time,* of the term "*hermeneutics,*" the abandonment which is to be accounted for much later in "A Dialogue On Language Between a Japanese and an Inquirer" [English title—TRANS.], in which the reference to *hermēneia,* according to Plato, is made.

It is these two indications which I would like to explore in succession.

*

*   *

In order to introduce the problematic of the hermeneutic circle and the reevaluation of "prejudice" as the condition of understanding which it involves, Gadamer invokes "the foundation by Heidegger of the circular structure of comprehension concerning the temporality of *Dasein.*"[15] In support of his analysis of the necessity of the circle, which is going to follow, he cites the following passage from *Being and Time:*

> It is not to be reduced to the level of a vicious circle, or even a circle which is merely tolerated. The circle reveals in itself the authentic possibility of the most primordial knowledge. One genuinely knows this possibility only if the first, last and permanent task given by interpretation [*explication*] does not allow our experiences and preliminary views [fore-havings, fore-sights, and fore-conceptions— TRANS.] to be presented by any intuitions and popular notions, but to secure the scientific theme by the development of these anticipations according to the "things themselves."[16]

Gadamer will pursue his analysis by submitting it to the obvious principles of this text: (1) to assume the circularity, that is to say, the anticipation of meaning having to be interpreted; (2) to regulate this anticipation on account of "non-transparent prejudices,"[17] but by a "grasp of consciousness" and a "control"[18] of anticipations, respecting "the things themselves," according to the phenomenological precept taken up again here by Heidegger.

At present, it is a question of asking oneself if Gadamer's understanding itself is, indeed, regulated by the "thing itself" in Heidegger—according to the standard at least where we make use of the image of the circle once again,which is precisely what is to be examined. For that, it is necessary, at least, to recall the combined major features of the "hermeneutic" problematic in *Being and Time.*

The question of the circle presents itself for the first time in Section 2, under the title "The Formal Structures of the Question of Being." Insofar as it is a question, this question recovers the mode of being of the being [*du mode d'être de l'étant*] who questions, of that being "which we are ourselves." Its position "requires, then, a preliminary and appropriate explication (*Explikation*) of a being (being-there [*Da-sein*]) relative to its own Being." In other words, it is necessary "to determine in its Being" the being who questions in order to be able to pose the question of being. Thus, it is necessary to anticipate the possibility of determining, and consequently of comprehending or precomprehending, the being of the being who questions in order to question the being of the being in general. Heidegger adds immediately: "But is not such an undertaking manifestly circular?"—At first he discards the objection in the name of the general sterility of all "formal" objections, which leaves open the possibility, then, of another, non-"formal" apprehension of the circle, which no longer will be an objection. He continues: "Moreover, this manner of posing the question, in fact, comprises no circle." What justifies it in this way is that the determination of the being of a being does not presuppose the disposal of a concept of being. Without that "no ontological knowledge could have ever been constituted." Thus, there is no presupposition of a *concept,* or of "the object of investigation." There is clearly a presupposition, but in the sense that "we always operate necessarily" in "the ordinary comprehension of Being." This comprehension appears "*as the essential constitution of being-there itself [l'être-là lui même].*"

Here, then, the presupposition does not beg the question regarding the concept of being, nor, in general, the anticipation of a meaning of being (nor, more generally, the anticipation of a meaning of meaning). It is the "position" of "the object in question (Being)," already given with "the questioner as the mode of Being of a being." Being is questioned, there is a question (thus an "end") of being. Moreover, more simply and more fundamentally, it is the question of being (which perhaps withdraws not only from the form of deductive inquiry, but from the more extensive form of the question-response as such) because the being of being-there does not consist of anything other than this: "it is in its Being that this being relates itself to its Being" (section 9). What is presupposed is this relation to being. But it is not presupposed by the person, by any preliminary orientation of inquiry (perhaps the "question of Being" is not a *question* and perhaps it is not *oriented*). Being is not presupposed as another thing, only as the relation to being—of being-there. Thus, it is not presupposed as the object or the term *to which* this *relation* would have to be made, as if by premonition, a vague intuition,[19] or the common property of a tradition which would have to be supplied to anticipate this object. Let us say here that being is infinitely less anticipated than according to this classical interpretive model, and nevertheless infinitely more presupposed: it is presupposed *as the relation itself.* Being is presupposed as the relation to being which makes the being of being-there. It is presupposed as being-there itself, as the facticity of being-there.

One would have to be tempted to say that nothing is presupposed: being-there is only posed. Indeed, but this position *is the position of the presupposition* which creates the relation to being as the being of being-there. "To pose" being-there is "to presuppose" nothing: this is neither to give credit to an empirical position presupposed as that of being-there (this is because being-there is not to be named "man"), nor to presuppose whatever is the subject of "being" with which being-there is in relation. That which signifies, or inversely, which presupposes the being of being-there, poses nothing: neither a determination, nor an anticipation. The "presupposition" of being is neither position, nor supposition, nor presupposition. It is that in which being-there is preceded always already, without, for all that, anything to pose or to anticipate, except *the* "presupposition" (of being) itself. This "presupposition" is not one: when one speaks of a presupposition, one supposes it anterior to that subject of which there is a presupposition. In reality, it is implied in this way as *posterior* to a position, whatever it is (ideal, imaginary, etc.), to that subject which one can "presuppose." But here, nothing precedes the presupposition, there is no "that"—and above all not so much as a "being," which is nothing without [*en dehors:* outside] the presupposition. "That," it is the "presupposition" which is posterior and anterior only to itself—that is to say, to being-there. On this account, one would be able to call it, as well, the "absolute" presupposition, but this "absolute" will be the only pure and simple beginning given in being-there and by being-there. In other words, the "absolute" presupposition is tied essentially to "absolute" finitude.

Finally—but this will not be an *end*—the only being presupposed is the being of the presupposition. That gives, if you will, an extreme form to the circle: but with this extreme, the circle as such flies into pieces; it contracts to a certain point, or else it disconnects [*affole*] its circularity to the point of rendering impossible the coincidence of a beginning and a result. It will not be a question, in the investigation, of leading to the meaning of a being that one would have anticipated (that would have *supposed,* for once, an origin of being as anterior to being-there—or to the *there* of being—or what would have come to the same thing, a being as origin of being-there, rendering possible its anticipation by intuition, reminiscence, or any other form of *conjecture* [mode de *visée*]). It will be a question of letting the inquiry—the "question"—to display itself *insofar as it is* the "meaning" of being which is "pre-supposed" in the being of the questioning-being (in the end, perhaps we will not have to answer what the question has "pre-judged," but will have the question itself as a response, and because of that perhaps it is removed from the status of a "question").

That is why, if it must be a question of being guided by "the things themselves," the thing-itself, here, reveals no being other than the thing-itself of the presupposition—that is to say, this "thing-itself so deeply veiled" that Heidegger returns to in Kant (BT, section 6). This signifies that the *thing* is to be determined here by its "concealment," in the sense that this cannot be measured or estimated in an anticipated fashion. The "thing-itself" of being, *that is* the indeterminate [*inassignable*] character of its "thing-itself." It is not the presupposition of its own concealment; rather it is the concealment of its being-presupposed, to an extent that no interpretive anticipation would be known to reach there, but that this profundity, on the other hand, is always already anticipated in every position of questioning, and a fortiori in every attempt of interpretation.

That is why Heidegger, at the time, comes a little further in explicating the task of the investigation as one of a hermeneutic. It is immediately that he calls for a "primordial" meaning of hermeneutics (as opposed to " 'hermeneutic' in a derivative sense: the methodology of the historical sciences of the mind" (BT, section 7, C), by which he designates no less than, via Dilthey, everything that has been understood up to that time under the name of hermeneutics).

The primordial meaning is attained through the determination of *Auslegung:* "the methodological meaning of phenomenological description is *Auslegung,*" translated here as *clarification* [*explicitation*]. This translation, in contrast with the possible translation by "interpretation," gives a very good account of what the context brings to the word *Auslegung,* which goes on to characterize "hermeneutic in the primordial meaning of this word." Thus, Heidegger describes *Auslegung:*

> The λόγος of the phenomenology of being-there has the character of an ερμηνεύειν which *announces* to the comprehension of Being, included in being-there, the authentic meaning of Being in general and the fundamental structures of its own being. [BT, section 7, C— TRANS.]

According to what had been established in the preceding section, *logos* designates *letting-something-be-seen* [*le faire-voir*], the unconcealment of a thing as revealed (*alèthés*). The *logos* of *phenomeno*-logy is the "letting of that which shows itself be seen just as it makes itself manifest from itself" [*le "faire voir de soi-même ce qui se manifeste, tel que, de soi-même, cela se manifeste"*]. This letting-something-be-seen (*sehen lassen*) is first of all a *letting* to be seen. It does not have the character of an operation, nor an envisioning, but a receiving, a welcoming. What it must let be seen, that is, what "remains concealed" in the manifestation as its very meaning—that is being. Here phenomenology receives a discreet but decisive inflection—that is the least one can say. It is no longer a question of showing the constitution of a world for a subject, but of letting be seen what the manifestation *is*, on the one hand, and, on the other hand, of letting it be seen that a comprehension is *already* comprehension of being. Thus, it is much less a question of deciphering a meaning (that of being) that traverses the phenomena than of letting the phenomenon of understanding (the "exemplary" being that is being-there) apprehend (receive) its own comprehension. Thus, there is nothing there to found any interpretation; there is this *hermēneuein* which "*announces* to the understanding of being . . . the meaning of being." "To announce" (*Kundgeben*) is neither to interpret nor to anticipate. It is simply, so to speak, to bring to speech and, thus, to be made known. There is nothing to be interpreted; there is to be announced the meaning to that (he) which [who—TRANS.] already understands it. Far from *hermēneuein* being related to this pre-understanding, it consists in *Auslegung,* in which it announces what it comprehends.[20]

*

* *

The question of the circle reappears considerably farther along in the framework of the analysis of *Auslegung* as characteristic of being-there, as a continuation of understanding. (This analysis is a prelude to the entire analysis of language.) Heidegger writes:

> In *Auslegung* understanding appropriates that which it has understood out of a new mode of understanding. *Auslegung* does not transform understanding into something different, but it becomes itself (BT, section 32).[21]

This transformation of understanding in-itself is brought about by "the acquisition of the structure of the *als* [as] (of the 'in so far as' [*l'en tant que*]": that is to say, that the interpreted [*ausgelegt*] being is known *as* such a being ("a table, a door, a carriage, or a bridge") according to its purpose [according to its "in order to"—TRANS.]. But there is no understanding which does not comprehend this *als* already. The *als* of *Auslegung* is not second, derived, added at a subsequent stage to the first seizure of the being. It does not depend, in particular, on linguistic enunciation. Rather, it is the *als* which renders linguistic enunciation possible. Contrary to Husserl, this paragraph affirms that there is no "pure perception" which is not already *Auslegung* (reciprocally, although not explicitly, it affirms, contrary to Hegel, that "sensible perception" does not begin with language, but rather that it begins with the former, well within itself, that is to say, well within the linguistic system and consciousness of the subject). Enclosed within the most primitive understanding, *Auslegung* forms the anticipation of language well within the explicit expression (the precise expression, it must be said): this singular and decisive situation indicates involuntarily the French translation which juxtaposes here *clarification* [*l'explicitation*] for *Auslegung* and the *explicit* adjective in order to designate *Ausdrücklichkeit* [explicitness], the precise character, expressed in language, of a statement.[22]

Auslegung forms the clarification of the explicit prior to its expression, or, again, clarification of the implicit while it is still implicit. Here language as articulation is not first: there is first a kind of language-in-addition-to [*d'outre-langue*] which only distinguishes the articulation of *Auslegung in* understanding. Thus, this last articulation *is* the being of being-there, as it is *in-the*-world. Therefore, this being is determined in this way: for being-there there is no pure and absolute implicit. The fact that it is for being-there, in its being, a question of being (and of its own being) is precisely such: it is in its being always already articulation that gives the explication of the meaning of being (as meaning the *als* of such and such a being). It is being according to and as this articulation: being *there* or being *in-the*-world, this differential style of the *als* which no longer pronounces anything but which articulates the understanding in it-self. *Auslegung* does not proceed, then, without an *anticipation* (*Vorgriff*) which "founds it." Each *als* is anticipated beginning with the understanding of everything as a finalized whole, or as a totality of involvements (*Bewandtnisganzheit*). This understanding itself "does not need to be explicitly (*explizit*) secured by an *Auslegung* thematic." That does not obstruct—on the contrary—what this understanding, which furnishes the preliminary release from which a determined meaning (let us say, global meaning) is anticipated, necessarily carries in itself, as does every understanding—the articulation of a nonexplicit *Auslegung*. In other words, *Auslegung does not proceed from a pregiven anticipation, but, by its structure and in its fundamental meaning, Auslegung anticipates itself.* Its anticipation is the very structure of *meaning*, by this meaning "structure by anticipation," as it is said a little farther along in the text.

Because of that, the meaning which articulates *Auslegung* is nothing given in advance of it, nor in advance of being-there. It structures "the disclosure (or the opening, *Erschlossenheit* [disclosiveness]) that belongs to the understanding." *Auslegung* anticipates nothing other than the opening of meaning as the ontological property of being-there.

Thus, that is why there is a circle: "*Auslegung* must have already understood what is *auslegen* [displayed]." Heidegger recalls that philological interpretation (*Interpretation*) (therefore, in a derived fashion) already knows the phenomenon of the circle. He recalls as well that in good logic it is a question of a *"circulus vitiosus."* But he declares that the circle to which he has been headed "is the expression (*Ausdruck*) of the *existential* structure of anticipation of being-there." And this declaration is made while he pronounces the "defense" of the circle which we have cited already with Gadamer. One sees a little better how to read, henceforth, this "defense." The "circle" is only an "expression." And the paragraph draws to a close in the following manner:

> If, however, one takes into account that [the image of] the circle ontologically recovers the mode of being of a subsistant being (subsistence) (*Vorhandenheit/Bestand*), one must avoid characterizing ontologically anything like being-there with the aid of this phenomenon (BT, section 32 [HT, p. 126.—ED.]).

The circle, the expression or the image of the circle, the appellation "circle," and consequently the figure and the concept of the circle will have only formed then a temporary privilege, in a manner of speaking, like philological (and religious) interpretation, and in a dangerous fashion because it returns to the determination of being as permanent-subsistence (that is, the Cartesian determination, cf. sections 20 and 21), as substance and as subject. It lacks the *existential* determination of being, of being-there, and, thus, it lacks as well understanding, *Auslegung* and anticipation as such. The "circle" ontologically lacks the existential circularity (so to speak . . .) of being-there. Or again: *the "hermeneutic circle" fundamentally lacks the hermeneutical anticipation of meaning in being-there.*

If the "circle" lacks this *hermēneuein*, it is because *hermēneuein* is not *part* of a preliminary belief or "participation in meaning" in order to recover it in an educated understanding. Existential *hermēneuein* consists in what meaning—which is not in anything anterior (and if it was, then what will be its being?)—*announces itself* to being-there, as its own announcement and as its own opening, and by which being-there ex-ists: that is to say, it does not *subsist on its own* as the subject of an act of understanding and interpretation.[23] The being of meaning announces itself—it is being-*there* that this announcement determines and structures. That meaning announces or displays itself constitutes a "most originary" or, if one wishes, "archi-originary" determination: that is to say, it constitutes an archi-archaic determination of the origin which undoes, in that way, the very assignment of an origin of meaning, and the infinite origin of the circle. For what is more archaic than the archaic is no longer archaic nor archonic, without being, for all that, posterior or derived. That which opens itself [*s'ouvre*: discloses itself] (it is always an opening [*une bouche*: a mouth]) is neither first nor second, and that which announces itself (it is always meaning) neither precedes nor succeeds itself. It will not suffice to say that we are always-already caught in the circle, if one understands by that, that we are always-already the origin. It is the origin itself (one that is the meaning as much as the opening [the mouth] of the interpreter) which is always-already detached from itself by the opening and the announcement according to which there is meaning which occurs.—In an analogous manner, where hermeneutics, as it has been said, implies that the participation in meaning is never interrupted to any extent, *hermēneuein* does not permit itself even to envisage such an implication. There is a question of neither discontinuity nor continuity, but a question of an interval [*un battement*]— the general effect of eclipse and bursting forth, the *syncopation* of the musical score of meaning—where meaning discloses itself. An overture—in the active sense of the term—is neither interrupted nor uninterrupted: it opens, it discloses itself. The *history* which engages *hermēneuein*, or in which it is engaged, is consequently quite different from the historic process of hermeneutics. *Hermēneuein* appears at the *time* as opening, beginning, sending—not History as the dialectical or asymptomatic fulfillment of the times.

In a word, hermeneutics anticipates meaning, whereas *hermēneuein* creates the anticipatory or "annunciative" structure of meaning itself. The first is possible only on the ground of the second. The latter does not define interpretation, nor in all rigor something like "pre-understanding." *Hermēneuein* defines this: understanding is possible only by the anticipation of meaning which creates meaning itself. And, it must be added, this *ontological* anticipation is, in such a manner, anterior to all anticipation as "pre-judgment" of meaning, which no doubt does not break away from the circular perspective of the final return to the original meaning, recovered and "understood." There is no end nor origin to the "anticipating" opening or announcement of meaning. In its "circle" (which Heidegger places between quotation marks once, which he defends), meaning collapses much farther on this side or beyond every origin. And it could be that what discloses and announces itself with meaning is precisely this, *that meaning "consists" in the absence of an origin and of an end.*—In this sense, in principle meaning diverts every *interpretation*—although its *hermēneuein* also, in principle, opens the possibility of determined interpretation in determined fields (of belief, history, texts, or artworks). For instance, in this way, the possibility, and the necessity, of interpreting what which names existential *hermēneuein*—that is to say, the text of Heidegger—is opened. That is what I am doing here, proceeding unquestionably according to the circle of belief or pre-understanding (coming from Heidegger himself, and others who are themselves interpreting Heidegger and who I reinterpret across Heidegger . . .) But what I am doing here, then, is possible precisely because *hermēneuein* is open already, or has been announced already, not only in this text of Heidegger (which is itself only a determined *Auslegung*—prisoner still of the hermeneutics which it challenges—and of which the determination will vary, moreover, in the rest of the work), but in *the text* in general, in the text of philosophy in any case, and insofar as this text to this day carries—while from the outset it has forgotten it—the question of the meaning of being.

*

*   *

Being and Time strives to understand this question of meaning as the meaning of a question which precedes itself "hermeneutically," that is to say, a question which is disclosed or announced already in being-there out of which it structures existence. *Hermēneuein* designates this constitutive antecedence, which is neither one of intention, one of belief, nor one of a participation in meaning—but which *is* meaning. The "meaning" of *hermēneuein* holds onto itself in this advance of meaning, an advance which one would be able to repeat endlessly if it had the distinctive mark of finitude, of being-there. And, from this fact, it would be able to take hold of itself, therefore, in a[n] (infinite/finite) delay of meaning concerning itself, in a *différance* which it would be necessary to import here from the "interpretation" of Heidegger by Derrida. Antecedent-differant, *hermēneuein* does not name the opposite of a "hermeneutic circle," but every other thing: everything which the hermeneutic circle, whether it desires it or not, finds itself, as a circle, paradoxically *opening*: that is to say, that alterity or that alteration of meaning, without which the identification of a meaning— the return to *itself* in the circle —would not even be able to take place.

The opening of *hermēneuein* is, in this sense, the opening of the meaning and in the meaning as *other:* not an "other" meaning, superior, transcendent, or more original, but a meaning itself as other, an alterity defining meaning. Just as the being-in-question of being in its own being defined being-there, according to an alterity and an alteration of its presence, its subsistence, and its identity, *hermēneuein* determines—or rather announces—that the meaning, this meaning *in question,* is always *other,* in every sense of the expression.[24]

What is other or what becomes the other ("being," in this case, is necessarily "becoming" . . . ["*venir*" . . .]) is not interpreted itself at first, but announces itself. Now we know that it is with respect to the *announcement* that the entire emphasis of the explication is given later on, in a "Dialogue on Language," *à propos* of *hermēneia.*

Even though it is not a question of commenting here on the whole text, it is necessary to recall that hermeneutics does not play an episodic role in it: it is the conducting thread of the dialogue itself, sometimes visible, sometimes hidden. The first question addressed in the thought of Heidegger carries over the hermeneutic motif out of *Being and Time*. Heidegger solicits a response by recalling the origin of this motif, for him, in the theology and the writings of Dilthey, but also in making reference to Schleiermacher, from whom he cites the definition of hermeneutics ("the art of comprehending completely the discourse of another"), whereas he indicates that in *Being and Time* "the name hermeneutics" "neither signifies the doctrine of the art of interpretation nor interpretation itself, but rather the attempt to determine what is interpretation, first of all, from what is hermeneutics."[25] His interlocutor asks what "hermeneutics" means. It is from there that the motif disappears explicitly, only in order to reappear much later, when he realizes that the question has not been elucidated. At the same time, it is recalled that Heidegger, since *Being and Time*, has abandoned the word "hermeneutics." The abandonment of a name does not prevent—on the contrary—the intended significations adopted by this name from being made explicit. Heidegger furnishes this clarification when referring to the Greek *hermēneia* in the following passage:

> The expression "hermeneutic" derives from the Greek *hermēneuein* [ερμηνεύειν]. That verb is related to the substantive noun *hermēneus* [ἑρμηνεύς], which can be related to the name of the God *Hermēs* ['Ερμῆς] by a play of thinking more binding than the rigor of science. Hermes is the messenger of the Gods. He brings the announcement of destiny; *hermēneuein* [ερμηνεύειν] is the manifestation which brings as much by way of knowledge as it is in the proper condition to listen to an announcement. Such a bringing to light becomes afterward an interpretation of what has been said by the poets—who, according to Socrates in Plato's dialogue *Ion* (534e), "are messengers [interpreters] of the Gods [ἑρμηνῆς εἰσιν τῶν θεῶν] ."
>
> J.—I love that short dialogue of Plato's. In the passage that you mention, Socrates extends the affinities [relations] even further: he conjectures that the rhapsodes are those who bring knowledge of the poets' word.
>
> D.—All this throws into relief clearly that what is hermeneutics does not mean merely interpretation, but, even, before that, carrying the announcement and communicating knowledge.[26]

The dialogue continues by sliding over hermeneutics to "the word which gives voice to the hermeneutic relation," as well as the dialogue itself, which appears as the exchange or the "liberation" of two questions which address themselves to the "same": the Japanese inquirer's question alludes to hermeneutics, and the question of his interlocutor, previously interrupted, is on the word used for "speech" [*"la parole"*]. This "sameness" [*"mêmeté"*] of hermeneutics and speech [language] displaces the relationship established in *Being and Time* between *hermēneia* and the statement. This was an imperceptible displacement (because the dialogue claims section 34 of *Being and Time* as having introduced already what is presently at stake). But this "sameness" is not thematically elucidated. When the Japanese asks a last time, "At present how would you lay bare the hermeneutic relation?" he is answered:

I would like to avoid a straightforward exposition then, as it is necessary to avoid speaking *about* speech.[27]

Instead of a discourse on speech—or on hermeneutics —, it is the dialogue [*le Gespräch*] itself that the dialogue, which goes on to draw to a close, will propose as "the meaning of speech in counterpoint to speaking." As such, the *Gespräch* would have to proceed, not from men who speak it, but from an address, from a challenge to men by *Sprache* [language] itself. Thus, the dialogue would have to be—it is, at least, all that is allowed to be understood—the hermeneutic announcement of speech, and by the same stroke the announcement of what is "the hermeneutic relation" which does not allow itself "to be exposed" (to be presented, *darstellen* [to be represented]) by a discourse. But that supposes a determination of the *dialogue* which is not satisfied by "any conversation," and which, perhaps, according to the Japanese, "the dialogues of Plato themselves" would not be able to satisfy. His interlocutor responds: "I would like to leave the question open . . . "

If, consequently, thanks to a violent setting apart of the text for which I assume authority,[28] one can only maintain that the "Dialogue" explicitly evokes the subject of hermeneutics, by neglecting the other motifs that it develops, one ends up in a strange and complex situation. The word *"hermeneutics"* is pulled from its abandonment by the question of the other—by the staging of a question from the other, who is at the same time the Western other and the former representative of a former Japanese disciple of Heidegger. The question of hermeneutics has been raised by the reminder of the fact that this former disciple—from the epoch of *Being and Time*—takes hold of it before anything else. This question is reactivated, then, by a double mediation: one of the understanding, or the interpretation, of the master's thought by a disciple, and one of the understanding, or the translation, of the word from this thought in a language which takes the appearance of the language of the other *par excellence*. One can add also that it is a question of understanding the disciple by his actual representative, who was his student: between the languages and in each language, there is only an indefinite return to the understanding of understanding. Thus, one analyzes all the details of the staging[29] (and from the very first the choice of the *genre* of the dialogue, which supposes a staging) in order to end in this: that which is staged is hermeneutics itself, in its infinite presupposition and in its "enigmatic" character, which has been announced by Heidegger in his first response on this subject.[30] He does not *respond* to the question because the dialogue—the text—is itself the response. It is the response insofar as it offers itself as the interpretation, as the deciphering of these figures, signs, or symbols, which are figures, signs, and symbols of interpretation itself. The dialogue is both enigma and the figure of enigma.

But, now this situation is, formally, classic: in principle it is no different from that of the Platonic dialogue in general—that is to say, if not from the workings of all the texts of Plato, at least from all those where the staging is very precisely calculated in order to place the object of the inquiry in the "abyss of representation" [*"mettre en abyme"*: the representative-placing-in-the-abyss].[31] If the "Dialogue" refers to the *Dialogues* of Plato, and leaves open the question of knowing whether there are *Gespräche* [conversations], this fact signifies nothing less than this: the present "Dialogue" replays the entire Platonic (philosophic) scene of the dialogue, this time not for the sake of staging [or producing] such or such an object of inquiry, but, if one can say, the "dialogicity" itself, or the *Gesprächheit* [conversationality] as such. Hermeneutics, as "the art of understanding well the discourse of another," is performed, that is say, carried out, executed, represented, and presented in the work of art which is the "Dialogue." But in the same way, it is not certain that this is not the case already with the Platonic dialogues (the object of the *Meno*, the *Theatetus*, the *Sophists*, the *Symposium*, in order only to cite them, is it not always *likewise* the dialogue or the dialogicity as such?), likewise, and in an inverse sense, whether one will be able to establish if the "Dialogue" does not replay in effect, simply, up to a certain point, the philosophic scene: that is to say, the scene of the *mise-en-abyme*, the scene of the text which shows nothing other than itself, the scene of the presentation of being presented in the same form of the presentation (or representation)[32]—in a word, that which has always been associated with philosophy under the haunting motif of a living, animated, auto-exposition of the exchange of thoughts, of that exchange—maieutic, didactic, interrogative, or mediative—which is itself thinking as the free life of thought.

Thus it could be established that, by the same stroke, this scene presents itself also as the classic scene of interpretation: the dialogue, which puts into play the alterity of the discourses or the speeches, shows itself as this *other* discourse, neither explicative, demonstrative, nor a statement "about," but giving up to its errant course, to the advantage of its indetermination.[33] What makes this discourse *other* is that it gives itself; it wants to give itself in this way for the discourse *of the Other* (of *Meaning*). No one speaks it—without fictions—but *the* essential dialogue dialogues itself; the "Dialogue" maintains itself. *Das Gespräch spricht von sich selbst:* the dialogue speaks of itself, from itself, in every sense of the expression. And moreover, undoubtedly *das Gespräch* is to be understood, more originally than as "dialogue," as the *Ge-spräch,* the essential reassembling of Language [*la Parole:* Speech]. That is to say that the Meaning *interprets itself,* in some roles, and gives itself in this way to be interpreted and comprehended. After all, according to the circle, it sets itself: it is necessary to have posed the dialoging essence of thinking (again Plato . . .) in order to comprehend the staging of the dialogue.

Paradoxically, the circle of interpretation will close itself up in this way because hermeneutics must open it.[34] Or again, and more exactly, it is the hermeneutic opening—or the announcement—itself which will determine itself as the circle. When Heidegger proclaims to object to an "explanation *about*" hermeneutics, he comes to recall that "to speak of a circle," although that proceeds from a necessary recognition, "remains in the foreground." As in *Being and Time,* the circle is superficial and inaccurate, only an expression or an image. Is it not necessary, then, to understand that this superficial and necessary circle, which will not be able to be replaced by another exposition, is itself to be *comprehended* and *interpreted* from and with a view to authentic hermeneutics? "Hermeneutics" is then the *meaning* of the circle, which is necessary to be able to interpret. In order to be able to interpret the circle, it is necessary to have recognized in the preceding that hermeneutics is its meaning, although this meaning can be reached only by the interpretation of the circle, which is to say, according to the duality (circularity) inscribed in the very same syntax of the genitive "the interpretation of the circle," by the interpretation that the circle gives of hermeneutics, and by the interpretation of the meaning of hermeneutics that traverses the comprehension of the circle. The interpretation of interpretation is indeed, then, hermeneutics, that is to say, the circle itself as the meaning which escapes interpretation because it precedes it, and which is *recovered* from and in interpretation because it follows it.

This can be said again in other words: the circle "itself" is nothing other than the relation of interpretation which circulates in the circle as the inaccurate expression in the primordial circle of meaning. At last, the circle recovers its own form [*figure*].[35]—Here likewise, the dialogue is dialectical.

II

Thus, in the circle composed of a circle, or in the placement in the abyss of all the circles which the "Dialogue" offers, the great philosophic scene of interpretation is replayed. Nevertheless, Heidegger pushes it to the extreme—to the limit of the circle, if one can speak in this way. He does so in two ways simultaneously: on the one hand, primordial "hermeneutics" itself becomes here, by an imprisonment of the problematic of *Being and Time, the* meaning which is to be understood, which it is necessary to presuppose, and, to depart from being "brutal," which it is necessary *to believe,* and on which we impose the setting of belief that the two interlocutors believe. According to this standard, his "enigma" possesses something of the sacred, and, moreover, the tone of the dialogue is not exempt from a certain complicity of piety or of devotion between accomplices in a belief itself. *Hermēneia* becomes the sacred name, primordial and originary in meaning. With this assumption and with this identification under this name, for which thanks is due to the primordial language of thought and to the refined "play" of this thought with the godlike Hermes, the *alterity* of meaning is, in passing, being reabsorbed.

But, on the other hand, this authentic assumption does not take place, if it takes place, in such a simple manner. It is the return to Plato which has given the primordial meaning to *hermēneia.* Thus, this primordial meaning (submitted to elsewhere by the circular understanding of the conversation) is found in one of these dialogues, of which it has not been decided whether they have the character of an authentic "dialogue." A second reading imposes itself from there: if the Platonic dialogue places the abyss at the center of this dialogue, and as its figure, the *Ion* is decidedly not an authentic "dialogue." Perhaps it is the case that it cannot be decided of any dialogue if it is an authentic conversation [*entretien*]: not any, and consequently no longer the one that we read, "A Dialogue on Language." It's title—*Aus einem Gespräch von der Sprache*—wants to make it understood that we read only an extract of the dialogue, as a partial transcription. The "genuine" dialogue is unreadable, inaudible, missing in the errance of contingency where it had been . . . It is there, still, a proceeding of a Platonic type, and at the same time the indication of a generalized "inauthenticity": but not to the extent that every readable dialogue will be inauthentic. Rather it will be a question of this, and not the authenticity of the "dialogue"—*hermeneutic* authenticity is not *determined.* It will be anterior to or exterior to the order of discussion which, rightly, permits ascribing the exactness of an interpretation and the authenticity of a meaning. By the same gesture (and if it is permissible to speak a language so ungrammatical [*barbare*]), the "Dialogue" would originate [*originerait*] and would terminate [*désoriginerait*] the *Gespräch* regarding what it signifies by referring to the *hermēneia* of the *Sprache*.

If this suspicion would have to be verified, it would be necessary for it to verify a corollary hypothesis: namely, that the return to the *Ion*, charged with furnishing the primordial meaning of *hermēneia*, has in truth a function other than the simple appeal to the authority of an authentic origin. (Already, the appeal to the etymology of *hermēneia* by *Hermēs*,— the "playfulness" of etymology itself is borrowed, without saying so, from Plato[36]—is a slight indication in this direction, insofar as a faint difference distinguishes this gesture from the seriousness and from the "belief" which coincide in the other etymologies—that is to say, in the other interpretations—of Heidegger.) But on the one hand, the return to the *Ion* does not provide only a passage to an abstract definition of the text. The text as such, in its entirety, is evoked: as soon as the Japanese adds that, for Socrates, not only are the poets the interpreters of the gods, but the rhapsodes are the interpreters of the poets, the entire structure of the *Ion* is in place, without the necessity of this indication being visible in the economy of the "Dialogue." On the other hand, *as a dialogue* this text creates the object from a designation and from an express fondness ("I love this little dialogue of Plato's"), which overflows, in some way, its placement in the abyss of interpretation. (And how can it not be noticed that the "Dialogue" is itself also a "little dialogue"?)

Thus, the hypothesis must be made that it is necessary to take hold of these indications of seriousness, and to treat, without reservation, their placement in the abyss of interpretation: in other words, that it is necessary (that Heidegger had wanted to make us) to read *Ion* in the "dialogue"— and that only the reading of the *Ion* can operate in another way within the circle of the primordial meaning of *hermēneia*. Perhaps the enigma is not, in that case, a sacred riddle which would have escaped already from Plato, but it would consist in this: a certain reading of Plato—that is to say, a certain path *from* philosophy as well as *in* philosophy—takes into account the excess of philosophical interpretation to which *hermēneia* is invited as "announcement." It is to an announcement and to an opening of the very text of philosophy that we are guests: from Plato to us, the hermeneutical, philosophical circle would have not ceased from breaking off . . .

What is it that *Ion* announces as the subject of the announcement? Let us read, let us interpret.

*

* *

Socrates meets Ion. Who is this Ion from Ephesus? Who knows him? Would he be there in order to take the place of Ion from Chios, author of tragedies and philosophic texts, like Plato, and a contemporary of Socrates? Would he, by homonymy, take the place of the one who has written these lines: "the *gnôthi seauton* [*"the know thyself"*] is a brief speech, but an action such that only Zeus, among all the Gods, is capable"?[37] Would he have, in short, the role of a rival—or of a double, more or less grotesque or contemptible—of Socrates and of Plato at the same time? It is necessary to keep this question alive.

Ion returns for a contest of rhapsodes. The rhapsodes are the orators [*déclamateurs:* declaimers, bombastic interpreters] of poems, or if one prefers—and this will be more correct—the orators of the poets.[38] Ion has won first prize. Socrates envies less the prize than the act of the rhapsode as such. These people must be well dressed and have a beautiful appearance: it is, as one knows, the contrary of Socrates himself. (This is the first touch of irony that will not cease to be directed toward Ion—at least in appearance. It will be necessary to question it in terms of its import.) But above all, they pass their time in the company of the great poets, of whom they "thoroughly understand the thought, and not merely the verse" [530c–d—TRANS.]. Indeed, the rhapsode must be *the hermēneus* [interpreter] of the *dianoia* [understanding] of the poets (that is to say, in the first approximation at least, of his thought). "But it is impossible to be a good interpreter if one does not know what the poet means to say (*o ti legei*)." *Hermēneia* is, then, distinct from the acquisition of understanding relating to this *logos;* this understanding renders possible a beautiful or good *hermēneia,* which is to be directed to "the listeners." *Hermēneuein*—that is to interpret the meaning of the orator and to produce the *logos* of the poet. The *logos* (and/or the *dianoia*) distinguishes itself from the verse (*epê*) as such, and the good *hermēneus* is the one who makes heard [*fait entendre:* makes understood] the *logos* in the delivery of the verse.

From the start, the situation is then clearly one of a distinction between the form and the content, between the sound and the meaning. It implies, as the preliminary condition of clear and theatrical interpretation, an activity of interpretation in the most classic sense: the rhapsode must comprehend the poet; he must give an exegesis. But this activity is not precisely *hermēneia.* It consists here in "learning completely" (*ekmanthanein*). Moreover, this acquisition of knowledge presents itself as simple and direct (even if it is not reached without arduous work): it does not consist in deciphering hidden meanings.[39] *Hermēneia,* on the other hand, is more complex, but as will be seen, it is not acquired. It is the activity (declamatory and imitative: the rhapsode will be sometimes associated with the actor) which delivers the meaning of the poem in delivering the poem itself. Or, once again, if *ekmathesis* consists in what the poet says through what he says, *hermēneia* consists in restoring the poet in his verse, in *making him speak* in his own words.

Ion declares, then, that he possesses this "competence"[40] only with respect to Homer. So that just as the other poets treat the same subjects as his exclusive poet, he remains ineffectual before their poems. The others "do not sing like Homer," but "clearly far worse" (531d). And Ion, who by this very affirmation seems nevertheless to play the part of an expert technician regarding poetry, affirms that he is skilful only in Homeric material.—In the passage, Socrates mentions, as the first example of a subject common to several poets, the divinatory art, the science of divination, prophecy [*la mantique:* from the Greek *mantis* meaning seer, prophet, "he who is mad"]. And the first example of these experts whom Ion does not resemble will have been the soothsayer or prophet: a prophet will be able to judge the work of all the poets from what they say on the subject of divination. As one will see, this example is not chosen by chance.

The question, then, is posed, as it were, about two types of expert knowledge: that of technicians or qualified scholars in a domain (divination, medicine, etc.; it has been admitted even that there must exist something like a "poetics" ["*poiétique*": from the Greek *poiétikē*, a productive science or art]), and that of this hermeneut, expert solely in Homer. What is supposed is an expert *à propos* everything spoken by Homer, without preference for particular domains, but only when it is Homer who has spoken about it, and, be that as it may, only because the other poets speak of the same subject. The hermeneut has, first of all and essentially—if not exclusively—a knowledge which is not about "content," nor about meaning, but which is nothing more than a "form." The strange thing is that it is a knowledge, and an excellent knowledge, indeed complete, of the meaning, of every meaning that one will want, of everything that can be made an object of a *dianoia* in the work of a single poet. The *o ti legei,* which is a question of knowing thoroughly, owes less to being understood as a "*what* he says, or intends to say (in the same way the translator interprets it)" than as a "what *he says,*" himself, Homer, and himself alone: it is a question less of the content of the announcement than of the singularity of a statement (and consequently, it is not a question of an "intent to say," but of the uniqueness of what one says). This knowledge is the knowledge *of meaning in a single form.* It is this strange thing that Socrates has dislodged, and which he wants to examine.

His judgment is formulated very quickly: the *hermēneia* of the rhapsode is neither a *technē* nor an *epistēmē.* That which is neither one nor the other is perhaps *sophia:* Socrates declares that he is not *sophos* [a sage], but it is "the rhapsodes and actors, and those whose poems they sing"

(532d). Here again, the place of irony must not be made too simple. Like elsewhere and often (always perhaps?) in the writings of Plato, a competition is established between the philo*sopher* and another. But it is not aimed at simply submitting the other to the philosopher. It aims, in a manner more twisted [*retorse:* artful, crafty, cunning] and less decidable, to show that the philosopher is better than the other *in the domain of the other,* or that he is the truth of the other, a truth which appears to the other, as such, consequently, but only insofar as this truth is his own. The philosopher submits, then, *also* to that which he appropriates, to this truth of the other and to this other truth.[41] The problem of *hermēneia,* and the reason for devoting himself to a dialogue,[42] is not perhaps anything other than the problem of the announcement of this other truth *by* philosophy and *to* philosophy (which simultaneously takes the form of an announcement *to* poetry and *by* poetry).

   That *hermēneia* is neither an art nor a science, that is to say, that it has no one general competence or uniformity (in regard to "poetics" as "a whole," 532c), but that it is, in the strongest sense of the word, a *singular* competence—that is what entirely defines the investigation of the dialogue.

   Likewise, it is not without a ruse that Socrates places in relief the exceptional nature of Ion's case, in that anyone who is equal to a competent judge in painting, sculpture, music, singing, or else in rhapsodic prestation finds himself in a similar situation. Each has a general competence in his domain. But *hermēneia* is not an activity of judgment, of discernment; it is not a *critical* activity, nor, in this sense, an interpretive activity. Socrates' ruse risks sliding toward critical competence, a sliding to which Ion is invited, but in which he is not himself truly engaged. Socrates' last example makes the ruse visible: to judge the prestations of rhapsodes is indeed something other than being it-self an rhapsode.—Elsewhere, in the system of fine arts through which the summary comes to be discretely given under the pretext of simple examples, it lacks poetry. Its place is doubly reserved: one will speak of the poets later, but here their position is held by the rhapsode. In the same way, here the classic commentary of the dialogue has rehearsed the longing; the rhapsode is a detour in order to attack the poet. To him alone, nevertheless, this argument is weak, because Socrates will speak directly of the poets. If the rhapsode doubles the poet, it is, one will see, because poetry cannot be acted without its *hermēneia,* and one can only act poetry through its *hermēneia.*

*

* *

   Socrates gives, then, his interpretation [*explication*] of this competence: it is not one, it does not have its own domain of jurisdiction, and it is not a mastery itself. It is a "divine power" that moves Ion. This power acts like the magnet which attracts iron rings. The characteristic of magnetism—because it is here, in the main, the premier philosophic trait of magnetism, and which indeed serves as a prelude to others[43]—is how this force is communicated: it passes through the rings, which are able to act (*poiein*) in their turn like the magnet, and attract other rings. Thus, one can have "a very long series of rings suspended from one another" (533c)[44]—and not one "chain" as the translator said, precisely because the rings are not enchained. They are *unchained* (in every manner one can imagine it), and they hold together: here the magnetism is the riddle.

An interpretation of the image is given: the magnet is the Muse. She produces (*poiei*) "inspired men" (*entheous,* enthusiasts) who inspire others in their turn. Thus, the poets are presented, because they are the first "inspired and possessed," and, thus, the first not to proceed "by *technē.*" It is very remarkable that magnetism, finally, will be employed less in order to represent allegorically the mysterious nature of rhapsodic rapture (certainly, everything depends on this mystery: but precisely, it is not to be explained; it is that which explains everything) than to present the "chain." Or else: what is signified in this mystery is of less exceptional character, "nonnatural"[45] because of the power, than its communicability, its transitivity. The mystery is, in this way, before everything through which it passes: in a receptivity that gives rise to an activity, or to a spontaneity, indeed, in a receptivity that is at the same time a spontaneity. Magnetism responds to the determination of a "receptive spontaneity," such as Heidegger, after *Being and Time,* would elicit from Kant, thanks to the violence of interpretation. It responds to the determination of finitude. Could it be that finitude will be [*soit:* is] the state of *hermēneia*? And could it be that finitude has been the stake since Plato? Will Ion be the first name of finite being-there? In order to finish, one will not be able to escape these questions. But let us proceed with the reading.

The poets are, then, the first hypnotists [*magnétisés*]. They are not in their right minds when they enter "into harmony and rhythm" (534a). They are similar to the Corybantian revellers or the Bacchian maidens. They themselves speak of it when they are to be compared to bees gathering in the gardens of the Muses.

> And they tell the truth: the poet is a light, winged, and holy thing, and out of his mind in *poiein* before being enthusiastic . . . (534b)

One can consider what is engaged in the ordinary manner of citation, that is to say, of interpretation: "the poet is a light thing" is far from being plainly and simply a contemptuous or suspicious judgment from Plato. It is thus, and first of all, what the poet himself says.[46] And, in this manner, he speaks the truth—the truth, this all-too-simple thing that Socrates himself says as a simple man. The poet speaks the truth on what is more than or other than the simple truth, on a kind of "sophia." At least the philosopher is there in order to say that the poet tells the truth about himself. But if this "verification" of what the poet says does not consist of anything other than its conversion in critical judgment, of what use, then, will any analysis be in which it is assumed, and of which, one will see, the essential point is not yet developed? In reality, it is indeed a question here of another truth that the philosopher announces and allows to be announced at the same time.

"Light, winged, holy thing": the ordinary citation-interpretation has the general effect, rightly or wrongly, of engaging only the first epithet, because it is the "light" which interprets the "holy," and not the inverse. The "holy" (or the "saint") is the light, floating, aerial thing which submits only to good fortune or the chance of the encounter.[47] The chance is what can place the self outside itself—in the other, *en-theos*—in delirium. The chance light-mindedness is the logic of being-outside-of-oneself. How will one be outside oneself in science, calculation, and volition? It is necessary that there be passivity, a saintly passivity which gives way to the magnetic force. The lightness of the poet is made of this passivity, responsive to the inspiration and the fragrance of the Muse's garden. It is from these risks or these indulgences in these "gardens or valleys" that they must find the honey which they furnish to us. They do not *make* the honey, they retrieve it, and poetic spontaneity does not consist in fabricating or in creating (for it would be necessarily *technē*), but "in furnishing us" with what they gather. It is a gift—and it is a gift which is given by the Muses. The lightness and the saintliness of the chance are, in this way, the gifts. (On the other hand, this is not an accident if what is valuable is presented here in this way, from the poets to us, *à propos* the *melopoioi* (which can be translated as "lyric poets"), whose verse or songs—*melê*—create assonance with the honey—*meli*—and with the bees—*melittai*. It is not by chance if Plato becomes the poet.)

Poiein (which does not, then, mean "to make") is the privilege of that state of being possessed, equal to or equivalent with *chresmodein*, "the singing of the oracles." *Chrèsmos*, oracle in the sense of the response given by the gods, is nothing other than "to inform (*chraô:* [*faire savoir*]), to hear and to declare knowledge. It is an other and similar mode of giving what at first was received from the gods. The oracular, the divinatory, the poetic, and the hermeneutic converse from these narrow bonds. First of all, they share "being beside oneself, out of his sense" (*ekphrôn*), which is the absolute condition for poetic "creation."[48] The poet must no longer be possessed of his mind in order to be able to give what he is given. The absence of *technē* (and *epistēmē*) corresponds as such to the absence of one's *own* capacity. A self-same *technē* prepares one for making, for producing, for fabricating—and by the effect of exchanging his products—but not for receiving, nor for giving the gift received. It is not of his own [*en propre*] that the poet is the poet; it is the standard, itself without a standard, of a deprivation and a dispossession of oneself. It is in the limit where the *poiein* itself is given to itself. It is necessary that he has nothing of his own—and that from the very first he is not in possession of himself—so that the Muse can "incite" him or "excite" him (*ormaô*) to *poiein,* and to *poiein* in a determined genre (dithyrambic, epic, iambic, etc.), which is the only one in which, because of that, the poet is able to excel.

In its principle, consequently, the enthusiastic outburst of frenzy does not correspond solely to the elevation and the divine possession of the poets' speech. The enthusiasm is necessary in order to enter into a genre which the Muse imposes. There is no gift of poetry in general (and perhaps there is never the gift "in general," nor possession "in general": both are conceived as particulars). There is then a sharing, an originary difference between genres or poetic voices—and perhaps, behind the scenes, a sharing of poetic and philosophic genres. There is no general poetry, and with regards to general poetics, the existence of which has been admitted in principle, it remains undiscoverable: but it is here, of course, that it exposes itself. There are only contrasting singular voices, and the enthusiasm is first of all the entrance into one such singularity.

Such is "divine sharing" (*theia moira* [divine fate or divine lot], 534c; the expression occurs several times) according to which the communication of "divine power" takes place. This force is to be communicated to make a difference, and this is only to traverse these differences so that we, "the listeners," can perceive the divine character of the poems: it is not in fact the poets who speak, but "the god himself is the speaker" (*o theos autos esti o legôn*). When it is a matter of knowing the *o ti legei* of a poet, it is a matter of knowing the *o ti legei* of the god. Thus, the god "makes himself heard" through the poets: *phthengetai,* he resounds, he speaks, in the clear and articulated sense of the term.

So it is that whereas the poets come to be designated as the *hermeneuts* of the divine—which induces identification with the rhapsodes—it is poetic *hermēneia* (the first, then), very far from consisting in the comprehension of a *logos* of the gods (to the contrary, fixed elsewhere in Plato, "the prophet and hermeneutics in general *know what is spoken but they do not know if it is true*"[49]), which consists in the consonant delivery of such a *logos. Hermēneia* is the *voice* of the divine. And this voice is first of all, principally (but that does not make it a *principle; it is only given* in this way), shared voices, the differentiation between singular voices. In other words, there is no *one* divine voice, nor perhaps a divine voice in general, because these "divine poems" are spoken in the language or languages of men. But *the voice*, for the divine, is the sharing and the difference. Is this difference itself divine or human? The question is not posed? This difference is the articulation of the divine with respect to and in the human. The man who is the poet is outside of himself, but the divine is there also outside himself—in the sharing of voices. (Likewise one must ask if what the Muse communicates, if what the magnetic force gives, is, in the end, anything other than that itself: being-outside-of-oneself, as the only "form" and the only "meaning" of divine *logos*.)

Insofar as "god himself is the speaker," he speaks and proclaims himself in singular genres, and the singular genre is divine. The divine does not speak directly; it is no longer a single voice. But the plural and indirect voice *is his voice*, and not a transcription, a translation, nor an interpretation.

That the plural and human voice is the voice itself of the divine is what makes the *theia moira*, at the same time, the lot [the sharing] which befalls each poet—one's fate (*Moira*) as poet, of *this* poet—and the fate of the divine itself. The divine is what gives itself, what divides itself in voice and in *hermēneia:* it is what signifies "en-thusiasm."[50] In this sense, the divine, or god himself, *is* enthusiasm. And perhaps one should go as far to say that the divine, in this way, means that there would be the gift and the sharing of voices. *Hermēneia* is the articulation and the announcement of this sharing.

*

* *

Now the rhapsode is, in his turn, the *hermēneus* of the poets. He is, then, the *hermēneus* of the *hermēneus* (535a). The "chain" constitutes itself. The *dunamis theia* [divine power] and *theia moira* [divine fate] communicate through the subsequent rings: the rhapsode is himself, in this way, inspired, enthusiastic, and *destined* to the *interpretation* of a singular poet. (He is not even the rhapsode of a single genre, but of a single poet: the "genres" do not have a true existence because they are not "interpreted" by the singular voice of *a* poet.) The singularity of Ion's talent receives its principle explanation. But the mark of the operation is only partially in this explanation—which would poorly justify the enterprise of the dialogue, and which elsewhere would allow one to suppose something like an increasing passivity and debasement in this transmission of *hermēneia* (after all, the rhapsode does not create the poems, and the poet does not create the divine *logos*). It is indeed on this idea of debasement that the classic commentary, according to which Plato "reascends" from the rhapsode to the poet, is ordered. But Plato does not reascend; he "descends" entirely to the series of rings. No part evokes a debasement of the magnetic force, the length of the series (which has been said to be capable of being "very long"). The main point is what happens in this "descent."

On the one hand, the divine force is transmitted intact—but exactly as it *is to be transmitted,* and it is with the second ring that it manifests entirely this property. The transmission requires the plurality of rings (the attendant will be us, the public). If the magnetic force is valued before everything for the sake of its transitivity, it implies the procession, and, thus, the difference of the rings as essential. The sharing of voices responds, as if on a perpendicular axis, to the sharing of hermeneutic instances. In the same way as there is no *one* divine voice, there is no *one* hermēneia. But there is the *hermēneia* of *hermēneia.* Perhaps that signifies a "receptive spontaneity" *to address* oneself necessarily, essentially, to an other receptivity, to whom it communicates its spontaneity. *Hermēneia* does not only give voice and resonance to a *logos:* it addresses this voice, it directs it—to a public (to "us, the listeners," as if to repeat the text)—but it directs it to this pubic in order to reproduce in itself that which is its fate. Otherwise, why would it have been determined and why would it be destined?

But that supposes, on the other hand, that the rhapsode does not reproduce simply, does not echo in a second hand and derived manner the *hermēneia* of the poet, and that the rhapsodic *hermēneia* equally plays a role, let us say a "positive" role, in the transmission of the divine *logos.* Such is the case indeed—and, in conclusion, it is necessary that the rhapsode is here the representative of a singularly complex problem of *mimēsis:* it would appear that he ought to copy, to reproduce the poem (or the poet? already this will be a primary form of the complexity in question). In one sense, he does nothing other. But, in doing this, he *represents* it, or he *interprets* it, that is to say, he makes it, in fact, through *hermēneia.* *Hermēneia* is a *mimēsis* . . .

Hermeneutic *mimēsis* forms, without a doubt, the determining feature: the problematic of the "hermeneutic circle" is implied according to every necessity (as a *mimēsis* of meaning, or of the author, or of the work itself), but it is not considered as such. (The *circle,* as circle, is, to the contrary, both the position and the *annulation* of the question of *mimēsis.*) *Hermēneia* is *mimēsis,* but an active, creative, or re-creative *mimēsis.* Or, again, it is a mimetic creation, effected through a *mimēsis* which proceeds from *methexis,*[51] from the participation itself due to the communication of enthusiasm—unless *mimēsis* is the condition of this participation. (Be that as it may, the "participation in meaning," which makes use of the hermeneutic circle, is by nature mimetic: it is what the circle dissembles.)

This particular *mimēsis*, then, will be placed in comparison to the two genres of *mimēsis* which take into consideration, in a general manner, Plato, and of which R. Brague gives a suggestive characterization by designating them as the *mimēsis* that operates "practically" and the mimēsis that operates "poetically."⁵² In the first, the imitating conforms *itself* to a model; in the second, it produces, outside of itself, a copy of a model. Similar to the *mimēsis* of the times, analyzed by Brague, the *mimēsis* of the rhapsode would combine the two.—It is not certain, moreover, if it is not to err to ask oneself, with or without Plato, if the combination of these two is not inevitable in every case of *mimēsis:* can one conform without producing this structure as a work? Can one, in copying for the sake of the work, not conform oneself to something of a model? . . . Be that as it may, the distinction is formulated in other terms by the *Sophist* (267a: or else the fantastic [*phantasma*] is made by means of the *organôn* [instrument], or else that which makes it lends itself as *organôn*), and it is *mimēsis* "by itself" which will be able to give the good or the "learned" *mimēsis*. Of this type is the *mimēsis* of Ion: for him, as for the sophist or for the philosopher, it is a question of imitating, if not the physical person of Homer, at least, "the design and the voice" of the poet. It is, indeed, a "learned" *mimēsis*, the science of which remains, no doubt, unseizable, but no more nor less than the one which is required in the *Sophist* for philosophic *mimēsis*.⁵³

How does the *mimēsis* of Ion present itself? This is recognized without difficulty as it is in the enthusiasm, at the moment he interprets Homer, when he recites it and when he "clearly speaks his words" (*eu eipès epè*, 535b). If it is a question of skipping from Ulysses or Achilles, from Hecuba or the misfortune of Priam, his soul rises to be there: it identifies itself; it weeps or it shudders with these individuals. The schema of the *Paradoxe sur le comédien* is there completely, because, some lines further, Ion explains how, during his enthusiastic declamation, he observes the spectators "high from his stage," in order to survey the effects that he produces, because his wages depend on his success. He is, then, capable of "participating in" and of "remaining" at a distance at the same time. This particular capacity of dividing into two itself proceeds from the absence of a *proper* ability, of art or of technique proper which characterizes Ion.⁵⁴

It is in Ion's enthusiasm that the enthusiasm of Homer is *interpreted,* staged, and not only imitated but seen. (*Hermēneia* is always, at the same time, *theatrical*.) The enthusiasm is communicated to the spectators, who experience with Ion the emotions or the passions of the Homeric heros. In this way, the spectator is the last ring in the "chain." The "rhapsode and actor" is, with respect to himself, the "intermediate link." Indeed, it is this middle position which accounts for Ion's choice as speaker and as object of the dialogue: the rhapsode embodies, overall, the very transitivity, even the

transit of the enthusiasm, the *passage* of communication, in that it is necessary to listen to the meaning of the magnetic communication and to the
meaning of the communication of the divine logos. What is to be communicated in this way—what delivers itself, announces itself, and gives itself
to be interpreted or participated in—is, with the enthusiasm, *hermēneia*
itself. The spectator, to make a long story short, becomes a hermeneut himself—and the hermeneutic state, reciprocally, is a state of enthusiasm.

*
* *

Nevertheless, Ion does not accept the frenzy—*the mania*—which is
attributed to him. Socrates must proceed to a second demonstration. In reality, this will repeat the major argument: each *technē* has a proper domain,
whereas *hermēneia* does not have one; it has only the singular and passive
"property" of letting itself communicate the magnetism of a poet, of a
singular voice.

In order to persuade Ion, Socrates makes him recite the lines of
Homer where it is a question of *technē:* one about the coachman, one about
the physician, and one about the fisherman [537–538]. In each case, it is
up to the specialist of this *technē* regarding what one says if Homer says it
well. Ion must admit it. It does not divulge Socrates' ruse, which consists
in making him identify his *hermēneia* with a technical commentary or with
a kind of expertise about the technical contents of Homeric poetry. Ion does
not know, in effect, what *the hermēneia* is; he confuses it with the gloss of
a hippological or medical treatise: in that way he proves that he no longer
knows what is the *hermēneia* of which he is the hermeneut, that is to say,
the poetry. It is not with respect to the meaning that a modern Ion will be
able to reply to Socrates that it is not a question of contents, in poetry, but
a question of a beautiful form. It is precisely that to which Ion does not
respond, and which Plato no longer seeks to induce (although a precise
analysis would be able to show it, his text contains as well, embossed or in
a state of rough outline, the elements for such a distinction, for this distinction which, indeed, later, will solidly distribute "form" in literature and
"content" in philosophy). Ion does not understand what the situation is
with poetry in this sense, where it is the *hermēneia* of divine *logos*—that is
to say, the meaning where "poetry" is less a sort of literary specialty (precisely, here there are no "specialists") than the generic name of what the
divine act (*poiei*) makes it by the enthusiasts, that is to say, the *hermeneuts*.
Poetry—which, perhaps, is not to be limited to "poetry," and of which
Plato, in an underhanded fashion, is, without a doubt, in the act of showing
to his reader (to his hermeneuts) that philosophy not only withholds itself in
the clef, but is part of, and, by this double motif, excels there—poetry is

the "making" of the *hermēneia,* the "making" of the sharing, of the destination of the *mimēsis,* and of the announcement of divine *logos.*

Socrates proves immediately that he understands it, himself, by returning to the situation: he pretends to become the one who is being questioned—that is to say, the rhapsode. And he pretends to be questioned about passages from Homer concerning another *technē:* this is soothsaying [*mantique*] (divination), the name which he has slipped very quickly into the conversation, and which participates in the same frenzy as the oraculatory act and hermeneutics.[55]

Presented with an insistence which does not deceive, this reversal of roles opens into a demonstration, the irony of which completely escapes Ion. Socrates cites two passages about divinatory voices, both of which will be applied to Ion himself: the first [539a], where the soothsayer sees the figures of the suitors who laugh with tears on their faces, recalls the divided and doubling posture of Ion who describes himself in the act of laughing up his sleeve while he imitates the tears and weeps; the second [539b–c], which concerns the foreboding defeat of a conqueror, announces to Ion (who, one recalls, presents himself as the prize-winner of a competition] his defeat, which the philosopher is in the act of consummating. Ion understands nothing here; he does possess the ironico-philosophical *hermēneia.* The representative-placement-in-the-abyss-of-representation [*la mise-en-abyme*] and the irony are on an equal footing with philosophical mastery: playing the rhapsode, Socrates interprets, *à propos* the rhapsode, the divination staged by the poet, exclusive of the rhapsode. There is, now at least, the *interpretation:* it is necessary to know in order to comprehend, that is to say, it is necessary to be persuaded by Plato's intention in order to unravel his text.

It is not very difficult to recognize this intention, which is, very evidently, that of the master of *hermēneia,* that of an interpretation mastering *hermēneia* by a "learned" *mimēsis* of the rhapsode (it is a question, then, also of mastering enthusiasm . . .).

The end of the dialogue, which is near, will force Ion to accept Socrates' thesis, to acknowledge that he is not in possession of a *technē,* and that he is a "divine-man," praise by which the philosopher himself signifies his formal permission to depart. However, the situation is not entirely so simple. Because what the philosopher masters in this way is only a designation of the uncontrollable nature of the hermeneut. To master the uncontrollable, I have said already, creates the stake and the most learned play of the philosopher. There is not a better speculative trap raised by the discourse assigning the dominant place to the incomprehensible. In order to construct it, however, it will have been necessary to stage, to assume roles, to interpret the rhapsode and to recite Homer, to divide the philosopher in two, *to interpret* philosophy. It will have been necessary to write, to choose a genre (a genre of *mimēsis*), to compose the dialogue. The *hermēneia* of the dialogue irresistibly overflows the mastery that the dialogue thinks and presents, and which is the mastery of the hermeneutic process. The staging or the declamation of the discourse assuredly forms the pure speculation of discourse—of *logos*—on the staging and on the declamation. But this *logos* stages nothing other than this: *logos* itself (divine *logos*, or *logos* absolutely, or the divinity of *logos*) makes itself understood [heard] only as it is staged, declaimed, hermeneuticized. Moreover, there is not one part of it *logos*, another part an interpretation (a declamation); but "god speaks" in the interpretation. In this way, the discourse on "interpretation" can be itself, already, only an "interpretation" of *logos*. But it is not, thus, an issue of an "interpretation of interpretation" as it is understood in a modern Nietzschean sense. It is a question of this, that *logos* interprets itself, and that it is only or is made only in *hermēneia*, indeed as *hermēneia*. Thus, only a philosophic rhapsode permits a philosophy of the rhapsode. Here it ends, ineluctably, in the same place where it established itself, a certain mastery.

Ion is constrained by his "divine" self-recognition, because he must acknowledge that he cannot assume any technical role, although he attempts to make it so by assuming it of himself. Among the roles inspected is the skilfulness of the strategist, which gives vent to Socrates' passion, before he is finished, by treating Ion of "Proteus." Proteus is not another role; he is the interpreter of all the roles; he is the patron of hermeneuts. (But Proteus, in the legend, joins mimetic transformation with his gift, a gift of divination, of clairvoyance, and of the oracle.) By naming it, Socrates names nothing other than the *theia moira*, according to which is to be communicated the *theia dunamis* [divine power], the sharing and the difference of roles and voices in which *logos* is to be communicated. The *dia-logue* can only be, perhaps, another name for the *theia moira*, that is to say, *hermēneia*, this dialogue in which Plato himself is Proteus, in turn Socrates and Ion, in turn Ion and Homer, in turn Homer and Plato. This sharing, this dia-logue, does not allow itself to be seized—and the mastery of Socrates is, in a sense, nothing more than, if one can speak in this way, the mastery of this recognition . . .

Moreover, it could be that the final episode of the rhapsode as strategist has been interpreted, once more, otherwise than as a comic pretension of Ion in the highest technical function. Ion recognizes himself, in effect, in the act of the strategist *à propos* what this person must say to his soldiers in order to exhort them. Thus, he does not recognize himself in "the military act" as such, as Socrates slides over it afterwards, but in the ability to hold a suitable discourse, not as technical discourse, but as directed encourage-

ment, exhortation, as speech having to communicate something as enthusiasm (rapture, ecstasy). This identification is, in the end, an identification
of the hermeneutic with the *parénétique* (the discourse of council, of exhortation). And it concludes the last episode of the dialogue on the subject of
the *technai* produced in Homer's texts. Socrates has asked Ion to cite the
passages on the *technē* of the rhapsode. Ion responds that it would be necessary to cite all of Homer, and, one more time, he has stated precisely
what he would understand there, not the diverse technical contents but "the
language which is agreeable to the man or woman, slave or freeman, to the
subordinate or the master." The *technē*, undiscoverable by the hermeneut,
then, is concerned with the propriety of the discourses, not their competence. It concerns the propriety of the delivery, and this propriety is, by
essence, multiple, shared according to the roles. The undiscoverable *technē*
will have been found in what is not any one *technē*, but in the multiplication of voices, in their deliveries, and in their addresses. The "proper self-
sameness" of *hermēneia;* that is the difference between the singular
characteristics [*propriétés*] of the voices.

*
* *

In the matter of multiplying voices, there is no way for them to be
known to each other. In order for each voice to be known to the others, it
would be necessary to be on this side or beyond this sharing. Socrates is no
more there than Ion. Plato, perhaps, attempts to simulate that he is there,
and that he knows himself to be there. But he divides himself, in order to
speak himself, between Ion and Socrates. "Plato" interprets himself, stages
himself; Plato is the hermeneut of Plato, but Plato himself is the only difference between the voices of his characters, and the general difference—
general and always singular—between each voice of the *logos*.

According to this difference, the *logos* is not one voice. But, consequently, it is no more than one silent voice. It is conjoined [*s'articule*] in
solitude and silence, and through one voice. It conjoins every voice in advance, multiplying it in other voices, in the manner of an expression before
the expression, in the position of the *Auslegung* "anterior" to the *Ausdrücklichkeit*. In this *Auslegung,* or in this *hermēneia,* one not only has the form
of the *als* of the "as such being," but also an other: the one of the "as such
and such voice." Not only is the being always composed of such and such,
but the voice of this understanding is always-already such and such, epic or
lyric, poetic or philosophic, etc.

Logos is not a *phonē sēmantikē* [signifying voice], it is not a voice
endowed with signification, it is not a meaning, and it will not be able to be
"interpreted." It is, on the other hand, the articulation before the voices, in

which, nevertheless, the voices are conjoined already, and divided (separated). It is both the "anticipatory" and participating structure of the voice in general.[56] "The" voice, always plural, is the sharing, the lot, the *theia moira* of *logos:* its fate and its destination are in the execution, in the singular interpretation of each voice. "Hermes bears the announcement of destiny," it is said in the "Dialogue": it is necessary to add that the destiny is nothing other than the announcement, and the sharing of the announcement of *logos.* What has been called "logocentrism," the nature of which is here confirmed by a "theo-logo-centrism," turns out to be, at the same time, dedicated to the most powerful decenterings, a destinal (fatal [inevitable]) division of *logos* itself.

Herméneia is the *theia moira* of *logos.* It is neither the understanding nor the pre-understanding of a meaning—and if it is "participation in meaning," it is, in this sense, only where the meaning does not pre-exist, and does not come to pass away any more in the end, but where the meaning *is* this sharing, this multiplication of *logos.* (We are the meaning, in the sharing, in the distribution, in the multiplication of our voices.) That is to say that meaning "is" the gift of itself in the sharing—this gift which is neither a pre-donation nor a pre-position, because *it is the sharing which makes the gift.* That the meaning is given signifies as well that it is abandoned in the sharing, to the hermeneutic law of the difference between voices, and that it is not *a gift,* anterior and exterior to our voices and our orations.

Meaning gives itself; it abandons itself. There is, perhaps, no other meaning of meaning than this generosity, where it neither sets itself up nor holds itself back; responding to itself, the generosity of the hermeneut is the only meaning of hermeneutics.

It is from there that it is necessary, from now on, to understand the hermeneutic opening of the question of being, and its circular character. If we are in motion always already "in the everyday understanding of being," it is not that we have in an ordinary fashion—nor extraordinary!—*the* meaning of being, nor *a* meaning of being, nor *the* meaning in order to be. It is that we are, we exist, in multiplying voices, and that this sharing is what we *are:* we give it, we share it, we announce it. "To be" already in the understanding of being is not to be already in the circulation, not in the circularity of meaning: it is "to be," and it is to be abandoned in this sharing, and to its difficult community, where being is that which we announce to ourselves one to another, unless being is only announcing ourselves to one another, in a "long" poetic, magnetic, and rhapsodic "chain."

*

*   *

Hermeneutics is a gift: interpreted in all its meanings, and beyond this proposition is "the announcement" of the *Ion*. Nothing else is announced, only the gift, and the gift is the announcement itself. "Announcement" would be to say here that it is neither a question of, nor entirely a philosophical thesis on, hermeneutics, nor entirely the assumption of a pure, primordial riddle. Between the two, quite otherwise, the hermeneutic announcement of the gift is only a difference of voice, the voice as different, and shared. "Heidegger" miming "Plato," and reinscribing Plato's dialogue in his conversation, does not allow for anything other than a new dividing, the multiplying of the hermeneutic voice, between the voices, the roles, the scenes and the dialogues. He converses by dialogues, and this is no longer what one understands by a "dialogue," nor by a "representative-placement-in-the-abyss-of-representation," but it forms a proximity to the spacing [the separation] itself, a dia-logue as the sharing of *logos*. By no means does Heidegger interpret Plato: he always allows himself to be Plato's hermeneut. They announce the same thing; they make the *hermēneia:* that *logos* is a sharing, our sharing, which only we reassemble in our sharing. This sharing is, in this way, one of philosophy and poetry, but it does not assign their place nor meaning. Proteus can assume all the roles, in philosophy and in poetry. In this way, he can blur the roles, no longer permitting a decision between them. But this cannot be, because it would lead to a monological identity. The voice of each is singular, which speaks the same announcement as the voice of the other. And for each Ion, there is only *one* Homer.—The gift: that is the singularity of *my* voice, of *yours*, and of *our* dialogue.

What is the oneness and singularity of a voice? What is this formation or conformation which has nothing of a "universal particular," from a Hegelian model, but which executes (interprets), on the contrary, this sharing in which, paradoxically, everything universal disappears? What is this syncopation of the universal in multiplying voices? The *interpretation* of the universal is its division in singular voices, in singular scenes, infinitely approaching and infinitely isolating the one from the others. No meaning originates there, nor is any achieved there, but an always different (other) announcement is delivered there: that of the other, exactly: Not a grand-other who will assume the origin of the Discourse-of-the-other in general, but the announcement that the other is other (never "in general," and always in the singular), and that it is not speech which communicates itself from this alterity and in this alterity, each singular and finite time.

In the "Dialogue," as it has been announced already, the *other* is the question of "understanding" returned to, after having disappeared from the hermeneutic problem in *Being and Time*. It is returned to even under the mark of its hermeneutic tradition, with the citation from Schleiermacher.

But this other is no longer an anthropological other. It no longer refers to subjectivity, indeed, to the psychology of "understanding." This other—who is the Japanese, but also "the one who questions," who is Plato, but as well "Hermes"—this other is no longer the other man, the interlocutor of a dialogue. But it is not another thing, nor some-One else. It is, in the other of every dialogue, the one which makes it other, and which is not human, which is not one's human identity, comprehensible and comprehensive. It is this other of the other which never reappears as the same thing, and solely by which the possibility, the necessity, and the impossibility of the dialogue installs itself. (Heidegger has asked elsewhere: "If and when dialogue is necessarily dialectic?" and he responds in the same manner as in the "Dialogue" to the subject of Plato's dialogue: "Let us leave the question open."[57])

The finitude of the other is, without a doubt, in its singularity and its delimitation, with the Japanese, with Plato, or with Heidegger. But it is not, thus, its *"finité"* (according to the term proposed by Birault in order to qualify the end of metaphysics): it does not consist in a limitation (sensible, empirical, individual, as one would like) which will set itself up dependent upon infinity and in an imminent relation of sublimation or of recovery in this infinity. The finitude of the other maintains that with which its alterity is not finished—precisely, of being other, in that it defers [*diffère:* differs] itself incessantly or in that it defers its identity. *Others* cannot be identified as *the* other. On the other hand, it announces itself, or it is announced. Infinitely adulterated, and infinitely announced, the other puts an end, unceasingly, to the identification and to the assumption of the absolute, perfect understanding.—In the *Entretien d'un philosophe chrétien avec un philosophe chinois* by Malbranche, the Chinese philosopher, to make a long story short, found himself identifying with the thought of his interlocutor, though he did so without knowing it, without the truth having been revealed to him (he would become the object of an *interpretation*). It is not certain whether the Japanese philosopher of Heidegger did not submit to the same identificatory violence, anything like Ion in the face of Socrates, nor whether this is not, then, a rule of the philosophic "dialogue." But the "Dialogue" acknowledges in this way that perhaps any "dialogue" is the "the dialogue of language," or rather that this does not allow itself to be summoned or identified. It indicates the finitude of the dialogue, that is to say, once again, not the limited status of every effective dialogue, depending on an infinite dialogue, but that the essence of the dia-logue is in the infinite alteration of the other, and in that puts an end without end to the end of the dialogue. At each time it is put to an end, the announcement is renewed. The announcement—*hermēneia*—articulates the finitude, that of genres, of languages, of interlocution. One more time:

logos is a sharing, it is *our* sharing, as it is of the "divine"; it shares what *we* mean. In the singularity of voices and announcements, the finitude of the sharing [divided] *logos* inscribes itself. *Hermēneia* is the announcement of the other by the other, and it is to this extent that the other can neither be signified, nor presented, but only announced. The announcement is, in this way, the mode of the proper presence of the other. Thus, *hermēneia* is the announcement of finitude by way of finitude: its division is infinite.

This division is that of the dialogue, in every sense of the word, which is not solely literary, but ethical, social, and political. Once again: the question of the dialogue is a literary question—indeed, *the* question— concerning philosophy, that is to say, the question of its *Darstellung* [representation, presentation, performance], of the exhibition of thought (or of *logos*), because in this question it is a question of "understanding the discourse of the other." If philosophy poses the question of its presentation (and if the age of hermeneutics coincides with the age of the speculation on *Darstellung*), and it has posed this question since its birth, it is not only in terms of an address to the other (to the nonphilosopher); it is that its concern is directly an alterity of discourse: the other discourse, or the other of the discourse, poetry, or divine *logos*. In the question of the dialogue, it is both a question of interpretation and what we call "communication."[58] Every conception of interpretation is, in conclusion, a conception of communication.

But then, it has been a long time that the one and the other have been comprehended in the "hermeneutic" manner, that is to say, in the manner of the circle which presupposes the propriety of a meaning, that is to say, which pre-appropriates, fundamentally, the interpreter of the meaning (and the meaning of the interpreter), on the whole, by pre-appropriating the partners of the dialogue, the one by the other; the conception (thought) does not come close to, even far from, multiplying voices—and the hermeneutic circle can only give rise to an-other circle—ethical and political— or to an evasion. The sharing (the dialogue) is understood here as a provisional necessity, whether this is fortunate or unfortunate, whether it is an enrichment or an impediment to the community of interlocutors. On the horizon resides a communion, lost or still to come, in meaning. But, in truth, that which is the communion is only to be involved in communication. It is neither a horizon, nor an end, nor an essence. It is made of and by the sharing; it understands the sharing to be infinitely finished (completed) in the other by the other, in you by me, in us by us. And it is comprehended by the sharing. The community remains to think according to the sharing of the *logos*. This surely cannot be a new *groundwork* for the community. But perhaps it indicates a new task with regards to the community: neither its reunion, nor its division, neither its assumption, nor its dispersion, but its *sharing*. Perhaps the time has come to withdraw every *logical* or teleological founder of the community, to withdraw from interpreting our being-together, in order to understand, on the other hand, that this being-together is only, for all that it is, the shared-being of the *"divine logos."* We communicate in this sharing and we present ourselves in this sharing, "since we are a dialogue and we are heard from one another" (Hölderlin).

Translated by Gayle L. Ormiston

Notes

*Originally published as *Le partage des voix* (Paris: Éditions Galilée, 1982).—ED.

1. The motifs, or the more particular interests, which I am content to indicate from memory rather than to develop here, thus will be engaged behind the scenes. (1) In fact, the whole question of a precise history of interpretation, from antiquity to the present, which would not be satisfied with an enumeration of concepts, doctrines, and procedures, but which would attempt to follow the main theme of an incessant overflowing of interpretation by *hermēneia:* one will find some very succinct elements in this passage. (2) In the most determined manner, the question is the following: the historico-theoretical framework of modern philosophical hermeneutics is defined by landmarks which, from Schleiermacher to Gadamer, by way of Dilthey, Bultmann, and Ricoeur, in particular, abandons what I would like to call, quickly, two thoughts constructed on "interpretation" that represent Nietzsche and Freud. No doubt they are not absent, but ordinarily they are not examined in the writings of the "hermeneuts," which signifies the upheaval of such thinking in which "interpretation" sustains perhaps a disorder which is not foreign to its unsettledness in Heidegger's texts. On this subject it is necessary to recall that Ricoeur's *De l'interprétation* (Paris: Les Éditions du Seuil, 1965) is dedicated to Freud [cf. *Freud and Philosophy: An Essay on Interpretation*, translated by Denis Savage (New Haven: Yale University Press, 1970)—TRANS.]. But there, Freudian interpretation is summoned and criticized from within the hermeneutic framework. In a certain respect, it is the same with the study of Nietzsche by J. Granier, *Le problème de la vérité dans la philosophie de Nietzsche* (Paris: Les Éditions du Seuil, 1966), which is ruled by a grasp of Nietzschean interpretation according to an ordinary conception of "interpretation." Sarah Kofman, on the other hand, insists on the complexities and the ambivalence of interpretation in the texts of Nietzsche (*Nietzsche et la métaphore* [Paris: Payot, 1982]) and Freud (*Quatre romans analytiques* [Paris: Éditions Galilée, 1973]).—Outside the framework of hermeneutics, the Nietzschean-Freudian motif of interpretation is scarcely given space in modernity, which makes a kind of jubilatory assumption about "infinite interpretation," and which definitely does not broach the most classical concept of interpretation. Cf. for

example, among others, Christian Descamps: "There are only interpretations of interpretations; and it is very well and very happy like that" (*Le Semblant*, Congrès de psychanalyse de Milan [Paris and Milan: Éditions Galilée/Spirali, 1981], p. 47).

2. The Greek verb *hermēneuein* and the noun *hermēneia* appear in Nancy's text untranslated into the French. For this reason, they remain in their Greek formations in the English translation. In general, *hermēneuein* would be rendered as "to interpret," and *hermēneia* would be understood as "interpretation." For a general, introductory discussion of *hermēneuein* and *hermēneia*, and three basic meanings attached to their ancient usage—to announce, to explain, and to translate—, see Richard Palmer, *Hermeneutics* (Evanston, Ill.: Northwestern University Press, 1969), chapter 2, "*Hermēneuein* and *Hermēneia:* The Modern Significance of Their Ancient Usage," pp. 12–32.—TRANS.

3. All of these questions are related very narrowly, without a doubt, to the Benjaminian theory of language, translation, literary criticism, and the relation of art to history and to the city. But here I can only envisage Benjamin.

4. Which, in this respect, is not at all the case of dissociating it from everything that follows after it in Heidegger's writings, as if that will prove it to be a much later text concerning *hermēneia* than the *Ion*. I cannot take into consideration here the problems of the "*Kehre*," and I take the liberty of referring to it simply in terms of the continuity explicitly affirmed in the second of these texts together with the first. [Hereafter, references to Martin Heidegger, *Being and Time*, translated by John Mcquarrie and Edward Robinson (New York: Harper and Row, 1962) will appear by abbreviation, BT, in brackets.—TRANS.]

5. According to the word, and the concept, of Derrida. By way of a reminder: "But one can conceive the closure of that which is without end. The closure is the circular limit within which the repetition of difference infinitely repeats itself" (*L'écriture et la différence* [Paris: Les Éditions du Seuil, 1967], p. 367 [*Writing and Difference*, translated by Alan Bass (Chicago: University of Chicago Press, 1978), p. 250]—TRANS.). Further, it is in terms of this repetition of difference in that closure, that we will have to read the "hermeneutic" inscription of Heidegger.—On the subject of interpretation, the difference will be, for Derrida, the following: "there are two interpretations of interpretation (. . .). The one seeks to decipher, dreams of deciphering a truth or an origin which escapes play (. . .) The other, which is no longer turned towards the origin, affirms the play" (*Ibid.*, p. 427 [*ibid.*, p. 292—TRANS.]). It must be a question of the closure and the difference of interpretation, with this supplementary difference, if I may venture to say so, which no longer will be the same concern of an interpretation of interpretation, or else, moreover, passing to the limit, the second "interpretation" itself becomes the *other* of interpretation.—Concerning Derrida, one should consult Jean Greisch, *Herméneutique et grammatologie* (Paris: Éditions du CNRS, 1977).

6. *Finitude et culpabilité, tome II (Paris: Aubier, 1960), p. 327. [cf. The Symbolism of Evil*, translated by Emerson Buchanan (Boston: Beacon Press, 1969), p. 351, and *Freud and Philosophy: Essay on Interpretation*, p. 525.—TRANS]

7. It is explicated even in *De l'interprétation* (*op. cit.*, p. 504ff. [*Freud and Philosophy*, p. 525ff.]—TRANS.), where it is met with again beside the problematic of the hermeneutic circle. Nevertheless, a complex and concise discussion will have to be opened here. It is arrived at also by Ricoeur as he rigorously separates the philosophical model of interpretation ("allegorical") and the Christian interpretation of the "Kerygma." Thus he can write: "Stoicism and Platonism will furnish only a language, indeed a compromising and misleading surplus" (according to the interpretive report of the *Nouvelle à l'Ancienne Alliance*—in the small, very dense, and suggestive text which is the preface to Bultmann's *Jésus* (Paris: Les Éditions du Seuil, 1968), p. 11. [Cf. "Preface to Bultmann," *The Conflict of Interpretations*, edited by Don Ihde, translated by Peter McCormick (Evanston: Northwestern University Press, 1974), p. 383.—TRANS] But the "Kerygma" is *announced* essentially ("interpellation," "good news," *ibid.* p. 16 [*ibid.*, pp. 386 and 388— TRANS.]). It is in the direction of the "announcement" that we will engage further the attention of Heidegger, and Plato. Thus, it is not certain whether the intermeshing of the philosophical and the religious will not be more profound and more established than thought by Ricoeur. (But the difference in faith consists in relating the announcement of a privileged person.)—By that remark, however, I can extend only in a certain way, at least concerning his philosophical side, the exigency manifested by Ricoeur (in the same text), contra Bultmann or beyond Bultmann, of a more exacting attention—and without premature theological design—conveyed as that which gives Heidegger's writings the exact system of "pre-understanding," an analytical knowledge of being-*there*. We will see that it is completely this analytic which imposes an excess on the model of the circle, comprehending it in the different statement (no longer "psychological" but "methodological") that Ricoeur gives it here: "It is the circle constituted by the object that regulates faith and the method that regulates understanding (. . .). Christian hermeneutics is moved by the announcement which is at issue in the text" (*ibid.*, p. 17 [*ibid.*, p. 389—TRANS.]). The analysis will go on to show what strays, philosophically, from this model without possible convergence. But in this deviation, no one "truth" triumphs over another. It is a question solely of the reciprocal incommensurability of faith and philosophy.

8. Again, said otherwise: it is not religion which has given philosophy an appearance of hermeneutics; it is philosophy—that is to say here, onto-theology as understood by Heidegger—which has determined hermeneutics in religion. The "hermeneutic circle" is without a doubt (onto)-theological by nature and in every circumstance, and which elsewhere permits no conclusion concerning religious "interpretation" *outside* of onto-theology (but of what could one speak in that case?). Perhaps it will be necessary to take the risk of extending the preceding note by saying that *faith*, so far as it is concerned, will be able to be indeed, in spite of the appearances, entirely foreign to hermeneutics (without, let us say, filling up the abyss that separates it from philosophy or from thought).

9. Hence, the dominant motif of the *tradition*, lost and resuscitated, such that it dominates the general hermeneutics of Gadamer (*Vérité et méthode—les*

grandes lignes d'une herméneutique philosophique—, first edition, French translation by Etienne Sacre [Paris: Les Éditions du Seuil, 1975] [*Wahrheit und Methode* (WM) (Tübingen: J. C. B. Mohr, 1973); and *Truth and Method* (TM), second edition, translated by Garrett Barden and John Cumming (New York: Seabury Press, 1975)—TRANS.]), preceded in this respect by the thought of Dilthey, which it strives to go beyond by having access to the true means of an anticipated understanding of the tradition: that is to say, by substituting the pre-understanding furnished by the socio-political and cultural "grand structures," by way of Diltheyan correspondence, for individual *Erlebnisse*.

10. Concerning the place of Schleiermacher at the opening of modern hermeneutic thought, see two quite different works besides Gadamer: Pierre Barthel, *Interprétation du langage mythique et théologie biblique* (Leiden: Brill, 1963) and Manfred Frank, *Das individuelle Allgemeine* (Frankfurt: Suhrkamp, 1977)—It will be necessary, above all, to presuppose here the analysis of Schleiermacher made by Werner Hamacher in "Hermeneutische Ellipsen: Schrift und Zirkel bei Schleiermacher," in *Texthermeneutik: Geschichte, Aktualität, Kritik,* edited by Ulrich Nassen (Paderborn: Schöningh, 1979), pp. 113–148; [see "Hermeneutic Ellipses: Writing the Hermeneutical Circle in Schleiermacher," pp. 177–210 above.—ED.]. As its title announces it, this study succeeds at putting out of shape and "opening" the "circle" of Schleiermacher (this "primitive" circle whose enunciation is that the whole is to be comprehended beginning with the part and the part is to be comprehended beginning with the whole) with respect to the size [*dimension*] of a hermeneutics as an unachievable [*inachevable*] relation to the other.

11. Cf. the characterization of Schleiermacher by Gadamer under the concept of "reconstruction," *op. cit.*, pp. 96–97 [WM, pp. 159–161: TM, pp. 147–148—TRANS.].

12. Without a doubt, these brief indications simplify to death the content of Schleiermacher's texts. In a more general fashion, I also simplify the complex facts of the history of hermeneutics, of its schools and its conflicts, from Schleiermacher to the present. I have in view only the entirely general stake of what distinguishes *all* interpretation from *hermēneia*.

13. The Hegelian traits thus accumulated around hermeneutics are abundantly justified by the return that Gadamer himself maintains with Hegel, and which is valuable, without a doubt, as a coherent and pertinent explication for all hermeneutics.

14. Cf. *op. cit.*, Ricoeur, Gadamer, Barthel, Greisch.

15. *Op. cit.*, p. 103 [WM, p. 250; TM, p. 235—TRANS.]. Without a doubt, he is justified in taking this work as evidence of the hermeneutic reading of Heidegger: it is, in effect, that which brings together, on the whole, modern hermeneutics in order to constitute it in the form of philosophy. Nevertheless, it remains well within philosophical precaution, marked out most prominently by Ricoeur, who would call for another examination (but who would confront, at once, another problem, that of faith).

16. *Ibid.*, p. 104 [*ibid.*, WM, p.251; TM, p. 235—TRANS].

17. *Ibid.*, p. 108 [*Ibid.*, WM, p. 255; TM, p. 239—TRANS.].

18. *Ibid.*, p. 107 [*Ibid.*, WM, p. 254; TM, p. 239—TRANS.]. Recalling the motto from the Husserlian order, "to the things themselves," indicates that the analysis of Heideggerian hermeneutics is parallel to that which concerns the relation between Heidegger and phenomenology. Cf. on this subject, in addition to Heidegger, Ernst Tugendhat, *Der Wahrheitsbegriff bei Husserl und Heidegger* (Berlin: Walter de Gruyter, 1970); and see also the relation, in Derrida's writings, between the analyses of Husserl and those of Heidegger. A precise and valuable study by Jean-François Courtine, "La cause de la phénoménologie," appeared after the editing of this text (in *Exercices de la patience,* numbers 3/4, "Heidegger" (Paris: Obsidiane, 1982); it passes on everything about the hermeneutic motif without making it its object.

19. Heidegger has spoken of the "average and vague comprehension of Being" which "is a fact" (BT, section 2), and it is certain that the analysis of *Being and Time* only disengages itself, in a certain respect, with difficulty from an interpretive-circular model. It presupposes, however, because of the style of the presupposition which it endeavors to manifest, the transgression of this model—to which it would have to lead finally.

20. I stand by this determination—the most general and the most formal—of *hermēneuein.* The remainder of the text would be engaged in demonstrating how, determined by the existential analytic of being-there, *Auslegung* consists entirely in the *announcement* to being-there from its own possibility in or beginning with "its average everydayness" ["*son être ordinaire et moyen*"] (BT, section 9), in contrast to an "interpretation" as "construction" "according to the difference in the determined manner of existing." Nothing is anticipated, so to speak, than the being-*there* of the *being-*there.—And that is *everything* this analytic is, which is placed under the title of "Part One" (continued as one knows without repeating it): "The Interpretation (*Interpretation*) of being-there . . . "

21. [See *The Hermeneutic Tradition: From Ast to Ricóeur,* edited by Gayle L. Ormiston and Alan D. Schrift (Albany: State University of New York Press, 1990), p. 121; hereafter HT—ED.]

22. In the following paragraph (section 33), Heidegger will write: "Thus the statement cannot deny that it takes its ontological origin from a comprehensive *Auslegung.* The primordial '*als*', which according to the fore-sight proper to a comprehensive *Auslegung* (*hermēneia*—written, in the text, in Greek), will be called an existential and hermeneutical '*als*' in order to distinguish it from the *apophantical* '*als*' of the statement." [See HT, p. 131—ED.]

23. As one can see, the stake of *hermēneuein* is nothing other than the general stake, from a methodological point of view (but that means identically from an ontological point of view; cf. the text of Courtine cited in note [18]), of the under-

taking of *Being and Time*. Consequently it will be necessary to complete this sketch with consideration of the *presupposition* as it appears as the *truth* [*à la vérité*] (BT, section 14, C: "We must make the presupposition of truth because this presupposition *is* made already with being under 'we' "), and the ultimate return, in section 63, of the question of the "circle" in light of the determination of being-there as *Selbstauslegung* [self-interpretation] and of the ontological meaning of care. With regards to the circle, the form of argumentation remains the same, and "the inadequate expression of the 'circle' " is preserved only in order to indicate "the fundamental structure of care, by which originally constituted being-there is always already in-advance-of-it-self."The "hermeneutic situation" appears there entirely as the existential situation of being-there, opposed to every proceeding which " 'would depart' from a worldless 'I' [*un moi privé de monde*] in order to fabricate afterwards an object for it and an ontologically unfounded relation to this object." But it will be necessary to go as far as inscribing the "hermeneutical situation" in "the temporality of understanding" (BT, section 68, a), in order to rejoin, in this way, the last question of *Being and Time,* which must open into the analysis of time as "the horizon of Being": "*How is a revealing (opening) understanding of Being, according to being-there, possible in general?*" The last question is, indeed, a hermeneutic question, or, more rigorously, it is the question which constitutes being-there, as such, that is to say, according to temporality, in a fundamentally "hermeneutic" fashion. It is presupposed there that temporal constitution and hermeneutical constitution are the "same": no doubt, not because interpretation takes place in time and according to time, but perhaps because time itself "is" *hermēneuein.*

24. To be sure, the motif of the other appears likewise in the foundation of modern hermeneutics, in the writings of Schleiermacher, for whom interpretation is the understanding of the discourse of others, whereby the average, and not the exceptional, situation is one of noncomprehension, or of misunderstanding (cf. Frank, *op. cit,* p. 152ff.). In a different way, one finds it again with the "Wholly Other" [*"Tout-Autre"*] of Ricoeur (cf. *De l'interprétation,* p. 505 [cf. *Freud and Philosophy,* p. 525—TRANS.], and no doubt with the Lacanian interpretation of Freudian hermeneutics in the problematic of "the discourse of the other." In each of these cases it would be necessary to analyze up to what point the alterity *of* meaning is put into play, and not only an originating meaning of an identified other (and because of that, endowed with an unchanged other [*non-altéré*]). With respect to what concerns Heidegger, it is necessary to remark with J. Greisch (*op. cit.,* p. 33) that the hermeneutic problematic of *Being and Time* separates itself from its antecedents also in that it abandons the motif of the union with others, at least explicitly, and under the heading of a nonanthropological position on the question. But, beyond the very "alterity" of meaning, which is for the moment the question, one will see, in the "Dialogue" nonanthropological others appear and reappear.

25. In *Acheminement vers la parole,* translated by F. Fedier (Paris: Éditions Gallimard, 1976), p. 96 [cf. *On the Way to Language,* translated by Peter D. Hertz (New York: Harper and Row, 1971), p. 11—TRANS.]. I pass over the problems

that the translation would pose for a thorough commentary of this text; they are not decisive for the necessary passages here.

26. *Ibid.*, p. 115 [*ibid.*, p.29—TRANS.].

27. *Ibid.*, p. 137 [*ibid.*, p. 51—TRANS.].

28. But I have deliberately abandoned the question of the violence of inter-pretation, which appears in *Being and Time.*—In the present case at least, it is necessary to be precise on this point: the violence consists in neglecting the very important network of themes which form the essential material of the "Dialogue." It carries the major themes of Heidegger's thought after *Being and Time* (the text is from 1953 to 1954), and it is on them or between them that the question of the abandoned word,"*hermeneutics*" is set adrift. I have neither the competence nor the interests to apply myself to these themes. I am content to note that this text calls forth once again the abandoned word at least, up to a certain point, in order "to explicate" by new motifs, in order to give it over, finally, to a new abandonment which is tantamount to the restoration of its original destination—that which is in-volved already in *Being and Time.* It is produced, therefore, as an auto-interpretive violence of Heidegger's, of which I attempted only to follow the indications. It produces itself as, it is true, a circle: I attempted, with or in spite of Heidegger, to do violence to him . . .

29. Thus, Schleiermacher's book is held "in his hand" and is not cited from memory by "he who questions." [cf. pp. 10–11, *On the Way to Language*—TRANS.].

30. *Ibid.* p. 97 [*ibid.*, p. 11—TRANS.].

31. It remains to be examined whether all the texts of Plato are, in this sense, *dialogues.* Let us recall here only the trilogy, *Theatetus-Sophist-Statesman* (cf. on the *Sophist*, J.-L. Nancy, "Le Ventriloque," in *Mimesis des articulations* (Paris: Aubier-Flammarion, 1976)); the *Phaedrus* (cf. J. Derrida, "La Pharmacie de Pla-ton," in *La dissemination* (Paris: Les Éditions du Seuil, 1972 [cf. "Plato's Phar-macy," in *Dissemination,* translated by Barbara Johnson (Chicago: University of Chicago Press, 1981), pp. 63–171—TRANS.]), the *Timeaus,* and the *Symposium.* Cf. equally, on the philosophical dialogue, Ph. Lacoue-Labarthe and J.-L. Nancy, "Le dialogue des genres," in *Poétique,* no. 21.

32. On this ensemble of motifs, and their philosophical overdetermination, cf. Ph. Lacoue-Labarthe, *Le sujet de la philosophie* (Paris: Aubier-Flammarion, 1979).

33. Heidegger, "A Dialogue on Language," p. 114 [p. 28, English—TRANS.].

34. Paradoxically besides—if at least there is any sense to speaking in these terms—the "progress" of the thought of the "Dialogue," with regards to *Being and Time,* will be, in this respect, "regressive."

35. And it is undoubtedly in the direction, suggested by Heidegger, to which contemporary hermeneutics has been faithful.

36. In the *Cratylus,* 407e.—If this word can have the meaning of translation or explication (*Theatetus* 163c, 209a, *Philebus* 16a, *Laws* 966b), let us state precisely that the meaning (. . .) of the announcement, of the deliverance of a message, of information, is attested to largely in Plato's writings (for example, *Epinomis* 984e, *Republic* 524b, *Symposium* 202e, *Laws* 907a), by the meaning of the expression, or by speaking-in-the-name-of (*Republic* 453e, *Letters* VIII, 355a). Announcement, signal, or information also form the meaning of the word in Aristotle's works (*de Partibus Animalium* 660a 35, *De Anima* 420b 19); in the *Poetics* 50b 14, the *lexis* is defined as *hermēneia dia tès onomasias:* the announcement, the presentation of a meaning by nomination. Indeed, it is a matter of a "knowing-how" of which language is only an essential means (in *de Partibus Animalium,* it is the song of the birds that signals). As for the title, *Peri Hermēneias,* it designates, evidently, a treatise on the expression or on the signifying exposition.

37. Cited in Pauly-Wissowa, "Ion of Chios."

38. Cf. other doubles or pseudonyms, C. G. Nietzsche, *Platonis dialogus Ion* (Leipzig, 1822).

39. Thus, it is not a question in *Ion* of the allegorical interpretation of the poets: cf. the restatement of this subject by L. Meridier in his *Notice on Ion* Belles-Lettres, 1964). In a general way, it is not a question of the interpretation of meaning or meanings.—But the acquisition of knowledge regarding the poet is "simple" in this sense, and yet it has asked Ion for "his greatest effort": an effort proportional, perhaps, to that which distinguishes Ion from the allegorical interpreters he names at this spot (530d). That way, he is, thus, in the position to take his turn at the *dianoiai concerning* Homer. But these are not interpretations. Meridier sees them as "eulogistic paraphrases." In any case, they do not make up the object of *hermēneia* as such; they are signs of the knowledge which depends on good *hermēneia.* And it is the status of the "hermeneutic knowledge" which comes to be discussed.

40. One can render the idea of *deinos* in this way, by the most frequent translation: "able" [clever; adroit; capable; skilful—TRANS.]. It is the word that the dialogue always takes up again in order to speak of those who are skilful in some knowledge or art.

41. Socrates says: you are *sophoi,* whereas to me "it is proper, as a simple private man, that I speak other than the truth." There is irony here to the extent to which this truth controls the *sophia* of the others; but the latter will not be exactly masterable. Without a doubt there is always, on the philosophic horizon, a master of the incomprehensible. And yet, on the contrary, it puts into play an incomprehensible mastery, where philosophy is no longer recovered, but exceeded.

42. Which is not confused, as it has been thought by many commentators, and Schleiermacher first of all, but which is not any longer, as it has been thought

by nearly all the others, a simple critique and disqualification, more or less, of the rhapsodists and the poets.

43. The trait given in Hegel, notably, and, through Hegel and his period, to the consideration of the psychic magnetism of hypnosis, and from there to the Freudian treatise which displays a complex network between hypnosis, interpretation, and poetry . . .

44. Why rings precisely? The interpretation is easy: it is an allegory of hermeneutic circles . . .

45. But this expression does not have this meaning for Plato—no more, although for other reasons, for the modern science of magnetism.

46. Of course, the part is ready-made for the irony involved in Plato's interpretation of the poet's words. But the irony, it is time to understand (as Hegel understood it already), is not anything other than the relation of the same to the same.

47. Light and airy is also the resonant voice, vehicle of *hermēneia* for Aristotle, *De Anima, loc. cit.*—It will be only a question, in everything that follows, of the voice(s) (*voix*), never of writing. Without a doubt, the poems of Homer are written, but they are not valued as this *text* to interpret which always forms, from Schleiermacher to Gadamer, the condition of departure from hermeneutics. With this condition is, in fact, posed something like an opacity of the text, which the interpreter must elucidate or penetrate. Contemporary thinking on writing and the text (Blanchot, Barthes, Derrida) considers under these works, on their account, what announces itself here, under the species of the "voice(s)." What this means, at least, is that, before other analyses which it will be necessary to make, the *voice(s)* of a text is that which itself is always perfectly clear in that it gives itself free from the care of the transcription of meaning. Every text, as such, even the most hermeneutic or the most poetic, possesses at first this perfect "clarity," which is not visual (significant), but "resonant," "aerial," "hermeneutic."

48. Regarding mantic delirium and delirium in general in Plato's work, cf. Luc Brisson, "Du bon usage du dérèglement" ["On the Good Practice of Disorder"], in *Divination et rationalité*, collective (Paris: Les Éditions du Seuil, 1969). It will be equally necessary to return to this motif of hermeneutic "divination" in Schleiermacher's text (cf. Hamacher, *op. cit.*).

49. *Epinomis*, 975c.

50. Cf. Pico della Mirandola, "Le propre de la bonté (divine) est de se départir" ("Traité de l'imagination," in *Poésie*, no. 20, 1982).—In the passage Socrates mentions a very bad poet who has nevertheless composed an admirable paean [a song of joy or triumph]: no irony here, but the whole of a "theory" of the chance of poetic sharing.

51. One knows how Levy-Bruhl returns to this couple of Platonic terms in his last conception of the "primitive mentality"; cf. his *Carnets* (Paris: Presses Universitaires de France, 1949).

52. *Du temps chez Plato et Aristote* (Paris: Presses Universitaires de France, 1982), p. 60.

53. The whole problematic of the *ventriloquist* in the *Sophist* (cf. note [30; and cf. *Sophist* 252c.]), that is to say, the problem of an "authenticity" which consists precisely in a *mimēsis*, is proper, then, to the rhapsode. In other words, the ventriloquist of the *Sophist*, Eurycles, is a soothsayer, an "interpreter" as well.

Moreover, the difference between the two kinds of *mimēsis* appears in the two successive treatments that *The Republic* imposed on poetry. A brief explanation asserts itself at the same time with regard to the relations of *Ion* with this double treatment. Whether Plato, at the time of *The Republic,* had modified his attitude for political reasons (a consideration which will be parallel to that proposed by Hannah Arendt for the theory of ideas in "What is Authority" [in *Between Past and Future* (New York: Viking Press, 1954), pp. 91–142—TRANS.], or whether the two attitudes toward poetry coexist—the one of the *Ion* being protected precisely by the irony—, it is still necessary, as such, to take into account the *Ion* (but also, and in other ways, the *Phaedrus*) to expose what *The Republic* condemns. Does one not find in this, besides, the acknowledgment of a fondness and a respect for Homer (595b–c)? No doubt this acknowledgment only prefigures the critique of ignorance in which Homer is included based on the things he says: ignorance that veils "the marvels of the standard, of the rhythm, and the harmony," and after that, *à propos* the tragedy of which Homer is said to be the father, the critique of emotions experienced with pleasure at the spectacle of the affliction. On the whole, then, the correspondences with *Ion* are evident—and are permitted *likewise* in reading *Ion* from the perspective of *The Republic*. But this only treats poetry as *mimēsis,* and as "productive" [*"poiétique"*] *mimēsis* and not as "active" [*"praxique"*] (I go on to state this point precisely). It keeps silent about *hermēneia*. In Book X, poetry is seen as a making (pedagogical, instructive, political) dangerous to the philosophical *making* of or in the city. This excludes nothing from its consideration as *hermēneia,* as mimetic "praxis," and as seduction. Moreover, the deceitful attraction for which it is reproached does not exclude recalling its intrinsic charm, contrary to which nothing will be objected if it can justify itself morally and politically (607c–d).— The condemnation of poetry, on the other hand, first of all, has been pronounced, in Books II and III, under the kinds of "active" [*"praxique"*] *mimēsis* for the delivery of the poet and for the imitation of the actor (and additionally for the rhapsode). But this condemnation was, then, before the whole condemnation of injurious objects of imitation (here I neglect the distinction between the styles of poetic imitation, which does not appear to be my concern expressly, although it encompasses the question of the *dialogue* itself). It will end in returning everything to the poet, "rendering homage to him as a holy, charming, and wonderful being" (398a), a triple epithet which evidently echoes the one from *Ion*. On the whole, the situation, then, is very complex, and the condemnation (which takes place twice, very removed from both, perhaps, for this reason) each time, as if involuntarily, overlooks something so that one can rediscover exactly the *hermeneutic* position of poetry in *Ion* (which does not contain any less the germ of *The Republic*'s critiques, *if* one allows oneself to be caught in the trap in which Ion allowed himself to be caught: that of considering poetic texts as technical and pedagogical texts).

54. In Diderot's *Paradoxe*, analyzed from the point of view of *mimēsis*, cf. Philippe Lacoue-Labarthe, "Diderot, le paradoxe et la mimesis," in *Poétique*, no. 43, 1980.—In order to be precise, it is necessary to recall that the rhapsode and the actor (of comedy or of tragedy) are entirely technically distinct (cf. *Republic* 395a), but they do not belong any less together in the spectacular *mimēsis*, and in the "procession which follows the poets: rhapsodists, actors, members of the chorus, entrepreneurs of the theatre."

55. Besides the references already given, consider this one: in the *Statesman* 290c, the *diviners* are called the *hermeneuts* of the gods near to men: and at 260d, four examples are given of the idea of a directive act which is not autodirective (as is the royal act). This is the act of the hermeneut, of the master oarsman, of the divine, of the herald. However, the four announce, proclaim, or stage something which they have not decided themselves.

56. The structure of writing, consequently, according to the Derridean concept of the word. In this sense, the shared dialogue of voices never restores, by way of the tradition which, from Schleiermacher to Gadamer, assigns to hermeneutics the privileged place of the dialogue as the living and full exchange of voices (cf. Hamacher, *op. cit.*, pp. 118–119). It is a question of "interpreting" this tradition, of translating it, of betraying it, of transporting it.

57. *Qu'est-ce que la philosophie?* (Paris: Gallimard, 1957), p. 35. [cf. *What is Philosophy?* translated by Jean T. Wilde and William Kluback (New Haven: College and University Press, 1955), p. 67. *Was ist das-die Philosophie?* was a lecture given in Cerisy-la-salle, Normandy, in August 1955.—TRANS.] It is necessary to push deeper yet into the research on the subject of dialogue in Heidegger's text: its motif is present, in a discrete but insistent fashion, in *Le chemin vers las parole* ["The Way to Language," in *On The Way to Language, op. cit.*, pp. 111–136—TRANS.] (the last of the texts which comprise *Acheminement vers la parole, op. cit.*). It decides in particular, according to a carefully calculated paradox, the assignment of speech (of *Sprache*) as a "monologue," to the extent that this "monologue," in opposition to the *Monologue* of Novalis which "dialectically represents speech proceeding from subjectivity" [English reference, p. 134—TRANS.], corresponds to the fact that "speech *alone* speaks. And it speaks *solitarily*. However, only he can be solitary who is *not* alone; not alone, that is to say separated, isolated, without any relations" (p. 254). A little farther along, Heidegger cites a line from Hölderlin: "we are a dialogue." This is pretty nearly the point of the text. But, in its first appearance, this text must have it in this way to pass through a "circle": a circle of the thought of speech as *information* which "finds itself constrained to think of information as spoken." This is, in short, this time, the hermeneutic circle of *Sprache* itself. And then again, the circle will have been both recognized as "inevitable" and deranged, overflowing or open, by which its circularity is "governed, from speech itself, by a movement which is in it." But this movement is not

determined from the circle. It is restored by the interlacing (*Geflecht*) in which "the circle is a particular case." (Cf. some remarks of Derrida's on the *Geflecht* in "Le retrait de la metaphore," *Poésie*, no. 7, 1978, p. 113 ["The *Retrait* of Metaphor," *Enclitic*, vol. 11, no. 2, Fall 1978, pp. 16–17—TRANS.]. *Gespräch* implies *Geflecht*, or is caught within the *Ge-flecht*. Perhaps it will be necessary to say that the *Geflecht* is what provides the order or the nature of the *Ge* of *Gespräch:* that is to say, a "collective" (that is the ordinary nature of the *Ge-*), but with the function of "*between*" [*entre-*] (interlacement, dialogue), and finally of an *dia-* which is not dialectical, but which shares and divides. What we interlace we share; what we share we interlace.)

58. It is not an accident if, after the tradition already summoned (and which, because of its theological leanings, supposes something like dialogue with God, which is quite different from the "divinity" of the dia-logue), the hermeneutic of Gadamer culminates in a general theory of the dialogue as truth, and if, in this way, it can agree with, theoretically and politically, the "communicational" vision of J. Habermas. In the same way as interpretation is thought to be the reappropriation of a meaning, communication is, then, thought to be the—at least Utopian—appropriation of a rational consensus . . . Much closer to what is in question here would be the thought of "communication" in the texts of Bataille, and, even if the rapprochement is intercepted, that political exchange on speech in the writings of Hannah Arendt. It will be necessary to return to them elsewhere.

Selected Bibliography

A. Works Authored by Contributors

Blondel, Eric. *Nietzsche: le "cinquième 'évangile'"?* Paris: Bergers et Mages, 1980.

——— . *Nietzsche, le corps et la culture.* Paris: Presses Universitaires de France, 1986.

——— . "Nietzsche: Life as Metaphor." In *The New Nietzsche: Contemporary Styles of Interpretation,* edited by David Allison. Cambridge, Mass.: MIT Press, 1985, pp. 150–75.

——— . "Nietzsche's Style of Affirmation: The Metaphors of Genealogy." In *Nietzsche as Affirmative Thinker,* edited by Yirmiyahu Yovel. Dordrecht: Nijhoff, 1986, pp. 132–46.

Caws, Peter. *The Philosophy of Science, a Systematic Account.* Princeton, N.J.: Van Nostrand, 1965.

——— . *Sartre.* London and New York: Routledge and Kegan Paul, 1979.

——— . *Science and the Theory of Value.* New York: Random House, 1967.

——— , editor. *Two Centuries of Philosophy: American Philosophy Since the Revolution.* Totowa, N.J.: Rowman and Littlefield, 1980.

——— . "Flaubert's Laughter." *Philosophy and Literature* 8 (October 1984): 167–80.

——— . "Oracular Lives: Sartre and the 20th Century." *Revue Internationale de Philosophie* 39 (1985): 172–83.

Derrida, Jacques. *Dissemination.* Translated by Barbara Johnson. Chicago: University of Chicago Press, 1981.

——— . *The Ear of the Other: Otobiography, Transference, Translation.* English edition edited by Christie V. McDonald. Translated by Avital Ronell and Peggy Kamuf. New York: Schocken, 1985.

——— . *Glas.* Translated by John P. Leavey, Jr. Lincoln: University of Nebraska Press, 1987.

——— . *Margins of Philosophy.* Translated by Barbara Johnson. Chicago: University of Chicago Press, 1981.

——— . *Memoires for Paul De Man.* Translated by Cecile Lindsay, Jonathan Culler, and Eduardo Cadava. New York: Columbia University Press, 1986.

——— . *Of Grammatology.* Translated Gayatri Chakravorty Spivak. Baltimore, Md.: Johns Hopkins University Press, 1974.

——— . *Otobiographies: L'enseignement de Nietzsche et la politique du nom propre.* Paris: Éditions Galilée, 1984.

————. *Positions.* Translated by Alan Bass. Chicago: University of Chicago Press, 1981.

————. *The Post Card: From Socrates to Freud and Beyond.* Translated by Alan Bass. Chicago: University of Chicago Press, 1987.

————. *Speech and Phenomena.* Translated by David B. Allison. Evanston, Ill.: Northwestern University Press, 1973.

————. *Spurs: Nietzsche's Styles/Éperons: Les Styles de Nietzsche.* Translated by Barbara Harlow. Chicago: University of Chicago Press, 1979.

————. *Truth in Painting.* Translated by Geoff Bennington and Ian McLeod. Chicago: University of Chicago Press, 1987.

————. *Writing and Difference.* Translated by Alan Bass. Chicago: University of Chicago Press, 1978.

————. "Fors." *Georgia Review* 31 (Spring 1977): 64–116.

————. "Limited Inc a b c . . ." *Glyph* 2 (1977): 162–254.

————. "The *Retrait* of Metaphor." *Enclitic* 2, no. 2 (Fall 1978): 5–33.

Foucault, Michel. *The Archaeology of Knowledge* and *The Discourse on Language.* Translated by A. M. Sheridan Smith. New York: Pantheon, 1972.

————. *Discipline and Punish: The Birth of the Prison.* Translated by Alan Sheridan. New York: Vintage Books, 1977.

————. *The History of Sexuality,* vol. 1: *An Introduction.* Translated by Robert Hurley. New York: Vintage Books, 1980.

————. *The History of Sexuality,* vol. 2: *The Uses of Pleasure.* Translated by Robert Hurley. New York: Pantheon, 1985.

————. *The History of Sexuality,* vol. 3: *The Care of the Self.* Translated by Robert Hurley. New York: Pantheon, 1987.

————. *Language, Counter-Memory, Practice.* Edited by Donald F. Bouchard. Translated by Donald F. Bouchard and Sherry Simon. Ithaca, N.Y.: Cornell University Press, 1977.

————. *Madness and Civilization: A History of Madness in the Age of Reason.* Translated by Richard Howard. New York: Vintage, 1973.

————. *The Order of Things: An Archaeology of the Human Sciences.* New York: Pantheon, 1970.

————. *Power/Knowledge.* Edited by Colin Smith. New York: Pantheon, 1977.

————. *This Is Not A Pipe.* Translated and edited by James Harkness. Berkeley: University of California Press, 1983.

Frank, Manfred. *Das individuelle Allgemeine. Textstrukturierung und–interpretation nach Schleiermacher.* Frankfurt: Suhrkamp, 1977.

————. *Das Problem 'Zeit' in der deutschen Romantik. Zeitbewusstsein und Bewusstsein von Zeitlichkeit in der frühromantischen Philosophie und in Tiecks Dichtung.* Munich: Winkler, 1972.

————. *Das Sagbare und das Unsagbare. Studien zur neuesten französischen Hermeneutik und Texttheorie.* Frankfurt: Suhrkamp, 1980.

————. *Die unendliche Fahrt. Ein Motiv und sein Text.* Frankfurt: Suhrkamp, 1979.

————. *Der unendliche Mangel an Sein. Schellings Hegelkritik und die Anfänge der Marxschen Dialektik.* Frankfurt: Suhrkamp, 1975.

——— . *Die Unhintergehbarkeit von Individualität. Reflexionen über Subjekt, Person und Individuum aus Anlass ihrer 'postmodernen' Toterklärung.* Frankfurt: Suhrkamp, 1986.

——— . *What is Neostructuralism?* Translated by Sabine Wilke and Richard T. Gray. Minneapolis: University of Minnesota Press, 1989.

——— . "The Infinite Text." Translated by Michael Schwerin. *Glyph 7* (1980): 70–101.

——— . "The Text and Its Style: Schleiermacher's Hermeneutic Theory of Language," *boundary 2* 11, no. 3 (Spring 1983): 11–28.

Hamacher, Werner. " 'Disgregation of the Will': Nietzsche on the Individual and Individuality.'' Translated by Jeffrey Librett. In *Reconstructing Individualism: Autonomy, Individuality, and the Self in Western Thought,* edited by Thomas C. Heller, Morton Susna, and David E. Wellberg. Palo Alto, Calif.: Stanford University Press, 1986, pp. 106–39.

——— . "Journal Politics: Notes on Paul de Man's Wartime Journalism." Translated by Susan Bernstein, et al. In *Responses: On Paul de Man's Wartime Journalism,* edited by Werner Hamacher, Neil Hertz, and Thomas Keenan. Lincoln, Neb.: University of Nebraska Press, 1989, pp. 438–67.

——— . "*Pleroma*—zu Genesis und Struktur einer dialektischen Hermeneutik." In G. W. F. Hegel, *Der Geist des Christentums. Schriften 1796–1800,* edited by Werner Hamacher. Berlin: Ullstein, 1978.

——— . "The World *Wolke*—If It Is One." *Studies in Twentieth Century Literature* II, no. 1 (Fall, 1986): 133–62.

Kristeva, Julia. *Desire In Language: A Semiotic Approach to Literature and Art.* Edited by Leon S. Roudiez. Translated by Thomas Gara, Leon Roudiez, and Alice Jardine. New York: Columbia University Press, 1980.

——— . *Powers of Horror: An Essay on Abjection.* Translated by Leon Roudiez. New York: Columbia University Press, 1984.

——— . *Revolution in Poetic Language.* Translated by Alice Jardine and Leon Roudiez. New York: Columbia University Press, 1984.

——— . *Semeiotikē: Recherches pour une sémanalyse.* Paris: Éditions du Seuil, 1969.

——— . *Le Texte du Roman: Approche sémiologique d'une structure discursive transformationnelle.* The Hague: Mouton, 1970.

——— . "Women's Time." Translated by Alice Jardine and Harry Blake. *Signs: Journal of Women in Culture and Society* 7, no. 1 (1981): 13–35.

Nancy, Jean-Luc. *Das aufgegebene Sein.* Berlin: Alphäus, 1982.

——— . *Le discours de la syncope. I. Logodaedalus.* Paris: Flammarion, 1976.

——— . *Ego Sum.* Paris: Flammarion, 1979.

——— . *Des lieux divins.* Paris: T. E. R., 1987.

——— . *L'oubli de la philosophie.* Paris: Éditions Galilée, 1986.

——— . *Le partage des voix.* Paris: Éditions Galilée, 1982.

——— . *La remarque spéculative.* Paris: Éditions Galilée, 1973.

——— . "Philosophie und Bildung," in *Wer hat Angst vor des Philosophie?* Paderborn: Schöningh, 1981.

——— . "La thèse de Nietzsche sur la téléologie." In *Nietzsche aujourd'hui,* Vol.

1. Paris: Union Générale de' Éditions, 1973; pp. 57–80.

Nancy, Jean-Luc, and Lacoue-Labarthe, Philippe. *The Literary Absolute: The Theory of Literature in German Romanticism.* Translated by Philip Barnard and Cheryl Lester. Albany: State University of New York Press, 1988.

Nietzsche, Friedrich. *Beyond Good and Evil.* Translated by Walter Kaufmann. New York: Vintage Books, 1966.

———. *Daybreak.* Translated by R. J. Hollingdale. Cambridge: Cambridge University Press, 1982

———. *The Gay Science.* Translated by Walter Kaufmann. New York: Vintage Books, 1974.

———. *Nietzsche, Werke, Kritische Gesamtausgabe.* Edited by Giorgio Colli and Mazzino Montinari. Berlin: Walter de Gruyter, 1967.

———. *On The Genealogy of Morals* and *Ecce Homo.* Translated by Walter Kaufmann. New York: Vintage Books, 1969.

———. *Twilight of the Idols* and *The Anti–christ.* Translated by R. J. Hollingdale. New York: Penguin, 1968.

———. *The Will to Power.* Edited by Walter Kaufmann. Translated by R. J. Hollingdale and Walter Kaufmann. New York: Vintage Books, 1968.

B. General Works

Abel, Elizabeth, editor. *Writing and Sexual Difference.* Chicago: University of Chicago Press, 1982.

Abel, Theodore. "The Operation Called *Verstehen.*" *American Journal of Sociology* 54 (1948): 211–18.

Abrams, M. H. "How to Do Things with Texts." *Partisan Review* 64 (1979): 566–88.

Adorno, Th. W., Popper, K., et al. *The Positivist Dispute in German Sociology.* Edited by Glyn Adey and David Frisby. London: Heinemann, 1976.

Albert, Hans. *Pladoyer für Kritischen Rationalismus.* Munich: Piper, 1971.

———. *Transzendentale Träumereien: Karl-Otto Apels Sprachspiele und sein hermeneutischer Gott.* Hamburg: Hoffmann und Campe, 1975.

Albrecht, Erhard. *Beiträge zur Erkenntnistheorie und das Verhältnis von Sprache und Denken.* Halle: Niemeyer, 1959.

Allison, David B. "Destruction/Deconstruction in the Text of Nietzsche." *boundary 2* 8 (Fall 1979): 197–222.

———, editor. *The New Nietzsche: Contemporary Styles of Interpretation.* 2nd ed. Cambridge, Mass.: MIT Press, 1985.

Altenhofer, Norbert. "Geselliges Betragen-Kunst-Auslegung. Anmerkungen zu Peter Szondis Schleiermacher Interpretation und zur Frage einer Materialen Hermeneutik." In *Studien zur Entwicklung einer materialen Hermeneutik.* Edited by Ulrich Nassen. Munich: Fink Verlag, 1974, pp. 165–211.

Althusser, Louis, and Balibar, Étienne. *Reading Capital.* Translated by Ben Brewster. London: New Left Books, 1972.

Altieri, Charles. *Act and Quality: A Theory of Literary and Humanistic Understanding.* Amherst: University of Massachusetts Press, 1981.

———. "The Hermeneutics of Literary Indeterminacy: A Dissenting From the Orthodoxy." *New Literary History* 10 (1978–79): 71–99.

Apel, Karl-Otto. *Analytic Philosophy of Language and the Geisteswissenschaften.* Dordrecht: D. Reidel, 1967.

———. *Die Idee der Sprache in der Tradition des Humanismus von Dante bis Vico.* 2nd ed. Bonn: Bouvier, 1975.

———. *Towards a Transformation of Philosophy.* Translated by Glyn Adey and David Frisby. London and Boston: Routledge and Kegan Paul, 1980.

———. *Understanding and Explanation: A Transcendental Pragmatic Perspective.* Translated by Georgia Warnke. Cambridge, Mass.: MIT Press, 1985.

———. "The Common Presuppositions of Hermeneutics and Ethics," *Research in Phenomenology* 9 (1979): 35–53.

———. "Types of Social Science in the Light of Human Interests of Knowledge." *Social Research* 44, no. 3 (1977): 425–70.

———. "Das Verstehen." *Archiv für Begriffsgeschichte* 1 (1955): 142–99.

Arac, Jonathan, editor. *Postmodernism and Politics.* Minneapolis: University of Minnesota Press, 1986.

Argyros, Alex. "The Warp of the World: Deconstruction and Hermeneutics." *Diacritics* 16, no. 3 (Fall 1986): 46–55.

Aristotle. *The Basic Works.* Edited by Richard McKeon. New York: Random House, 1941.

———. *Categories* and *De Interpretatione.* Translation with notes by J. L. Ackrill. London: Clarendon Press, 1966.

Arthur, Christopher E. "Gadamer and Hirsch: The Canonical Work and the Interpreter's Intention." *Cultural Hermeneutics* 4 (1977): 183–97.

Ast, Friedrich. *Grundlinien der Grammatik, Hermeneutik und Kritik.* Landshut: Thomann, 1808.

———. *Grundriss der Philologie.* Landshut: Krull, 1808.

Attridge, Derek, Bennington, Geoff, and Young, Robert, editors. *Post-Structuralism and the Question of History.* Cambridge: Cambridge University Press, 1987.

Auerbach, Erich. *Mimesis: The Representation of Reality in Western Literature.* Princeton, N.J.: Princeton University Press, 1953.

Ball, Terrence, editor. *Political Theory and Praxis: New Perspectives.* Minneapolis: University of Minnesota Press, 1977.

Ballard, Edward G. *Principles of Interpretation.* Athens: Ohio University Press, 1983.

Bar-Hillel, Y. "On Habermas' Hermeneutic Philosophy of Language," *Synthese* 26 (1973): 1–12.

Barnes, Annette. *On Interpretation: A Critical Analysis.* Oxford: Basil Blackwell, 1986.

Barthes, Roland. *Critical Essays.* Translated by Richard Howard. Evanston, Ill.: Northwestern University Press, 1972.

———. *Mythologies.* Translated by Richard Howard. Evanston, Ill.: Northwestern University Press, 1972.

————. *The Pleasure of the Text*. Translated by Richard Miller. New York: Hill and Wang, 1975.

————. *On Racine*. Translated by Richard Howard. New York: Hill and Wang, 1977.

————. *Roland Barthes*. Translated by Richard Howard. New York: Hill and Wang, 1977.

————. *Sade/Fourier/Loyola*. Translated by Stephen Heath. New York: Hill and Wang, 1977.

————. *S/Z*. Translated by Richard Miller. New York: Hill and Wang, 1975.

————. *Writing Degree Zero/Elements of Semiology*. Translated by Annette Lavers and Colin Smith. Boston: Beacon Press, 1970.

Bauman, Zygmunt. *Hermeneutics and Social Science*. New York: Columbia University Press, 1978.

Bernstein, Richard J. *Beyond Objectivism and Relativism: Science, Hermeneutics, and Praxis*. Philadelphia: University of Pennsylvania Press, 1983.

————. *Praxis and Action*. Philadelphia: University of Pennsylvania Press, 1971.

————. *The Restructuring of Social and Political Theory*. New York: Harcourt Brace Jovanovich, 1976.

————. "From Hermeneutics to Praxis." *Review of Metaphysics* 35 (1982): 823–45.

————. "Philosophy in the Conversation of Mankind." *Review of Metaphysics* 33 (1980): 745–76.

————. "Why Hegel Now?" *Review of Metaphysics* 31 (1977): 29–60.

Betti, Emilio. *Allgemeine Auslegungslehre als Methodik der Geisteswissenschaften*. Tübingen: Mohr (Siebeck), 1967.

————. *Die Hermeneutik als allgemeine Methodik der Geisteswissenschaften*. Tübingen: Mohr (Siebeck), 1962.

————. *Teoria generale della interpretazione*. 2 vols. Milan: A. Guiffrè, 1955.

————. "The Epistemological Problem of Understanding As An Aspect of the General Problem of Knowing." Translated by Susan Noakes. In *Hermeneutics: Questions and Prospects*, edited by Gary Shapiro and Alan Sica. Amherst: University of Massachusetts Press, 1984, pp. 25–53.

————. "Problematik einer allgemeinen Auslegungslehre als Methode der Geisteswissenschaften." In *Hermeneutik als Weg heutiger Wissenschaft*, edited by Viktor Warnach. Salzburg-Munich: Anton Pustet, 1971, pp. 15–30.

Binswanger, Ludwig. *Grundformen und Erkenntnis menschlichen Daseins*. Munich and Basel: Ernst Reinhardt Verlag, 1962.

Blanchette, Oliva. "Language, the Primordial Labor of History: A Critique of Critical Social Theory in Habermas." *Cultural Hermeneutics* 1 (February 1974): 325–82.

Bleicher, Josef. *Contemporary Hermeneutics: Hermeneutics as method, philosophy, and critique*. London: Routledge and Kegan Paul, 1980.

————. *The Hermeneutic Imagination: Outline of A Positive Critique of Scientism and Sociology*. London: Methuen, 1982.

Bloom, Harold. *A Map of Misreading.* New York: Oxford University Press, 1975.

Bloom, Harold, de Man, Paul, Derrida, Jacques, Hartman, Geoffrey, and Miller, J. Hillis, editors. *Deconstruction and Criticism.* New York: Seabury Press, 1979.

Blumenberg, Hans. *The Legitimacy of the Modern Age.* Translated by Robert Wallace. Cambridge, Mass.: MIT Press, 1983.

Boeckh, Philip August. *On Interpretation and Criticism.* Translated and edited by John Paul Pritchard. Norman: University of Oklahoma Press, 1968.

Boehler, Dietrich. "Das Dialogische Prinzip als Hermeneutische Maxime." *Man and World* 11 (1978): 131–64.

———. "Zum Problem des 'Emancipatorischen Interesses' und seiner gesellschaftlichen Wahrnehmung." *Man and World* 3 (1970): 26–53.

Bollnow, Otto Friedrich. *Dilthey: Eine Einführung in seine Philosophie.* 3d rev. ed. Stuttgart: Kohlhammer, 1968.

———. *Die Lebensphilosophie.* Berlin: Springer, 1958.

———. *Die Methode der Geisteswissenschaften.* Mainz: Gutenberg, 1950.

———. *Das Verstehen: Drei Aufsätze zur Theorie der Geisteswissenschaften.* Mainz: Kirchheim, 1949.

———. "Über das Kritische Verstehen." *Deutsche Vierteljahresschrift für Literaturwissenschaft* 22 (1972): 1–29.

———. "What Does it Mean to Understand a Writer Better than He Understood Himself?" *Philosophy Today* 23 (1979): 16–28.

Bontekoe, Ron. "A Fusion of Horizons: Gadamer and Schleiermacher." *International Philosophical Quarterly* 27 (March 1987):3–16.

Bornkamm, Günther. "Die Theologie Rudolf Bultmanns in neueren Diskussion. Zum Problem der Entmythologisierung und Hermeneutik." *Theologische Rundschau,* n.s. (1963): 33–141.

Borsche, Tilman. *Sprachansichten. Der Begriff der menschlichen Rede in der Sprachphilosophie Wilhelm von Humboldts.* Stuttgart: Klett-Cotta, 1981.

Bourdieu, Pierre. *Outline of a Theory of Practice.* Translated by Richard Nice. Cambridge: Cambridge University Press, 1977.

Bové, Paul. *Destructive Poetics: Heidegger and Modern American Poetry.* New York: Columbia University Press, 1980.

Brandt, Reinhard. *Die aristotelische Urteilslehre: Untersuchungen zur "Hermeneutik."* Marburg: Görich und Weiershäuser, 1965.

Brenkman, John. *Culture and Domination.* Ithaca: Cornell University Press, 1987.

Brinckmann, Hennig. *Mittelalterliche Hermeneutik.* Tübingen: Niemeyer, 1980.

Brunner, August. *Geschichtlichkeit.* Bern and Munich: Francke, 1961.

Bubner, Rüdiger. *Essays in Hermeneutics and Critical Theory.* Translated by Eric Matthews. New York: Columbia University Press, 1987.

———. *Modern German Philosophy.* Translated by Eric Matthews. Cambridge: Cambridge University Press, 1981.

———. *Theorie und Praxis, eine nachhegelsche Abstraktion.* Frankfurt: Klostermann, 1971.

———. "Action and Reason." *Ethics* 83 (1973): 224–36.

———. "Transzendentale Hermeneutik?" In *Wissenschaftstheorie in den Geistes-*

wissenschaften. Konzeptionen, Vorschläge, Entwürfe, edited by R. Simon Schaefer and W. Ch. Zimmerli. Hamburg: Hoffmann und Campe, 1975.

————. "Was ist Kritische Theorie?" *Philosophische Rundschau* (December 1969): 213–48.

Bubner, Rüdiger, Cramer, K., and Weihl, R., editors. *Hermeneutik und Dialektik.* Vols. 1 and 2. Tübingen: J. C. B. Mohr, 1970.

Buck, Günther. "Hermeneutics of Texts and Hermeneutics of Action." *New Literary History* 4, no. 1 (1980): 87–96.

————. "The Structure of Hermeneutic Experience and the Problems of Tradition." *New Literary History* 10, no. 1 (1978): 31–47.

Bultmann, Rudolf. *Essays, Philosophical and Theological.* Translated by J. C. G. Greig. London: SCM Press; New York: Macmillan, 1955.

————. *Existence and Faith: Shorter Writings of Rudolf Bultmann.* Selected, translated, and introduced by Schubert M. Ogden. New York: Meridian Books, 1960.

————. *Faith and Understanding.* Edited and introduced by Robert W. Funk. Translated by Louise Pettibone Smith. New York: Harper and Row, 1969.

————. *Jesus and the Word.* Translated by Louise Pettibone Smith and E. Huntress. New York: Charles Scribner's Sons, 1958.

————. *Theology of the New Testament.* 2 vols. Translated by K. Grobel. New York: Charles Scribner's Sons, 1951–55.

Byrum, Charles Stephen. "Philosophy as Play." *Man and World* 8 (1975): 315–26.

Capurro, Rafael. *Hermeneutik der Fachinformation.* Freiburg: Alber, 1986.

Caputo, John D. *Radical Hermeneutics: Repetition, Deconstruction, and the Hermeneutic Project.* Bloomington: Indiana University Press, 1987.

————. "Hermeneutics as the Recovery of Man." *Man and World* (1982): 343–67.

————. "Husserl, Heidegger, and the Question of a 'Hermeneutic' Phenomenology." *Husserl Studies* 1 (1984): 157–78.

Carr, David. *Phenomenology and the Problem of History.* Evanston, Ill.: Northwestern University Press, 1974.

————. "Interpretation and Self-Evidence." *Analecta Husserliana* 11 (1980): 133–48.

Cassirer, Ernst. *The Philosophy of Symbolic Forms.* 3 vols. Translated by Ralph Manheim. New Haven, Conn.: Yale University Press, 1953–57.

Castelli, Enrico, editor. *Herméneutique et tradition.* Paris: Vrin, 1963.

Chladenius, Johann Martin. *Einleitung zur richtigen Auslegung vernünftiger Reden und Schriften.* Facsimile reprint of the Leipzig edition of 1742. With an introduction by Lutz Geldsetzer. Vol. 5 of the Series Hermeneutica, Instrumenta Philosophica. Düsseldorf: Stern Verlag, 1969.

Chomsky, Noam. *Aspects of the Theory of Syntax.* Cambridge, Mass.: MIT Press, 1963.

————. *Cartesian Linguistics. A Chapter in the History of Rationalist Thought.* New York: Harper and Row, 1966.

Cicourel, Aaron. *Cognitive Sociology: Language and Meaning in Social Interaction.*

New York: The Free Press, 1974.

Coreth, Emrich. *Grundfragen der Hermeneutik*. Freiburg: Herder, 1969.

Corngold, Stanley. *The Fate of the Self*. New York: Columbia University Press, 1986.

―――. "Error in Paul de Man." *Critical Inquiry* 8 (Spring 1982): 489–513.

Corrington, Robert S. "Horizontal Hermeneutics and the Actual Infinite." *Graduate Faculty Philosophy Journal* 8 (Spring 1982): 36–97.

Cosgrove, Stephen. "Styles of Thought: Science, Romanticism, and Modernization." *British Journal of Sociology* 29 (1978): 358–71.

Crother, Paul. "Experience of Art: Some Problems and Possibilities of Hermeneutical Analysis." *Philosophy and Phenomenological Research* 43 (1983): 347–62.

Crowley, Charles B. *Universal Mathematics in Aristotelian-Thomistic Philosophy: The Hermeneutics of Aristotelian Texts Relative to Universal Mathematics.* Washington, D.C.: University Press of America, 1980.

Culler, Jonathan. *On Deconstruction*. Ithaca, N.Y.: Cornell University Press, 1982.

Dallmayr, Fred R. *Critical Encounters: Between Philosophy and Politics*. Notre Dame, Ind.: University of Notre Dame Press, 1987.

―――. *Polis and Praxis: Essays in Contemporary Political Theory*. Cambridge, Mass.: MIT Press, 1985.

―――, editor. *Materialien zu Habermas' Erkenntnis und Interesse*. Frankfurt: Suhrkamp, 1974.

―――. "Hermeneutics and Historicism: Reflections on Winch, Apel, and Vico." *The Review of Politics* 39 (1977): 60–81.

―――. "Reason and Emancipation: Notes on Habermas." *Man and World* (Fall 1972): 79–109.

Dallmayr, Fred R., and McCarthy, Thomas A., editors. *Understanding and Social Inquiry*. Notre Dame, Ind.: University of Notre Dame Press, 1977.

Dannhauer, Johann Conrad. *Idea boni interpretis (1670)*. Strasbourg: n.p., 1670.

Danto, Arthur C. "Deep Interpretation." *Journal of Philosophy* 78 (1981): 691–706.

―――. "Philosophy as/and/of Literature." In *Post-Analytic Philosophy,* edited by John Rajchman and Cornel West. New York: Columbia University Press, 1985, pp. 63–83.

Davidson, Donald. *Inquiries into Truth and Interpretation*. Oxford: Oxford University Press, 1984.

De George, Richard T., and Fernande, M., editors. *The Structuralists: From Marx to Lévi-Strauss*. Garden City, N.Y.: Anchor Books, 1972.

Deleuze, Gilles, and Guattari, Félix. *Kafka: Toward a Minor Literature*. Translated by Dana Parker. Minneapolis: University of Minnesota Press, 1986.

De Man, Paul. *Allegories of Reading*. New Haven, Conn.: Yale University Press, 1979.

―――. *Blindness and Insight*. 2nd ed. Minneapolis: University of Minnesota Press, 1983.

Descombes, Vincent. *Modern French Philosophy*. Cambridge: Cambridge University Press, 1981.

Diderot, Denis, and d'Alembert, Jean Le Rond. "Interpretation." *Encyclopédie*. Vol. 8. 1765.

Dilthey, Wilhelm. *Descriptive Psychology and Historical Understanding*. Translated by Richard M. Zaner and Kenneth L. Heiges. The Hague: Nijhoff, 1977.

————. *Gesammelte Schriften*. 18 vols. Stuttgart: B. G. Tübner; Göttingen Vandenhoeck und Ruprecht, 1914–77.

————. *Pattern & Meaning in History: Thoughts on History & Society*. Edited and introduced by H. P. Rickman. New York: Harper and Row, 1962.

————. *Selected Writings*. Edited, translated, and introduced by H. P. Rickman. Cambridge: Cambridge University Press, 1976.

————. *Selected Writings: Poetry and Experience*. Edited by Rudolf A. Makkreel and Frithjof Rodi. Princeton: Princeton University Press, 1985.

Diwald, Hellmut. *Wilhelm Dilthey: Erkenntnistheorie und Philosophie der Geschichte*. Göttingen: Musterschmidt, 1963.

Dockhorn, Klaus. "Hans-Georg Gadamer's *Truth and Method*." *Philosophy and Rhetoric* 13 (1980): 160–80.

Doppelt, Gerald. "Kuhn's Epistemological Relativism: An Interpretation and Defense." *Inquiry* 21 (1978): 33–86.

Dostel, Robert J. "The World Never Lost: The Hermeneutics of Trust." *Philosophy and Phenomenological Research* 47 (March 1987):413–34.

Dray, William H. *Laws and Explanations in History*. Oxford: Oxford University Press, 1957.

————. "Explaining What Is History." In *Theories of History*, edited by Patrick Gardiner. Glencoe, Ill.: The Free Press, 1959.

Dreyfus, Hubert L. "Holism and Hermeneutics." *Review of Metaphysics* 34 (1980): 3–55.

Dreyfus, Hubert, and Rabinow, Paul. *Michel Foucault: Beyond Structuralism and Hermeneutics*. Chicago: University of Chicago Press, 1982.

Droysen, Johann Gustav. *Historik: Rekonstruktion der ersten vollständigen Fassung der Vorlesungen (1857), Grundriss der Historik in der ersten handschriftlichen (1857/1858) und in der letzten gedruckten Fassung (1882)*. Historical and critical edition by Peter Leyh. Stuttgart–Bad Cannstatt: Frommann-Holzboog, 1977.

————. *Outline of the Principles of History*. Translated and Introduced by E. Benjamin Andrews. Boston: Ginn and Co., 1897.

Dufrenne, Mikel. *The Notion of the A Priori*. Translated by Edward S. Casey. Evanston, Ill.: Northwestern University Press, 1966.

————. *The Phenomenology of Aesthetic Experience*. Translated by Edward S. Casey et al. Evanston, Ill.: Northwestern University Press, 1973.

————. *La Poétique*. Paris: Presses Universitaires de France, 1963.

Ebeling, G. "Hermeneutik." *Religion in Geschichte und Gegenwart*. 3 (1959): 242–62.

Ebner, Ferdinand. *Schriften*. 3 vols. Munich: Kösel, 1963, 1965.

Eco, Umberto. *The Role of the Reader: Explorations in the Semiotics of Texts*. Bloomington: Indiana University Press, 1979.

————. *A Theory of Semiotics*. Bloomington: Indiana University Press, 1976.

Ermarth, Michael. *Wilhelm Dilthey: The Critique of Historical Reason.* Chicago: University of Chicago Press, 1978.

————. "The Transformation of Hermeneutics." *Monist* 64, no. 2 (April 1981): 175–194.

Ernesti, Johann August. *Institutio interpretis Novi Testamenti.* 4th ed. With observations by Christopher Fr. Ammon. Leipzig: Weidmann, 1792. English translation by Moses Stuart, *Elements of Interpretation,* 3rd ed.; Andover, England: M. Newman, 1827. 4th ed.; New York: Dayton and Saxton, 1842. Another English translation by Charles H. Terrot, *Principles of Biblical Interpretation,* 2 vols.; Edinburgh: T. Clark, 1832–33.

Farrar, Fredric W. *History of Interpretation.* Grand Rapids, Mich.: Baker Book House, 1961.

Felman, Shoshana, editor. *Literature and Psychoanalysis: The Question of Reading: Otherwise.* Baltimore, Md.: Johns Hopkins University Press, 1982.

Feyerabend, Paul. *Against Method: Outline of an Anarchistic Theory of Knowledge.* London: NLB, 1975.

Figl, Johann. *Interpretation als philosophisches Prinzip: Friedrich Nietzsches universale Theorie der Auslegung im späten Nachlass.* Berlin: Walter de Gruyter, 1982.

————. "Nietzsche und die philosophische Hermeneutik des 20. Jahrhunderts." *Nietzsche-Studien* 10–11. Berlin: Walter de Gruyer, 1981–82, pp. 408–30.

Fink, Eugen. *Sein, Wahrheit, Welt. Vor-Fragen zum Problem des Phänomen-Begriffs.* The Hague: Nijhoff, 1958.

————. *Spiel als Weltsymbol.* Stuttgart: Kohlhammer, 1960.

Fischer-Lichte, Erika. *Bedeutung. Probleme einer semiotischen Hermeneutik und Aesthetik.* Munich: C. H. Beck, 1979.

Fish, Stanley. *Is There A Text In This Class?* Cambridge, Mass.: Harvard University Press, 1980.

————. "Literature in the Reader: Affective Stylistics." *New Literary History* 1 (1970): 123–62.

Flanagan, Kieran. "Hermeneutics: A Sociology of Misunderstanding," *Philosophical Studies* (Ireland) 30 (1984): 270–81.

Flashar, Hellmut, Gründer, Karlfried, and Horstmann, Axel, editors. *Philologie und Hermeneutik im 19. Jahrhundert. Zur Geschichte und Methodologie des Geisteswissenschaften.* Göttingen: Vandenhoeck and Ruprecht, 1979.

Forget, Phillipe, editor. *Text und Interpretation.* Munich: Fink Verlag, 1984.

Foster, Hal, editor. *The Anti-Aesthetic: Essays on Postmodern Culture.* Port Townsend, Wash.: Bay Press, 1983.

Franklin, James. "Natural Sciences of Textual Interpretation: The Hermeneutics of the Natural Sign." *Philosophy and Phenomenological Research* 44 (1984): 509–20.

Frei, Hans W. *The Eclipse of Biblical Narrative: A Study of Eighteenth and Nineteenth Century Hermeneutics.* New Haven, Conn.: Yale University Press, 1974.

Friedrich, Christoph. *Sprache und Geschichte. Untersuchungen zur Hermeneutik von Johann Martin Chladenius.* Meisenheim am Glan:Hain, 1978.

Freundlieb, Dieter. *Zur Wissenschaftstheorie der Literaturwissenschaft: eine Kritik der transzendentalen Hermeneutik*. Munich: Fink Verlag, 1978.

Fruchon, Pierre. *Herméneutique, langage et ontologie: Un disiernment du Platonisme chez H.-G. Gadamer*. Paris: Éditions du Seuil, 1975.

Fuchs, Ernst. *Hermeneutik*. Bad Cannstatt: R. Müllerschön, 1963.

Funk, Robert W., editor. *History and Hermeneutic* (Journal for Theology and the Church, vol. 4). Tübingen: J. C. B. Mohr, 1967; and New York: Harper and Row, 1967.

――――. *Schleiermacher as Contemporary* (Journal for Theology and the Church, Vol. 7). New York: Herder & Herder, 1970.

Funke, Gerhard. "Problem und Theorie der Hermeneutik: Auslegen, Verstehen in E. Betti 'Teoria generale della interpretazione.' " *Studi in Onore di Emilio Bettis*. Milan: A. Giuffrè, 1962.

Fynsk, Christopher. *Heidegger: Thought and Historicity*. Ithaca, N.Y.: Cornell University Press, 1986.

Gallop, Jane. *The Daughter's Seduction: Feminism and Psychoanalysis*. Ithaca, N.Y.: Cornell University Press, 1982.

――――. *Reading Lacan*. Ithaca, N.Y.: Cornell University Press, 1985.

Gadamer, Hans-Georg. *Die Aktualität des Schönen: Kunst als Spiel, Symbol und Fest*. Stuttgart: Reclam, 1977.

――――. *Dialogue and Dialectic*. Translated by P. Christopher Smith. New Haven, Conn.: Yale University Press, 1980.

――――. *Hegel's Dialectic: Five Hermeneutical Studies*. Translated by P. Christopher Smith. New Haven, Conn.: Yale University Press, 1976.

――――. *The Idea of the Good in Platonic-Aristotelian Philosophy*. Translated by P. Christopher Smith. New Haven, Conn.: Yale University Press, 1986.

――――. *Kleine Schriften*. Tübingen: J. C. B. Mohr, 1967-.

――――. *Philosophical Apprenticeships*. Translated by Robert R. Sullivan. Cambridge, Mass.: MIT Press, 1985.

――――. *Philosophical Hermeneutics*. Edited and translated by David E. Linge. Berkeley: University of California Press, 1976.

――――. *Philosophische Lehrjahre*. Frankfurt: Klostermann, 1977.

――――. *Plato und die Dichter*. Frankfurt: Klostermann, 1934.

――――. *Plato. Texte zur Ideenlehre*. Frankfurt: Klostermann, 1978.

――――. *Poetica*. Frankfurt: Klostermann, 1977.

――――. *Reason in the Age of Science*. Translated by Frederick G. Lawrence. Cambridge, Mass.: MIT Press, 1981.

――――. *The Relevance of the Beautiful and Other Essays*. Translated by Nicholas Walker. Edited by Robert Bernasconi. Cambridge: Cambridge University Press, 1986.

――――. *Truth and Method*. Translated by Garrett Barden and John Cumming. New York: Seabury, 1975.

――――. "The Continuity of History and the Existential Moment." *Philosophy Today* 16 (Fall 1971): 230–40.

――――. "Heidegger and the History of Philosophy." *The Monist* 64 (1981): 423–38.

———. "Heidegger's Paths." *Philosophie Exchange* 2 (1979): 80–91.

———. "The Hermeneutics of Suspicion." *Man and World* 17 (1984): 313–24.

———. "Historical Transformations of Reason." In *Rationality Today.* Edited by Theodore F. Geraets. Ottawa: University of Ottawa Press, 1979.

———. "On the Problematic Character of Aesthetic Consciousness." *Graduate Faculty Philosophy Journal* 9 (1982): 31–40.

———. "The Problem of Historical Consciousness." In *Interpretive Social Science: A Second Look,* edited by Paul Rabinow and William Sullivan. Berkeley: University of California Press, 1987, pp. 103–62.

———. "The Power of Reason." *Man And World* 3 (February 1970): 5–15.

———. "Summation." *Cultural Hermeneutics* 2 (1975): 329–30.

Gasché, Rodolphe. *The Tain of the Mirror.* Cambridge, Mass.: Harvard University Press, 1987.

Geertz, Clifford. *The Interpretation of Culture.* New York: Basic Books, 1973.

———. *Local Knowledge: Further Essays in Interpretive Anthropology.* New York: Basic Books, 1985.

———. "From the Native's Point of View: On the Nature of Anthropological Understanding." In *Interpretive Social Science: A Second Look,* edited by Paul Rabinow and William Sullivan. Berkeley: University of California Press, 1987.

Gethmann, C. F. *Verstehen und Auslegung: Das Methodenproblem in der Philosophie Martin Heideggers.* Bonn: Bouvier, 1974.

Giddens, Anthony. *New Rules of Sociological Method.* London: Hutchinson, 1976.

———. *Profiles and Critiques in Social Theory.* Berkeley: University of California Press, 1982.

Glowinski, Michael. "Reading, Interpretation, Reception." *New Literary History* (Anniversary Issue II) 9 (1980): 76–81.

Gooch, G. P. *History and Historians in the Nineteenth Century.* Boston: Beacon Press, 1959.

Goodman, Nelson. *Ways of Worldmaking.* Indianapolis, Ind.: Hackett Press, 1978.

Greisch, Jean. *Herméneutique et grammatologie.* Paris: Éditions du CNRS, 1977.

Griswald, Charles. "Gadamer and the Interpretation of Plato." *Ancient Philosophy* 2 (1981): 121–28.

Grondin, Jean. *Hermeneutische Wahrheit?* Königstein: Athenäum, 1982; Bern: Francke, 1947.

Grunbaum, Adolf. *The Foundations of Psychoanalysis.* Berkeley: University of California Press, 1984.

Gründer, K. R. "Hermeneutik und Wissenschaftstheorie." *Philosophisches Jahrbuch der Gorres-Gesellschaft* 75: 152–65.

Guattari, Félix. "Postmodern Impasse and Postmodern Transition." *Filozof Istraz* 16 (1986): 97–102.

Gusdorf, Georges. *Speaking (La Parole).* Translated and introduced by Paul T. Brockelman. Evanston, Ill.: Northwestern University Press, 1965.

Gutting, Gary. "Paradigms and Hermeneutics: A Dialogue on Kuhn, Rorty and the Social Sciences." *American Philosophical Quarterly* 21 (1984): 1–16.

Güttinger, Fritz. *Zielsprache: Theorie und Technik des Übersetzens.* Zürich: Manesse, 1963.

Habermas, Jürgen. *Communication and the Evolution of Society.* Translated by Thomas McCarthy. Boston: Beacon Press, 1979.

————. *Knowledge and Human Interests.* Translated by Jeremy J. Shapiro. Boston: Beacon Press, 1971.

————. *Legitimation Crisis.* Translated by Thomas McCarthy. Boston: Beacon Press, 1975.

————. *On the Logic of the Social Sciences.* Translated by Shierry Weber Nicholsen and Jerry A. Stark. Cambridge, Mass.: MIT Press, 1988.

————. *The Philosophical Discourse of Modernity.* Translated by Frederick G. Lawrence. Cambridge, Mass.: MIT Press, 1987.

————. *Philosophical-Political Profiles.* Translated by Frederick Lawrence. Cambridge, Mass.: MIT Press, 1981.

————. *Protestbewegung und Hochschulreform.* Frankfurt: Suhrkamp, 1969.

————. *Technik und Wissenschaft als 'Ideologie'.* Frankfurt: Suhrkamp, 1969.

————. *Theory and Practice.* Translated by John Viertel. Boston: Beacon Press, 1973.

————. *The Theory of Communicative Practice.* vol. 1: *Reason and the Rationalization of Society.* Translated by Thomas McCarthy. Boston: Beacon Press, 1984.

————. *The Theory of Communicative Practice.* vol. 2: *Lifeworld and System, a Critique of Function and System.* Translated by Thomas McCarthy. Boston: Beacon Press, 1987.

————. *Toward a Rational Society: Student Protest, Science, and Politics.* Translated by Jeremy J. Shapiro. Boston: Beacon Press, 1970.

————. "A Reply to My Critics." In *Habermas: Critical Debates,* edited by John B. Thompson and David Held. Cambridge, Mass.: MIT Press, 1987, pp. 219–83.

Haering, Theodor. *Philosophie des Verstehens. Versuch einer systematisch-erkenntnistheoretischen Grundlegung alles Erkennens.* Tübingen: Niemeyer, 1963.

Handleman, Susan. "Jacques Derrida and the Heretic Hermeneutic." In *Displacement: Derrida and After,* edited by Mark Krupnick. Bloomington: Indiana University Press, 1983, pp. 98–129.

Harari, Josué. *Textual Strategies: Perspectives in Post-Structuralist Criticism.* Ithaca, N.Y.: Cornell University Press, 1979.

Harney, Maurita. "Psychoanalysis and Hermeneutics." *Journal of the British Society for Phenomenology* 9 (1978): 71–81.

Hartmann, Eduard von. *Über die dialektische Methode. Historisch-kritische Untersuchungen.* Darmstadt: Wissenschaftliche Buchgesellschaft, 1963.

Hass Jaeger, H.-E. "Studien zur Frühgeschichte der Hermeneutik." *Archiv für Begriffsgeschichte* 18 (1974):35–84.

Haw, Alan R. "Dialogue as Productive Limitation in Social Theory: The Habermas-Gadamer Debate." *Journal of the British Society for Phenomenology* 11 (1980):131–43.

Heelan, Patrick A. "Continental Philosophy of Science." In *Current Research in*

Philosophy of Science, edited by P. Asquith. Ann Arbor, Mich.: Edwards, 1979.

————. "Horizon, Objectivity and Reality in the Physical Sciences." *International Philosophical Quarterly* 7 (Summer 1967): 375–412.

————. "Perception as a Hermeneutical Art." *Review of Metaphysics* 37 (1983): 61–76.

————. "Towards a Hermeneutics of Science." *Main Currents* 28 (January–February 1971): 85–93.

Heeschen, Volker. *Die Sprachphilosophie Wilhelm von Humboldts.* Ph.D. diss., Bochum, 1972.

Heidegger, Martin. *The Basic Problems of Phenomenology.* Translated by Albert Hofstader. Bloomington: Indiana University Press, 1982.

————. *Basic Writings.* Edited by David Farrell Krell. New York: Harper and Row, 1977.

————. *Being and Time.* Translated by John Macquarrie and Edward Robinson. New York: Harper and Row, 1962.

————. *Discourse on Thinking.* Translated by John M. Anderson and E. Hans Freund. New York: Harper and Row, 1966.

————. *Early Greek Thinking.* Translated by David Farrell Krell and Frank A. Capuzzi. New York: Harper and Row, 1975.

————. *The End of Philosophy.* Translated by Joan Stambaugh. New York: Harper and Row, 1973.

————. *The Essence of Reasons.* Translated by Terrence Malick. Evanston, Ill.: Northwestern University Press, 1969.

————. *Existence and Being.* Edited and introduced by Werner Brock. Chicago: Henry Regnery Company,1949.

————. *Hegel's Concept of Experience.* Translated by J. Glenn Gray and Fred D. Wieck. New York: Harper and Row, 1970.

————. *Identity and Difference.* Translated by Joan Stambaugh. New York: Harper and Row, 1969.

————. *An Introduction to Metaphysics.* Translated by Ralph Manheim. New York: Doubleday-Anchor Books, 1961.

————. *Kant and the Problem of Metaphysics.* Translated by James S. Churchill. Bloomington: Indiana University Press, 1962.

————. *The Metaphysical Foundations of Logic.* Translated by Michael Heim. Bloomington: Indiana University Press, 1984.

————. *Nietzsche*, vol. 1: *The Will to Power as Art.* Edited and translated by David Farrell Krell. New York: Harper and Row, 1979.

————. *Nietzsche*, vol. 2: *The Eternal Recurrence of the Same.* Edited and translated by David Farrell Krell. New York: Harper and Row, 1984.

————. *Nietzsche*, vol. 3: *The Will to Power as Knowledge and Metaphysics.* Edited by David Farrell Krell. Translated by Joan Stambaugh, David Farrell Krell, and Frank Capuzzi. New York: Harper and Row, 1987.

————. *Nietzsche*, vol. 4: *Nihilism.* Edited by David Farrell Krell. Translated by Frank Capuzzi. New York: Harper and Row, 1982.

————. *On the Way to Language.* Translated by Peter D. Hertz and Joan Stambaugh. New York: Harper and Row, 1971.

————. *On Time and Being.* Translated by Joan Stambaugh. New York: Harper and Row, 1972.

————. *Poetry, Language, Thought.* Translated by Albert Hofstader. New York: Harper and Row, 1971.

————. *The Question Concerning Technology and Other Essays.* Translated by William Lovitt. New York: Harper and Row, 1979.

————. *The Question of Being.* Translated by William Kluback and Jean T. Wilde. New Haven, Conn.: College and University Press, 1958.

————. *Schelling's Treatise on the Essence of Human Freedom.* Translated by Joan Stambaugh. Athens: Ohio University Press, 1985.

————. *What is a Thing?* Translated by W. B. Barton, Jr. and Vera Deutsch. Chicago: Henry Regnery Company, 1967.

————. *What is Called Thinking?* Translated by Fred D. Wieck and J. Glenn Gray. New York: Harper and Row, 1968.

————. *What is Philosophy?* Translated by William Kluback and Jean T. Wilde. New Haven, Conn.: College and University Press, 1958.

Heinrich, D., Schultz, W., and Volkmann-Schluck, K-H., editors. *Die Gegenwart der Griechen im neueren Denken: Festschrift für Hans-Georg Gadamer zum 60, Geburtstag.* Tübingen: J. C. B. Mohr, 1960.

Hekman, Susan J. *Hermeneutics and the Sociology of Knowledge.* Notre Dame, Ind.: University of Notre Dame Press, 1986.

Henn, Claudia. " 'Sinnreiche Gedanken.' Zur Hermeneutik des Chladenius." *Archiv für Geschichte der Philosophie* 58 (1976): 240–63.

Henrichs, Norbert. *Bibliographie der Hermeneutik und ihrer Anwendungsbereiche seit Schleiermacher. Kleine Bibliographien aus dem Philosophischen Institut der Universität Dusseldorf.* Dusseldorf: Philosophia-Verlag, 1968.

Herrmann, Friedrich Wilhelm Von. *Die Selbstinterpretation Martin Heideggers.* Meisenheim: Anton Hain, 1964.

————. *Subjekt und Dasein. Interpretationen zu 'Sein und Zeit'.* Frankfurt: Klostermann, 1974.

Hinman, Lawrence M. "Quid facti or quid juris?: The Fundamental Ambiguity of Gadamer's Understanding of Hermeneutics." *Philosophy and Phenomenological Research* 40 (1980): 512–35.

Hirsch, E. D., Jr. *The Aims of Interpretation.* Chicago: University of Chicago Press, 1976.

————. *Validity in Interpretation.* New Haven, Conn.: Yale University Press, 1967.

Hodges, H. A. *The Philosophy of Wilhelm Dilthey.* London: Routledge and Kegan Paul, 1952.

Hogan, John. "Gadamer and the Hermeneutical Experience." *Philosophy Today* 20 (1976): 3–12.

Hollinger, Robert, editor. *Hermeneutics and Praxis.* Notre Dame, Ind.: University of Notre Dame Press, 1985.

————. "Practical Reason and Hermeneutics." *Philosophy and Rhetoric* 18, no. 2 (1985): 113–22.

Hookway, Christopher, and Pettit, Philip, editors. *Action and Interpretation.* Cambridge: Cambridge University Press, 1978.

Howard, Roy J. *Three Faces of Hermeneutics: An Introduction to Current Theories of Understanding.* Berkeley: University of California Press, 1982.

Hoy, David Couzens. *The Critical Circle. Literature, History, and Philosophical Hermeneutics.* Berkeley: University of California Press, 1978.

———. "Forgetting the Text: Derrida's Critique of Hermeneutics." *boundary 2* 8 (Fall 1979): 223–35.

———. "Hermeneutic Circularity, Indeterminacy and Incommensurability." *New Literary History* 10, no. 1 (1978):161–73.

———. "Must We Say What We Mean?" *Review of the University of Ottawa* 50 (1980): 411–26.

———. "Taking History Seriously: Foucault, Gadamer, Habermas." *Union Seminary Quarterly Review* 34 (Winter 1979): 85–95.

Hufnagel, E. *Einführung in die Hermeneutik.* Stuttgart: Kohlhammer, 1976.

Humboldt, Wilhelm von. *Gesammelte Schriften.* Edited by A. Leitzmann et al. Academy of Sciences. 17 vols. Berlin: B. Behr, 1903–1916. Rpt. Berlin: Walter de Gruyter, 1968.

Humphrey, Laurentius. *De ratione interpretandi libris III.* Basel: n.p., 1559.

Husserl, Edmund. *Cartesian Meditations: An Introduction to Phenomenology.* Translated by Dorion Cairns. The Hague: Nijhoff, 1960.

———. *The Crisis of European Sciences and Transcendental Phenomenology: An Introduction to Phenomenological Philosophy.* Translated and introduced by David Carr. Evanston, Ill.: Northwestern University Press, 1970.

———. *Ideas: General Introduction to Pure Phenomenology.* Translated by W. R. Boyce Gibson. New York: Collier Books, 1962.

———. *Logical Investigations.* 2 vols. Translated by J. N. Findlay (from the second German edition). London: Routledge and Kegan Paul; New York: The Humanities Press, 1976.

———. *The Phenomenology of Internal Time Consciousness.* Edited by Martin Heidegger. Translated by James S. Churchill. Introduction by Calvin O. Schrag. Bloomington: Indiana University Press, 1964.

Hyde, Michael J. "Philosophical Hermeneutics and the Communicative Experience," *Man and World* 13 (1980): 81–98.

Ihde, Don. *Hermeneutic Phenomenology: The Philosophy of Paul Ricoeur.* Evanston, Ill.: Northwestern University Press, 1971.

———. "Interpreting Hermeneutics." *Man and World* 13 (1980): 325–44.

IJsseling, Samuel. "Hermeneutics and Textuality." *Research in Phenomenology* 9 (1979): 1–16.

Ineichen, Hans. *Erkenntnistheorie und geschichtlichgesellschaftliche Welt: Diltheys Logik der Geisteswissenschaften.* Frankfurt: Klostermann, 1975.

Ingarden, Roman. *The Cognition of the Literary Work of Art.* Translated by Ruth Ann Crowley and Kenneth R. Olson. Evanston, Ill.: Northwestern University Press, 1973.

———. *The Literary Work of Art. An Investigation on the Borderline of Ontology, Logic, and Theory of Literature. With an Appendix on the Functions of*

Language in the Theater. Translated and with introduction by George G. Grabowicz. Evanston, Ill.: Northwestern University Press, 1973.

Ingram, David B. *Habermas and the Dialectic of Reason.* New Haven, Conn.: Yale University Press, 1987.

———. "Hermeneutics and Truth." *Journal of the British Society for Phenomenology* 15 (1984): 62–76.

———. "The Historical Genesis of the Gadamer-Habermas Controversy." *Auslegung* 10 (1983): 86–151.

Iser, Wolfgang. *The Act of Reading: A Theory of Aesthetic Response.* Baltimore, Md.: Johns Hopkins University Press, 1978.

———. *The Implied Reader.* Baltimore, Md.: Johns Hopkins University Press, 1974.

Jalbert, John E. "Hermeneutics or Phenomenology: Reflections on Husserl's Historical Meditations as a 'Way' into Transcendental Phenomenology." *Graduate Faculty Philosophy Journal* 8 (1982): 98–132.

Jameson, Fredric. *Marxism and Form: Twentieth-Century Dialectical Theories of Literature.* Princeton, N.J.: Princeton University Press, 1971.

———. *The Political Unconscious: Narrative as a Socially Symbolic Act.* Ithaca, N.Y.: Cornell University Press, 1981.

———. *The Prison House of Language: A Critical Account of Structuralism and Russian Formalism.* Princeton, N.J.: Princeton University Press, 1974.

———. "Figural Relativism, or the Poetics of Historiography." (Review of Hayden White's *Metahistory*). *Diacritics* 6 (Spring 1976): 2–9.

———. "Ideology, Narrative Analysis, and Popular Culture." *Theory and Society* 4 (1977): 543–59.

———. "Magical Narratives: Romance as Genre." *New Literary History* 7 (Autumn 1975): 135–63.

———. "Marxism and Historicism." *New Literary History* 11 (Autumn 1979): 41–73.

———. "Postmodernism, or the Cultural Logic of Late Capitalism." *New Left Review* 146 (July–August, 1984): 53–92.

Japp, Uwe. *Hermeneutik. Der theoretische Diskurs, die Literatur und die Konstruktion ihres Zusammenhanges in den philologischen Wissenschaften.* Munich: Fink Verlag, 1977.

Jauss, Hans Robert. *Aesthetic Experience and Literary Hermeneutics.* Translated by Michael Shaw. Minneapolis: University of Minnesota Press, 1982.

———. *Toward an Aesthetic of Reception.* Translated by Timothy Bahti. Minneapolis: University of Minnesota Press, 1982.

———. "The Limits and Tasks of Literary Hermeneutics." *Diogenes* 17 (1980): 92–119.

Jay, Martin. "Should Intellectual History Take a Linguistic Turn? Reflections on the Habermas-Gadamer Debate." In *Modern European Intellectual History,* edited by Dominick LaCapra and Stephen L. Kaplan. Ithaca, N.Y.: Cornell University Press, 1982, pp. 86–110.

Jeanrond, Werner G. *Text and Interpretation as Categories of Theological Thinking.*

Translated by Thomas J. Wilson. New York: Crossroad Publishing Company, 1988.

Johnson, Barbara. *The Critical Difference*. Baltimore, Md.: Johns Hopkins University Press, 1982.

———. *A World of Difference*. Baltimore, Md.: Johns Hopkins University Press, 1987.

Jolles, Andre. *Einfache Formen: Legende, Sage, Mythe, Rätsel, Spruch, Kasus, Memorabile, Märchen, Witz*. Darmstadt: Wissenschaftliche Buchgesellschaft, 1958.

Juhl, P. D. *Interpretation: An Essay in the Philosophy of Literary Criticism*. Princeton, N.J.: Princeton University Press, 1980.

Kainz, Friedrich. *Psychologie der Sprache*. 4 vols. Stuttgart: Ferdinand Enke Verlag, 1940–56.

Kamper, Dietmar. "Hermeneutik-Theorie einer Praxis?" *Zeitschrift für Allgemeine Wissenschaftstheorie* 5 (1974): 39–53.

Kemp, Peter. "Phänomenologie und Hermeneutik in der Philosophie Paul Ricoeurs." *Zeitschrift fr Theologie und Kirche* 67 (1970): 335–47.

Kermode, Frank. *The Genesis of Secrecy: On the Interpretation of Narrative*. Cambridge, Mass.: Harvard University Press, 1979.

———. "Institutional Control of Interpretation." *Salmagundi*, no. 43 (Winter 1979): 72–86.

Kimmerle, Heinz. *Philosophie der Geisteswissenschaften als Kritik ihrer Methoden*. The Hague: Nijhoff, 1978.

———. "Die Funktion der Hermeneutik in den positiven Wissenschaften." *Zeitschrift für allgemeine Wissenschaftstheorie* 5 (1974): 54–73.

———. "Hermeneutische Theorie oder ontologische Hermeneutik." *Zeitschrift für Theologie und Kirche* 61 (1962): 114–30.

———. "Metahermeneutik, Application, hermeneutische Sprachbildung." *Zeitschrift für Theologie und Kirche*. 63 (1964): 221–35.

Kirkland, Frank M. "Gadamer and Ricoeur: The Paradigm of the Text." *Graduate Faculty Philosophy Journal* 6 (Winter 1977): 131–44.

Kisiel, Theodore. "The Happening of Tradition: The Hermeneutics of Gadamer and Heidegger." *Man and World* 2 (1969): 358–85.

Klassen Grover, Julie Ann. "August Boeckh's *Hermeneutik* and its relation to contemporary scholarship." Ph.D. diss., Stanford University, 1972.

Klein, Jürgen. *Beyond Hermeneutics: Zur Philosophie der Literatur und Geisteswissenschaften*. Essen: Blaue Eule, 1985.

Kockelmans, Joseph J. *Hermeneutic Phenomenology—1988*. Lanham, Md.: University Press of America, Inc., 1988.

———. *Martin Heidegger: A First Introduction to His Philosophy*. Pittsburgh: Duquesne University Press, 1965.

———. *On Heidegger and Language*. Evanston, Ill.: Northwestern University Press, 1972.

———, editor. *Phenomenology. The Philosophy of Edmund Husserl and Its Interpretation*. Garden City, N.Y.: Anchor Books (Doubleday), 1967.

———. "Destructive Retrieval and Hermeneutic Phenomenology in *Being and*

Time." *Research in Phenomenology* 7 (1977): 106–37.

————. "On Myth and Its Relationship to Hermeneutics." *Cultural Hermeneutics* 1 (April 1973): 47–86.

————. "Toward an Interpretive or Hermeneutic Social Science." *Graduate Faculty Philosophy Journal* 5 (1975): 73–96.

Kortian, Garbis. *Metacritique: the Philosophical Argument of Jürgen Habermas.* Translated by John Raffan. Introduction by Charles Taylor and Alan Montefiore. Cambridge: Cambridge University Press, 1980.

Krüger, Gerhard. *Freiheit und Weltverwaltung: Aufsätze zur Philosophie der Geschichte.* Freiburg and Munich: Alber, 1958.

————. *Grundfragen der Philosophie: Geschichte, Wahrheit, Wissenschaft.* Frankfurt: Klostermann, 1958.

Kuhn, Thomas S. *The Essential Tension: Selected Studies in Scientific Tradition and Change.* Chicago: University of Chicago Press, 1977.

————. *The Structure of Scientific Revolutions.* 2nd ed. Chicago: University of Chicago Press, 1970.

Kunne-Ibsch, Elrud. "Rezeptionsforschung: Konstanten und Varianten eines literaturwissenschaftlichen Konzepts in Theorie und Praxis." *Amsterdamer Beiträge.* (1974):1–36.

Kuypers, K. "Hermeneutik und die Interpretation der Logos-Idee." *Revue Internationale de Philosophie* 29 (1970): 52–77.

Labroisse, Gerd. "Überlegungen zu einem Interpretations-Modell." *Amsterdamer Beiträge* (1974): 149–61.

Lacan, Jacques. *Écrits de Jacques Lacan: le champ freudien.* Paris: Éditions du Seuil, 1967.

————. "The Insistence of the Letter in the Unconscious," *Yale French Studies,* nos. 36–37 (1967). 112–47.

LaCapra, Dominick. *Rethinking Intellectual History: Texts, Contexts, Language.* Ithaca, N.Y.: Cornell University Press, 1983.

Lawson, Hilary. *Reflexivity: The Post-Modern Predicament.* La Salle, Ill.: Open Court Press, 1985.

Leibfried, E. *Kritische Wissenschaft vom Text.* Stuttgart: Metzler, 1970.

Lentricchia, Frank. *After the New Criticism.* Chicago: University of Chicago Press, 1980.

Levi, Albert William. "De interpretatione: Cognition and Context in the History of Ideas." *Critical Inquiry* 3, no.1 (1976): 153–78.

Licher, Edmund. "Kommunikationstheoretische Aspekte der Analyse einiger Gedichte Bertolt Brechts." *Amsterdamer Beiträge* (1974): 163–211.

Linge, David E. "Dilthey and Gadamer: Two Theories of Historical Understanding." *Journal of the American Academy of Religion* 41 (1973): 536–53.

Llewelyn, John. *Beyond Metaphysics? The Hermeneutical Circle in Contemporary Continental Philosophy.* Atlantic-Highlands, N.J.: Humanities Press, 1985.

————. *Derrida on the Threshold of Sense.* New York: St. Martin's Press, 1986.

Lyotard, Jean-François. *The Differend: Phrases in Dispute.* Translated by Georges Van Den Abbeele. Minneapolis: University of Minnesota Press, 1988.

————. *The Postmodern Condition: A Report on Knowledge.* Translated by Geoff

Bennington and Brian Massumi. Minneapolis: University of Minnesota Press, 1984.

MacCannell, Dean, and MacCannell, Juliet Flower. *The Time of the Sign: A Semiotic Interpretation of Modern Culture.* Bloomington: Indiana University Press, 1982.

McCarthy, Thomas. *The Critical Theory of Jürgen Habermas.* Cambridge, Mass.: MIT Press, 1978.

———. "On Misunderstanding 'Understanding.' " *Theory and Decision* 3 (June 1973): 351–69.

Macquarrie, John. *An Existentialist Theology. A Comparison of Heidegger and Bultmann.* London: SCM Press, 1955.

Magliola, Robert. *Phenomenology and Literature.* West Lafayette, Ind.: Purdue University Press, 1977.

Makkreel, Rudolf. *Dilthey, Philosopher of the Human Studies.* Princeton, N.J.: Princeton University Press, 1975.

———. "Dilthey and Universal Hermeneutics." In *European Philosophy and the Human and Social Sciences,* edited by Simon Glynn. Hampshire: Gower Press, 1984, pp. 1–19.

———. "Hermeneutics and the Limits of Consciousness." *Nous* 21 (March 1987): 7–18.

———. "Tradition and Orientation in Hermeneutics." *Research in Phenomenology* 16 (1986): 73–85.

Malet, André. *The Thought of Rudolf Bultmann.* Translated by R. Strachan. Preface by Rudolf Bultmann. New York: Doubleday, 1971.

Maraldo, John C. *Der Hermeneutische Zirkel: Untersuchungen zu Schleiermacher, Dilthey und Heidegger.* Freiburg and Munich: Verlag Karl Alber, 1974.

Marassi, Massino. "The Hermeneutics of Rhetoric in Heidegger." Translated by Kiaran O'Malley. *Philosophy and Rhetoric* 19, No.2 (1986): 79–98.

Marx, Werner. *Heidegger and the Tradition.* Translated by Theodore Kisiel and Murray Greene. Introduced by Theodore Kisiel. Evanston, Ill.: Northwestern University Press, 1972.

Mazzeo, John Anthony. *Varieties of Interpretation.* Notre Dame, Ind.: University of Notre Dame Press, 1978.

Meier, Georg Friedrich. *Versuch einer allgemeinen Auslegungskunst.* (Halle, 1757) Dsseldorf: Stern-Verlag, 1965.

Meinecke, Friedrich. *Historism: The Rise of a New Historical Outlook.* Translated by J. E. Anderson. London: Routledge and Kegan Paul, 1972.

Melville, Stephen W. *Philosophy Beside Itself: On Deconstruction and Modernism.* Minneapolis: University of Minnesota Press, 1986.

Mendelson, Jack. "The Habermas/Gadamer Debate." *New German Critique* 18 (1979): 44–73.

Merleau-Ponty, Maurice. *Phenomenology of Perception.* Translated by Colin Smith. London: Routledge and Kegan Paul, 1962.

———. *Signs.* Translated and with an introduction by Richard C. McCleary. Evanston, Ill.: Northwestern University Press, 1964.

———. "Eye and Mind." Translated by Carleton Dallery. In *The Primacy of Per-*

ception and Other Essays, edited by James M. Edie. Evanston, Ill.: Northwestern University Press, 1964.

Misch, Georg. *Lebensphilosophie und Phänomenologie: Eine Auseinandersetzung der Diltheyschen Richtung mit Heidegger und Husserl.* Leipzig: Teubner, 1931.

Misgeld, Dieter. "Critical Hermeneutics Versus Neo-Parsonianism." *New German Critique* 35 (Spring–Summer 1985): 55–82.

Mohanty, J. N. *Edmund Husserl's Theory of Meaning.* The Hague: Nijhoff, 1964.

Mueller-Vollmer, Kurt. *Towards a Phenomenological Theory of Literature. A Study of Wilhelm Dilthey's Poetik.* The Hague: Mouton, 1963.

———. "From Poetics to Linguistics: Wilhelm von Humboldt and the Romantic Idea of Language." In *Le Groupe de Coppet. Actes et documents du deuxième Colloque de Coppet, 1974.* Paris and Geneva: Champion and Slatkine, 1977, pp. 195–215.

———, editor. *The Hermeneutics Reader.* New York: Continuum Books, 1985.

Murphy, John W. "Cultural Manifestations of Postmodernism." *Philosophy Today* 30 (Winter 1986):346–53.

Nassen, Ulrich, editor *Studien zur Entwicklung einer materialen Hermeneutik.* Munich: Fink Verlag, 1979.

———, editor. *Texthermeneutik: Geschichte, Aktualität, Kritik.* Paderborn: Schöningh, 1979.

Natanson, Maurice. *Edmund Husserl. Philosopher of Infinite Tasks.* Evanston, Ill.: Northwestern University Press, 1973.

———. *Literature, Philosophy, and the Social Sciences: Essays in Existentialism and Phenomenology.* The Hague: Martinus Nijhoff, 1962.

Nehamas, Alexander. *Nietzsche: Life as Literature.* Cambridge, Mass.: Harvard University Press, 1985.

Nicholson, Graeme. *Seeing and Reading.* Atlantic Higlands, N.J.: Humanities Press, 1984.

———. "The Role of Interpretation in Phenomenological Reflection." *Research in Phenomenology* 14 (1984): 57–72.

———. "Transforming What We Know." *Research In Phenomenology,* 16 (1986): 57–71.

Nida, Eugene A. *Toward a Science of Translating: With Special Reference to Principles and Procedures Involved in Bible Translating.* Leiden: Brill, 1964.

Niebuhr, Richard R. *Schleiermacher on Christ and Religion: A New Introduction.* New York: Charles Scribner's Sons, 1964.

Nielson, Kai. "Probing Critical Theory." *International Studies in Philosophy* 13 (1981): 81–92.

Noakes, Susan. "Literary Semiotics and Hermeneutics: Towards a Taxonomy of the Interpretant." *American Journal of Semiotics.* 3, no. 3 (1985): 109–119.

Noller, Gerhard. *Sein und Existenz: Die Überwindung des Subjekt-Objektschemas in der Philosophie Heideggers und in der Theologie der Entmythologisierung.* Munich: Kaiser, 1962.

Norris, Christopher. *Derrida.* Cambridge, Mass.: Harvard University Press, 1988.

O'Hara, Daniel T. *Tragic Knowledge: Yeat's Autobiography and Hermeneutics.* New

York: Columbia University Press, 1981.
——— , editor. *Why Nietzsche Now?* Bloomington: Indiana University Press, 1985.
Olson, Alan. *Transcendence and Hermeneutics.* Boston: Kluwer, 1979.
O'Neill, John. *Essaying Montaigne: A Study of the Renaissance Institution of Writing and Reading.* Boston: Routledge and Kegan Paul, 1982.
——— , editor. *On Critical Theory.* New York: Seabury, 1976.
Ormiston, Gayle L. "Already Not-Yet: Shoreline Fiction Metaphase." In *The Poetry of the Elements: The Sea, Analecta Husserliana,* vol. 19, edited by Anna-Teresa Tymieniecka. Dordrecht: D. Reidel, 1985, pp. 343–51.
——— . "Binding Withdrawal." In *Hermeneutics and Deconstruction,* edited by Hugh J. Silverman and Don Ihde. Albany: State University Press of New York, 1985, pp. 247–261.
——— . "The Economy of Duplicity: *Différance.*" In *Derrida and Différance,* edited by David Wood and Robert Bernasconi. Evanston, Ill.: Northwestern University Press, 1988, pp. 41–50.
——— . "Hermeneutic: A Question of Understanding Sign Iteration, *Et Caetera.*" *Ars Semeiotica* 3, no. 2 (1980): 137–58.
——— . " 'I am no-thing'—The Name and Cleft Reference of Wo/Man." *Journal of the British Society for Phenomenology* 18, no. 2. (May 1987): 149–161.
Ormiston, Gayle L., and Schrift, Alan D., editors. *The Hermeneutic Tradition: From Ast to Ricoeur.* Albany: State University of New York Press, 1990.
Orth, Ernest Wolfgang. *Bedeutung, Sinn, Gegenstand. Studien zur Sprachphilosophie Edmund Husserls und Richard Hönigswalds.* Bonn: Bouvier, 1967.
——— . "Historical and Systematic Remarks on the Relation between Description and Hermeneutics in Phenomenology: A Critique of the Enlarged Use of Hermeneutics." *Research in Phenomenology* 14 (1984): 1–18.
Page, Carl. "Axiomatics, Hermeneutics, and Practical Rationality." *International Philosophical Quarterly* 27 (March 1987): 81–100.
Palmer, Richard. *Hermeneutics: Interpretation Theory in Schleiermacher, Dilthey, Heidegger, and Gadamer.* Evanston, Ill.: Northwestern University Press, 1969.
——— . "Allegorical, Philological and Philosophical Hermeneutics." *Review of the University of Ottawa* 50 (1980): 338–60.
——— . "Phenomenology as Foundation for a Post-Modern Philosophy of Literary Interpretation." *Cultural Hermeneutics* 1 (July 1973): 207–22.
Palmer, Richard, and Michelfelder, Diane, editors. *Dialogue and Deconstruction: The Gadamer-Derrida Encounter.* Albany: State University of New York Press, 1989.
Pannenberg, Wolfhart. "Hermeneutic and Universal History." In *Basic Questions in Theology,* vol. 1, translated by George H. Kehm. Philadelphia: Fortress Press, 1970.
Pavlovic, Karl R. "Science and Autonomy: The Prospects for Hermeneutic Science." *Man and World* 14 (1981): 127–40.
Pepper, Stephen C. *The Basis of Criticism in the Arts.* Cambridge: Harvard University Press, 1956.
Pettit, Philip, editor. *Action and Interpretation: Studies in the Philosophy of the So-*

cial Sciences. Cambridge: Cambridge University Press, 1978.

Phillips, Leslie, and Smith, Joseph G. *Rorschach Interpretation.* New York: Grune and Stratton, 1959.

Plantinga, Theodore. *Historical Understanding in the Thought of Wilhelm Dilthey.* Toronto: University of Toronto Press, 1980.

Pöggeler, Otto. *Martin Heidegger's Path of Thinking.* Translated by Dan Magurshak and Sigmund Barber. Atlantic Highlands, N.J.: Humanities Press, 1987.

———. "Hermeneutik und semantische Phänomenologie." *Philosophische Rundschau* 13 (1965): 1–39.

———. "Hermeneutische Philosophie und Theologie." *Man and World* 7 (1974): 158–176.

Prauss, Gerold. *Erkennen und Handeln in Heidegger's 'Sein und Zeit.'* Freiburg, Munich: Alber, 1977.

Rabinow, Paul, and Sullivan, William M., editors. *Interpretive Social Sciences: A Second Look.* Berkeley: University of California Press, 1987.

Radnitzky, Gerard. *Contemporary Schools of Metascience.* 2 vols. 2nd ed. Göteborg: Akademiförlaget/Gumpert, 1968. 3rd. enlg. ed.; Chicago: Regnery, 1973.

Ramm, Bernard L. *Hermeneutics.* Grand Rapids: Baker Book House, 1971.

Rasmussen, David M. *Mythic-Symbolic Language and Philosophical Anthropology: A Constructive Interpretation of the Thought of Paul Ricoeur.* The Hague: Nijhoff, 1971.

———. "Between Autonomy and Sociality." *Cultural Hermeneutics* 1 (April 1973): 3–45.

Raulet, Gerard. "La Fin de la 'Raison dans l'Histoire'." *Dialogue* 22 (Decembre 1983): 631–46.

Reagan, Charles E. *Studies in the Philosophy of Paul Ricoeur.* Athens: Ohio University Press, 1979.

Reisinger, P. "Über die Zirkelstruktur des Verstehens in der traditionellen Hermeneutik." *Philosophisches Jahrbuch* 81 (1974): 88–104.

Rickman, H. P. *Dilthey Today: A Critical Appraisal of the Contemporary Relevance of His Work.* New York: Greenwood Press, 1988.

Ricoeur, Paul. *The Conflict of Interpretations: Essays in Hermeneutics.* Edited by Don Ihde. Evanston, Ill.: Northwestern University Press, 1974.

———. *Freud and Philosophy: An Essay on Interpretation.* Translated by Denis Savage. New Haven, Conn.: Yale University Press, 1970.

———. *History and Truth.* Translated by Charles A. Kelbley. Evanston, Ill.: Northwestern University Press, 1965.

———. *Husserl: An Analysis of His Phenomenology.* Translated by Edward G. Ballard and Lester E. Embree. Evanston, Ill.: Northwestern University Press, 1967.

———. *Interpretation Theory: Discourse and the Surplus of Meaning.* Fort Worth, Texas: Texas Christian University Press, 1976.

———. *Hermeneutics and the Human Sciences.* Edited and translated by John B. Thompson. Cambridge: Cambridge University Press, 1981.

————. *The Philosophy of Paul Ricoeur.* Edited by Charles Reagan and David Stewart. Boston: Beacon Press, 1978.

————. *The Rule of Metaphor: Multi-disciplinary Studies of the Creation of Meaning in Language.* Translated by Robert Czerny. Toronto: University of Toronto Press, 1977.

————. *The Symbolism of Evil.* Translated by Emerson Buchanan. New York: Harper and Row, 1967.

————. *Du Texte à l'action: Essais d'hermnéutique, II.* Paris: Éditions du Seuil, 1986.

————. *Time and Narrative I.* Translated by Kathleen McLaughlin and David Pellauer. Chicago: University of Chicago Press, 1984.

————. *Time and Narrative II.* Translated by Kathleen McLaughlin and David Pellauer. Chicago: University of Chicago Press, 1986.

————. *Time and Narrative III.* Translated by Kathleen McLaughlin and David Pellauer. Chicago: University of Chicago Press, 1988.

————. "Ethics and Culture: Habermas and Gadamer in Dialogue." *Philosophy Today* 17 (1973): 153–65.

————. "Narrative and Hermeneutics." In *Essays on Aesthetics: Perspectives on the Work of Monroe C. Beardsley,* edited by John Fisher. Philadelphia: Temple University Press, 1983.

————. "Phenomenology and Hermeneutics." *Nous* 9 (1975): 85–102.

————. "Schleiermacher's Hermeneutics." *Monist* 60 (1977): 181–97.

Ricoeur, Paul, and Gadamer, Hans-Georg. "The Conflict of Interpretations." In *Phenomenology: Dialogues & Bridges,* edited by Ronald Bruzina and Bruce Wilshire. Albany: State University of New York Press, 1982.

Riedel, Manfred. *Verstehen oder Erklären? Zur Theorie und Geschichte der hermeneutischen Wissenschaften.* Stuttgart: Klett-Cotta, 1978.

Riffaterre, Michael. "Interpretation and Undecidability." *New Literary History* 12 (1981): 227–42.

Robinson, James M., and Cobb, John B., Jr., editors. *The New Hermeneutic.* New York: Harper and Row, 1964.

Rockmore, Tom. "Ideality, Hermeneutics and the Hermeneutics of Idealism." *Idealistic Studies* 12 (1982): 92–102.

Rodi, Frithjof. "Diesseits der Pragmatik: Gedanken zu Einer Funktionsbestimmung der Hermeneutischen Wissenschaften." *Zeitschrift für Allgemeine Wissenschaft* 10 (1979): 288–315.

————. " 'Erkenntis des Erkannten'—August Boeckhs Grundformel der hermeneutischen Wissenschaften." In *Philologie und Hermeneutik im 19. Jahrhundert. Zur Geschichte und Methodologie des Geisteswissenschaften,* edited by H. Flashar, K. Gründer, and A. Horstmann. Göttingen: Vandehoeck and Ruprecht, 1979, pp. 68–83.

Rorty, Richard. *Consequences of Pragmatism.* Minneapolis: University of Minnesota Press, 1982.

————. *Philosophy and the Mirror of Nature.* Princeton, N.J.: Princeton University Press, 1979.

————. "Deconstruction and Circumvention." *Critical Inquiry* 11 (1984): 1–23.

————. "Habermas and Lyotard on Post-Modernity." *Habermas and Modernity*, edited by Richard J. Bernstein. Cambridge, Mass.: MIT Press, 1985, pp. 161–175.

Rosen, Stanley. *Hermeneutics as Politics*. New York: Oxford University Press, 1987.

Rothacker, Erich. *Einleitung in die Geisteswissenschaften*. 2nd ed. Tübingen: J. C. B. Mohr, 1930.

————. *Logik und Systematik der Geisteswissenschaften*. Bonn: Bouvier, 1948.

Rüsen, Jörn. *Für eine erneuerte Historik. Studien zur Theorie der Wissenschaft*. Stuttgart—Bad Cannstatt: Frommann-Holzboog, 1976.

Ryan, Michael. *Marxism and Deconstruction: A Critical Articulation*. Baltimore, Md.: Johns Hopkins University Press, 1982.

Said, Edward W. *The World, the Text, and the Critic*. Cambridge: Harvard University Press, 1983.

Sallis, John. *Delimitations*. Bloomington: Indiana University Press, 1987.

————, editor. *Deconstruction and Philosophy: The Texts of Jacques Derrida*. Chicago: University of Chicago Press, 1987.

Sandkühler, Hans-Jörg. *Praxis und Geschichtsbewusstsein: Studien zur materialistischen Dialektik, Erkenntnistheorie und Hermeneutik*. Frankfurt: Suhrkamp, 1973.

Savile, Anthony. "Historicity and the Hermeneutic Circle." *New Literary History* 10 (Autumn 1978): 49–70.

Schleiermacher, Friedrich D. E. *Dialektik*. Edited by Andras Arndt. Hamburg: Meiner, 1986.

————. *Hermeneutics: The Handwritten Manuscripts*. Edited by Heinz Kimmerle. Translated by James Duke and Jack Forstman. Missoula, Mont.: Scholars Press, 1977.

————. *Hermeneutik*. Edited and introduced by Heinz Kimmerle. Heidelberg: Carl Winter Universitätsverlag, 1959.

————. *Hermeneutik und Kritik mit besonderer Beziehung auf das Neue Testament*. Edited by F. Lücke. *Sämmtliche Werke*. Vol. 7. Berlin: Reimer 1838.

————. *Hermeneutik und Kritik: Mit einem Anhang sprachphilosophischer Texte Schleiermachers*. Edited and introduced by Manfred Frank. Frankfurt: Suhrkamp, 1977.

————. *Kritsche Gesamtausgabe*. Edited by Hans-Joachim Birkner, et al. Berlin: Walter de Gruyter, 1980.

Schmitt, Richard. *Martin Heidegger on Being Human: An Introduction to "Sein und Zeit."* New York: Random House, 1969.

Schrag, Calvin O. *Communicative Praxis and the Space of Subjectivity*. Bloomington: Indiana University Press, 1986.

————. *Radical Reflection and the Origin of the Human Sciences*. West Lafayette, Ind.: Purdue University Press, 1980.

Schrift, Alan D. "Between Perspectivism and Philology: Genealogy as Hermeneutic." In *Nietzsche-Studien*, Band 16. Berlin: Walter de Gruyter, 1987, pp. 91–111.

————. "Genealogy and/as Deconstruction: Nietzsche, Derrida and Foucault on Philosophy as Critique." In *Postmodernism and Continental Philosophy*, edited by Hugh J. Silverman and Donn Welton. Albany: State University of New York Press, 1988, pp.193–213.

————. "Language, Metaphor, Rhetoric: Nietzsche's Deconstruction of Epistemology." *Journal of the History of Philosophy* 23, no. 3 (July, 1985): 371–395.

————. "Reading, Writing, Text: Nietzsche's Deconstruction of Author-ity." *International Studies in Philosophy* 18, no. 2 (1985): 55–64.

Seebohm, Thomas M. *Zur Kritik der hermeneutischen Vernunft*. Bonn: Bouvier, 1972.

————. "Boeckh and Dilthey: The Development of Methodical Hermeneutics." *Man and World* 17 (1984): 325–46.

————. "The Problem of Hermeneutics in Recent Anglo-American Literature: Part I." *Philosophy and Rhetoric* 10 (1977): 180–98.

Seigfried, Hans. "Phenomenology, Hermeneutics and Poetry." *Journal of the British Society for Phenomenology* 10 (1979): 94–100.

Seung, T. K. *Semiotics and Thematics in Hermeneutics*. New York: Columbia University Press, 1982.

————. *Structuralism and Hermeneutics*. New York: Columbia University Press, 1982.

Shapiro, Gary, and Sica, Alan, editors. *Hermeneutics: Questions and Prospects*. Amherst: University of Massachusetts Press, 1984.

Shapiro, Michael J. *Language and Political Understanding: The Politics of Discursive Practices*. New Haven, Conn.: Yale University Press, 1981.

Silverman, Hugh J. *Inscriptions: Between Phenomenology and Structuralism*. New York and London: Routledge and Kegan Paul, 1987.

————. "For a Hermeneutic Semiology of the Self." *Philosophy Today* 23 (1979): 199–204.

————. "Phenomenology: From Hermeneutics to Deconstruction." *Research in Phenomenology* 14 (1984): 19–34.

Simmel, Georg. *Vom Wesen der historischen Verstehens*. Berlin: E. S. Mittler, 1918.

Simon-Schaefer, Roland, and Zimmerli, Walter. *Theorie zwischen Kritik und Praxis. Jürgen Habermas und die Frankfurter Schule*. Stuttgart–Bad Cannstatt: Friedrich Frommann Verlag, 1975.

Simpson, Evan, editor. *Antifoundationalism and Practical Reasoning: Conversations Between Hermeneutics and Analysis*. Edmonton, Alberta: Academic Printing and Publishing, 1987.

Sims, Stuart. "Lyotard and the Politics of Antifoundationalism." *Radical Philosophy* 4 (Autumn 1986): 8–13.

Singleton, Charles, editor. *Interpretation: Theory and Practice*. Baltimore, Md.: Johns Hopkins University Press, 1969.

Smith, P. Christopher. "Gadamer on Language and Method in Hegel's Dialectic." *Graduate Faculty Philosophy Journal* 5 (1975): 53–72.

————. "H.-G. Gadamer's Heideggerian Interpretation of Plato." *Journal of the British Society for Phenomenology* 12 (1981): 211–30.

Sokolowski, Robert. *Husserlian Meditations. How Words Present Things.* Evanston, Ill.: Northwestern University Press, 1974.

Sontag, Susan. *Against Interpretation, and Other Essays.* New York: Farrar, Straus, and Giroux, 1966.

Spanos, William. V. *Repetitions: The Postmodern Occasion in Literature and Culture.* Baton Rouge and London: Louisiana State University Press, 1987.

————. editor. *Martin Heidegger and the Question of Literature: Toward a Postmodern Literary Hermeneutics.* Bloomington: Indiana University Press, 1980.

Spieler, Karl-Heinz. *Untersuchungen zu Johann Gustav Droysens "Historik."* Berlin: Duncker und Humbolt, 1970.

Spivak, Gayatri Chakravorty. *In Other Worlds: Essays in Cultural Politics.* New York: Methuen, 1987.

Steiner, George. *After Babel: Aspects of Language and Translation.* New York: Oxford University Press, 1975.

————. *On Difficulty and Other Essays.* New York: Oxford University Press, 1978.

Steinmetz, Horst. "Rezeption und Interpretation. Versuch einer Abgrenzung." *Amsterdamer Beiträge* (1974): 37–81.

Steinthal, Heymann. "Darstellung und Kritik der Boeckschen Enzyklopädie und Methodologie der Philologie." *Zeitschrift für Völkerpsychologie und Sprachwissenschaft* 11 (1880): 303–26.

Störig, Hans Joachim, editor. *Das Problem des Übersetzens.* Darmstadt: Wissenschaftliche Buchgesellschaft, 1963.

Strasser, Stephen. *Phenomenology and the Human Sciences.* Pittsburgh: Duquesne University Press, 1963.

Sullivan, William, and Rabinow, Paul. "The Interpretive Turn: Emergence of an Approach." *Philosophy Today* 23 (1979): 29–40.

Symposium. "Hermeneutics and Critical Theory." *Cultural Hermeneutics* 2 (1975): 307–90.

Symposium. "Hermeneutics, Post-Structuralism, and Objective Interpretation." *Papers on Language and Literature* 17 (1981): 48–87.

Szondi, Peter. *Einführung in die literarische Hermeneutik.* Edited by J. Bollack and H. Stierlin. Frankfurt: Suhrkamp Verlag, 1975.

————. *On Textual Understanding, and Other Essays.* Translated by Harvey Mendelsohn. Minneapolis: University of Minnesota Press, 1986.

————. "Introduction to Literary Hermeneutics." *New Literary History* 10, no. 1 (1978): 17–29.

————. "Über philologische Erkenntnis." *Schriften.* Vol. 1. Frankfurt: Suhrkamp, 1978.

Thompson, John B. *Critical Hermeneutics: A Study in the Thought of Paul Ricoeur and Jürgen Habermas.* Cambridge: Cambridge University Press, 1981.

Thompson, John B., and Held, David, editors. *Habermas: Critical Debates.* Cambridge, Mass.: MIT Press, 1982.

Tice, Terrence N. *Schleiermarcher Bibliography: With Brief Introductions, Annotations, and Index.* Princeton Pamphlets, No. 12. Princeton, N.J.: Princeton Theological Seminary, 1966.

Todorov, Tzvetan. *The Poetics of Prose.* Translated by Richard Howard. Ithaca, N.Y.: Cornell University Press, 1977.

Tracy, David. *The Analogical Imagination: Christian Theology and the Culture of Pluralism.* New York: Crossroad, 1981.

————. *Plurality and Ambiguity: Hermeneutics, Religion, and Hope.* New York: Harper and Row, 1987

Turner, Stephen, and Carr, David. "The Process of Criticism in Interpretive Sociology & History." *Human Studies* 1 (1978): 138–52.

Tuttle, Howard Nelson. *Wilhelm Dilthey's Philosophy of Historical Understanding: A Critical Analysis.* Leiden: E. J. Brill, 1969.

Ulmer, Gregory L. *Applied Grammatology: Post(e)–Pedagogy from Jacques Derrida to Joseph Beuys.* Baltimore, Md.: Johns Hopkins University Press, 1985.

Vattimo, Gianni. *The End of Modernity. Nihilism and Hermenentics in Postmodern Culture.* Translated by Jon R. Snyder. Baltimore, Md.: Johns Hopkins University Press, 1989.

————. "The End of (Hi)story." *Chicago Review* 35, no. 4 (1987): 20–30.

————. "Nietzsche and Contemporary Hermeneutics." In *Nietzsche as Affirmative Thinker,* edited by Yirmiyahu Yovel. Dordrecht: Nijhoff, 1986, pp. 58–68.

Velkley, Richard. "Gadamer and Kant: The Critique of Modern Aesthetic Consciousness in *Truth and Method.*" *Interpretation* 9 (1981): 353–64.

Versñyi, Laszlo. *Heidegger, Being, and Truth.* New Haven, Conn.: Yale University Press, 1965.

Von Wright, Georg Henrik. *Explanation and Understanding.* Ithaca, N.Y.: Cornell University Press, 1971.

Wach, Joachim. *Das Verstehen: Grundzüge einer Geschichte der hermeneutischen Theorie im 19. Jahrhundert.* 3 vols. Tübingen: J. C. B. Mohr, 1926–1933. Vol. 1: *Die grossen Systeme,* 1926. Vol. 2: *Die theologische Hermeneutik von Schleiermacher bis Hoffmann,* 1929. Vol. 3: *Das Verstehen in der Historik von Ranke bis zum Positivismus,* 1933. Reprinted, 1 vol., Hildescheim: Georg Olms, 1965.

Wachterhauser, Brice, editor. *Hermeneutics and Modern Philosophy.* Albany: State University of New York Press, 1986.

Wallulis, Jerald. "Philosophical Hermeneutics and the Conflict of Ontologies." *International Philosophical Quarterly* 24 (1984): 283–302.

Warminski, Andrzej. *Readings in Interpretation: Hölderlin, Hegel, Heidegger.* Minneapolis: University of Minnesota Press, 1987.

Warnach, Viktor, editor. *Hermeneutik als Weg heutiger Wissenschaft.* Munich–Salzburg: Anton Pustet, 1971.

Warnke, Georgia. *Gadamer: Hermeneutics, Tradition and Reason.* Palo Alto, Calif.: Stanford University Press, 1987.

Watson, Stephen. "Jürgen Habermas and Jean-François Lyotard: Post Modernism and the Crisis of Rationality." *Philosophy and Social Criticism* 10 (Fall 1984): 1–24.

Weber, Max. *Economy and Society: An Outline of Interpretive Sociology.* Edited by G. Roth and C. Wittich. Berkeley: University of California Press, 1978.

Weber, Samuel. *Institution and Interpretation.* Minneapolis: University of Minnesota Press, 1987.

———. *The Legend of Freud.* Minneapolis: University of Minnesota Press, 1982.

Weimar, Klaus. *Historische Einleitung zur literaturwissenschaftlichen Hermeneutik.* Tübingen: J. C. B. Mohr, 1975.

Weinsheimer, Joel C. *Gadamer's Hermeneutics: A Reading of Truth and Method.* New Haven, Conn.: Yale University Press, 1985.

———. " 'London' and the Fundamental Problem of Hermeneutics." *Critical Inquiry* 9 (1982): 303–22.

Wellek, René. "Wilhelm Dilthey." *A History of Modern Criticism.* 1750–1950. Vol. 5. New Haven: Yale University Press, 1965, pp. 320–335.

Wellmer, Albrecht. *Critical Theory of Society.* Translated by John Cumming. New York: Herder and Herder, 1971.

———. "On the Dialectic of Modernism and Postmodernism." *Praxis International* 4 (January 1985): 337–362.

West, Philip. "The Redundant Labyrinth." *Salmagundi,* no. 46 (Fall 979): 58–83.

Westphal, Merold. "Hegel, Pannenburg, and Hermeneutics." *Man and World* 4 (1971): 276–93.

White, Hayden. *Metahistory: The Historical Imagination in Nineteenth-Century Europe.* Baltimore, Md.: Johns Hopkins University Press, 1974.

———. *Tropics of Discourse: Essays in Cultural Criticism.* Baltimore, Md.: Johns Hopkins University Press, 1978.

———. "The Problem of Change in Literary History." *New Literary History* 7 (Autumn 1975): 97–111.

Whorf, Benjamin L. *Language, Thought, and Reality: Selected Writings.* Cambridge, Mass.: Technology Press of MIT, 1956.

Wimsatt, William K., Jr. *The Verbal Icon: Studies in the Meaning of Poetry.* Lexington: University of Kentucky Press, 1954.

Winch, Peter. *The Idea of a Social Science and Its Relation to Philosophy.* London: Routledge and Kegan Paul, 1958.

Wittgenstein, Ludwig. *Philosophical Investigations.* Translated by G. E. M. Anscombe. Oxford: Basil Blackwell, 1958.

Wolf, Friedrich August. *Vorlesung über die Enzyklopädie der Altertumswissenschaft.* Leipzig: Lehnhold, 1831.

Wolff, Christian. *Vernünftige Gedanken. Von den Kräften des menschlichen Verstandes und ihrem richtigen Gebrauche. Gesammelte Werke.* Edited by H. W. Arndt. Hildescheim: Olms, 1965.

Wolff, Janet. *Hermeneutic Philosophy and the Sociology of Art.* London: Routledge and Kegan Paul, 1975.

Wood, Charles Monroe. *Theory and Religious Understanding: A Critique of the Hermeneutics of Joachim Wach.* Missoula, Mont.: Scholars Press, 1975.

Zedler, J. H. ''Hermeneutik.'' *Grosses vollständiges Universallexicon aller Künste und Wissenschaften.* Vol. 12. Halle and Leipzig: J. H. Zedler, 1735, pp.1729–33.

Zimmermann, Jörg. *Wittgensteins sprachphilosophische Hermeneutik.* Frankfurt: Klostermann, 1975.

Zockler, Christofer. *Dilthey und die Hermeneutik.* Stuttgart: Metzler Verlag, 1975.

Contributors

Eric Blondel (1942–) teaches philosophy at the Université de Nancy II. In addition to his numerous and influential articles and books on Nietzsche, he has translated Nietzsche's *Götzen-Dämmerung, oder: Wie man mit dem Hammer philosophirt* into French in 1983 and recently has published a book on humor.

Peter Caws (1931–) is University Professor of Philosophy at George Washington University in Washington D.C. His work has covered a broad array of areas in contemporary philosophy including issues in philosophy of science, the history of twentieth-century thought, a book on Sartre, and most recently a book on structuralism.

Jacques Derrida (1930–) taught for many years at the École Normale Supérieure, was founding director of the College Internationale de Philosophie, is currently Director of Studies at the École des Hautes Études en Sciences Sociales in Paris, and has held visiting appointments at several American universities including Yale, Cornell, and the University of California at Irvine.

Michel Foucault (1926–1984) held the Chair of History and Systems of Thought at the Collège de France. He held a visiting appointment for many years at the University of California at Berkeley. His published works addressed issues related to semeiotics, hermeneutics, history, psychology, psychiatry, and sexuality, as well as the nature of the knowledge in the human and natural sciences.

Manfred Frank (1945–), Professor of Philosophy at the Universität in Tübingen, has published widely in German, French, and English. His particular research interests are Idealism and German Romanticism, Hermeneutics and Neostructuralism, and theories of self-consciousness, areas in which he has published numerous influential books and articles.

Werner Hamacher (1948–) is Professor in the Department of German and the Humanities center at The Johns Hopkins University. His many publications include work on Kant, Fichte, Schlegel, Schleiermacher, Hegel, Heidegger and Derrida, and literary theory, and have appeared in numerous anthologies, and journals. His most recent published work examines the wartime journals of Paul deMan.

Julia Kristeva (1941–) has held for many years a visiting appointment at Columbia University. She is currently Professor of Linguistics at the Université de Paris VII (U.E.R. de Sciences des Textes et Documents). One of the most influential figures in the field of semiotics and feminists studies today, Kristeva's work focuses on the relations between language, consciousness, desire, and ''political'' action.

Jean-Luc Nancy (1942–) teaches philosophy at the Université de Strasbourg where he is co-founder (with Philippe Lacoue-Labarthe) of the Group de recherches sur les theories du signe et du texte; he has held visiting appointments in the United States at the University of California at San Diego and the University of California at Berkeley. His books and articles on Plato, Descartes, Rousseau, Kant, Hegel, Nietzsche, and Heidegger have been published in French, German, and English.

Friedrich Nietzsche (1844–1900) was trained as a philologist at the University of Basel where he held the Chair of Classical Philology from 1869 until his retirement from teaching 1879. It was during this period that Nietzsche laid the ground for the later work that would come to influence twentieth-century deliberations on interpretation theory and semeiotic.

Gayle L. Ormiston (1951–) is Associate Professor in the Department of Philosophy and the Institute for Applied Linguistics at Kent State University. His published books and articles span a wide range of interests in contemporary philosophy, especially the relation between questions of postmodernity, narrative and discourse analysis and the study of science and technology.

Alan D. Schrift (1955–) teaches at Grinnell College where he is Assistant Professor of Philosophy. His published articles treat issues in contemporary German and French philosophy, especially those of interpretation, authority, and textuality in Nietzsche, Heidegger, Derrida, Foucault, and Sartre. He is completing a book-length manuscript entitled *Nietzsche and the Question of Interpretation: Between Hermeneutics and Deconstruction*.

Index